MW00658309

The Postcolonial Biblical Reader

The Postcolonial Biblical Reader

Edited by R. S. Sugirtharajah

Blackwell Publishing

BLACKWELL PUBLISHING
350 Main Street, Malden, MA 02148-5020, USA
9600 Garsington Road, Oxford OX4 2DQ UK
550 Swanston Street, Carlton, Victoria 3053, Australia

First published 2006 by Blackwell Publishing Ltd

1 2006

Library of Congress Cataloging-in-Publication Data

The postcolonial Biblical reader/edited by R. S. Sugirtharajah.
p. cm.
Includes bibliographical references and indexes.
ISBN-13: 978-1-4051-3349-4 (hardcover: alk. paper)
ISBN-10: 1-4051-3349-X (hardcover: alk. paper)
ISBN-13: 978-1-4051-3350-0 (pbk.: alk. paper)
ISBN-10: 1-4051-3350-3 (pbk.: alk. paper) 1. Bible—Criticism, interpretation, etc. 2. Christianity—Politics and government—History. I. Sugirtharajah, R. S. (Rasiah S.)

BS511.3.P67 2006
220.6—dc22

2005012643

A catalogue record for this title is available from the British Library.

Set in 10/12pt Sabon
by SPI Publisher Services, Pondicherry, India
Printed and bound in the United Kingdom
by TJ International, Padstow, Cornwall

The publisher's policy is to use permanent paper from mills that operate a sustainable forestry policy, and which has been manufactured from pulp processed using acid-free and elementary chlorine-free practices. Furthermore, the publisher ensures that the text paper and cover board used have met acceptable environmental accreditation standards.

For further information on
Blackwell Publishing, visit our website:
www.blackwellpublishing.com

Contents

Contributors

Jon L. Berquist, is Senior Academic Editor, Westminister John Knox Press, Louisville, KY.

Philip Chia is a visiting scholar at Chung Chi College, Chinese University of Hong Kong.

Laura E. Donaldson is Associate Professor of English, Cornell University.

Musa W. Dube is Associate Professor of Religion, Scripps College, Claremont, California.

Eleazar S. Fernandez is Associate Professor of Constructive Theology, United Theological Seminary of the Twin Cities.

Richard A. Horsley is Distinguished Professor of Liberal Arts and the Study of Religion, University of Massachusetts, Boston.

Mary Huie-Jolly teaches biblical studies and theological reflection at the Presbyterian School for Ministry, Dunedin, New Zealand.

Hephzibah Israel is lecturer in English at Lady Shri Ram College, University of Delhi.

Werner H. Kelber is Isla Carroll Turner and Percy E. Turner Professor of Biblical Studies, Rice University.

Karen L. King is Winn Professor of Ecclesiastical History, Harvard Divinity School.

Kwok Pui-lan is William F. Cole Professor of Christian Theology and Spirituality, Episcopal Divinity School, Cambridge, Massachusetts.

Kari Latvus is Principal Lecturer in Diaconia, Diaconia Polytechnic, Finland.

Dora R. Mbuwayesango is Associate Professor of Old Testament Studies, Hood Theological Seminary, Salisbury, North Carolina.

Stephen D. Moore is Professor of New Testament, Drew University.

Itumeleng J. Mosala is Director-General, Department of Arts and Culture, Government of South Africa.

Erin Runions is Assistant Professor, Department of Religious Studies, Pomona College, Claremont, California.

Mayra Rivera is a visiting scholar at the Drew University.

Fernando F. Segovia is Oberlin Graduate Professor of New Testament and Early Christianity at Vanderbilt University Divinity School.

R. S. Sugirtharajah is Professor of Biblical Hermeneutics, University of Birmingham, England.

Tat-siong Benny Liew is Associate Professor of New Testament, Chicago Theological Seminary.

Acknowledgments

First, I would like to sincerely thank all the copyright holders for giving permission to reproduce the material. I am also most grateful to Rebecca Harkin of Blackwell for initiating the project and trusting my judgment, and to Karen Wilson, the Editorial Controller, for her patience and professionalism in guiding the project through various stages of production.

As with my previous publishing projects, I have benefited immensely from the encouragement of Dan O'Connor, the support of Ralph Broadbent, and from the intellectual and spiritual strength of Sharada, my wife.

R. S. Sugirtharajah

The editor and publisher gratefully acknowledge the permission granted to reproduce the copyright material in this book:

Gloria Anzaldúa for "Canción de la diosa de la noche," in *Borderlands/La Frontera: The New Mestiza*, p. 218 (San Francisco: Aunt Lute Books, 1999), reprinted by permission of the publisher;

Jon L. Berquist, "Postcolonialism and Imperial Motives for Canonization," pp. 15–33, 33–5, from *Semeia: An Experimental Journal for Biblical Criticism* 75, 1996, copyright © 1996 by Jon L. Berquist, reprinted by permission of the author;

Philip P. Chia, "On Naming the Subject: Postcolonial Reading of Daniel 1," pp. 17–35, from *Jian Dao* 7, 1997, copyright © 1997 by *Jian Dao*, reprinted by permission of the Alliance Bible Seminary;

Laura E. Donaldson, "The Sign of Orpah: Reading Ruth through Native Eyes," pp. 20–36 from R. S. Sugirtharajah, *Vernacular Hermeneutics* (Sheffield: Sheffield Academic Press, 1999), copyright © 1999 by The Continuum International Publishing Group, reprinted by permission of the publisher;

Musa W. Dube, "Rahab says Hello to Judith: A Decolonizing Feminist Reading," pp. 54–71, from Elisabeth Schussler Fiorenza and Fernando Segovia, *Toward a New*

Heaven and a New Earth: Essays in Honor of Elisabeth Schussler Fiorenza (Maryknoll: Orbis Books, 2003), copyright © 2003 by Orbis Books, reprinted by permission of the publisher;

Simeon Dumdum for "America," copyright © 1998 by Simeon Dumdum, reprinted by permission of the author;

Eleazar S. Fernandez, "Exodus-toward-Egypt: Filipino-Americans' Struggle to Realize the Promised Land in America," pp. 167–81, from Eleazar S. Fernandez and Fernando F. Segovia, *A Dream Unfinished: Theological Reflections on America from the Margins* (Maryknoll: Orbis Books, 2001), copyright © 2001 by Orbis Books, reprinted by permission of the publisher;

Richard A. Horsley, "Renewal Movements and Resistance to Empire in Ancient Judea," pp. 74–92, 146–9, from *Religion and Empire: People Power and the Life of the Spirit* (Minneapolis: Fortress Press, 2003), copyright © 2003 by Augsburg Fortress, reprinted by permission of the publisher;

Mary Huie-Jolly, "Mori 'Jews' and a Resistant Reading of John 5.10–47," pp. 94–110, from Musa W. Dube and Jeffrey L. Staley, *John and Postcolonialism* (London: Continuum, 2002), copyright © 2002 by The Continuum International Publishing Group, reprinted by permission of the publisher;

Hephzibah Israel, "Cutchery Tamil Versus Pure Tamil: Contesting Language Use in the Translated Bible in the Early Nineteenth-Century Protestant Tamil Community," unpublished paper;

Werner H. Kelber, "Roman Imperialism and Early Christian Scribality," pp. 135–53, 219–38, from J. Draper, *Orality, Literacy, and Colonialism in Antiquity* (Atlanta: Society of Biblical Literature, 2004), copyright © 2004 by The Society of Biblical Literature, reprinted by permission of The Society of Biblical Literature;

Karen L. King, "Canonization and Marginalization: Mary of Magdala," pp. 29–35, 35–6, from *Concilium 3*, 1998, copyright © 1998 by *Concilium*, reprinted by permission of the journal;

Kwok Pui-lan, "Making the Connections: Postcolonial Studies and Feminist Biblical Interpretation," pp. 77–99, from *Postcolonial Imagination and Feminist Theology* (Westminster John Knox Press, 2005), copyright © 2005 by Kwok Pui-lan, reprinted by permission of Westminster John Knox Press and SCM Press;

Kari Latvus, "Decolonizing Yahweh: A Postcolonial Reading of 2 Kings," unpublished paper;

Tat-Siong Benny Liew, "Tyranny, Boundary and Might: Colonial Mimicry in Mark's Gospel," pp. 7–27, 27–31, from *Journal for the Study of the New Testament* 73, 1999, copyright © 1999 by Sage Publications, reprinted by permission of Sage Publications Ltd;

Dora R. Mbuwayesango, "How Local Divine Powers Were Suppressed: A Case of Mwari of the Shona," pp. 63–75, 76–7, from Musa W. Dube, *Other Ways of Reading: African Women and the Bible* (Atlanta: Society of Biblical Literature, 2001), copyright © 2001 by The Society of Biblical Literature, reprinted by permission of The Society of Biblical Literature;

Stephen D. Moore, "Mark and Empire: 'Zealot' and 'Postcolonial' Readings," pp. 134–48, from Catherine Keller et al., *Postcolonial Theologies: Divinity and Empire* (St Louis: Chalice Press, 2004), copyright © 2004 by Chalice Press, reprinted by permission of the publisher;

Itumeleng J. Mosala, "The Implications of the Text of Esther for African Women's Struggle for Liberation in South Africa," pp. 129–37, from *Semeia: An Experimental Journal for Biblical Criticism* 59, 1992, copyright © 1992 by Itumeleng Mosala;

Mayra Rivera, "God at the Crossroads: A Postcolonial Reading of Sophia," pp. 186–203, from Catherine Keller et al., *Postcolonial Theologies: Divinity and Empire* (St Louis: Chalice Press, 2004), copyright © 2004 by Chalice Press, reprinted by permission of the publisher;

Erin Runions, "Desiring War: Apocalypse, Commodity Fetish, and the End of History," from *The Bible and Critical Theory* 1 (1), 2004, copyright © 2004 by Monash University ePress (www.epress.monash,edu), reprinted by permission of the publisher;

Fernando F. Segovia, "Biblical Criticism and Postcolonial Studies: Toward a Postcolonial Optic," pp. 49–65, from R. S. Sugirtharajah, *Postcolonial Bible* (Sheffield: Sheffield Academic Press, 1998), copyright © 1998 by The Continuum International Publishing Group, reprinted by permission of the publisher;

R. S. Sugirtharajah, "Charting the Aftermath: A Review of Postcolonial Criticism," pp. 11–42, 208–24, from *Postcolonial Criticism and Biblical Interpretation* (Oxford: Oxford University Press, 2001), copyright © 2001 by R. S. Sugirtharajah, reprinted by permission of Oxford University Press;

David Tracy for epigraph to chapter 11, from *On Naming the Present* by David Tracy, copyright © 1995 by David Tracy, reprinted by permission of Orbis Books.

Every effort has been made to trace copyright holders and to obtain their permission for the use of copyright material. The publisher apologizes for any errors or omissions in the above list and would be grateful if notified of any corrections that should be incorporated in future reprints or editions of this book.

Introduction

R. S. Sugirtharajah

This Reader is a natural development from my earlier volume, *Voices from the Margin: Interpreting the Bible in the Third World* (1991). It is complementary to and in some respects engages with, while going beyond, the concerns of the minority hermeneutics introduced there. I hope to bring out at a later date a study of the changes that have occurred in methodological issues, in reading practices, and in the profile of the contributors, between these two publications. This present volume is designed to introduce postcolonialism and its application to biblical studies. While there is a considerable scholarly literature which deals with how other academic disciplines have appropriated postcolonialism into their theoretical universe, there has been a reluctance within theology to embrace the methodological maneuvers of postcolonialism except in the field of biblical studies. Here, there has been a vigorous engagement with postcolonial criticism. This has been in part because of the mobilization of the Bible for modern imperialism, but also because of the pervasive presence of various empires from the Persian to the Roman within the biblical writings. What Adolf Deissmann said of the New Testament, that it is the "book of the imperial age," could be reworded to include both testaments. This Reader is a sampling of the attempts by biblical scholars to incorporate insights from postcolonial criticism and so take biblical studies beyond their Euro-centric tutelage.

The Reader is coming out at a time when, ominously, there is a rapid rise of colonialism with biblical accompaniments. What we are witnessing now is not only a replay of the nineteenth century and the return of sometimes latent, sometimes patent imperialism, but also the return of the Bible as the textual motor behind the empire, and once again underpinning the imperial vision. We have entered a world with a single superpower in the form of the American administration. Like the colonialism of old, it is not only fueled by a sense of moral virtue, but is also sustained by a biblical vision for the re-ordering of the world's power-relations. It is here that postcolonialism proves significant. The past entanglements of the Bible with imperialism enable postcolonialism to point out the deeply problematic and pliable nature of biblical texts, and a tainted colonial legacy. At the same time, past

anti-colonial strategies of defiance and struggle with their biblical legitimations offer tools to engage with the new colonizing forces.

This volume brings together both some well-established practitioners of postcolonial criticism and a few scholars who may not call themselves postcolonial but whose work resonates with the preoccupations of postcolonialism. All of them have been affected by one form of empire or another – British, Russian, or American. Some of them have been exiled, or are diasporic, living on and between borders. A few are part of the current empire but sensitive to its predatory nature. Hence their articulations presented here offer a complex of interactions and negotiations. As the reader will note, although these essays were written on different occasions and for different publishing needs, there is a conversation going on among them. This dialogical aspect provides a compelling overview of the nuanced applications of postcolonial criticism to biblical studies. Naturally, there is a certain amount of repetition and overlapping within these essays, and inevitably it is a partial and uneven collection.

The volume is organized and unified around four themes, each of which has its own brief introductory preface. It opens with a selection of essays which deal with the transformative energies of postcolonialism, and how its theoretical maneuvers impinge on biblical studies and on cognate disciplines such as feminist biblical interpretation. The second section, "Empires: Old and New," addresses the menacing presence of empires both ancient and current, how subject peoples defied it in the past, and how they seek to mobilize against today's domination. The third section, "Empire and Exegesis," offers practical examples of how postcolonial criticism is applied to biblical studies and how in the process such an exegesis not only disrupts the nicely finessed Western readings and undermines their claim to universality, but also uncovers the tacit colonial biases within such readings. The last section, "Postcolonial Concerns," deals with such issues generated by postcoloniality as the importance of translation in the colonial civilizing mission, mistaken recognitions of the other, and the dislocation of people. These four sections are not tightly sealed off compartments, and an essay which is located in one segment might well find itself at home in another.

This volume does not aim to bring resolution to ongoing debates surrounding the profitability or pointlessness of postcolonialism. These debates are so enmeshed in theoretical jargon that it is a daunting task for the uninitiated to decipher them. If the volume succeeds, it will not be in championing or contradicting the theory, but in fostering whatever response is possible in the field of political action. Ultimately, as the late Edward Said made abundantly clear in his writings, political responsibility must take priority over theoretical engagement.

Part I Theoretical Practices

Introduction: Theoretical Practices

R. S. Sugirtharajah

Biblical studies have often used external sources to illuminate biblical texts. Even historical criticism, allegedly bias-free, has made use of nineteenth-century European cultural traditions. Using its own external sources, postcolonial criticism is a new critical ally in helping to unravel biblical texts.

This section opens with Sugirtharajah's "Charting the Aftermath: A Review of Postcolonial Criticism." His essay offers a conspectus of postcolonialism, with an explanation of the leading concepts encountered in the discourse. This is followed by his account of the emergence of this category in the discussion of theory. In its earlier appearances it was essentially an expression of a moral rejection of imperialism, taking the form of resistant creative writing, following which it entered the academy, becoming an analytic instrument not least among diasporan scholars. His essay also discusses postcolonialism's relation to two significant critical movements of our time – feminism and globalization. The essay more crucially examines the vexed status of the United States of America and its current international standing as it is emerging as a sole superpower.

Fernando Segovia's essay "Biblical Criticism and Postcolonial Studies: Toward a Postcolonial Optic" interweaves the author's complicated personal history at the receiving end of four distinct forms of imperialism and colonialism, and his own work as a biblical critic, constructive theologian, and cultural critic. In the light of his experience, Segovia concludes that postcolonialism proves to be the "most appropriate, most enlightening and most fruitful" tool. He identifies three postcolonial "optics" – the inescapable and omnipresent reality of the empires which shaped the construction of the texts of Judaism and early Christianity; the colonial impulses which fuel Western interpretation of Jewish and Christian writings, and the emergence of biblical critics from the former empires who are trying to destabilize received readings. The essay concludes with a summary of the advantages of applying postcolonialism to biblical studies.

The essay by Kwok Pui-lan, "Making the Connections: Postcolonial Studies and Feminist Biblical Interpretation" focuses on postcolonialism and feminist biblical scholarship. After a brief narration of the emergence of postcolonialism in

biblical studies, she examines the writings of Musa Dube and Gale Yee. She then goes on to show how postcolonialism can open up new avenues for studying gender relations in early Christianity, especially in the Gospels and Pauline writings. Her contention is that by studying how gender, class, and race functioned in the Roman empire one gets a clearer picture of these early Christian texts. The essay ends with a call for cooperation between practitioners of postcolonial feminist criticism and Jewish feminist criticism, in order to avoid the deeply entrenched anti–Semitic elements prevalent in some Christian discourse. These not only dehumanize Jewish people but also lend themselves to a form of colonial ideology. Such a cooperative reading would, in Pui-lan's view, challenge one's bias and "investment in a particular method."

These three essays reinforce the value of using theories and criticism forged outside the biblical field. These enable biblical scholars to ask questions which the traditional discipline failed or was reluctant to address, relating to issues such as sexism, racism, and colonialism, and to engage with wider debates outside the discipline of biblical scholarship.

1

Charting the Aftermath: A Review of Postcolonial Criticism

R. S. Sugirtharajah

The colonialist likes neither theory nor theorists.

(Albert Memmi 1990: 136)

We are surrounded by theories. They grow as thick as trees around us, everyday new saplings sprout up among the hoary old veterans.

(*In the Garden Secretly and Other Stories*, Arasanayagam 2000: 87)

Postcolonial studies emerged as a way of engaging with the textual, historical, and cultural articulations of societies disturbed and transformed by the historical reality of colonial presence.[1] In this respect, in its earlier incarnation, postcolonialism was never conceived as a grand theory, but as creative literature and as a resistance discourse emerging in the former colonies of the Western empires. Postcolonialism as a methodological category and as a critical practice followed later. There were two aspects: first, to analyze the diverse strategies by which the colonizers constructed images of the colonized; and second, to study how the colonized themselves made use of and went beyond many of those strategies in order to articulate their identity, self-worth, and empowerment. Postcolonialism has been taking a long historical look at both old and new forms of domination. Its insight lies in understanding how the past informs the present.

As a field of inquiry, postcolonialism is not monolithic but rather a field which provides and caters to a variety of concerns, oppositional stances, and even contradictory positions. Nonetheless, it generates a noticeable theoretical strength. It provides valuable resources for thinking about those social, cultural, political, and historical contexts in which domestication takes place. As a style of inquiry, it emerged more or less simultaneously in a variety of disciplines including Anthropology, Geography, International Studies, History, English, Music, and Medieval Studies. When

First published in *Postcolonial Criticism and Biblical Interpretation*. Oxford: Oxford University Press, 2001, 11–42.

used in conjunction with "theory" or "criticism," the term "postcolonialism" signifies a distinct methodological category and acts as a discursive force. In its reconsideration of colonialism and its aftermath, it draws on poststructuralism, Marxism, cultural studies, linguistics, and literary studies. In its application, postcolonial criticism differs not only from location to location but also from discipline to discipline. In his essay "The Scramble for Post-Colonialism" Stephen Slemon remarks:

> "Postcolonialism", as it is now used in its various fields, describes a remarkably heterogenous set of subject positions, professional fields, and critical enterprises. It has been used as a way of ordering a critique of totalising forms of Western historicism; as a portmanteau term for a retooled notion of "class"; as a subset of both postmodernism and post-structuralism (and conversely, as the condition from which those two structures of cultural logic and cultural critique themselves are seen to emerge); as the name for a condition of nativist longing in post-independence national groupings; as a cultural marker of non-residency for a Third World intellectual cadre; as the inevitable underside of a fractured and ambivalent discourse of colonialist power; as an oppositional form of "reading practice"; and... as the name for a category of "literary" activity which sprang from a new and welcome political energy going on within what used to be called "Commonwealth" literary studies. (Slemon 1994: 16–17)

Postcolonialism is a discipline in which everything is contested, everything is contestable, from the use of terms to the defining of chronological boundaries. Postcolonialism, as one would expect, is a much disputed term. Inevitably it has chronological dimensions attached to it. In popular perception, postcolonialism is seen as a period which began in the 1960s after the demise of formal European colonialism following the struggle for independence waged by the colonized people. The term as used at present is ineluctably tied to modern European imperialism. It does not allow an understanding of colonialism outside modern European colonialism. It is seen as a condition of no longer being what one was, a colony, but as finding a space in the world as a newly independent nation state, and its citizens referred to as postcolonials. In postcolonial discursive practice, several critics contend and recognize that, when it is used with a hyphen, "post-colonial," the term is seen as indicating the historical period aftermath of colonialism, and without the hyphen, "postcolonial," as signifying a reactive resistance discourse of the colonized who critically interrogate dominant knowledge systems in order to recover the past from the Western slander and misinformation of the colonial period, and who also continue to interrogate neo-colonizing tendencies after the declaration of independence. It is in this latter sense that the term will be employed in this volume. Homi Bhabha sums up what postcolonial criticism is about:

> Postcolonial criticism bears witness to the unequal and uneven forces of cultural representation involved in the contest for political and social authority within the modern world order. Postcolonial perspectives emerge from the colonial testimony of Third World countries, and the discourses of "minorities" within the geopolitical divisions of East and West, North and South. They intervene in those ideological discourses of modernity that attempt to give a hegemonic "normality" to the uneven development and the differential, often disadvantaged, histories, of nations, races, communities, people. (Bhabha 1994: 171)

As with the case of the other critical category, postmodernism, which is no longer seen as implying a linear progression from modernism, but as a continuum, postcolonialism too is no longer perceived as a chronological progression from colonialism but as a perpetual set of critical possibilities which were already available with the formal advent of modern colonialism. It is an instrument or method of analyzing situations where one social group dominated another.

One of the vexing questions which bedevils the debate is whether to treat postcolonialism as theory or as criticism. If one applies the Foucaultian parameter that theory is "the deduction, on the basis of a number of axioms, of an abstract model applicable to an indefinite number of empirical descriptions,"[2] then postcolonialism will not fit. Postcolonialism is essentially a style of inquiry, an insight or a perspective, a catalyst, a new way of life. As an inquiry, it instigates and creates possibilities, and provides a platform for the widest possible convergence of critical forces, of multi-ethnic, multi-religious, and multicultural voices, to assert their denied rights and rattle the center. It is an assemblage of interests and attitudes and is remarkably productive because it offers a perspective complementing and in some ways transcending the Enlightenment's modernizing project. As postcolonialism is not a theory in the strict sense of the term, but a collection of critical and conceptual attitudes, an apt description would be to term it criticism. Criticism is not an exact science, but an undertaking of social and political commitment which should not be reduced to or solidified into a dogma. It is always oppositional. Edward Said sees criticism "as life-enhancing and constitutively opposed to every form of tyranny, domination, and abuse, its social goals are noncoercive knowledge produced in the interests of human freedom" (Said 1991: 29). Put at its simplest, criticism is always contextual; it is paradoxical, secular, and always open to its own contradictions and shortcomings. And, to cite Said again: "I take criticism so seriously as to believe that, even in the very midst of a battle in which one is unmistakably on one side against another, there should be criticism, because there must be critical consciousness if there are to be issues, problems, values, even lives to be fought for" (Said 1991: 28). It is in this sense that "postcolonial" is used in this volume.

The Arrival of Postcolonial Criticism

Theorizing, contrary to popular perception, is not necessarily a Western phenomenon. Writers from the Third World have used abstract logic in narrative forms to intellectualize and analyze art, literature, and theatre. Indians and Chinese have evolved sophisticated and sustained analyses of how meaning is constructed in texts. For instance, Indians have a well-developed system of *śāstra paddhati*, "which employs different interpretative instruments, including philosophy, grammar, etymology, logical reasoning, theory of meaning, and metarules" (Kapoor 1998: 15).[3] Similarly, Barbara Christian has noted, people of color have developed their own theorizing, using their experiences of the struggle of everyday life, distinct from the abstract theoretical fashion practiced in the West. Her implication is that theories can arise not only in intellectual and academic institutions: "I am inclined to say that our theorizing (and I intentionally use the verb rather than the noun) is often in narrative forms, in the stories we create, in riddles and proverbs, in the play with

language, since dynamic rather than fixed ideas seem more to our liking" (Christian 1995: 457). The crucial question is not where theories originate or who owns them but whether they have diagnostic capabilities to promote the cause of the marginalized.

The considerable presence and recognition of postcolonial thinking in Western academia is due to the favorable intellectual environment for the rise of resistance theories in the 1980s. The arrival and acceptance of postcolonialism, especially in the United States, is noticeably different from that of any other minority discourse such as African-American, Chicano, gender, even though these interventionary disciplines share some common political preoccupations and theoretical presuppositions. Ethnic-minority studies were introduced into the US academy as a result of student demonstrations against white institutions which excluded minority cultures from college syllabi and racial minorities from the faculty and student bodies. Postcolonialism, on the other hand, according to Jenny Sharpe, "constitutes an institutional reform from 'within' " (Sharpe 2000: 108). The text which paved the way was Edward Said's *Orientalism*, published in 1978. Said defined "Orientalism" as a Western way of "dominating, restructuring, and having authority over the Orient" (Said 1985: 3). What was noticeably different about Said's work was that it was able to establish the connection between the production of academic knowledge and colonialism, which earlier interpreters of the history of ideas failed to acknowledge and expose. The key to power is knowledge, and true power is held with the conviction that the ruler knows better than the ruled, and must convince the ruled that whatever the colonial master does is for the benefit of the ruled. The assumption undergirding this thinking is the belief that "knowledge of subject races or Orientals is what makes their management easy and profitable; knowledge gives power, more power requires more knowledge, and so on in an increasingly profitable dialectic of information and control" (Said 1985: 36).

There are other factors, too, that promoted the arrival of postcolonialism. The 1980s saw the emergence of theorizing and literary analysis gaining a fresh lease in the academy. At a time when the socialist experiment advocated by the Soviet bureaucracy failed to produce the expected results, the fortunes of Marxist criticism took a deep dive, and, with the arrival of Reaganism and Thatcherism, a new form of literary analysis arrived on the scene. Reflecting the multicultural mood of the period, these literary analyses and theorizings were irredeemably eclectic, hybridized, and cross-disciplinary in character and in execution. They borrowed critically and fused imaginatively from a variety of disciplines ranging from philosophy, psychology, politics, anthropology, to linguistics (McLeod 2000: 23–4).

Though postcolonial criticism was not minted in the academy, the imprimatur accorded by the guild raised its status and authority. In the current theoretical foundry, the names of Edward Said, Homi Bhabha, and Gayatri Spivak, occupy an important place, and they are generally spoken of as being influential in fomenting the theory. The trouble with such a notion is that none of these writers, however indispensable they are to the theoretical cause, ever set out to be postcolonial in their writings. It was only after postcolonial analysis had reached its momentum that Said, Spivak, and Bhabha were identified and hailed as instigators. The other difficulty with such a narrowing of the list of personalities is that it overlooks anti-colonial liberationist writings which emerged outside the academy long before

they were accorded academic appreciation. They were considered lacking in academic pedigree. These discourses were spearheaded by Amilcar Cabral, Frantz Fanon, C. L. R. James, Aimé Césaire, Albert Memmi, and Ananda Coomarswamy, who were openly anti-colonial in their writings and praxis. Each in his own way tried to articulate the psychological, cultural, and political damage that European colonialism had inflicted on millions of people. Recently, there is a move to bring others into the postcolonial framework, figures like the African-American W.E.B. Du Bois, and the Cuban José Marti, both intellectuals with socialist leanings, who in their literary and political activities engaged in national emancipation for African-Americans and Cubans, and denounced the global imperial policies of the United States (Cooppan 2000: 1–35).

The articulations of these earlier writers are too extensive to be dealt with here in a way that would do justice to their work. More importantly, they have been analyzed perceptively elsewhere.[4] But to give a flavor, let me briefly look at the works of two writers, one pre-eminent, the other less so. Frantz Fanon was born in Martinique. He was a psychiatrist and activist who involved himself in the Algerian War of Independence. In his writings, Fanon argued that colonialism instilled deep in the minds of the native population that before its advent their history was dominated by savagery and internecine tribal warfare, and that if the colonialists were to leave they would fall back into "barbarism, degradation and bestiality" (Fanon 1990: 169).[5] The trick of colonialism, according to Fanon, was to project itself as a mother, but not as a gentle and loving mother who sheltered and steered her child from situations surrounded with hostility, but rather as a mother who reigned over and restrained her wayward child from practicing evil deeds. To put it bluntly, what the colonial mother did was to "protect the child from itself, from its ego, and from its physiology, its biology and its own unhappiness which is its very essence" (Fanon 1990: 170). In other words, for colonialism, it was not merely sufficient for the colonizer to manage the present and the future of the native population, their past also must be rewritten, creating a cultural vacuum:

> [C]olonialism is not simply content to impose its rule upon the present and the future of a dominated country. Colonialism is not satisfied merely with holding a people in its grip and emptying the native's brain of all form and content. By a kind of a perverted logic, it turns to the past of the oppressed people, and distorts, disfigures and destroys it. (Fanon 1990: 169)

For colonialism the vast continent of Africa was a "haunt of savages", replete with "superstitions and fanaticisms", and was held in contempt and cursed by God. Fanon's answer was to urge Africans to recover their history and reassert their identity and culture. Fanon advocated the reclamation of aspects of the past culture conscious of the fact that an idealized past can be problematic. For him there was no point in reviving "mummified fragments" of the past because, when people are involved in a struggle against colonialism, the significance of the past changes. The aim was not to replace colonial European culture with an uncomplicated, celebratory, and uncritical negro culture (his word). For Fanon, culture and nation are not isolated entities but are at the core of every national and cultural consciousness which develops into an international cosmpolitan consciousness. His work provides

tools for the former colonized to conceptualize and take control of their identities and rectify the falsification and harm done by colonial misrepresentation.

In a list riddled with African personalities, the work that is often overlooked in postcolonial critical thinking is that of a Sri Lankan, Ananda Coomaraswamy. His essays on nationalism were published in 1909, at the height of classical colonialism. He recognized that what was needed more than political and economic freedom was cultural liberation. Anticipating Ngũgĩ wa Thiong'o, Coomaraswamy called for an active decolonizing of the mind:

> For this struggle is much more than a political conflict. It is a struggle for spiritual and mental freedom from the domination of an alien ideal. In such a conflict, political and economic victory are but half the battle; for an India, "free in name, but subdued by Europe in her inmost soul" would ill justify the price of freedom. It is not so much the material, as the moral and spiritual subjugation of Indian civilisation that in the end impoverishes humanity. (Coomaraswamy 1909: p.i)

For Coomaraswamy, the regeneration of India had to be expressed in art and spirituality. He spoke about nationalism too, but he saw it as a service and a duty to be undertaken by the subjugated people.

These brief descriptions of Fanon and Coomaraswamy are little more than caricatures, but they point to the significant contribution of their work.

Creative Literature

Unlike metropolitan practitioners of theory who concentrate on representation of the other in colonial history and literature, the liberationist writings of Fanon, Memmi, C. L. R. James, and others like them, were concerned with studying how decolonization destabilized the exotic images fixed within the Western imagination. It is crucial to acknowledge these writers as intellectual antecedents of postcolonial studies, though they cannot be pressed into the service of a simple and single reading of colonialism because, before academic institutions became infatuated with their work and bestowed recognition, their concerns and constituencies were varied and specific.

Along with resistant discourse, creative literature also, which emerged from Commonwealth countries, played a critical role as a precursor to the current postcolonial thinking. Current studies of postcolonial work focus largely on the writings of Chinua Achebe, Ngũgĩ wa Thiong'o, Wole Soyinka, and V.S. Naipaul. One novel which has been overlooked in postcolonial discussion and is relevant to our purpose, is Akiki Nyabongo's *Africa Answers Back* (Nyabongo 1936).[6] Its importance lies in the fact that it contains a heady mixture of colonialism and the Bible. The author, a descendant of the Toro kings, was born in Uganda. The novel is autobiographical, and mixes both fact and fabrication, chronicle and memoirs. The story is set in Buganda at the turn of the nineteenth century and spans 50 years. As the title indicates, it is a subversive African tale which talks back to colonial discourse by rupturing and remolding it. The novel reverses a seemingly successful missionary story into a narrative of the empowerment and emancipation of the missionized. The

novel is about the hero, Abala Stanley Mujungu, and his journey of self-discovery as he tries to straddle both the ancient culture his parents want to maintain, and the modern Western culture introduced by the missionary, Hubert, and how the latter transformed Mujungu from being an exemplary mission-school student into an African rebel.

The interesting aspect of the novel, for us, takes place in part III, where the text introduced by the missionary – the Bible, which symbolizes and legitimizes Western culture – comes under a heavy hermeneutical bombardment. Curiously, the Bible, the Englishman's book, loses its authority at the beginning of the novel, when Stanley, the first missionary to Buganda, reads the story of the Israelites crossing the Red Sea to the King. The King's response is, "Hm, that's just like our story, because when the Gods came from the north they reached the River Kira and the waters stopped flowing, so that they could get across. Isn't it strange that his story and ours should be the same" (Nyabongo 1936: 10). Instead of confronting and dislodging the heathen world, now the "White man's mythology" as the King called it, has a parallel story, to vie with the "heathen" version, for attention and authority. At school, besides the Bible, Mujungu is introduced to other monumental texts of Western literary supremacy, Gibbon's *Rise and Fall of the Roman Empire* and the works of William Shakespeare. But it is over the Bible that hermeneutical contestations take place. Mujungu, who has acquired the modernist habit of writing and reading, and, more importantly, rational thinking, at a school run by the missionary Hubert, refuses to succumb to interpretations imposed by him, thereby challenging monopoly of the interpretative authority enjoyed by the missionary. The Bible's legitimizing power melts away on two particular occasions.

One such is when Hubert tries to introduce biblical stories to the class, with the condescending attitude that his students will not "grasp the full significance of the White Man's Bible" (Nyabongo 1936: 223). Whatever the story, Jonah, Adam and Eve, or the Virgin Birth, Mujungu continues to question it. He disputes the Jonah story by asking "how could a whale swallow a man whole?" And wonders "how could a man go through so small a throat unharmed?" (Nyabongo 1936: 224). He questions the story of the Creation in Genesis by pointing out that "no woman came from a man's rib". His biggest suspicion is reserved for the story of the Virgin Birth. For him it is a fairy-tale, since it was recorded only by two of the evangelists and in any case it was a biologically impossible feat: "Sir, how could the seed of a man get into the womb of a woman without intercourse?" (Nyabongo 1936: 226). When Hubert tries to get out of the difficulty by saying that Mary had two husbands, God and Joseph, Mujungu's immediate riposte is: "You won't baptize the children of men with two wives, yet John baptized Jesus" (Nyabongo 1936: 226), an obvious reference to the missionary practice of not baptizing Africans engaged in polygamous relationships.

The second occasion is when Mujungu is on holiday, and he reads aloud from the Hebrew Scripture about King Solomon and his 700 wives and 300 concubines, in order to prove to his parents that he has acquired the new skill of reading. Ati, his father and his wives are astonished to find that the practice of polygamy, the very practice condemned elsewhere in the Englishman's book, is approved of here. The book and the missionary are as they see it now exposed for their double standards. After hearing the story read, one of the wives of Ati exclaims: "Ha, ha, your son will

find him out. He can read his books, too! The Reverend Mr. Hubert can't tell us lies any more" (Nyabongo 1936: 207).

The final straw is when Mujungu, deprived of his holidays as a punishment for asking impertinent questions, accompanies the missionary as his interpreter on his visits to different churches. Mujungu uses his experience in the mission school and his knowledge of the Bible to warn his listeners that Hubert's intentions to teach people "the new ways" will result in disrespect to their elders and their culture. Handicapped by not being able to speak the native language, the missionary accepted defeat and announces that further evangelizing mission activities are over (Nyabongo 1936: 234).[7]

Arguing from what he regarded as a commonsensical and rational point of view, Mujungu undermines, if only temporarily, God's word, the English book. Hubert, instead of engaging in dialogue with Mujungu, dismisses him as jeopardizing evangelization and retreats into the safety of authoritative dogma and the missionary homiletical practice of denunciation: "There is no hope for you. You are dangerous to the faith of the rest of the class. I shall pray for you" (Nyabongo 1936: 228). Hubert found that Mujungu had read "too much" and the only way to stop him from further "misreadings" is to ask him to withdraw from the class. It was only by refusing to dialogue with Mujungu, that Hubert managed to maintain his own authority and pre-empted any further question: "I will not tolerate your talking back to me, as you have just done. I am the master of the school" (Nyabongo 1936: 218–19). The superiority of the Christian text is established through Hubert's assertion of his power as headmaster of the school rather than by cogently presenting its case. Hubert's desire to produce spiritually Christian Africans, even though, as he saw it, they looked like heathens, ends with his decision to make no further converts.

It was the resistant discourse of political activists and imaginative literature by novelists such as Nyabongo which sowed the seeds of the current postcolonial thinking.

The Contours of Postcolonial Criticism

What postcolonialism did was to introduce power and politics into the world of literary criticism in such a way as to expose how some literature, art, and drama were implicitly linked to European colonialism. As indicated earlier, the text which initiated this kind of thinking was Edward Said's *Orientalism* (Said 1985).[8] Though not always consistent, the core proposal of the book was to expose the connection between imperial power and the production of literary and historical traditions. According to John McLeod, this literary analysis manifested itself in three ways (McLeod 2000: 17–29).

First, there was a rereading of Western canonical texts to detect conscious or dormant colonial elements in them. This involved scouring texts, some of which were set in a colonial context, as in the case of Conrad's *Heart of Darkness*, or which, as in the case of Jane Austen's *Mansfield Park*, apparently had nothing to do with colonialism but unwittingly espoused colonialist intentions.

Secondly, literary analysis encouraged critics to search not just literary but other texts such as historical discourses, official documents, missionary reports, to see

how the colonized were represented and how they resisted or accepted colonial values. It was the post-structuralist thought of Jacques Derrida, Michel Foucault, and Jacques Lacan which provided the theoretical impulse here. The critics who were at the forefront were Homi Bhabha, Gayatri Spivak, and the historians who belonged to the "Subaltern studies" group. Bhabha argued that hybridity and mimicry were strategies forged by the colonized as ways of responding to colonial rule. Hybridity is an "in-between space" in which the colonialized translate or undo the binaries imposed by the colonial project: "From the perspective of the 'in-between', claims to cultural authenticity and sovereignty – supremacy, autonomy, hierarchy – are less significant 'values' than an awareness of the hybrid conditions of inter-cultural exchange" (Bhabha 2000: 139). For Bhabha, the significant characters in Naipaul's novels are those who, in spite of their defeat and degradation, transgress the conformity enforced by colonialism through mimicry and fusion. Spivak, in her oft-quoted essay, "Can the Subaltern Speak?" problematizes the difficulties of recovering the voices constructed in colonial texts, especially those of the women, and reads them as potentially insurrectionary (Spivak 1993: 66–111). This unnecessarily complicated essay has to be read in conjunction with the interview with the author in *The Spivak Reader* to get a fuller picture. Her concern is that speaking should not be taken literally as talk. Women did speak, but the problem was with the constrictions placed on translating their speech through the accepted conceptual mindset: "The actual fact of giving utterance is not what I was concerned about. What I was concerned about was that even when one uttered, one was constructed, by a certain kind of psychobiography, so that the utterance itself – this is another side of the argument – would have to be interpreted in the way in which we historically interpret anything" (Landry and Maclean 1996: 291). In other words, the marginalized can make themselves known only in relation to metropolitan conceptual practices. The central aim of those scholars who are involved in the Subaltern Studies project is to rectify the disproportionate space accorded to the interests of the elite in the writings of South Asian history. They redefine subaltern as the non-elite, rural section of Indian society, ranging from destitutes to the upper ranks of the peasantry, and see their task as amplifying the contribution made by "the people *on their own*, that is, *independently of the élite* to the making and development of this nationalism" (Guha 1988: 39; italics in original).

Thirdly, there was literary analysis of literature which emerged from the colonies, as a way of writing back to the center, questioning and challenging colonialist discourses, and in the process producing a new form of representation. The work which pioneered such an analysis was *The Empire Writes Back* (Ashcroft, Griffiths, and Tiffin 1989). It opened up the debate surrounding the explosion of powerful and diverse writings especially those emerging from the former Commonwealth countries, their interrelatedness, their politicization, and their use of language as subversion. Ashcroft, Griffiths, and Tiffin identify four modes of "writing back" – national or regional (reflecting and emphasizing the country's culture), black writing (by Africans in diaspora), comparative (literatures of the past and present Commonwealth countries which emerge out of shared history), and hybridized or syncretic (eclectic use of theories, histories, forms, and concepts) (Ashcroft, Griffiths, and Tiffin 1989: 15–37). Despite their different emphases, and variant needs, what binds

these literatures together is their recognition and challenge of the notion of the ruler and the ruled, and the dominating and dominated.[9]

The advent of postcolonial theory in the late 1980s, nearly two decades after the formal ending of territorial colonialism, is indicative of the fact that postcolonial thinking was not a direct critique of colonial devastation. The delay suggests that postcolonialism was an "intellectual symptom" a reaction against the failure of the newly independent nation states to initiate pluralistic democratic structures and environmentally balanced development, to bridge the gap between rich and poor, and meet the needs of indigenous peoples. Postcolonial studies are not simply about what went wrong during colonial days and what went wrong in the anticolonial struggle where gender and class went unnoticed or were subsumed under the nationalist cause, but has also to do with the non-materialization after the euphoria of freedom of greater democracy, justice for indigenous people, and minorities like Dalits and *burakumins*, gender equality and the end of poverty and hunger. The Subaltern Studies initiative is a salient example of this newer approach.

To conclude this section: postcolonial criticism, like the hybridity it celebrates, is itself a product of hybridity. It is an inevitable growth of an interaction between colonizing countries and the colonized. It owes its origin neither to the First nor the Third World, but is a product of the contentious reciprocation between the two.

Clarification of the Lexicon

In postcolonial writing, terms such as "imperialism" and "colonialism" are often lumped together, and tend to be used interchangeably. Edward Said has returned to the standard distinction between the two. In this usage, "the term 'imperialism' means the practice, the theory, and the attitudes of a dominating metropolitan center ruling a distant territory; 'colonialism', which is almost always a consequence of imperialism, is the implanting of settlements on distant territory" (Said 1993: 8). Put differently, imperialism is often taken to mean literally "of empire" and indicates the control exercised by one nation state over another and its inhabitants to exploit and develop the resources of the land, for the benefit of the imperial government. It is often accompanied by an imperial propaganda in the form of ceremonies, coronations, parades, pageants, and military supremacy. Colonialism, on the other hand, implies settlement, but also necessitates controlling and "civilizing" indigenous people. The predatory nature of imperialism, namely acquiring distant territories for economic and political reasons only became unambiguous in the later nineteenth century. Prior to that, empire was seen as a humanitarian enterprise where an amiable form of civilization was pressed upon the hapless and ignoble races. The revival of the Roman empire as a model helped to provide an articulation of the aims of high imperialism. The ideology of the Roman empire consolidated the notion that superior races are entitled to power over savage races because the natives are unruly and incapable of ruling themselves.

The other term which has a high purchase in postcolonial discourse is neo-colonialism. Its first usage was attributed to the first president of Ghana, Kwame Nkrumah. "The essence of neo-colonialism", he wrote, "is that the state which is subject to it is, in theory, independent and has all the outward trappings of inter-

national sovereignty. In reality its economic system and thus its political policy is directed from outside" (Nkrumah 1965: p.ix). In his view, this was a new form of economic hegemony exercised by former colonizers through international banks and multinational corporations, after territorial freedom had been gained by newly independent countries. Unlike the earlier colonialism, which was visible, the new form of indirect control was much more subtle and less visible. Recently, with the former colonial European countries losing their hold on the international political scene, the term has been transferred to indicate principally the influence and intervention of the United States in the economic and political affairs of the world. In essence, what neo-colonialism means is the inability of the Third World countries to work out an economic policy and strategy without the interference of Western powers, although Nkrumah went on to warn that neo-colonialism was injurious not only to the dominated but also to the dominating countries: "Neo-colonialism is a mill-stone around the necks of the developed countries which practise it. Unless they can rid themselves of it, it will drown them" (Nkrumah 1965: xvi).

Postcolonialism and Biblical Studies

The greatest single aim of postcolonial biblical criticism is to situate colonialism at the center of the Bible and biblical interpretation. What we find in both the historical and the hermeneutical literature of biblical scholarship over the last 400 years is the impact of the Reformation or the Counter-reformation, or the effects of the Enlightenment in defining and shaping the discipline by rationalistic thinking or its offshoot, historical criticism. But there has been a remarkable unwillingness to mention imperialism as shaping the contours of biblical scholarship. What postcolonial biblical criticism does is to focus on the whole issue of expansion, domination, and imperialism as central forces in defining both the biblical narratives and biblical interpretation.

Postcolonial criticism opens up potential areas for biblical studies to work in tandem with other disciplines. Biblical scholars have in other ways been open to trends from elsewhere and have used insights from other disciplines with profit. Postcolonialism's ongoing battle for emancipation, and continuing attempt to dismantle imperial institutions and dominating structures offers a valuable field for collaboration. The overlapping areas in which biblical scholars can cooperate with the postcolonial agenda include: race, nation, translation, mission, textuality, spirituality, representation. It can also explore plurality, hybridity, and postnationalism, the hallmarks of the postcolonial condition. Related identity categories are undergoing vigorous rethinking, including: slaves, sex-workers, the homosexual/heterosexual divide, people of mixed race. Each of these topics deserves attention, although in this volume, we will confine ourselves to a few of the issues which are critical to biblical interpretation, such as textuality, translation, and diasporic hermeneutics.

Another area where biblical studies could benefit from postcolonial discourse is the place and function of criticism in the contemporary world. What Said says of the American literary scene is equally true of biblical studies. Biblical studies, as in the case of literary studies, is enmeshed in the labyrinth of textuality, and obsessed with

professionalism and specialization: "As it is practised in the American academy today, literary theory has for the most part isolated textuality from the circumstances, the events, the physical senses, that made it possible and render it intelligible as the result of human work" (Said 1991: 4). There are two greater dangers within the field. One is an uncritical acceptance of the principal tenets of the discipline, and the other, its failure to relate it to the society in which its work is done. Biblical studies is still seduced by the modernistic notion of using the rational as a key to open up texts and fails to accept intuition, sentiment, and emotion as a way into the text. By and large, the world of biblical interpretation is detached from the problems of the contemporary world and has become ineffectual because it has failed to challenge the status quo or work for any sort of social change. Recently, feminist and liberation hermeneutics have reacted with increasing impatience to the way mainstream biblical scholarship has detached itself from real social and political issues.

Empire and Theological Reflections

Scholars of biblical studies, or, for that matter, scholars working in the field of theological studies have yet to address the relation between European expansionism and the rise of their own discipline. More importantly, there is yet to be a theological critique of the empire, especially among English theologians. Precisely in the 1960s when the process of decolonization was taking place, Western theologians spent their creative energies addressing issues such as secularization and its impact on Christian faith. They were eloquent in their silence when it came to assessing the role of the West in the colonial domination, the one exception being the British theologian and missiologist, M. A. C. Warren. In his 1955 Reinecker Lectures at the Virginia Theological Seminary, *Caesar the Beloved Enemy*, he acknowledged the link between colonialism and mission, at that time an unusual admission: "Christianity in Asia and Africa is associated with the past political, economic and cultural 'aggression' of the West" (Warren 1995: 12). Warren's contention in the lectures was that the attack on imperialism had been largely misconceived, and one "cannot just dismiss it as 'an organized selfishness' or 'something minted in hell' " (Warren 1955: 28). His thesis was that to gain a true knowledge about colonialism one had to look at and appreciate the concrete examples of benefits it brought to the natives, rather than treat imperialism as an abstract notion, which Warren thought was an illegitimate way to study the subject. For him imperialism had to be evaluated theologically, in terms of God's purpose in history, which, among other things was "to bring mankind to a true knowledge of Himself who is Love, Power and Justice" (Warren 1955: 24).[10] In his view, imperialism could "be the vehicle of great good to a subject people" (Warren 1955: 36), and functioned as a "diffusion of good life" (Warren 1955: 21), and more importantly as "a *preparatio* for God's good will for the world" (Warren 1955: 28). The imperium was set as the providence of God to establish law and order and to forge unity among people driven by anarchy, by enlarging the idea of neighborhood for all those who came under the wings of the empire. Instead of being a citizen of a tribe, what colonial rule offered was a chance to be a citizen of the world and share in a common culture. He reminded his audience that African culture with its practice of witchcraft, ritual murder, and tribal warfare would not have prepared Africans to

face the modern world. To justify his claim biblically, Warren cited examples from the Hebrew Scripture as evidence of God operating in and through the great concentrations of power exercised by the empires of the ancient world. He also summoned the exegetical comments of Edward Selwyn on 1 Peter 2: 14 about the authority of the emperor and the state. But this concentration of power, in Warren's view, was positively a better alternative than the unruliness which prevailed in the colonies before the introduction of the Roman orderliness. The control and consolidation of power was an instrument to do justice. The role of the empire was teleological. Warren claimed: "It can, I think, be fairly argued that successive imperialisms have made a significant contribution to the realization of the vision of the time when 'the earth shall be filled with the knowledge of God as the water covers the sea' " (Warren 1955: 27). Under colonial rule, "love, power and justice have been seen to take shape redeeming some tragic situation" (Warren 1955: 31). Then he went on to claim that "at least, up till today, no other method has been devised for so successfully keeping the peace and making progress possible" (Warren 1955: 28). If there were any fault in the imperial enterprise it was because "imperialism is an activity of fallen humanity" (Warren 1955: 40). Quoting Paul Tillich, Warren also went on to remind the American audience of America's "vocational consciousness," the American dream, "namely to establish the earthly form of the kingdom of God by a new beginning" which was meant first for America alone but now "is meant explicitly for one-half of the world and implicitly for the whole world" (Warren 1955: 30).

Warren echoes the views of those who saw the empire with touching fondness, as the personification of grandeur and as the instigator of civilizing values. It is these facets of imperial glory that Warren wanted to rescue from the clutches of postcolonial revisionism. I have taken time over the work of Warren to reiterate two points. One, that in spite of all atrocities, which he calls aberrations, the empire was a good thing and the other, the notable absence of the empire in English theological reflections. Warren's main thesis is that, despite the involvement of Christian mission with colonialism, its praiseworthy achievements speak for themselves. This view is still prevalent among many who look at missionary activities with nostalgia (Coote 2000: 100). I will come back to this point and try to offer a response in the concluding section. Western theologians have yet to offer a sustained theological analysis of the impact of colonialism. Colonialism has not received anything like as much attention as the Holocaust in recent theological reflection in the West. There is no admission of the place of colonialism in the shaping of English theology.[11]

Postcolonial Criticism and Cognate Disciplines – Feminism

Some of the critical undertakings pursued by postcolonialism coincide with such liberative movements as feminism. What unites feminist and postcolonial critique is their mutual resistance to any form of oppression – be it patriarchy or colonialism. In their strategies of resistance, both feminist and postcolonial critics are of one accord. They seek to uncover the subjugation of both men and women in colonial texts, and the modes of resistance of the subjugated, and expose the use of gender in both colonial discourse and social reality. In spite of their cordial collaboration, however, there is an in-house debate within the field, which manifests itself in three

forms. First, there is a concern among feminists, of both the First and Third Worlds that in building up the larger picture of colonialism, male-centered postcolonial work tends to overlook and underplay gender differences, women's concerns, and their role in emancipatory struggles. Secondly, Third World feminist scholars are of the view that, notwithstanding their solidarity, First World biblical scholars still work within and often replicate male colonial tendencies. Thirdly, recently, postcolonial feminist biblical scholars have joined in the criticism of the First World feminist biblical scholars, in pointing out that in the noble aim of feminist construction of biblical narratives, they often compromise and overlook the colonial context of these texts, and their exegetical conclusions are often arrived at without problematizing the colonial agenda embedded in the biblical narratives.[12]

While conceding that, just as there are many forms of patriarchy, there are many forms of colonialism. First World feminists tend to conflate them. Third World feminist scholars, on the other hand, make it clear that they are not identical. Though women are doubly victimized by patriarchy and colonialism, the former is seen as male domination of the female, whereas the latter is defined as nation states which include both men and women who subjugate and control men and women of other nation states. Third World feminists complain that collapsing them into one category, fails to acknowledge different strategies of subjugation. Third World feminists criticize First World feminists for homogenizing Third World women in their works and portraying them as perpetual and hapless victims, or in some cases, failing to recognize the contribution Third World women have made in different fields.

Third World feminists have acted as a necessary corrective to mainstream postcolonial thinking. They have extended their work to include issues overlooked by the dominant postcolonial thinking. Rajeswari Sunder Rajan and You-me Park have outlined the following as the postcolonial feminist agenda: the retrieval and investigation of the role of women in independence movements, social roles of women, motherhood, and relations among women of different castes, class, and religious communities. They also include how these were reformulated under modernity and the colonial state's reformist legislation, women's role and contribution in economic development, the interface between the emancipatory goals of feminism and the agendas of nationalism, religious fundamentalism, communalism, the rights of immigrant women in metropolitan centres when they are pitched against modern, secular values, and the virulent nationalism of the host countries (Sunder Rajan and Park 2000: 53–71). To this one could add the link between race and gender in colonial expansion.

Though there is a potential tension between feminism and postcolonialism, feminism should not be seen as an adjunct to postcolonialism. Notwithstanding tensions within the field, feminist critical work should be seen as integral to postcolonial thinking.

Global Intentions and Postcolonial Concerns

The current globalization is not something that happened suddenly. Its roots go back to colonial history and it is a legacy of European colonialism and modernity. Syed Ahmed Khan, the Indian reformer, was able to detect how the combined efforts of

colonialism and the inventions of modernity were able to transform and shrink the world: "Railways, Steam Vessels and the Electric Telegraph, are rapidly uniting all the nations of the earth: the more they are brought together, the more certain does the conclusion become, that all have the same wants, the same anxieties, the same hopes, and the same fears, and therefore the same nature and the same origin" (Ahmed Khan 1873: 55). Globalization is not something new. It has been going on for ages. There is a world legacy of interchange and interaction. The influences have gone in different directions. Recently, the flow has been mainly from the West to the rest of the world. Previously it was the other way round. It was Europe which was assimilating Arabic science and technology and Indian mathematics, and consuming goods from China. Like most of the cultural forces of our time, globalization manifests itself in a variety of ways – economically, politically, and culturally – and all of these evolved over several centuries of European imperialism. In some ways, what the present globalization does, following the demise of the old colonialism, is to intensify the power relations in a more acute manner. The crucial difference between the old colonialism and the current globalization is the unrivalled grip of the United States on the world economy through military and foreign policies, its financial and mercantile corporations, and its hold on world culture through its massive media outputs – television, film, and publishing.

There is also another key difference between modernity's old universalizing tendencies and the current globalization. Zygmunt Bauman is of the view that universalization and globalization represent more than a shift in vocabulary. He sees a distinction between the two – one religiously espousing emancipation, rationality, and the autonomy of the individual, the other an experience which people unwittingly comply with because of its overpowering presence and its relentless impingement on their lives:

> Modernity once deemed itself *universal*. It now thinks of itself instead as *global*. Behind the change of terms hides a watershed in the history of modern self-awareness and self-confidence. Universal was to be the rule of reason – the order of things that would replace slavery to passions with the autonomy of rational beings, superstition and ignorance with truth, tribulations of the drifting plankton with self-made and thoroughly monitored history-by-design. "Globality" in contrast, means merely that everyone everywhere may feed on McDonald's burgers and watch the latest made-for-TV docudrama. Universality was a proud project, a herculean mission to perform. Globality in contrast, is a meek acquiescence to what is happening "out there";... Universality was a feather in philosophers' caps. Globality, exiles the philosophers, naked, back into the wilderness from which universality promised to emancipate them. (Bauman 1995: 24; italics in original)

Though Bauman's distinction between the missionizing project of the Enlightenment and current popular cultural practices may be contrived, his claim that both are culturally controlled by the West is important. One also needs to differentiate, as Arjun Appadurai has pointed out, between cultural imperialism and the globalization of culture. In his view, the former stands for uniformity in the global spread of Western consumer culture, whereas the latter demonstrates how Western

commodities are transformed into indigenous hybridized forms by local cultures (Appadurai 1990: 1–21).

There are two varieties of globalization: élite and grassroots. It is the latter which is of special interest to postcolonialism. The singular aim of elite globalization is to maximize profits for international corporations. It is this form of globalization which compels Third World countries to deregulate their markets and open up national economies to multinational companies, advocates drastic cutbacks in social welfare programs, promulgates laws against trade union rights, and preaches the virtues of privatization of state-owned utilities. It speaks the vocabulary of efficiency, profit, and competition. Its organizing principle is the market, and everything and everyone must be subject to its forces. But there is another form of globalization which operates on different values. It focuses on the quality of human life, sustaining the environment, upholding human rights, and safeguarding the cultures of indigenous people. This grassroots globalization consists of people from both First and Third Worlds. It is composed of expert scientists, officials of international agencies, activists of non-governmental organizations, environmentalists, farmers and consumers, and members of people movements.[13] It is they who agitate for fair trade and fight to protect ecological balance and conserve the forests. What these different campaigns and movements are trying to do is, to use Naomi Klein's phrase, to "reclaim the commons", such communal spaces as "town squares, streets, schools, farms and plants" (Klein 2001: 82). They are working against forces which are bent on privatizing every aspect of life – health, education, and natural resources – into commodities. The issue is not whether poor countries should be economically developed or benefit from trade. They are already in the process of development. The issue is also not whether such developments would change the character of these countries. The changes are already afoot. The issue is about the terms on which change takes place and who will benefit as a result. It is here that postcolonialism can a play a positive role in exposing the exploitative policies of donor countries and organizations which force the under-developed nations to adopt measures which would make them conducive to the investment of multinational corporations.

A postcolonial approach is useful in dealing with the issues generated by globalization. The strategies for transformation used in postcolonial responses to colonial discourse, such as representation, exposure of the link between power and knowledge, resistance, can become useful tools in the hands of local communities who engage with the forces of globalization. The earlier paradigms of how subjugated people under colonialism achieved agency, can provide models for local cultures and communities to compete and reassert and reclaim their agency under the pressures of global hegemony.

Is the United States Postcolonial?

Postcolonial studies have been largely seen as concerned with former colonies of Europe and generated by the hermeneutical efforts of a Commonwealth-led literary activity. The canon is in the main populated with literature from Africa and Asia, and spiced up with articulations of thinkers who were actively engaged in anti-colonial struggles, such as Fanon, Cabral, and James referred to above. Such

accepted notions tend to keep the United States of America, the present imperialist giant, outside the discursive loop. There is an uneasiness in associating the United States with postcoloniality.[14] Curiously enough, in their watershed book, *The Empire Writes Back*, Bill Ashcroft, Gareth Griffiths, and Helen Tiffin advanced the notion that the United States was "the first post-colonial society to produce a 'national' literature" and, to the great annoyance of other critics, the trio went on to claim the United States as an exemplar of postcolonial literary activity: "In many ways the American experience and its attempt to produce a new kind of literature can be seen to be the model for all later post-colonial writing" (Ashcroft, Griffiths, and Tiffin 1989: 16). In spite of advancing this proposition, Ashcroft, Griffiths, and Tiffin, did not, in their book, look at American literature or its role in the global cultural landscape. The question then is, does the United States become postcolonial simply because it broke its connection with England in the eighteenth century, and does this count for more than its neo-colonial position as an unrivalled financial, military, and political power in the world which has no equal competitors. However, there is a crucial difference between US and European colonialism. Malini Johar Schueller, who has studied the nineteenth-century American discourses, points out that for England and France the narrative of the empire needed to be undergirded by "firm national character", but in the United States the imperialism was constructed much more benevolently as a teleological project:

> Since the "discovery" of the Americas by Columbus was popularly transmitted as the outcome of a vision to reach the Orient, contemporary arguments about seizing Oriental trade or civilizing Orientals through missionary activity were accompanied by visionary statements about completing Columbus's original mission. Tropes of expansion and control over various specific Orients were thus mystified as "natural" through the complex genealogy of the country's intimate associations with the search for the Orient. (Schueller 1998: 9)[15]

Paul Tillich, whom Warren quoted enthusiastically, saw American expansion as a vocational consciousness which expressed itself in laws which embody love and justice. He also foresaw it as one of the great powers emerging as a "world centre, ruling the other nations through liberal methods and in democratic forms!" (Tillich 1954: 105).[16]

The question as to whether the United States is postcolonial or not depends more on how one defines postcolonialism than on the status of the United States. There is an attempt among some American scholars working in the field to extend the term "postcolonial" to cover not only the traditional catchment area of Europe and its colonies but also the United States. The strategy here is to redefine and advance notions of postcolonialism as a more processual, fluid, and dynamic concept. With such a reconfiguration in mind, Karen Piper defines postcolonialism as "after the imprint of colonialism". She goes on to claim: "The US, then, is postcolonial in the sense that its fundamental identity is wrapped in a colonizing project – whether settler or indigenous, the inhabitants of the US have been impacted by the colonial ideal of resource 'development' or exploitation" (Piper 1999: 19). The tendency is to disregard "post" in the term "postcolonial" as an evaluative term denoting "after colonialism," and appropriate it as a descriptive one and as a legacy which continues

to survive as an existential reality for many Americans. Two such legacies, according to Karen Piper, are "internal extermination," where the United States is engaged in displacing people, and the other is "successive waves of immigration," which still continues (Piper 1999: 14–28).

Another marker of colonialism which helps to redefine America as postcolonial is the marginalization faced by American ethnic minorities. If postcolonial discursive practices emerge from the experience of colonial dominance, then, according to Deborah Madsen, Native American, Chicano American, African American, and Asian American writers face precisely a similar kind of "marginalization and cultural erasure" to that which writers from Africa, India, and other settler colonies face. In Deborah Madsen's view, the US minorities are left out of the current discussion because of an obsolete concept of American literature as "originating in Massachusetts with the Winthrop and Bradford settlements and developing through the American resistance of the 1850s to a twentieth-century Modernist-Postmodernist literature" (Madsen 1999: 4). Since a sense of commonality runs through the writings of the Third World and American minority writers, based on experience of "imperial domination, cultural catastrophe, genocide, and erasure" (Madsen 1999: 11), there is no justification for excluding their texts:

> In comparison with the post-colonial expression of Australian Aboriginal writers, Canadian First Nations writers, New Zealand Maori writers, indigenous African writers, the work of American Indian writers assumes a new set of significances that is derived from a matrix of indigenous experience, and not from the stifling paradigm of sophisticated metropolitan centre versus primitive post-colonial margin. This is important, because the values assigned to literary expression in native cultures may share more in common with each other than with the values of Western literary representation. (Madsen 1999: 11)

The scenario is similar to the one the Ecumenical Association of Third World Theologians (EATWOT) faced in its formative years. The vexing question which tormented the original founders, who came from Asia and Africa and Latin America, was whether to include African Americans and Native Americans in their newly formed group. Their decision to allow them to be part of EATWOT was eventually decided on the basis of their marginality.

According a marginal status to American minority writers is not without problems. While concurring with, and at the same time not discounting the value of marginal status in the prevailing models of postcolonial studies, Jenny Sharpe observes that such a reduction of the field to discussions surrounding marginality and oppression in the texts of the past and present diasporic experience of African slaves, and diverse experiences of immigrants from the Third World to industrialized nations, offers explanations of past history but not of the present state of the United States as a neo-colonial power. Her proposal is that postcolonialism as a critical category should move beyond these accepted notions and be seen as the study of differential power and transnationalism: "I want to propose that the postcolonial be theorized as the point at which internal social relations intersect with global capitalism and the international division of labour. In other words, I want us to define the 'after' to colonialism as the neocolonial relations into which the United States

entered with decolonized nations" (Sharpe 2000: 106). Richard King, in a volume of essays which maps out and clarifies the applicability of postcolonialty to America, states: "Indeed, framing the United States as postcolonial, as emergent through its changing relations both with European imperialism and with its own imperial endeavours, directs attention to its production as an imperial nation-state" (King 2000: 5). Associating the United States with postcoloniality, captures many of the complicated experiences of contemporary American life.

Concerns, Temptations, Conclusions

Those engaged in postcolonial discourse are, among other things, constantly confronted with two questions. One, whether one should rake up the past and blame earlier generations and make their present successors feel guilty for the misdeeds of their forebears. The other side of this is to make all victims innocent and virtuous. The issue is not that one is at fault, and the other is blameless. The issue is how one makes use of the past and who benefits from it. If one is in the business of glorifying the past, and making use of stereotypical images from a bygone era to decide policies which affect the housing, education, and health of ethnic minorities, then one should recognize the ambivalence of past achievements. If the empire is portrayed as a magnificent achievement, then one should be reminded of the atrocities, ranging from the slave trade to planned genocide and forced resettlement, which were committed in the name of the empire. These heinous events should not be airbrushed out of the record because they make unpleasant reading but should be highlighted as integral to the achievement. If history books rhapsodize Victorian achievements, then it is reasonable also to recount colonial genocides which resulted in the killing of 60 million Asians, Latin Americans, and Africans, which Mike Davies calls the "Victorian Holocaust."[17] If Winston Churchill is portrayed as typifying the British bulldog spirit, then reverential accounts of his life should also refer to his part in perpetuating the famine in Bengal which killed nearly three million people because of his uncompromising stance on sending relief to help the victims. In order to further reveal his xenophobic nature, it would not be a bad idea to recall his extraordinary proposal that Gandhi should be bound hand and foot and trampled by viceregal elephants (Raychaudhuri 1999: x, xi). History books which highlight the wonderful achievements of the East India Company and its clerk Lord Clive should also point out the rapacious nature of their enterprise and his criminal deeds. Similarly, if Indian nationalists stress the Jalianwala Bagh incident of 1918, where innocent protesters were massacred by British troops under the command of General Dyer, it would also be right to recall that four years later 1,200 Gujarati tribals, more than three times the number killed in the Amritsar incident, were gunned down by the local landowners with the help of the British simply because they were demanding a lower levy by the landowners.

The second question which is often raised by apologists for colonialism is what is wrong in regenerating, renovating, and civilizing a people who were "living in darkness." This kind of argument was advocated by Warren, as we saw earlier. The supporters of this claim often point to the benefits bestowed by the Western powers upon people who were deemed to be uncivilized. One often hears about the

British abolishing *sati* in India, polygamy in Africa, human sacrifice in the Pacific, and how European clothes and Western knowledge were introduced. Or as Warren claimed: "Would a Nkrumah on the Gold Coast have sprung like an African Athene 'full-armed' from the bush?" (Warren 1955: 28). Tzvetan Todorov, who studied Western colonial atrocities in the Americas, provides an apt answer to such queries:

> A civilization may have features we can say are superior or inferior; but this does not justify their being imposed on others. Even more, to impose one's will on others implies that one does not concede to that other the same humanity one grants to oneself, an implication which precisely characterises a lower civilization. No one asked the Indians if they wanted the wheel, or looms, or forges; they were obliged to accept them. Here is where the violence resides, and it does not depend on the possible utility of these objects. (Todorov 1992: 179)

The current postcolonial discourse places a high emphasis on the nineteenth century and along with it the British empire and its achievements. The trouble with such a preoccupation is that it gives a distorted version of Britain, and is, to use Linda Colley's phrase, "over-flattering to the West" (Colley 2000: 19). True, Britain was at the zenith of its power in the nineteenth century, but it was from this highly advantageous position that the previous centuries of British history were interpreted. Postcolonial criticism often works on the premiss that, because of the scale of European dominance in the nineteenth century, the West was able to map out its responses to the Orient and to Islam from a towering position of might, belligerence, and military superiority. It was not the case, as Linda Colley has pointed out:

> British knowledge and preconceptions about Islam were not and could not be translated into durable colonizing ventures as far as the Ottomans or the North African powers were concerned before 1800. Until the mid-1700s at least, Ottoman Turkey was a more formidable and in many ways a more sophisticated state than Britain, while the North African powers not only remained independent of Europe but also preyed effectively on Western commerce and seized large numbers of European captives. (Colley 2000: 18)

Postcolonial criticism should abandon its obsession with the nineteenth century and widen its net to include other forms of colonialism and other influences before and since the nineteenth century. Nayantara Sahgal expressed aptly at the Silver Jubilee conference of the Association of the Commonwealth Literature and Language Studies:

> So is "colonial" the new Anno Domini from which events are to be everlastingly measured? My own awareness as a writer reaches back to x-thousand B.C., at the very end of which measureless timeless time the British came, and stayed, and left. And now they're gone, and their residue is simply one more layer added to the layer upon layer of Indian consciousness. Just one more. (Sahgal 1992: 30)

There is, further, a tendency among postcolonial critics to homogenize colonial experience. The sheer diversity of colonial encounters from settler to imperial projects is too complicated and complex to see as a single pattern. Often a certain

colonial experience is highlighted and it is from this prism that the rest of colonial encounters are read. For instance, Fanon's *Wretched of the Earth*, has become a paradigmatic text to judge and evaluate other colonialisms, often forgetting that it was tied to a particular locale. It was written in 1961 as a response to a specific Algerian context. It came out of and was addressed to a very specific group of people in French-speaking West Africa, the native intellectuals and the middle-class who were yet to be emancipated. Despite the different manifestations of colonialism with their different codes of practice and different styles of assimilation and different modes of power relations, there is a tendency to see all these experiences as a single, undifferentiated whole.

One of the most challenging and exciting aspects of postcolonial criticism has been its rereading of ancient documents and literary texts. Its application has produced unexpected results to those not familiar with this literature. It has brought to the fore some of the often neglected and even in some cases unrecognized aspects of well-known texts. Now it has become impossible to read texts such as Joseph Conrad's *Heart of Darkness*, or E. M. Forster's *A Passage to India*, or Jane Austen's *Mansfield Park* without noticing colonial allusions to, for example, slavery, sugar plantations, racial tensions, and the scramble for Africa, embedded in these novels. Such a preoccupation with tracking down ideologies in the plots and characterization has resulted in two things. One, it has re-emphasized and re-empowered the role of the critic. The critic is now invested with power and knowledge and acts as a broker between literature and the lay reader. Secondly, however, such an exercise can become an esoteric and an escapist activity. It might encourage the notion that deconstructing a narrative is the ultimate form of liberation, and lead to complacency and overlook continuing structural inequalities that are staring at us. Unless there is a serious effort to connect the interrogations of these narratives with the concerns of people, such as housing, education, health, human rights, and asylum, postcolonial criticism will lose its potency and credibility.

Postcolonialism has enabled those of us who were part of the former empires to see ourselves differently. It has helped us to go beyond thinking in contrastive pairs "us" and "them," "East" and "West." Such a duality reduces everyone to an undifferentiated entity. What postcolonialism does is to help us to free ourselves from such neatly drawn confines. At least it seems possible to throw off the victim syndrome. Positively, what postcolonial criticism does is to prevent interpretation from becoming too nativistic or nationalistic. One is freed from the cultural compulsion to assert one's own heritage and self-consciously interpret everything as an Indian or Sri Lankan or whatever. It also enables Western countries to recognize the extent to which European culture and knowledge were involved in and contributed to older and continuing forms of deprivation, exploitation, and colonization. Negatively, too much theory-chasing and too much enchantment with it, and a hope that modern theory will make up for the lack of imaginative hermeneutics, will not take us far. Its specific usefulness lies in its capacity to detect oppression, expose misrepresentation, and to promote a fairer world rather than in its sophistry, precision, and its erudite qualities as a critical tool. Postcolonial criticism will enhance its value if it can foster a greater interchange between theoretical fine-tuning in the academy and the wider world.

NOTES

1 There are a number of readers and introductions which deal with the history, theory, practice, and debates about postcolonialism. For history, see Bill Ashcroft, Gareth Griffiths, and Helen Tiffin, *The Empire Writes Back: Theory and Practice in Post-Colonial Literatures* (London: Routledge, 1989) and Robert J. C. Young, *Postcolonialism: An Historical Introduction* (Oxford: Blackwell Publishers, 2001); for explanation of terms, see Bill Ashcroft, Gareth Griffiths, and Helen Tiffin, *Key Concepts in Post-Colonial Studies* (London: Routledge, 1998); for various issues related to postcolonialism, see Henry Schwarz and Sangeetha Ray (eds), *A Companion to Postcolonial Studies* (Oxford: Blackwell Publishers, 2000) and Bill Ashcroft, *Post-Colonial Transformation* (London: Routledge, 2001); for an introduction and some of the debates surrounding postcolonialism, see Ania Loomba, *Colonialism/Postcolonialism* (London: Routledge, 1998), Peter Childs and Patrick Williams, *An Introduction to Post-Colonial Theory* (London: Prentice-Hall, 1997), Ato Quayson, *Postcolonialism: Theory, Practice or Process?* (Cambridge: Polity Press, 2000), Leela Gandhi, *Postcolonial Theory: A Critical Introduction* (Edinburgh: Edinburgh University Press, 1998), and John McLeod, *Beginning Postcolonialism* (Manchester: Manchester University Press, 2000); for anthologies, see Padmini Mongia (ed.), *Contemporary Postcolonial Theory: A Reader* (London: Arnold, 1996) and Bill Ashcroft, Gareth Griffiths, and Helen Tiffin, *The PostColonial Studies Reader* (London: Routledge, 1995). The journals which deal with postcolonial issues are: *Interventions: International Journal of Postcolonial Studies* and *Postcolonial Studies: Culture, Politics, Economy.*

2 I found this quotation in Robert J. C. Young, *Postcolonialism: An Historical Introduction* (Oxford: Blackwell Publishers, 2001), 64.

3 For other Indian theorizing, see V. K. Chari, *Sanskrit Criticism* (Delhi: Motilal Banarsidass Publishers, 1990) and K. Satchidanandan, *Indian Literature: Positions and Propositions* (Delhi: Pencraft International, 1999).

4 For an incisive introduction and critique, see Grant Farred (ed.), *Rethinking C. L. R. James* (Oxford: Blackwell Publishers, 1996) and Lewis R. D. Gordon, Dean T. Sharpley-Whiting, and Renée T. White (eds), *Fanon: A Critical Reader* (Oxford: Blackwell Publishers, 1996).

5 Frantz Fanon's other writings include: *A Dying Colonialism*, trans. H. Chevalier (Harmondsworth: Penguin Books, 1970) and *Black Skin, White Másks*, trans. C. L. Markmann (London: Pluto Press, 1986).

6 For essays on biblical themes on justice and liberation in the writings of Latin American and African novelists, see Susan VanZanten Gallagher, *Postcolonial Literature and the Biblical Call for Justice* (Jackson: University Press of Mississippi, 1994). For the use of the Bible in Ngũgĩi wa Thiong'o's novels, see Peter Wamulungwe Mwikisa, "The Limits of Difference: Ngũgĩ wa Thiong'o's Redeployment of Biblical Signifiers in *A Grain of Wheat* and *I Will Marry when I Want*," in G. O. West and M. W. Dube (eds), *The Bible in Africa: Transactions, Trajectories, Trends* (Leiden: Brill, 2000), 163–83.

7 For further examples of profuse use of the Bible in novels which deal with colonialism and newly independent nations in the Pacific, see Epeli Hau'ofa, *Tales of the Tikongs* (Honolulu: University of Hawaii Press, 1983). Also see Leñero's reworking of St Luke's gospel from a Mexican perspective, which also falls within the larger context of postcolonial literature and biblical interpretation, Vicente Leñero, *The Gospel of Lucan Gavilán*, trans. R. Mowry (Lanham, Md.: University Press of America, 1991). For a critique of Leñero's work, see Hector Avalos, "*The Gospel of Lucan Gavilán* as Postcolonial Biblical Exegesis," *Semeia: An Experimental Journal for Biblical Criticism*, 75 (1996): 87–105.

8 Said's work concentrates mainly on the Middle East. For a similar treatment of Latin America, see Tzvetan Todorov, *The Conquest of America: The Question of the Other*, trans. R. Howard (New York: Harper Perennial, 1992); and for Africa, see Walter Rodney, *How Europe Underdeveloped Africa* (Harare: Zimbabwe Publishing House, 1972).

9 For a succinct critique of the Ashcroft, Griffiths, and Tiffin model, see McLeod, *Beginning Postcolonialism*, 27–8. Since the publication of the *Empire Writes Back*, there has been a proliferation of literature which builds on and goes beyond issues related to literatures of the Third World. For a convenient entry into the subject, see Bruce King, *New National and Post-colonial Literatures: An Introduction* (Oxford: Clarendon Press, 1996).

10 This kind of view, acknowledging the grandeur of British achievement in India notwithstanding its failures, was held by some Indian Christians also. For instance, soon after Indian Independence, the renowned Indian theologian M. M. Thomas wrote that under God's providence, British imperialism in India was laying the foundation for political unity and social progress. Echoing Karl Marx's double vision of the British in India – one destructive and the other regenerative – Thomas wrote that God used British imperialism "to judge and correct traditional Indian life and put India on the path of progress" ("Indian Nationalism: A Christian Interpretation," *Religion and Society*, 6/2 (1959): 7). Interestingly, in his private correspondence with Warren, Thomas agreed with his main proposal but castigated Warren for his narrow understanding of theology which centred on creation but failed to take note of the fall, judgement, and redemption (ibid. 1617). For a trenchant critique of Warren's thesis by R. L. Hsu, the Chinese theologian, see ibid. 1924.

11 For the English Churches' attitude over the last four decades to race, immigration, nationality, and asylum, which are all interconnected with British colonialism, see Kenneth Leech, "From Chaplaincy towards Prophecy: Racism and Christian Theology over Four Decades," *Race and Class*, 41/1–2 (1999): 131–42.

12 For a vigorous critique of First World feminist biblical scholars by Third World feminist interpreters, see Musa W. Dube, *Postcolonial Feminist Interpretation of the Bible* (St Louis: Chalice Press, 2000) and Laura E. Donaldson, "Postcolonialism and Biblical Reading: Introduction," *Semeia: An Experimental Journal for Biblical Criticism*, 75 (1996): 114.

13 For the possibilities and dangers of such alliances, see Alan Thomas, "Modernisation Versus the Environment? Shifting Objectives of Progress," in T. Skelton and T. Allen (eds), *Culture and Global Change* (London: Routledge, 1999), 4557.

14 For a neat summary and critique of the debate and the personalities involved, see Jon Stratton, "The Beast of the Apocalypse: The Postcolonial Experience of the United States," in C. R. King (ed.), *Post-Colonial America* (Urbana: University of Illinois Press, 2000), 2164, esp. 51–61; Karen Piper, "Post-Colonialism in the United States: Diversity or Hybridity," in D. L. Madsen (ed.), *Post-Colonial Literatures: Expanding the Canon* (London: Pluto Press, 1999), 20; and C. Richard King, "Introduction: Dislocating Postcoloniality, Relocating American Empire," in C. Richard King (ed.), *Post-Colonial America* (Urbana: University of Illinois Press, 2000), 35.

15 For the absence of the American empire in American studies, see Amy Kaplan and Donald E. Pease (eds), *Cultures of United States Imperialism* (Durham, NC: Duke University Press, 1993).

16 To be fair to Tillich, he also warned that there would be a threat to the center of power, first from within and openly "driving towards separation from or towards radical transformation of the whole. They may develop a vocational consciousness of their own" (Paul Tillich, *Love, Power and Justice: Ontological Analyses and Ethical Applications* (London: Oxford University Press, 1954), 106). The current anti-capitalist movement may be a sign of this disruption and dissension which Tillich predicted.

17 From the review of Mike Davis's book, *Late Victorian Holocausts: El niño Famines and the Making of the Third World* (London: Verso, 2001), by Michael Watts, "Black Acts," *New Left Review*, 9 (2001): 125–40.

REFERENCES

Ahmed Khan, S. (1873; 2000). *The Causes of the Indian Revolt* (Oxford in Asia, Historical Reprints). Karachi: Oxford University Press.

Appadurai, Arjun (1990). "Disjuncture and Difference in the Global Cultural Economy." *Public Culture*, 2/2: 1–24.

Arasanayagam, Jean (2000). *In the Garden Secretly and Other Stories*. New Delhi: Penguin Books.

Ashcroft, Bill (2001). *Post-Colonial Transformation*. London: Routledge.

—— Griffiths, Gareth, and Tiffin, Helen (1989). *The Empire Writes Back: Theory and Practice in Post-Colonial Literatures*. London: Routledge.

—— —— —— (1995). *The Post-Colonial Studies Reader.* London: Routledge.

—— —— —— (1998). *Key Concepts in Post-Colonial Studies*. London: Routledge.

Avalos, Hector (1996). "*The Gospel of Lucan Gavilán* as Postcolonial Biblical Exegesis." *Semeia: An Experimental Journal for Biblical Criticism*, 75: 87–105.

Bauman, Zygmunt (1995). *Life in Fragments: Essays in Postmodern Morality.* Oxford: Blackwell.

Bhabha, Homi K. (1994). *The Location of Culture*. London: Routledge.

—— (2000). "The Vernacular Cosmopolitan," in F. Dennis and N. Khan (eds), *Voices of the Crossing: The Impact of Britain on Writers from Asia, the Caribbean and Africa*. London: Serpent's Tail, 133–42.

Chari, V. K. (1990). *Sanskrit Criticism*. Delhi: Motilal Banarsidass Publishers.

Childs, Peter, and Williams, Patrick (1997). *An Introduction to Post-Colonial Theory.* London: Prentice-Hall.

Christian, Barbara (1995). "The Race for Theory," in B. Ashcroft, G. Griffiths, and H. Tiffin (eds.), *The Post-Colonial Studies Reader.* London: Routledge, 457–60.

Colley, Linda (2000). "Britain and Islam: 1600–1800: Different Perspectives on Difference," *Yale Review*, 88/4: 1–20.

Coomaraswamy, Ananda K. (1909). *Essays in National Idealism*. Madras: G. A. Natesan.

—— (1983). "The Religious Basis of the Forms of Indian Society." *Studies in Comparative Religion*, 15/1–2: 9–29.

Cooppan, Vilashini (2000). "W(h)ither Post-colonial Studies? Towards the Transnational Study of Race and Nation," in L. Chrisman and B. Parry (eds), *Postcolonial Theory and Criticism*. Suffolk: D. S. Brewer, 1–35.

Donaldson, Laura E. (1996). "Postcolonialism and Biblical Reading: Introduction." *Semeia: An Experimental Journal for Biblical Criticism*, 75: 1–14.

—— (1999). "The Sign of Orpah: Reading Ruth through Native Eyes," in R. S. Sugirtharajah (ed.), *Vernacular Hermeneutics*. Sheffield: Sheffield Academic Press, 20–36.

Dube, Musa W. (2000). *Postcolonial Feminist Interpretation of the Bible*. St Louis: Chalice Press.

Fanon, Frantz (1970). *A Dying Colonialism*, trans. H. Chevalier. Harmondsworth: Penguin Books.

—— (1986). *Black Skin, White Masks*, trans. C. L. Markmann. London: Pluto Press.

—— (1990). *The Wretched of the Earth*, trans. C. Farrington. London: Penguin Books.

Farred, Grant (ed.) (1996). *Rethinking C. L. R. James*. Oxford: Blackwell.

Gallagher, Susan VanZanten (1994). *Postcolonial Literature and the Biblical Call for Justice*. Jackson: University Press of Mississippi.

Gandhi, Leela (1998). *Postcolonial Theory: A Critical Introduction.* Edinburgh: Edinburgh University Press.
Gordon, Lewis R., Sharpley-Whiting, T. D., and White, Renée T. (eds) (1996). *Fanon: A Critical Reader.* Oxford: Blackwell.
Guha, Ranajit (1988). "On Some Aspects of the Historiography of Colonial India," in R. Guha and G. C. Spivak (eds), *Selected Subaltern Studies.* New York: Oxford University Press, 37–44.
Hau'ofa, Epeli (1983; 1994). *Tales of the Tikongs.* Honolulu: University of Hawaii Press.
Kaplan, Amy, and Pease, Donald E. (eds) (1993). *Cultures of United States Imperialism.* Durham: Duke University Press.
Kapoor, Kapil (1998). *Literary Theory: Indian Conceptual Framework.* New Delhi: Affiliated East–West Press Private Limited.
King, Bruce (1996). *New National and Post-Colonial Literatures: An Introduction.* Oxford: Clarendon Press.
King, C. Richard (2000). "Introduction: Dislocating Postcoloniality, Relocating American Empire," in C. Richard King (ed.), *Post-Colonial America.* Urbana: University of Illinois Press, 1–17.
Klein, Naomi (2001). "Reclaiming the Commons." *New Left Review,* 7:81–9.
Landry, Donna and Maclean, Gerald (1996). *The Spivak Reader.* New York: Routledge.
Leech, Kenneth (1999). "From Chaplaincy towards Prophecy: Racism and Christian Theology over Four Decades." *Race and Class,* 41/1–2: 131–42.
Leñero, Vicente (1991). *The Gospel of Lucas Gavilan,* trans. R. Mowry. Lanham, Md: University Press of America.
Loomba, Ania (1998). *Colonialism/Postcolonialism.* London: Routledge.
McLeod, John (2000). *Beginning Postcolonialism.* Manchester: Manchester University Press.
Madsen, Deborah L. (1999). "Beyond the Commonwealth: Post-Colonialism and American Literature," in Deborah L. Madsen (ed.), *Post-Colonial Literatures: Expanding the Canon.* London: Pluto Press, 1–14.
Memmi, Albert (1990). *The Colonizer and the Colonized,* trans. H. Greenfeld. London: Earthscan Publications.
Mongia, Padmini. (ed.) (1996). *Contemporary Postcolonial Theory: A Reader.* London: Arnold.
Mwikisa, Peter Wamulungwe (2000). "The Limits of Difference: Ngũgĩ wa Thiong'o's Redeployment of Biblical Signifiers in *A Grain of Wheat and I Will Marry when I Want,*" in G. O. West and M. W. Dube (eds), *The Bible in Africa: Transactions, Trajectories, Trends.* Leiden: Brill, 163–83.
Nkrumah, Kwame (1965). *Neo-Colonialism: The Last Stage of Imperialism.* London: Thomas Nelson and Sons.
Nyabongo, Akiki K. (1936). *Africa Answers Back.* London: George Routledge & Sons Ltd.
Piper, Karen (1999). "Post-Colonialism in the United States: Diversity or Hybridity," in D. L. Madsen (ed.), *Post-Colonial Literatures: Expanding the Canon.* London: Pluto Press, 14–28.
Quayson, Ato (2000). *Postcolonialism: Theory, Practice or Process?* Cambridge: Polity.
Raychaudhuri, Tapan (1999). *Perceptions, Emotions, Sensibilities: Essays on India's Colonial and Post-Colonial Experiences.* New Delhi: Oxford University Press.
Rodney, Walter (1972). *How Europe Underdeveloped Africa.* Harare: Zimbabwe Publishing House.
Sahgal, Nayantara (1992). "The Schizophrenic Imagination," in A. Rutherford (ed.), *From Commonwealth to Post-Colonial.* Sydney: Dangroo Press, 30–6.
Said, Edward W. (1985). *Orientalism.* London: Penguin Books.

Said, Edward W. (1991). *The World, the Text, and the Critic*. London: Vintage.
—— (1993). *Culture and Imperialism*. London: Chatto & Windus.
Satchidanandan, K. (1999). *Indian Literature: Positions and Propositions*. Delhi: Pencraft International.
Schueller, Malini Johar (1998). *U.S. Orientalisms: Race, Nation, and Gender in Literature, 1790–1890*. Ann Arbor: University of Michigan Press.
Schwarz, Henry, and Ray, Sangeetha (eds) (2000). *A Companion to Postcolonial Studies*. Oxford: Blackwell.
Sharpe, Jenny (2000). "Is the United States Postcolonial? Transnationalism, Immigration, and Race," in R. C. King (ed.), *Post-Colonial America*. Urbana: University of Illinois Press, 103–21.
Slemon, Stephen (1994). "The Scramble for Post-Colonialism," in C. Tiffin and A. Lawson (eds), *De-Scribing Empire: Post-Colonialism and Textuality*. London: Routledge, 15–32.
Spivak, Gayatri Chakravorty (1993). "Can the Subaltern Speak?" in P. Williams and L. Chrisman (eds), *Colonial Discourse and Postcolonial Theory*. New York: Harvester Wheatsheaf, 66–111.
Stratton, Jon (2000). "The Beast of the Apocalypse: The Postcolonial Experience of the United States," in C. R. King (ed.), *Post-Colonial America*. Urbana: University of Illinois Press, 21–64.
Thomas, Alan (1999). "Modernisation Versus the Environment? Shifting Objectives of Progress," in T. Skelton and T. Allen (eds), *Culture and Global Change*. London: Routledge, 45–57.
Thomas, M. M. (1959). "Indian Nationalism: A Christian Interpretation." *Religion and Society*, 6/2: 4–26.
Tillich, Paul (1954). *Love, Power and Justice: Ontological Analyses and Ethical Applications*. London: Oxford University Press.
Todorov, Tzvetan (1992). *The Conquest of America: The Question of the Other*, trans. R. Howard. New York: Harper Perennial.
Warren, M. A. C. (1995). *Caesar: The Beloved Enemy: Three Studies in the Relation of Church and State*. The Reinecker Lectures at the Virginia Theological Seminary, Alexandria, Virginia, February 1955. London: SCM Press Ltd.
Watts, Michael (2001). "Black Acts." *New Left Review*, 9: 125–40.
— and Dube, M. W. (2000). *The Bible in Africa: Transactions, Trajectories and Trends*. Leiden: Brill.
Young, Robert J. C. (2001). *Postcolonialism: An Historical Introduction*. Oxford: Blackwell.

2

Biblical Criticism and Postcolonial Studies: Toward a Postcolonial Optic

Fernando F. Segovia

In previous delineations of the paradigm of cultural studies in biblical criticism, I have sought to bring to the fore the constellation of elements that I regard as fundamental to this most recent and still emerging umbrella model of interpretation in the discipline (Segovia 1995a; 1995b; 1998). Two of these I see as particularly relevant for the present study. The first involves a view of all interpretation, all recreations of meaning from texts and all reconstructions of history, as dependent upon reading strategies and theoretical models, with a further view of all such strategies and models and the resultant recreations and reconstructions as constructs on the part of real readers. The second concerns a view of real or flesh-and-blood readers as variously positioned and engaged within their respective social locations, with a further view of all such contextualizations and perspectives as constructs on the part of real readers as well.

Needless to say, such views regarding the character of interpretation and the role of critics bear immediate consequences for the dynamics and mechanics of the paradigm as a whole.

First, the task of interpretation is viewed in terms of the application of different reading strategies and theoretical models – whether produced or borrowed – by different real readers in different ways, at different times, and with different results (different readings and interpretations) in the light of their different and highly complex situations and perspectives.

Second, a critical analysis of real readers and their readings (their representations of themselves as well as their representations of the ancient texts and the ancient world) becomes as important and necessary as a critical analysis of the ancient texts themselves (the remains of the ancient world).

First published in R. S. Sugirtharajah, *Postcolonial Bible*. Sheffield: Sheffield Academic Press, 1998, 49–65.

Third, all recreations of meaning and all reconstructions of history are in the end regarded as representations of the past – recreations and reconstructions – on the part of readers who are themselves situated and interested to the core.

Finally, given its overriding focus on contextualization and perspective, social location and agenda, and thus on the political character of all compositions and texts, all readings and interpretations, all readers and interpreters, its mode of discourse may be described as profoundly ideological.

In this study I should like to proceed a step further in the definition and analysis of my own stance within the paradigm of cultural studies. In effect, I should like to lay the basic foundations and contours for what I have come to regard as a most appropriate, most enlightening, and most fruitful approach to biblical criticism, as I presently envision and practice the discipline. I have in mind the model of postcolonial studies, currently in vogue across a number of academic fields and disciplines.[1] This is a model that I find both hermeneutically rewarding and personally satisfying. On the one hand, I find that the model can shed precious, concomitant light on the various dimensions that I have posited as constitutive for my own vision and exercise of the discipline. On the other hand, I find that the model speaks to me in a very direct way, not only as a contemporary biblical critic but also as a constructive theologian as well as a cultural critic.[2]

Option for a Postcolonial Optic

This is not the first time that I have had recourse to the language and concepts of postcolonial studies. Indeed, I have done so in the past both as a biblical critic and as a constructive theologian. I should like to recall such previous appeals as a point of departure for the present proposal regarding the adoption of a systematic and fully fledged postcolonial optic.[3]

First, from the point of view of my work in biblical criticism, I have described the development of biblical criticism from its beginning as an academic discipline in the early nineteenth century through to its present formation at the end of the twentieth century as a process of "liberation" and "decolonization" (Segovia 1995a: 8–9; 1995b: 2–7). To begin with, the development itself, I argued, involved the sequential emergence of four paradigms or umbrella models of interpretation: (1) the initial turn to and long reign of historical criticism, from early in the nineteenth century through to the third quarter of the twentieth century; (2) the rapid rise and steady consolidation of literary criticism and cultural or social criticism, beginning in the mid-1970s and continuing right through the present; (3) the recent irruption of cultural studies, beginning in the late 1980s and early 1990s. This development, I further argued, resulted in the present stage of competing modes of discourse within the discipline. Finally, such historical development and disciplinary dénouement I classified in terms of "liberation" and "decolonization" on two grounds.

First, with reference to a fundamental transformation in theoretical orientation and reading strategy. In the process, I pointed out, the long-dominant construct of the scientific reader – the universal, objective and impartial reader, fully decontextualized and non-ideological – yielded, slowly but surely, to the construct of the real reader – the local, perspectival and interested reader, always contextualized and

ideological. Second, with reference to a fundamental transformation in the ranks of the discipline. In the process, I further pointed out, the male, clerical and European/Euro-American faces and concerns of the traditional practitioners of biblical criticism gave way, again gradually but steadily, to a variety of faces and concerns previously unknown to the discipline: at first, a large infusion of women from the West; subsequently, a growing presence of women and men from outside the West as well as from non-Western minorities in the West.

The end result of such transformations was not only enormous diversity in method and theory but also enormous diversity in faces and concerns within the discipline. This combined explosion of disciplinary perspectives and interpretive voices, I concluded, could and should be seen as a veritable process of liberation and decolonization: a movement away from the European and Euro-American voices and perspectives that had dominated biblical criticism for so long, toward a much more diversified and multicentered conception and exercise of the discipline. Biblical criticism, I observed, had become in the process but another example of a much more comprehensive process of liberation and decolonization at work in a number of different realms – from the political to the academic and, within the academy itself, across the entire disciplinary spectrum.

Second, from the point of view of my work in constructive theology, I have described the recent emergence of contextual theologies, both in the Two-Thirds World and among minorities of non-Western origin in the West, as an exercise in "liberation" and "decolonization" (Segovia 1992: 26–7). Thus, in setting out to formulate, as a distinctive expression within the rich matrix of US Hispanic American theology, a theology of the diaspora – a theology born and forged in exile, in displacement and relocation – I characterized it as both a "liberation" and a "postcolonial" theology (Segovia 1996a: 21–31; 1996b: 195–200).

Modern Christian theology, I argued, was a theology that emanated from the center, grounded as it was in Western civilization. As such, certain fundamental traits could be readily outlined: it was a systematic and universal theology, altogether reticent about its own social location and perspective; a theology of enlightenment and privilege, tacitly considered by nature superior to any theological production from outside the West – past, present, or future; a theology of hegemony and mission, with the effective control and progressive civilization of the margins in mind. In contrast, I further argued, diaspora theology – like any other contextual theology – was a theology that emerged from the margins, in this case from the margins within the West itself. Consequently, certain fundamental traits could be readily delineated as well: it was a self-consciously local and constructive theology, quite forthcoming about its own social location and perspective; a theology of diversity and pluralism, highlighting the dignity and value of all matrices and voices, including its own; a theology of engagement and dialogue, committed to critical conversation with other theological voices from both margins and center alike.

The rapid and widespread rise of contextual theologies, such as US Hispanic American theology and my own theology of the diaspora, I concluded, could and should be seen as an undeniable process of "liberation" and "decolonization": a movement away from the long-standing control of theological production by European and Euro-American voices and perspectives, toward the retrieval and revalorization of the full multiplicity of voices and perspectives in the margins. As in the

case of biblical criticism, therefore, theological studies, I observed, had also become in the process yet another example of the much more extensive process of liberation and decolonization at work in the world and in the academy.

Such past appeals on my part to the linguistic and conceptual apparatus of postcolonial studies have been, though quite useful and revealing to be sure, much too limited and unsystematic as well. A more fundamental grounding and deployment of the model is in order, therefore, and it is precisely this task that I should like to undertake in the present study, with biblical criticism specifically in mind. I do so, once again, because of the rich hermeneutical and personal dividends that I see as accruing from an explicit and sustained use of the model.

On the one hand, as I indicated earlier, this is a model that lends itself eminently to simultaneous application across the various dimensions that I see as central to my own conception and exercise of the discipline: first, the level of texts – the analysis of the texts of ancient Judaism and early Christianity; second, the level of "texts" – the analysis of readings and interpretations of such texts in the modern, Western tradition; third, the level of readers – the analysis of the modern and contemporary real readers of these texts and producers of the "texts" both inside and outside the West. In other words, postcolonial studies can function thereby as an excellent model for cross-cultural studies in the discipline, and in what follows I shall show how such is the case in terms of these three major dimensions of the discipline.

On the other hand, as I also stated earlier, this is a model that proves extremely appealing to me personally. The reason, I would readily acknowledge, has to do with my own social location and agenda: I come from the margins, from the world of the colonized; I reside in the center, in the world of the colonizers; and I have devoted myself to the struggle for liberation and decolonization, for the sake of both the colonized and the colonizer. For me, therefore, postcolonial studies not only comes from the heart, so to speak, it also refreshes and invigorates the heart. A colonial genealogy is in order.

The history of my own colonial mapping is quite complex. To begin with, I am a child of the Caribbean Basin, one of the most highly colonized and contested sites of the globe, as both the almost total absence of indigenous peoples and the presence of anglophone, francophone and hispanophone populations readily attest. Here the project of imperialism and colonialism was so immensely successful and so radically effective that, in a relatively brief period of time, the original local populations had disappeared and the original local languages had been replaced. Indeed, in the Caribbean archipelago one has to go almost island by island to explain the imperial and colonial dynamics at work over the five centuries since the European "discovery." Then, with emigration and exile, a further distinguishing mark of the Caribbean Basin, I became a child of the diaspora, a part of the Hispanic American reality and experience in the United States, a context of internal colonialism not unlike that facing other groups from outside the West now residing in the West (Segovia 1992: 27–33; 1996a: 21–31).

In my own case, therefore, as a native of the island of Cuba and an exile-immigrant in the United States, such mapping entails four distinctive experiences of imperialism and colonialism: (1) the after-effects of possession by the Spanish Empire, from the very beginning of its landfall in "the Americas" to the very demise of the empire itself – from the first voyage of Christopher Columbus to the Spanish–

American War (1492–1898); (2) the continuing effects of occupation by the American Empire at the very apex of its period of manifest destiny (1898–1902) followed by the period of the republic (1902–59), a period of neocolonial dependency, marked by the watchful supervision of the United States, a number of military interventions by US forces, and a series of cruel and corrupt dictatorships – from the declaration of independence to the triumph of the Cuban Revolution; (3) the new effects from the implantation of a socialist-Leninist system of government at the very height of the Cold War, under the neocolonial aegis of the Soviet Empire (1959–89) followed by the continuation of such a system of government even after the total collapse of the imperial center (1989–present); (4) the situation of internal colonialism affecting by and large the Hispanic American population as a whole in the United States.

In the light of such a long and distinguished pedigree, it should come as no surprise that I regard and construct myself as carrying imperialism and colonialism in my flesh and in my soul, as a human subject and as a real, flesh-and-blood reader – and hence as a biblical critic, as a constructive theologian and as a cultural critic. For me, therefore, the reality of empire, of imperialism and colonialism, constitutes an omnipresent, inescapable and overwhelming reality. My option for a postcolonial optic should thus be obvious: it is a model that I find most helpful, most revealing and most liberating. In what follows, therefore, I proceed to unpack its particular importance and relevance for biblical criticism.

Postcolonial Studies and Biblical Criticism

Postcolonial studies is a model that takes the reality of empire, of imperialism and colonialism, as an omnipresent, inescapable, and overwhelming reality in the world: the world of antiquity, the world of the Near East or of the Mediterranean Basin; the world of modernity, the world of Western hegemony and expansionism; and the world of today, of postmodernity, the world of postcolonialism on the part of the Two-Thirds World and of neocolonialism on the part of the West.

Postcolonial studies and ancient texts

A first dimension of a postcolonial optic in biblical criticism involves an analysis of the texts of ancient Judaism and early Christianity that takes seriously into consideration their broader sociocultural contexts in the Near East and the Mediterranean Basin, respectively, in the light of an omnipresent, inescapable and overwhelming sociopolitical reality – the reality of empire, of imperialism and colonialism, as variously constituted and exercised during the long period in question. Some preliminary observations regarding this phenomenon of empire are in order.[4]

First, the reality of empire should be seen as a structural reality that is largely defined and practiced in terms of a primary binomial: on the one hand, a political, economic, and cultural center – more often than not symbolized by a city; on the other hand, any number of margins politically, economically, and culturally subordinated to the center. This grounding binomial entails and engenders, in turn, any number of secondary or subordinate binomials: civilized/uncivilized; advanced/

primitive; cultured/barbarian; progressive/backward; developed/undeveloped – underdeveloped. Second, such a structural reality, despite the many and profound similarities in common, should not be seen as uniform in every imperial context across time and culture – say, for example, from the world of Assyria and Babylon, to the world of Greece and Rome, to the world of Western Europe and the United States – but as differentiated in constitution and deployment, though again with many and profound similarities in common. Third, this reality, I would argue, is of such reach and such power that it inevitably affects and colors, directly or indirectly, the entire artistic production of center and margins, of dominant and subaltern, including their respective literary productions.

From the point of view of ancient Judaism and its literature, it is necessary to speak not just of one empire but of a succession of empires involving, depending on the locality of the center in question, the Near East as well as the Mediterranean Basin: Assyria, Babylon, Persia, Greece, Rome. From the point of view of early Christianity and its literature, it is obviously the massive presence and might of the Roman Empire, master and lord of the entire Circum-Mediterranean, with its thoroughly accurate if enormously arrogant classification of the Mediterranean Sea as *mare nostrum*.

To begin with, therefore, the shadow of empire in the production of ancient texts is to be highlighted. A number of key questions come to the fore as a result: How do the margins look at the "world" – a world dominated by the reality of empire – and fashion life in such a world? How does the center regard and treat the margins in the light of its own view of the "world" and life in that world? What images and representations of the other-world arise from either side? How is history conceived and constructed by both sides? How is "the other" regarded and represented? What conceptions of oppression and justice are to be found? From the perspective of postcolonial studies, such questions – questions of culture, ideology, and power – emerge as crucial.

Postcolonial studies and modern readings

A second dimension of the proposed postcolonial optic in biblical criticism involves an analysis of the readings and interpretations of the texts of Jewish and Christian antiquity that takes seriously into account their broader sociocultural context in the West, whether by way of Europe or of North America, in the light of the same omnipresent, inescapable, and overwhelming sociopolitical reality that surrounded the production of the texts of ancient Judaism and early Christianity – the reality of empire, of imperialism and colonialism, now with regard to the Western imperial tradition of the last 500 years.

First, the imperial tradition of the West may be approached in terms of three different phases and periods:[5] (1) early imperialism, with reference to the initial, mercantile phase of European imperialism – from the fifteenth century through most of the nineteenth century, from the monarchical states of Portugal and Spain to the early modern states of England, France, and the Netherlands, among others; (2) high imperialism, involving monopoly capitalism with its integration of industrial and finance capital in the major capitalist nation-states – from the end of the nineteenth century through to the middle of the twentieth century, with England as prime

example; and (3) late imperialism, with reference to both the end of formal colonialism and the continued impact and power of imperial culture in the world – from mid-century to the present, with the United States as its prime example.

Second, this tradition of Western empire-building was accompanied by a very prominent socioreligious dimension as well. Thus, the Western missionary movement may be divided into two major waves and periods, represented by the highly symbolic dates of 1492 and 1792.[6] The first date stands, of course, for the first European landfall in the "New World." This first stage of the missions (1492–1792) is primarily Catholic in orientation, involves the massive evangelization of the Americas, and finds itself near exhaustion by the end of the eighteenth century. The second date, not as well known, recalls two different though related events: first, with regard to Asia (India), the publication of William Carey's *Enquiry into the obligation of Christians to use means for the propagation of the Gospel among the heathens* and concomitant formation of his missionary society; second, with regard to Africa (Sierra Leone), the establishment of the first church in tropical Africa in modern times (interestingly enough, by people of African birth or descent from North America). This second stage (1792–present) is at first primarily Protestant in nature, concerns the massive evangelization of Africa, Asia, and remaining areas of the Americas, and remains quite vigorous today. Over the last five centuries, therefore, the different phases of European imperialism and colonialism brought with them, wherever they turned, their respective religious beliefs and practices, whether Catholic or Protestant.

Third, a comparison of this twofold division of the missionary movement of the West with the previous threefold division of Western imperialism proves instructive. On the one hand, the first missionary wave of the fifteenth through the eighteenth centuries coincides with the first imperialist phase – the mercantile stage of early imperialism; on the other hand, the second missionary wave of the nineteenth and twentieth centuries coincides with the transition from the first to the second imperialist phase in the nineteenth century and its full bloom at the end of the nineteenth century and the beginning of the twentieth – the monopoly capitalist stage of high imperialism.

As such, the structural binomial reality of empire should be seen as involving a strong socioreligious component as well. The political, economic, and cultural center also functions as a religious center; that is to say, the practices and beliefs of the center are invariably grounded on, sanctioned, and accompanied by a set of religious beliefs and practices. Consequently, the primary binomial of center and margins entails and engenders a further binomial in this sphere as well: believers/unbelievers–pagans, which in turn gives rise to a number of other secondary and subordinate binomials, such as godly/ungodly (worshipers of the true God/worshipers of false gods) and religious/idolatrous–superstitious. As a result, the margins politically, economically, and culturally subordinated to the center must be brought into religious submission as well: their religious beliefs must be corrected and uplifted; their gods attacked and destroyed; their practices ridiculed and replaced.

Finally, such a reality, I would argue once again, further colors and affects, directly or indirectly, the entire artistic production of both center and margins, the dominant and the subaltern, including their respective literary productions.

From the point of view of biblical criticism, therefore, it is clear that the academic study of the texts of ancient Judaism and early Christianity, given the formation and consolidation of the discipline in the course of the nineteenth century, parallels the second major wave of the Western missionary movement as well as the transition period to the second, high phase of Western imperialism and colonialism: first, as Europe turns to Africa and Asia, in a renewed and frantic scramble for territories and possessions; second, as the United States turns West and beyond, with its eyes increasingly set on the islands of the Caribbean, the heart of Mexico, and territories in the Pacific.

Consequently, the shadow of empire in the production of modern readings of the ancient texts should also be underlined. In the process, certain crucial questions again come to the surface, not unlike those raised earlier but now from a different angle: How do such readings and interpretations, coming from the metropolitan centers of the West as they do, address and present such issues in the ancient texts as empire and margins, oppression and justice; the world and life in the world as well as the other-world and its inhabitants; history and "the other", mission and conversion, followers and outsiders; salvation, election and holiness? Once again, from the point of view of postcolonial studies, questions such as these – questions of culture, ideology, and power – prove all-important.

Postcolonial studies and readers

For this third dimension of the proposed postcolonial optic in biblical criticism, I would argue once more for an analysis of the readers of the texts of ancient Judaism and early Christianity that takes seriously into consideration their broader sociocultural contexts in the global sphere, whether in the West or outside the West, in the light of the same omnipresent, inescapable, and overwhelming sociopolitical reality that engulfed the texts of Jewish and Christian antiquity as well as the readings and interpretations of such texts in the West – the reality of empire, of imperialism and colonialism, now in terms of not only the Western imperial tradition of the last five centuries but also the reaction against such a tradition from outside the West within the context of the postcolonial yet neocolonial world of the last half-century. Some preliminary observations are once again in order.

First, despite what I have described as its omnipresent, inescapable, and overwhelming character, the structural binomial reality of imperialism and colonialism is never imposed or accepted in an atmosphere of absolute and undisturbed passivity. Always in the wake of the fundamental binomial of center/margins, and ultimately deconstructing it as well, in principle if not in praxis, lies the inverted binomial of resistance/fear. I say "inverted" because this is the one binomial opposition where the margins actually take the initiative, while the center is forced into a reactive position.

In effect, there is always – sooner or later, major or minor, explicit or implicit – resistance to the center on the part of the politically, economically, culturally, and religiously subordinated margins, even when such resistance brings about, as it inevitably does, further measures of control on the part of the center, designed to instil fear into the minds and hearts of the margins. Such measures, to be sure, only

serve to contribute to a further deconstruction of the binomial reality, as the civilized, advanced, cultured, progressive, developed, and believing center turns increasingly to measures of an uncivilized, primitive, barbarian, backward, undeveloped, and unbelieving order against the marginal groups. At some point, such resistance on the part of the margins may come to a climax, and this climax may involve in turn a variety of gradations: open challenge and defiance; widespread rebellion and anomie; actual overthrow and reorientation.

Second, I would argue that such resistance is precisely what has occurred in the discipline in the last quarter of the century, as more and more outsiders have joined its ranks. Such outsiders can be classified according to two groupings: women from the West; men and women from outside the West as well as from ethnic and racial minorities in the West. In both cases, a similar pattern of resistance can be observed: early stirrings in the 1970s – what could be called a situation of open challenge and defiance; maturation and solidification through the 1980s – a clear situation of widespread rebellion and anomie; sharpened sophistication in the 1990s – what could be compared to a situation of actual overthrow and reorientation.

Third, it should not go unobserved that such disciplinary changes take place not long after the commencement of the third major phase of Western imperialism and colonialism, marked by the end of formal colonialism, with wars of independence and the loss of colonies everywhere – the age of the postcolonial, and the continued impact of imperial culture everywhere – the age of the neocolonial. More specifically, such developments, one should recall, come soon after the crisis experienced by the West, both in Europe and North America, during the late 1960s and the early 1970s. Quite clearly, the upheaval in the world at large ultimately affects the discipline as well.

Finally, such a reality, I would argue yet again, does affect and color as well, directly or indirectly, the entire artistic production of center and margins, dominant and subaltern, including their respective literary productions.

From the point of view of biblical critics, then, it now becomes necessary to distinguish between two general groupings. On the one hand, those readers associated with the long imperial tradition of the West, especially from the time of transition to high imperialism to the present phase of neocolonialism within late imperialism – still the vast majority of critics; on the other hand, those critics associated with the colonies of the Western empires, what has come to be known as the "Two-Thirds World," now raising their voices for the first time during the present phase of postcolonialism within late imperialism – a growing minority of critics.

Therefore, the shadow of empire in the lives of modern as well as contemporary readers must, yet again, be highlighted in biblical criticism. In so doing, a number of crucial questions come to the fore, similar to those outlined before but formulated from yet another angle of approach: how do traditional (male) critics, from the metropolitan centers of the West, stand – and construct them-"selves" – with regard to the relationship between empire and margins, the West and the rest, Christendom and outsiders; mission and conversion, oppression and justice, history and the other; salvation, election and holiness; the this-world and life in the world as well as the

other-world? What is the position of Western women in this regard, in their role as previous outsiders from the West itself? How do men and women from outside the West as well as from ethnic and racial minorities in the West respond to such issues? Such questions – questions of culture, ideology, and power – emerge as all-important, from the point of view of postcolonial studies.

Concluding Comments

From the point of view of cultural studies, that paradigm within which I presently situate myself in the discipline, the model of postcolonial studies should be seen as one major line of approach, alongside others. Such a line of approach, furthermore, should also be seen as quite broad and quite rich – multidimensional, multicentered, multilingual. Not only is its theoretical apparatus immense and its range of reading strategies phenomenal, as reflected in the exploding corpus of critical literature, but also its scope and its reach prove to be radically global as well, drawing as it does on the discourses and practices of imperialism and colonialism across cultures and historical periods.

In the introduction I remarked that, as a model within cultural studies – an intermediate model within an umbrella model, as it were – postcolonial studies proves most appropriate, most enlightening, and most fruitful. The reasons should now be evident.

First, the model is not only thoroughly self-conscious of itself as a construct, dependent upon certain theoretical claims and reading strategies, but also calls for self-consciousness on the part of its would-be practitioners as constructs, dependent upon certain representations of themselves, of their own social locations and agendas, as real readers. Both with regard to interpretation and interpreters, therefore, the model presupposes and demands a specific optic with clear implications for both the representation of the past and the representation of the present.

Second, the model can address at one and the same time the various interrelated and interdependent dimensions of criticism: the analysis of texts – the world of antiquity; the analysis of "texts" – the world of modernity; the analysis of readers of texts and producers of "texts" – the world of postmodernity.

Finally, the model is profoundly ideological, for it looks upon the political experience of imperialism and colonialism as central to the task of criticism at all levels of inquiry.

In the end, however, as a model within cultural studies, postcolonial studies has no choice but to see itself and represent itself as *unus inter pares*; otherwise, it could easily turn into an imperial discourse of its own. It is an optic, not the optic, in full engagement and dialogue with a host of other models and other optics. Yet, even as one among equals, it proves most incisive and most telling, for it reminds us all, the children of the colonized and the children of the colonizer, that the discipline of biblical criticism as we know it and have known it must be seen and analyzed, like all other discourses of modernity, against the much broader geopolitical context of Western imperialism and colonialism. In so doing, furthermore, the goal is not merely one of analysis and description but rather one of transformation: the struggle for "liberation" and "decolonization."

NOTES

1 There is no comprehensive – that is, cross-imperial and cross-colonial – study of postcolonial studies as such: no encompassing account of its origins, histories, and discourses across the various imperial/colonial experiences of Europe and the United States. There are, however, two very good readers. The first of these (Williams and Chrisman 1994) focuses on theory, as a listing of its chapters readily reveals: "Theorizing Colonized Cultures and Anti-Colonial Resistance"; "Theorizing the West"; "Theorizing Gender"; "Theorizing Post-Coloniality: Intellectuals and Institutions"; "Theorizing Post-Coloniality: Discourse and Identity"; "Reading from Theory." The second (Ashcroft, Griffiths and Tiffin 1995) is organized according to themes, as again a listing of its chapters readily demonstrates: "Issues and Debates"; "Universality and Difference"; "Representation and Resistance"; "Postmodernism and Post-colonialism"; "Nationalism"; "Hybridity"; "Ethnicity and Indigeneity"; "Feminism and Post-colonialism"; "Language"; "The Body and Performance"; "History"; "Place"; "Education"; "Production and Consumption." There are also two excellent studies of literary production in the postcolonial context, both with an emphasis on the anglophone world of the former British Empire (Ashcroft, Griffiths and Tiffin 1989; Boehmer 1995).

2 I can no longer describe myself solely as a biblical critic, despite my specific hiring, assignment and location in a Department of New Testament and Early Christianity within the context of the highly compartmentalized academic divisions of a Graduate Department of Religion based in a liberal Protestant Divinity School. At the very least, I must now describe myself as a constructive theologian as well, not only because I presently regard the traditional distinction between critic and theologian as having altogether collapsed but also because I see myself as engaged in the task of discoursing about the "this-world" and the "other-world" in the light of my own sociocultural and sociohistorical context in the diaspora, both as a child of the non-Western World and a child of a minority group within the West. Indeed, in the end, I would have to describe myself further as a cultural critic, insofar as I am also interested in these various dimensions of my social context quite aside from their socioreligious aspect. From this point of view, I am quite in agreement with the view that the call of the minority scholar is to engage in academic border crossings (JanMohamed and Lloyd 1990).

3 Within the model of postcolonial studies, terminology itself proves quite varied and thus problematic. Suffice it to say for now that by "postcolonial" I mean ideological reflection on the discourse and practice of imperialism and colonialism from the vantage point of a situation where imperialism and colonialism have come – by and large though by no means altogether so – to a formal end but remain very much at work in practice, as neoimperialism and neocolonialism. Thus, the postcolonial optic is a field of vision forged in the wake of imperialism and colonialism but still very much conscious of their continuing, even if transformed, power.

4 For good, concise introductions to the phenomena of imperialism and colonialism in general, see Said (1990; 1993: 3–61 (Chapter 1: "Overlapping Territories, Intertwined Histories"); Deane 1994).

5 I find myself in agreement with the caution offered for postcolonial studies in general by Michael Sprinker (1996: 1–10), who insists on the need to offer and follow a historical periodization of the different types of imperialism at work in the West over this period of five centuries.

6 I follow here the thesis of Andrew Walls (1995).

REFERENCES

Ashcroft, Bill, Gareth Griffiths, and Helen Tiffin (eds) (1989). *The Empire Writes Back: Theory and Practice in Post-colonial Literatures*. London: Routledge & Kegan Paul.

——————(1995). *The Post-Colonial Studies Reader*. London: Routledge & Kegan Paul.

Boehmer, Elleke (1995). *Colonial and Postcolonial Literature: Migrant Metaphors*. Oxford: Oxford University Press.

Deane, Seamus (1994). "Imperialism and Nationalism," in Frank L. Lentricchia and Thomas McLaughlin (eds), *Critical Terms for Literary Study*. Chicago: University of Chicago Press, 2nd enl. edn, 354–68.

JanMohamed, Abdul R., and David Lloyd (eds) (1990). "Introduction: Toward a Theory of Minority Discourse: What Is to Be Done?", in *The Nature and Context of Minority Discourse*. Oxford: Oxford University Press, 1–16.

Said, Edward (1990). "Yeats and Decolonization," in Seamus Deane (ed.), *Nationalism, Colonialism, and Literature*. Minneapolis: University of Minnesota Press, 69–95.

——(1993). *Culture and Imperialism*. New York: Alfred A. Knopf.

Segovia, Fernando F. (1992). "Two Places and No Place on Which to Stand: Mixture and Otherness in Hispanic American Theology," in Fernando F. Segovia (ed.), *Hispanic Americans in Theology and the Church*. Special issue of *Listening: Journal of Religion and Culture*, 27: 26–40.

——1995a. " 'And They Began to Speak in Other Tongues': Competing Modes of Discourse in Contemporary Biblical Criticism," in F. F. Segovia and M. A. Tolbert (eds), *Reading from This Place*. I. *Social Location and Biblical Interpretation in the United States*. Minneapolis: Fortress Press, 1–32.

——1995b. "Cultural Studies and Contemporary Biblical Criticism: Ideological Criticism as Mode of Discourse," in F. F. Segovia and M. A. Tolbert (eds), *Reading from This Place*. II. *Social Location and Biblical Interpretation in Global Perspective*. Minneapolis: Fortress Press, 1–17.

——1996a. "Aliens in the Promised Land: The Manifest Destiny of U.S. Hispanic American Theology," in Ada María Isasi-Díaz and Fernando F. Segovia (eds), *Hispanic/Latino Theology: Challenge and Promise*. Minneapolis: Fortress Press, 15–42.

——1996b. "In the World but Not of It: Exile as a Locus for a Theology of the Diaspora," in Ada María Isasi-Díaz and Fernando F. Segovia (eds), *Hispanic/Latino Theology: Challenge and Promise*. Minneapolis: Fortress Press, 195–217.

——1998. "Pedagogical Discourse and Practices in Cultural Studies: Toward a Contextual Pedagogy of the Bible," in F. F. Segovia and M. A. Tolbert (eds), *Teaching the Bible: The Discourses and Politics of Biblical Pedagogy*. Maryknoll: Orbis Books.

Sprinker, Michael (1996). "Introduction," in R. de la Campa, E. Ann Kaplan and M. Sprinker (eds), *Late Imperial Culture*. London: Verso, 1–10.

Walls, Andrew (1995). "Christianity in the Non-Western World: A Study in the Serial Nature of Christian Expansion," *Studies in World Christianity* 1: 1–25.

Williams P., and L. Chrisman (eds) (1994). *Colonial Discourse and Post-Colonial Theory: A Reader*. New York: Columbia University Press.

3

Making the Connections:

Postcolonial Studies and Feminist Biblical Interpretation

Kwok Pui-lan

> In their feminist practices of reading and writing, Two-Thirds World women call for the decolonization of inherited colonial education systems, languages, literary canon, reading methods, and the Christian religion, in order to arrest the colonizing ideology packed in the claims of religious conversion, Western civilization, modernization, development, democratization, and globalization.
>
> *Musa W. Dube*[1]

Some time ago, when I was reading the writings of women missionaries in a library archive, I came across a fascinating story about a Chinese woman. A female missionary reported at the turn of the twentieth century that a Chinese woman who could barely read used a pin to cut from the Bible verses where Paul instructed women to be submissive and remain silent in church. I have long forgotten where I read the story, but it lodged in my mind as a vivid testimony to the fact that Chinese women were not passive recipients of biblical teachings. Instead of subscribing to Paul's sexist ideology, this woman exercised the freedom to choose and reject what she thought was harmful for women.

A postcolonial feminist interpretation of the Bible creates a space so that the reading of this and other women in similar colonial and semicolonial situations can be remembered in order to enliven our historical and moral imagination. For this story demonstrates how oppressed women have turned the Bible, a product introduced by the colonial officials, missionaries, and educators, into a site of contestation and resistance for their own emancipation. Continuing this critical task, postcolonial feminist critics not only recover the insights of ordinary women readers

First published in from *Postcolonial Imagination and Feminist Theology*. Westminster: JohnKnox Press, 2005, 77–99.

but also unmask the myriad ways in which biblical scholars, feminists among them, have been complicit with or oblivious to colonialism and neocolonialism.

Postcolonial Criticism and Feminist Biblical Interpretation

While postcolonial criticism has been used by literary critics and by those in humanities and social sciences for some time, its use in the field of religious studies and Christian studies is fairly recent. Postcolonial theories were introduced to the field of biblical studies in the 1990s, mainly through the works of critics from the Third World and from racial minorities in the United States. In *Decolonizing Biblical Studies*, Fernando Segovia traces the development of biblical criticism from the early nineteenth century through the end of the twentieth.[2] He argues that until the last quarter of the twentieth century, historical criticism was the reigning paradigm in the discipline. Beginning in the 1970s and continuing to the present, biblical studies experienced the rapid rise of literary criticism and cultural or social criticism. The late 1980s and early 1990s saw the irruption of cultural studies and the resulting competing modes of discourse. He characterizes such a development as a process of "liberation" and "decolonization," in which the universal, objective reader is gradually replaced by the interested, local, and perspectival reader. He notes that the field of biblical studies is no longer the monopoly of white, middle-class men. The addition of Western women, men and women from outside the West, as well as non-Western minorities in the West has resulted in a diversity of method and theory, an expansion of scope of inquiry, and an explosion of interpretive voices.

It is important to stress that postcolonial criticism does not reject the insights of historical criticism, because much of the work of the historical critics contributes to the understanding of the "worldliness" of the text, that is, the material and ideological backgrounds from which the texts emerged and to which the texts responded. The difference is that postcolonial critics pose new questions about the historical and literary contexts and thereby enlarge the moral imagination of the interpretive process. For example, postcolonial critics scrutinize the colonial entanglements in the texts, highlighting the impact of empire and colonization in shaping the collective memory of the Jewish people, the literary production and redaction of biblical texts, and the process of the formation of the canon. The cultural production and literary imagination of the Hebrew people and early Christians were invariably shaped by the social and political domination of successive empires: in Assyria, Babylon, Persia, Greece, and Rome. Postcolonial critics in their reconstructive readings of the text highlight the struggles and resistance in the different colonial contexts, lift up the voices of women and other subalterns, and are sensitive to postcolonial concerns such as hybridity, deterritorialization, and hyphenated or multiple identities.[3] Thus, postcolonial criticism has the potential to open up the interpretive process, making the Bible a highly relevant and invaluable resource for our postcolonial situation.

Some may wonder whether postcolonial analysis, developed largely from the experiences of modern colonialism, can be applicable to ancient situations, which may not be comparable to modern cases.[4] I would like to point out that history is interpreted according to the mental apparatus and framework we have constructed.

Since the 1970s, biblical scholars using social scientific methods, including those with a Marxist bent, have not shied away from employing "modern" theories to illuminate ancient societies. Postcolonial theories add a critical dimension by focusing on the empire and colonization, the center and the periphery, the exiled and the diasporized. For example, in his comparison of Trito-Isaiah with the postcolonial situation of Hong Kong, Archie Lee does not argue that imperial/colonial experience is similar across time and culture, though there may be resemblances.[5] What he seeks to show is that the problems facing the hybridized Hong Kong people in returning to China may shed new light on the meaning of return as well as the quarrels and disputes in the postexilic community. In doing so, he invites us to use a postcolonial imagination to enter into the cultural world of the returnees after the exile for a better comprehension of the complex and wrenching identity-formation process.

Besides illuminating ancient texts, postcolonial criticism makes visible the ways modern readings of the texts collude with colonial interests in the West. Emerging during the expansion of European powers, the historical-critical method gathered momentum as imperialism and colonization reached its zenith in the late nineteenth century. Shaped by the drive toward rationality and the development of historical consciousness begun in the Enlightenment, the historical-critical method was embedded in the sociocultural ethos of its particular time. Hailed as scientific, academic, and objective, its nineteenth-century practitioners employed Orientalist philology, racial theory, and an evolutionary understanding of "religions."[6] Once the historical-critical method was established as the norm for studying the Bible, it excluded the validity of other contextual readings and devalued the contributions of nonacademic interpretations.

In addition to scrutinizing biblical interpretive practices in the West, postcolonial studies also provide a useful framework to assess the history of biblical interpretation in the Third World. In the last three decades, biblical scholars and theologians from the Third World and from indigenous and Dalit communities have presented a wide array of biblical criticism using insights from oral hermeneutics, literary theory, reader-response criticism, and other indigenous methods. R. S. Sugirtharajah has provided a useful comparative framework to organize the growing data of biblical interpretations coming from Asia, Africa, and Latin America to discern their different hermeneutical interests, and to compare and contrast the many approaches.[7] Based primarily on biblical interpretation and commentaries from the South Asian context, Sugirtharajah proposes four different approaches to Asian hermeneutics, which he argues can also be found in other parts of the Third World. The Orientalist mode invokes the golden age of Indian civilization, based on Sanskrit and Brahmanical texts. Contrary to this, the anglicists try to replace the indigenous texts with Western learning, so that the colonized can be assimilated to the culture of the colonizers. The nativist mode challenges both Western theories and the elitist Orientalist approach by reviving the vernacular tradition and the use of popular resources. Sugirtharajah espouses the postcolonial approach, which he thinks can best analyze the colonial trappings in biblical texts; offer alternative readings that address nationalism, identity, ethnicity, and subaltern and feminist concerns; as well as interrogate both colonial and metropolitan interpretations.

Although the works of postcolonial male critics may include some discussion of women's scholarship, gender remains a marginal issue in their overall analysis.

Postcolonial feminist critics have stressed the intricate relationship between colonialism and patriarchy such that the analysis of one without the other is incomplete. Those male postcolonial critics who leave out gender run the risk of overlooking that colonialism involves the contest of male power and that patriarchal ideology is constantly reshaped and reformulated in the colonial process. On the other hand, those feminist critics who isolate gender from the larger economic and colonial context court the danger of providing a skewed interpretation that tends to reflect the interests of the socially and economically privileged. The exploration of the interstices of different forms of oppression under the shadow of the empire constitutes the exciting postcolonial feminist project. As Asian American biblical scholar Gale Yee has said, "I have become convinced in my feminist investigations of the Bible over the years that the study of gender must include race, class, and colonial status as categories of analysis."[8]

Feminist scholars interested in postcolonial criticism adopt different approaches of interpretation, from ideological criticism to literary-rhetorical method, but they share some common concerns. First, they want to investigate how the symbolization of women and the deployment of gender in the text relate to class interests, modes of production, concentration of state power, and colonial domination. In *Poor Banished Children of Eve*, Gale Yee uses a sophisticated ideological criticism to reveal how the "wicked women" in the Hebrew Bible function as "sexual metaphors" and "symbolic alibis" for the contests of male elites who wield political, economic, and social power. For instance, in Ezekiel 23, two sexually insatiable sisters were used to symbolize the two rival kingdoms, personified as Oholah (Samaria) and Oholibah (Jerusalem), in love with the foreign nations of Egypt, Assyria, and Babylon. Yee argues that the violent pornographic story must be situated in the context of colonial relation between Israel and Judah and the foreign powers, which led eventually to the conquest and exile of the elites.[9] The story was seen through the lens of a colonized male of the priestly elite during the final days of the nation and the imminent exile of the upper-class sector. In the text, the woman was used as a trope for the land and the nation, and sexual images became tropes for colonial dominance. Ezekiel subscribes to the patriarchal ideology of gender and depicts Judah and Israel as feminine, the subjugated colonial subjects, while the foreign aggressors are hypermasculine. The foreign Others were racialized and sexualized, with far superior male prowess and virility than that of the emasculated Judean leadership. For Yee, Ezekiel 23 was an attempt of the prophet to deal with the personal and collective trauma of colonization, conquest, and exile of the Judean royal and priestly aristocracy, of which he was a part. Her multiaxial interpretation demonstrates why focusing on gender and sexuality alone, as some feminist interpreters have done, fails to grasp the polyvalent signification of the sexual metaphors. She writes: "The pornography of these texts should be coded not simply as another form of patriarchal violence, but as colonial ethnic conflict framed as a sexualized encounter."[10]

Second, postcolonial feminist critics pay special attention to the biblical women in the contact zone and present reconstructive readings as counternarrative. A contact zone is the space of colonial encounters where people of different geographical and historical backgrounds are brought into contact with each other, usually shaped by inequality and conflictual relations.[11] One such figure is the prostitute Rahab in

Joshua 2 during the siege of Jericho. In the story, Rahab was rewarded for having protected the spies sent by Joshua, and as a Canaanite Other, she crossed over to live in Israel and was elevated to high status as the ancestress of David and Jesus (Matt. 1:5). Laura Donaldson reads the Rahab story not from the Jewish but from the Canaanite perspective, and situates it within the cultural and historical predicament of Native women during conquest. Rahab's story reminds her of the co-optation and exploitation of Native women's sexuality as an integral part of the white colonial myths and ideology.[12] The story of Rahab illustrates the double colonization of women: their bodies are open to taking by foreign men, and their land is possessed. Musa Dube of Botswana uses the story as a springboard for her postcolonial feminist method and calls it "Rahab's reading prism." She says Rahab's reading prism highlights "the historical fact of colonizing and decolonizing communities inhabiting the feminist space of liberation practices."[13] Dube argues that those feminist readers who belong to the colonizing community will need to adopt a decolonizing stance, while doubly colonized women will have to privilege imperial oppression over a patriarchal one. A decolonizing reading would need to present a counternarrative by lifting up the memory of the many "Rahabs" who have risen up against the colonizers and subverted the master's genre. Such a reading will cultivate new postcolonial spaces for spinning new narratives that speak of equality and freedom.

Third, postcolonial feminist critics scrutinize metropolitan interpretations, including those offered by both male and feminist scholars, to see if their readings support the colonizing ideology by glossing over the imperial context and agenda, or contribute to decolonizing the imperializing texts for the sake of liberation. Using the story of the Syrophoenician woman in Matthew 15:21–8 as a case study, Dube shows that white male scholars have not paid attention to how the divine claims of salvation history, Davidic kingship, and universal mission can be used as colonizing ideology. Moreover, they have shown no effort to investigate the relation among gender, mission, and empire. In short, their gender, race, and class privilege accounts for their lack of interest in problematizing the power relations inscribed in the text.[14] Although white feminist scholars have focused on gender as a major category of analysis, their works in general do not consider the imperial context of Matthew and how the different local groups were vying for the favor of the empire. They have also failed to question the ideology of mission in the text and continue to assume that biblical traditions are universally valid for all cultures. Thus, even with the good intention of reclaiming the Gentile woman as a foremother within the history of early Christianity, their reconstructive project does not deconstruct the power relation embedded in the mission passages. From her analyses of the works of male and female metropolitan interpreters, Dube concludes that, by and large, they have bracketed imperialism and thus subscribed to it. Moreover, her scrutiny of white feminist interpretations has shown that "the patriarchal category of analysis does not necessarily translate into imperial criticism."[15]

Fourth, in order to subvert the dominant Western patriarchal interpretations, postcolonial feminist critics, especially those in Africa, emphasize the roles and contributions of ordinary readers. As Dube explains, ordinary readers are not just nonacademic readers – they include most Third World readers, who are outside the accepted academic traditions of the biblical interpretation and who are relegated to the periphery of the global economic structures. The inclusion of ordinary readers is

meant to enlarge the interpretive community and to stress that these readers possess the "suppressed knowledges" that academic elites often dismiss. When Dube and her colleagues went to visit women in the African Independent Churches, they did not assume that as academically trained women they had the knowledge to teach the women. They went not just to *read with* the nonacademic women, but also to *read from* them, believing that these women offer strategies of interpretation born from their struggles with imperialism and sexism.[16] They find that these ordinary women readers are not preoccupied with a textual approach, but adopt communal and participatory modes of interpretation, through the use of songs, dramatized narration, and interpretation through repetition. As members of the professional guild, the academically trained women often find that they are not equipped to understand these lively oral modes of engaging the Bible, and have to retool and relearn from this experience.[17]

Finally, postcolonial feminist critics pay increasing attention to what Mary Ann Tolbert has called the politics and poetics of location. By politics of location, Tolbert means the complexity of one's social background, such as gender, race, and sexual orientation, as well as one's national and institutional context and economic and educational status, which determine who speaks and who is likely to listen. By poetics of location, she says, "Any interpretation of a text, especially a text as traditionally powerful as the Bible, must be assessed not only on whatever its literary or historical merits may be but also on its theological and ethical impact on the integrity and dignity of God's creation."[18] White women who participate in postcolonial interpretation are aware of their multiple identities as both oppressors and oppressed. For instance, Sharon Ringe has articulated how white feminists and others with power with the ambivalent status as both colonized and colonizers have to work to mitigate the practices of colonial authority and to share the table fellowship with others for greater inclusiveness.[19] Similarly, the African academically trained women are cognizant of the privileges they have over ordinary women readers because of their economic and educational attainment. They are very conscious of the ambivalent efforts of speaking on behalf of them or presenting their views in the academic setting.[20] In the case of Gale Yee, she notes that in American popular culture Asian and Asian American women are depicted as highly eroticized figures as a means to resolve racist anxieties and the fear of foreigners. Such stereotypical cultural representations make her sensitive to the symbolization of women as evil in the Hebrew Bible.[21] Her attention to the use of rhetoric of sexuality in the Bible is much influenced by her Asian American social location.

Postcolonialism, Gender, and Early Christianity

Postcolonial criticism offers critical insights to examine the intersection among gender, empire, and the formation of Christian communities in the New Testament. Yet, feminist scholars in the past have seldom utilized such insights in their studies of women's position or gender construction in early Christianity because they have not foregrounded the Roman imperial context within which both Jews and Christians lived. One of the reasons is that biblical scholarship in the nineteenth and twentieth centuries has dichotomized the cultural context of Christian origins into Judaism

versus Hellenism. A lot of effort has been devoted to determining whether the background of a Christian text could be traceable to its Jewish or Hellenistic sources or influences. When the discussion was framed in such a way, and frequently with an anti-Jewish bias, Roman imperial ideology and politics were largely obscured or deemed insignificant to the interpretive task at hand.[22] Furthermore, as Mary Rose D'Angelo has poignantly observed: "The nineteenth- and twentieth-century imperial cultures in which classical and biblical studies have been done (Germany, England, France, the United States) were deeply and explicitly identified either with the Roman Empire itself (Germany, England, France), or the imperial republic (France and the United States)."[23] Scholars tended to see the empire as either beneficial or neutral because of their social location, and did not question the political context harshly, as liberation theologians have done.

Without ignoring this larger cultural and political context of biblical scholarship, I would argue that there are also specific reasons why the interpretive models constructed by feminist scholars have downplayed the Roman imperial context. The historical-reconstructionist model debunks the claims of objectivity made by androcentric historians and sets to reclaim women's history at the center of the development of early Christianity. The focus is on reclaiming women's heritage, especially the stories of the Christian foremothers, who emerged as playing such important roles as apostles, prophets, missionaries, and founders and leaders of house churches. Since the emphasis is on recovering women's significant leadership in the early church, researchers tend to concentrate on women leaders, or the elite women of the church, sometimes to the neglect of women of the lower classes. As Musa Dube has pointed out, the emphasis on patriarchy and the resurrection of women's history might downplay the imperial setting of early Christianity and bracket the imperial prescriptions and constructions of biblical texts. The accent on the early Christian foremothers may lead to overlooking the lives of non-Christian women and to glossing over the power dynamics of mission strategies in biblical narrative.[24]

The second approach investigates women in the social world of the early church and attempts to present a feminist social history of early Christianity. While some scholars have borrowed from the honor and shame model of cultural anthropologists, others have deployed various sociological and theoretical frameworks. Instead of focusing on the female leaders and elite women, this approach yields a wealth of data concerning the ordinary lives of women in the period of the early church, from women's struggle for bread and money, women's work and occupation, to the lives of slave women and widows. Moreover, women's family life, work, income, illness, and resistance are set in the context of Roman imperial society, governed by the marriage institution, legal norms, and economic systems.[25] What I find missing is a nuanced understanding of the diversity of women's social worlds as shaped by local, regional, and submerged histories within the Roman Empire. Postcolonial historiography has increasingly paid attention to the danger of making generalized statements and has aimed to resurrect subaltern histories.[26] Another problem is that while women's oppression is highlighted, there is insufficient discussion of gender as a constitutive factor, intersecting with ethnicity, class, and social status, to uphold not only patriarchy, but also imperial control and authority.

The third model is the rhetorical model, which sees the text not as a window to historical reality, but as a social and linguistic construct performing particular

rhetorical functions to shape action and the ethos of the community. Rhetorical criticism focuses on the persuasive power of the text to motivate the audience to action and its communicative functions in specific historical and political contexts. Instead of accepting the androcentric language and reality construction of biblical texts, rhetorical criticism uncovers and points to women's struggles for participation and power in early Christianity. Its reading strategy does not define patriarchy as men dominating women, but as an interlocking system of oppression because of racism, classism, colonialism, and sexism. Its aim is to create an alternative feminist rhetorical space in which women can participate as equals to men, defined by the logic of radical democracy.[27] Feminist rhetorical criticism of the New Testament has so far focused much of its energy on unmasking the rhetoric of the patriarchal household and the patriarchalization of the early church. More work needs to be done to explore how the imperial rhetoric, cultus, propaganda, and ideology affected the interlocking system of oppression and influenced the rhetoric and proclamation of the early church. We may also need to ask, how can this feminist rhetorical space be an anti-imperial space so that it will welcome Third World women and women who belong to other faiths?

I think these different models of feminist studies of the New Testament can benefit from postcolonial insights into how gender, race, and sexuality interplay in colonial situations. The works of Ann Laura Stoler and Anne McClintock have pointed to the fact that gender inequalities were essential to maintain the structure of colonial racism and imperial authority. Stoler's studies of Southeast Asian colonies elucidate how imperial authority and racial distinctions were fundamentally structured in gender terms. The management of sexual activity of women, reproduction, and intermarriage was fundamental to maintain distinctions between the colonizers and colonized, and to signify imperial power.[28] Anne McClintock's work on colonial discourses in Britain shows that gender was used to mark cultural and racial differences as well as to secure class distinction. Gender is not "simply a question of sexuality but also a question of subdued labor and imperial plunder; race is not just a question of skin color but also a question of labor power, cross-hatched by gender."[29]

Several scholars of early Christianity have applied such a multilayered and interactive approach to the study of gender relations in the complex negotiation of cultural and religious identities within the Palestine Jewish community and the Hellenistic Jewish diaspora under the Roman Empire. For example, Mary Rose D'Angelo has insightfully broadened the debate on Jesus' reference to God as Abba within the context of Roman imperial theology. While feminist scholars have decried the predominant use of patriarchal and parental imagery for God, some liberal theologians tried to downplay such a critique by insisting that Jesus had a special and intimate "abba experience." The argument is largely based on the influential study of Joachim Jeremias, who claims that the word "abba" denoted an intimate relationship with God, which was something new and not found in Judaism.[30] Jewish scholars have contested that claim, arguing that the use of "father" for God could be found in Jewish piety and would have been easily communicable to the Jewish audience. While much discussion has focused on the Jewish context, D'Angelo adds a new dimension by tracing the use of "father" in the Roman imperial context. She points out that the title of father was awarded to Julius Caesar

and reflected "an understanding of the empire as a great *familia* in which the emperor functions as a *paterfamilias*."[31] During the reign of Augustus, the consolidation of his empire was reinforced with legal measures aiming at strengthening the patriarchal family. Given the fact that Jesus died at the hands of the Romans, D'Angelo surmises that Jesus' use of "abba" challenges imperial and paternal authority, for the father he refers to is not the Roman imperial father, but the father who rules heaven and earth. Still, she cautions that the use of "father" cannot be said to be nonpatriarchal, as the name still reflects a social system in which privileged males had power over women, children, slaves, and other lesser males.[32]

Richard Horsley's postcolonial reading of the Gospel of Mark also places gender relations in the larger economic-political power relations operative under Roman imperial rule.[33] As a story about Galileans' and Judeans' struggles in resistance against harsh Roman domination, Mark's Gospel describes women as playing pivotal and instrumental roles in the renewal movement, in sharp contrast to the lack of faith of the disciples. Horsley interestingly does not read the stories of the hemorrhaging woman (Mark 5:25–34) and the twelve-year-old daughter of the assembly leader (Mark 5:35–43) as individuals, but as figures representative of Israel, a people bleeding and virtually dying under Roman exploitation. He takes into account local histories and discusses how Magdala, the region where Mary of Magdala came from, suffered from severe military violence and enslavement under Roman armies, as well as financial hardship imposed on the family by heavy taxation. The conquest of Palestine by the Romans brought acute pressure and instability to village life and the patriarchal family, undermining the authority of many fathers as the head of household. Seen from this larger context, Jesus called the whole village to form a "familial" community based on the Mosaic convenantal commandment to provide the supportive functions that used to be performed by the family. Horsley thinks that it would be anachronistic to say that Mark's Jesus opposed patriarchal marriage and championed an egalitarian social order, but Jesus' covenantal understanding of marriage placed it on a less patriarchal footing when compared to the teachings of the Pharisees.[34] Jesus did not want to abolish the family, and his insistence on marriage as indissoluble (Mark 10:2–9) was not simply an incidence of teaching about sexual ethics, but an argument for the protection of the family as the fundamental socioeconomic unit. Such a provision guaranteed the economic security of women and children against the liberalization of divorce by the Pharisees, which facilitated the consolidation of landholdings of the Herodian and other elite. Reading gender and women's stories in the larger political plot of Mark's Gospel, Horsley presents the different forms of oppression as interlocking and multiplicative.

New Testament scholars have also paid more attention to the imperial culture and ideology in the interpretation of Paul's context and his corpus of writings. In the past, scholars have polarized the Jewish background and the Hellenistic influence in Paul, or bifurcated Paul as either a Jew or a Christian. The dominant interest has been to contrast between "particularistic" or "ethnocentric" Judaism with the "universalism" of Paul, as the apostle who established Gentile Christianity. But Paul's identity was never so clear-cut, and in today's postcolonial parlance, his identity must be considered as highly hybridized. Paul did not envisage he was joining a new religious movement, but rather saw it as a development of Israelite traditions, and

therefore needed to clarify his position vis-á-vis the Jewish leaders who held to a more traditional way of life. As a Greek-speaking diasporic Jew apparently born in exile, Paul joined a popular movement and moved out to the Gentiles, thus risking alienation from his fellow "Judeans."[35] Paul's debates with the other apostles on circumcision and eating food that had been offered to idols were of critical importance at the time, because circumcision and food served as crucial markers of religious and cultural difference. And at the same time, as Antoinette Clark Wire has observed, Paul as a freeborn and educated Jewish male, with other Greek-speaking city gentry, saw "their independence disintegrate under Roman rule."[36] Paul experienced a loss of status as a result of his joining the Jesus movement. By so doing, he compromised the privileges of his Jewish status as a Pharisee, and the Christian teachings of submission to Christ placed restrictions on his advancement in the Roman Empire.

Paul's political stance toward the state and empire has long been a bone of contention among biblical scholars and theologians. For some, Paul as a Roman citizen was a social conservative, who accepted the status quo and exhorted his followers to be subjects of governing authorities (Rom. 13:1–7). For others, Paul was anti-imperial, and the movement he participated in and the local communities he was building represented an alternative society in opposition to the Roman imperial order. Neil Elliott argues that Paul's remarks of submission were issued out of a particular historical context, and his aim was to safeguard the most vulnerable among the Roman Christians against the anti-Jewish sentiment in Rome.[37] Horsley, using rhetorical criticism to study 1 Corinthians, argues that Paul used terms and language of Greco-Roman rhetoric and Roman imperial ideology to oppose the imperial order.[38] But if we add the gender dimension to scrutinize Paul's anti-imperial stance, the picture emerging is more complicated, for Paul supported the subordination of women to men (1 Cor. 11:2–16; 14:33b–36, though some consider the latter as Deutero-Pauline). Some argue there is a "double standard" in Paul, for while he allowed for the transformation of the relationship between Jews and Gentiles and might have advocated resistance to the Roman order, he did not challenge gender roles and sexual relationships. In the study of modern anti-colonial movements, postcolonial feminists have also shown that the struggle against the colonial regime does not automatically lead men to give up their patriarchal privileges, and in many cases they want to reinscribe male-dominated norms to protect their "manhood."

In her analysis of the rhetoric of 1 Corinthians, Cynthia Briggs Kittredge argues that Paul used the language of the Roman patronage system to construct a pattern of linked hierarchical relationship in the Corinthian church. She says: "God's subjection of Christ is the ultimate symbolic legitimization of the father's position between the children and Christ and the husband's position between his wife and God."[39] Thus, she wonders whether Paul had replicated the language of subordination in the patronage system and thereby reinscribed imperial power relations. If Paul reinscribed gender inequality and preached about the submission of wives to their husbands in his letters, he was not alone in doing so. Mary Rose D'Angelo has shown that the authors of Luke-Acts, the Pastorals (Deutero-Pauline), and the *Shepherd of Hermas* had to construct masculinity and gender relations in the context of promulgation of imperial family values during the reigns of Trajan and Hadrian in

the late first and early second centuries. In order to maintain the harmony of the Roman order, proper governance of the household was seen to be necessary, which demanded the display of submission of women, children, and slaves. Because of the threat of persecution, these Christian writers wanted to argue that Christians demonstrated exemplary moral character and family life, to avoid denunciation. Thus, Roman family values cast their influence on the formulation of sexual ethics in the early Christian community.[40]

Sheila Briggs examines the rhetoric of Paul from another angle by focusing on his discourses on bondage and freedom.[41] Briggs's study would also complicate the claim of an anti-imperial stance for Paul, since Paul did not condemn the institution of slavery, which upheld the imperial order alongside the emperor cult, the paterfamilias, and the patronage system, and which pervaded the whole material and ideological domain. Of particular importance is her reading of the interplay among gender, sexuality, and slavery in Paul's rhetoric in Galatians 3–4 and 1 Corinthians 6–7. While scholars have used the baptismal formula in Galatians 3:28 to argue that Paul has a social egalitarian vision that abolishes all boundaries and differences, Briggs helpfully contextualizes the formula in the dual system of slaveholding patriarchy in Paul's time and highlights the plight of slave women living in such a society.[42] She notes that gender was always constructed through sexuality, and the inferior status of the slaves (both male and female) was marked by their sexual availability. Sexuality was deployed to maintain a hierarchical order and to denote legal and social status of persons. For example, the superiority of the free woman because of her honor and chastity was contrasted with the lack of honor and sexual degradation of the slave woman. Reading from such a context, Briggs eschews the consensual interpretation, which maintains that the baptismal formula speaks in parallel manner of three differences among human beings: ethnicity, class, and gender. Instead, she proposes that "an analogy is drawn between the common strife of Jew and Greek and the conflictual relationships inherent in the patriarchal dual system of slavery and gender."[43] The baptismal formula, for Briggs, sought to replace ethnicity in civic life and the household as sources of identity and conflict with the new identity in Christ.

Briggs notes that Paul did not draw the egalitarian and emanicipatory import from the baptismal formula in his construction of meaning of the Sarah and Hagar story, which he used to symbolize the two covenants (Gal. 4:21–31). He pitted Sarah against Hagar, and Sarah's children against Hagar's children, in the dual system of gender and slavery. While Christians were regarded as the true descendants of Abraham and shared in the covenant, the children of Hagar, born out of slavery, could not share the inheritance of God's promise. And in 1 Corinthians, Briggs finds it problematic that Paul used the discourse of evasion when he addressed but evaded the social institution of slavery. In particular, he condemned going to prostitutes (1 Cor. 6:15–16) as incompatible with Christian behavior, but did not criticize the sexual uses of slaves, which was seen as acceptable in the Roman moral and legal codes. In fact, most prostitutes were usually slaves coerced into this dishonorable occupation.[44] Paul also used slavery as a theological metaphor to describe Christians' relationship with Christ, asserting that Christians "were bought with a price" (1 Cor. 6:20; 7:23). Such a metaphor would sound very different to the freeborn than to the enslaved. What would it mean to a slave woman who would have experienced double slavery?

Having raised all these questions about Paul's position on the empire, women, and slavery, these feminist scholars insist that Paul was but one of the many voices in early Christianity. Elisabeth Schüssler Fiorenza argues for a hermeneutics of *ekklesia* that "seeks to displace the politics and rhetorics of subordination and otherness which [are] inscribed in the 'Pauline' correspondence with a hermeneutics and rhetorics of equality and responsibility."[45] Antoinette Clark Wire lifts up the submerged "voices within Paul's voice" and highlights the women prophets in Corinth.[46] Sheila Briggs reminds us to read gender and slavery as a dual system and to bear in mind the silent voices of the slave woman in the text. Early Christianity was a plurivocal movement of women and men from many social locations, and a postcolonial reading helps us to raise new questions and make connections.

Postcolonialism, Feminism, and Anti-Judaism

Postcolonial feminist interpreters of the Bible need to pay attention to deepseated anti-Jewish biases in Christian thought and their manifestations in different contexts. Amy-Jill Levine has charged that anti-Jewish readings can be found in the writings of Third World theologians and biblical scholars working out of a feminist-liberationist framework.[47] To make Jesus look like a feminist, the first-century Jewish context was described and labeled as blatantly misogynist. Jewish feminists, most notably Judith Plaskow and Susannah Heschel, have challenged such anti-Jewish tendencies in white Christian feminist biblical interpretation in the 1970s and early 1980s.[48] Levine is concerned about the resurfacing of such biases in the global feminist biblical discourse in the 1990s.

There has not been much conversation and dialogue between Third World feminist scholars coming out of postcolonial contexts, on the one hand, and Jewish feminists, on the other. Judaism and Christianity exist as two distinct traditions and operate within very separate orbits in the Third World. Even where there is a local Jewish population, there are few opportunities for Christian and Jewish feminists to mingle and work together. In most cases, the writings of Jewish feminists and other Jewish sources on first-century Judaism are not easily available, and there are few who have adequate training in using these materials. Further, combating anti-Judaism has not been a priority within global Christian feminist networks and in the ecumenical circles. And most importantly, Third World feminists may see the holocaust as the burden for Europeans only. Since their countries have not participated directly in persecuting the Jews, they have not been as pressed to see anti-Judaism as a critical issue to reckon with. Furthermore, in the continual Middle East conflict, they tend to stand in solidarity with the Palestinians, who are driven from their land and suffer under the military might of the state of Israel, supported by the government of the United States.

But Third World feminists and Jewish feminists have a lot to learn from one another to understand on a deeper level how anti-Semitism intersects with colonial discourse, especially during the nineteenth century and early twentieth century – how, for example, the Jews were treated by the Christian colonists as the Others within, who were persecuted and suppressed, while the colonized were the Others from without, who were enslaved and conquered. When Christianity was

brought to other parts of the world from the West, it was almost completely purged of its Jewish context, such that the universal tradition initiated by Jesus was seen as a new religion, supplanting the old tradition of Judaism. A postcolonial analysis will help Third World scholars see more clearly how such a mystification of Christian origins supports both anti-Semitism and Christian imperialism. If we were to see the Jesus movement not as an innovation of Jesus, but as a reform or emancipatory movement within Judaism, Christian feminists from the Third World could dialogue with Jewish feminists about how to assess the emancipatory nature of this movement.[49]

It is important, therefore, to pay attention to what Levine identifies as problematic and anti-Jewish in Third World women's biblical interpretation. First, there is often a blanket and monolithic portrayal of the Jewish tradition as patriarchal. Jewish women were depicted as marginalized and excluded from religious leadership and public roles, a view that has long been challenged by feminist historians who have studied that period. Second, against this negative foil of Judaism, Jesus is seen as either not influenced by or rejecting his Jewish context, a countercultural radical who befriended women, healed, and preached to them. Third, the demand of Jewish laws for ritual purity and cleanliness is highlighted, which is regarded as biased against women and non-Jews. Against such taboos of pollution and impurity, Jesus is seen as transgressing the boundaries between the clean and the unclean, and between Jews and Gentiles. Fourth, women's oppression and powerlessness in their modern social location was projected into Jewish antiquity, as if transcultural and transhistorical comparisons could be made. Fifth, Third World women who are outside the guilds of biblical studies and have no access to biblical scholarship tend not to reproduce anti-Jewish readings.[50]

When we examine these charges, we can see that some of them bear a close resemblance to what missionaries have taught the "native" Christians. Levine also astutely observes that "much of the anti-Judaism named in this paper thus appears to be another colonial product of global symbol capital, exported along with cured tobacco and DDT."[51] The claim that Jesus was a liberator of women who broke from Jewish tradition was first introduced to the Third World not by Western academic scholarship but by missionaries who wanted to convert native women to Christianity. For example, missionaries cited Jesus' befriending women, teaching profound spiritual truths to them, his healing the woman who suffered from hemorrhage, his sympathy for the woman caught in sin, and his appearance to women after his resurrection.[52] The subordination of women in the native traditions was regarded as symptomatic of the inferiority of their cultures. Many native women who leave their tradition to become Christians believe that Jesus does not discriminate against women and that Christianity offers women a better chance for life. Because of this long history of hailing Jesus as an iconoclastic hero in missionary and also native Christian women's discourses, I am not persuaded that only Western-educated Third World feminists are making anti-Jewish remarks, and that ordinary readers who are not theologically trained are not. Since ordinary readers tend to read the Bible more literally, it is difficult to believe that anti-Jewish statements found in the text itself, especially in the passion narratives, would not influence them.

So what are the causes of anti-Jewish readings in Third World feminist writings that Levine identifies as problematic? I agree with her that it is possible that Third World feminist theologians may simply reinscribe the colonialist position and

internalize the colonizers' abjection of the Jews. Or they may have repeated the kind of argument that "Jesus was a feminist" found in Western Christian feminist interpretation in the 1970s. But to lay blame on the colonists, missionaries, and early feminists may lead us to overlook some deeper cultural politics at work. Unlike in the West, the cultures in the Third World do not harbor a long animosity toward the Jews. Few Third World feminists have had sufficient sustained contact with the Jewish people or dialogue with Jewish feminists to know how they feel about the Jewish tradition. Levine suggests that the reproduction of anti-Jewish discourse by Third World feminists can be interpreted as a colonial mimicry and a repetition of what they have learned from their Western teachers. I want to highlight the ambivalent nature of mimicry, which Homi Bhabha has described as "almost the same, *but not quite*." Bhabha emphasizes the indeterminacy and double articulation of mimicry: on the one hand, it may reinscribe colonial authority (trying to be white); on the other hand, it may be a complex strategy to challenge identity and difference constructed by "normalized" knowledges ("*but not quite*") and to appropriate, fracture, and displace the dominant discourse for resistance.[53] Whereas Levine looks at mimicry as a repetition and reinscription of Western Christian anti-Jewish discourse (trying to be white), I want to probe in what ways Third World feminist writings are different ("almost the same but not white")[54] from those of their colonial masters and mistresses.

I suggest the critique of patriarchy in Jewish culture may have served as a rhetorical device not just to make Jesus look good, but also to bring into sharp relief patriarchy in their own cultures. As Jesus critiqued his own culture (some aspects of it, not all), these women find support and encouragement to challenge their own culture. As Elsa Tamez has said:

> The sometimes sharp criticism that Jesus thrusts at his own Jewish culture does not reflect an anti-Jewish stance. As we know, Jesus is a Jew and therefore places himself in a position of self-critique with respect to the patriarchy of Judaism and Roman culture as enacted in oppressive practices. Importantly, in this same way, women today engage in constructive criticism of their religious and social culture.[55]

From a liberationist perspective, Jesus is seen as attacking not only patriarchy alone, but also imperialism, colonialism, and militarism. Thus, these Third World feminists may not have engaged in a simple kind of colonial mimicry, but may have tried to refashion the dominant colonial discourse in order to create a language of resistance that challenges both patriarchy in native cultures and imperialism at once.

Still, we must question the ethics of portraying Judaism as blatantly sexist to serve as a negative foil to criticize patriarchy in native cultures. To heed Levine's call, we must avoid using generalized and monolithic descriptions about the Jewish tradition or about indigenous cultures. An important postcolonial insight is that what is so-called national culture is always constructed, contested, forged through debate, negotiation, and sometimes confrontation. This will require us to know much better the different groups and factions of first-century Judaism: their daily practices, local histories, and religious and political ideologies. Instead of singling out the patriarchal practices of the Jews, we need to place them in the wider contexts of the Roman imperial rule.

Levine has noted that Third World feminists have identified "the Jews" transhistorically and transculturally with their oppressors, but rarely with "the Romans." One plausible reason is that, in the colonial setting, the oppression of the colonialists is often not felt intimately and immediately, for the colonialists, as members of the upper class, rarely mix with the people. It is the disciplinary power of the indigenous elites employed as colonial agents and accomplices that is most keenly felt. At this juncture, postcolonial criticism may provide a corrective to a one-sided blaming of "the Jews," since postcolonial biblical studies focus on the impact of the empire, both ancient and modern, and on its representations in the text. For example, postcolonial feminist studies of the Bible can examine how Roman imperial rule had shaped and changed Jewish cultures and customs, especially regarding gender relationships and women's roles in their faith community. And, if the conflicts of Jesus with the Pharisees and the Jewish leaders were not Christian–Jewish conflicts but intra-Jewish arguments, it would be productive to explore the political implications of such conflicts under the shadow of the empire. A postcolonial interpretation will highlight the roles these religious leaders played in maintaining the traditional ways of Jewish life, while also serving as mediators between the Jewish people and the Roman order.[56] Furthermore, the Jesus movement must be recognized as a movement within the context of Judaism, and postcolonial feminists are interested to know if this movement provided opportunities for Jewish women to challenge not only patriarchy but also imperial rule.

Levine places the burden of detecting and correcting anti-Jewish interpretation on the shoulders of those who have been theologically trained, noting that mainstream New Testament scholarship has perpetuated and even promoted such readings. In the Third World, this problem is particularly acute, as some of the theological schools are still using "standard" Western dictionaries and commentaries published a generation ago. Some of these texts not only contain anti-Jewish remarks, but also present an outdated and skewed picture of Christian origins. For example, Susannah Heschel has noted that Rudolf Bultmann's highly negative depictions of Judaism's legalism had influenced New Testament scholarship after the Second World War, especially in the new quest for the historical Jesus.[57] Before the Third World libraries are updated, we must exercise caution and discretion in using these resources and maintain a healthy dose of suspicion whenever Jewish culture is portrayed in a negative light.

I support many of Levine's strategies for conscientizing people about anti-Jewish biases in biblical and theological studies: learning more about Jewish history, avoiding making generalized negative statements about Judaism, the inclusion of Jewish voices in anthologies, updating libraries (especially in the Third World) with Jewish resources, and naming the problem when we see it. Relating to the process are pedagogical issues regarding teaching the body of Third World feminist writings. Levine is concerned that the teaching of these multicultural voices with anti-Jewish contents will infect the next generation of students, and the infection would have global effects. I think these Third World writings must be taught with an understanding of the history and cultures of their contexts and the rhetorical strategies they use. At a time when American imperialism is on the rise, those of us teaching in the United States must insist on including voices outside the United States to challenge "sanctioned ignorance" perpetuated by the dominant white educational system, the mass media, and the state apparatus. A roundtable

discussion of Levine's work by some of the authors she criticizes can be used to help students understand the complex and multifaceted dimensions of the issues and to illustrate that those feminists are not afraid to dialogue on difficult issues across differences.[58]

I welcome Levine's invitation to feminists to read the biblical texts in community, so that we can confront our prejudices and be aware of how our social location influences our reading practices.[59] Reading in company with those who have not been our constant dialogical partners has the added benefit of shifting our location within a changing configuration of social relationships. For example, Levine, as a North American, is concerned that her critique of the work of an Asian, African, Australian, or Latin American woman might be seen as "patronizing racism."[60] But outside the United States, where the issues of racism and anti-Semitism are understood differently, her partners in conversation may respond to her in ways different from her American audiences. Similarly, her Asian, African, Australian, and Latin American colleagues will have an opportunity to redefine their hybridized Christian identity as they encounter diasporic Jewish feminists.

Feminist interpretation of the Bible has come a long way since the day when the Chinese woman excised from her Bible those Pauline passages that she considered misogynous. It has become a global movement, as women with different histories and cultures challenge patriarchal readings and articulate their faith and understanding of God. If the Bible has been the "great code" undergirding Western civilization as Northrop Frye has said,[61] women from all over the world are claiming the power and authority to retell, rewrite, and reinterpret this important document. In particular, they have pointed to the intersection of anti-Semitism, global racism, and sexism in the colonialist imagination. Women can benefit from reading together with others in community in order to challenge our own biases and investment in a particular interpretive method. We have the challenge to turn the postcolonial "contact zones" into places of mutual learning, and places for trying out new ideas and strategies for the emancipation of all.

NOTES

1 Musa W. Dube, "Postcoloniality, Feminist Spaces, and Religion," in Laura E. Donaldson and Kwok Pui-lan (eds), *Postcolonialism, Feminism, and Religious Discourse*. (New York: Routledge, 2002), 115.

2 Fernando F. Segovia, *Decolonizing Biblical Studies: A View from the Margins* (Maryknoll, NY: Orbis Books, 2000), 121–2.

3 R. S. Sugirtharajah, *The Bible and the Third World: Precolonial, Colonial and Postcolonial Encounters* (Cambridge: Cambridge University Press, 2001), 251–3.

4 See David Jobling's contribution to "*The Postcolonial Bible*: Four Reviews," *Journal for the Study of the New Testament*, 74 (1999): 117–19.

5 Archie C. C. Lee, "Identity, Reading Strategy and Doing Theology," *Biblical Interpretation*, 7 (1999): 156–73.

6 Kwok Pui-lan, "Jesus/The Native: Biblical Studies from a Postcolonial Perspective," in *Teaching the Bible: The Discourses and Politics of Biblical Pedagogy*, ed. Fernando F. Segovia and Mary Ann Tolbert (Maryknoll, NY: Orbis Books, 1998), 69–85.

7 Sugirtharajah, *The Bible and the Third World*; and R. S. Sugirtharajah, *Asian Biblical Hermeneutics and Postcolonialism: Contesting the Interpretations* (Maryknoll, NY: Orbis Books, 1998).
8 Gale A. Yee, *Poor Banished Children of Eve: Women as Evil in the Hebrew Bible* (Minneapolis: Fortress Press, 2003), 4.
9 Ibid., 111–34.
10 Ibid., 111.
11 Mary Louise Pratt, *Imperial Eyes: Travel Writing and Transculturation* (London: Routledge, 1992), 6.
12 Laura E. Donaldson, "The Sign of Orpah: Reading Ruth through Native Eyes," in (ed.) R. S. Sugirtharajah *Vernacular Hermeneutics* (Sheffield: Sheffield Academic Press, 1999), 29–32.
13 Musa W. Dube, *Postcolonial Feminist Interpretation of the Bible* (St. Louis: Chalice Press, 2000), 122.
14 Ibid., 168–9.
15 Ibid., 184.
16 Musa Dube, "Readings of *Semoya*: Batswana Women Interpretations of Matt. 15:21–28," *Semeia*, 73 (1996): 111–29; Gloria Kehilve Plaatjie, "Toward a Postapartheid Black Feminist Reading of the Bible: A Case of Luke 2:36–38," in Musa W. Dube (ed.), *Other Ways of Reading: African Women and the Bible* (Atlanta: Society of Biblical Literature, 2001), 114–42.
17 Dube, *Postcolonial Feminist Interpretation of the Bible*, 190–2.
18 Mary Ann Tolbert, "When Resistance Becomes Repression: Mark 13: 9–27 and the Poetics of Location," in Fernando F. Segovia and Mary Ann Tolbert *Reading from This Place*, (eds) vol. 2 (Minneapolis: Fortress Press, 1995), 333.
19 Sharon H. Ringe, "Places at the Table: Feminist and Postcolonial Biblical Interpretation," in R. S. Sugirtharajah (ed.), *The Postcolonial Bible*, (Sheffield: Sheffield Academic Press, 1998), 136–51.
20 Plaatjie, "Toward a Post-apartheid Black Feminist Reading," 119–20; Beverley G. Haddad, "Constructing Theologies of Survival in the South African Context: The Necessity of a Critical Engagement between Postmodern and Liberation Theology," *Journal of Feminist Studies in Religion*, 14/2 (1998): 5–18.
21 Yee, *Poor Banished Children of Eve*, 159.
22 Mary Rose D'Angelo, "Early Christian Sexual Politics and Roman Imperial Family Values: Rereading Christ and Culture," in Christopher I. Wilkins (ed.), *The Papers of the Henry Luce III Fellows in Theology*, 6 (Pittsburgh: Association of Theological Schools, 2003), 24–5. Warren Carter also notes that the study of the Gospel of Matthew has been preoccupied with its Jewish context to the neglect of the influence of the Roman Empire; see Warren Carter, *Matthew and Empire: Initial Explorations* (Harrisburg, Pa.: Trinity Press International, 2001).
23 D'Angelo, "Early Christian Sexual Politics," 30.
24 Dube, *Postcolonial Feminist Interpretation of the Bible*, 28–30.
25 See, e.g., Luise Schottroff, *Lydia's Impatient Sisters: A Feminist Social History of Early Christianity* (Louisville, Ky.: Westminster John Knox Press, 1995).
26 Richard A. Horsley has emphasized the need to foreground local histories; see, e.g., idem, "Subverting Disciplines: The Possibilities and Limitations of Postcolonial Theory for New Testament Studies," in Fernando F. Segovia *Toward a New Heaven and a New Earth: Essays in Honor of Elisabeth Schüssler Fiorenza*, (Maryknoll, NY: Orbis (ed.), Books, 2003), 93–4. For a discussion of regional differentiation of the Roman family, see Beryl Rawson, "'The Roman Family' in Recent Research: State of the Question," *Biblical Interpretation*, 11 (2003): 132.

27 Elisabeth Schüssler Fiorenza, *But She Said: Feminist Practices of Biblical Interpretation* (Boston: Beacon Press, 1992), 40–7, 150–1.
28 Ann Laura Stoler, *Carnal Knowledge and Imperial Power: Race and the Intimate in Colonial Rule* (Berkeley: University of California Press, 2002).
29 Anne McClintock, *Imperial Leather: Race, Gender, and Sexuality in the Colonial Contest* (New York: Routledge, 1995), 5.
30 Joachim Jeremias, *Abba: Studien zur neutestamentlichen Theologies und Zeitgeschichte* (Göttingen: Vandenhoeck and Ruprecht, 1966).
31 Mary Rose D'Angelo, "Abba and 'Father': Imperial Theology and the Jesus Traditions," *Journal of Biblical Literature* 111 (1992): 623.
32 Mary Rose D'Angelo, "Theology in Mark and Q: Abba and 'Father' in Context," *Harvard Theological Review* 85 (1992): 174.
33 Richard A. Horsley, *Hearing the Whole Story: The Politics of Plot in Mark's Gospel* (Louisville, Ky.: Westminster John Knox Press, 2001), 203–29; and a shorter version in idem, "Feminist Scholarship and Postcolonial Criticism: Subverting Imperial Discourse and Reclaiming Submerged Histories," in Shelly Matthews, Cynthia Briggs Kittredge, and Melanie Johnson-Debaufre *Walk in the Ways of Wisdom: Essays in Honor of Elisabeth Schüssler Fiorenza*, (Harrisburg, Pa.: Trinity Press International, 2003), 301–5.
34 For other readings of Jesus and the patriarchal family, see Elisabeth Schüssler Fiorenza, *In Memory of Her: A Feminist Theological Reconstruction of Christian Origins*, 10th ann. edn. (New York: Crossroad, 1994), 140–51; and a contrasting view, John H. Elliot, "Jesus Was Not an Egalitarian: A Critique of an Anachronistic and Idealist Theory," *Biblical Theology Bulletin*, 32. 3 (2002): 75–91.
35 Richard A. Horsley, "Submerged Biblical Histories and Imperial Biblical Studies," in Sugirtharajah, *The Postcolonial Bible*, 162–3.
36 Antoinette Clark Wire, *The Corinthian Women Prophets: A Reconstruction through Paul's Rhetoric* (Minneapolis: Fortress Press, 1990), 70.
37 Neil Elliott, "Romans 13:1–7 in the Context of Imperial Propaganda," in Richard A. Horsley (ed.), *Paul and Empire: Religion and Power in the Roman Imperial Society* (Harrisburg, Pa.: Trinity Press International, 1997), 184–204.
38 Richard A. Horsley, "Rhetoric and Empire – And 1 Corinthians," in Richard A. Horsley (ed.), *Paul and Politics: Ekklesia, Israel, Imperium, Interpretation*, ed. (Harrisburg, Pa.: Trinity Press International, 2000), 91.
39 Cynthia Briggs Kittredge, "Corinthian Women Prophets and Paul's Argumentation in 1 Corinthians," in Horsley, *Paul and Politics*, 107.
40 Mary Rose D'Angelo, " 'Knowing How to Preside over His Own Household': Imperial Masculinity and Christian Asceticism in the Pastorals, *Hermas*, and Luke-Acts," in Stephen D. Moore and Janice Capel Anderson (eds), *New Testament Masculinity* (Atlanta: Society of Biblical Literature, 2003), 265–95.
41 Sheila Briggs, "Paul on Bondage and Freedom in Imperial Roman Society," in Horsley, *Paul and Politics*, 110–23.
42 Sheila Briggs, "Slavery and Gender," in Jane Schaberg, Alice Bach, and Esther Fuchs *On the Cutting Edge: The Study of Women in the Biblical Worlds*, (New York: Continuum, 2003), 171–92.
43 Ibid., 182.
44 Briggs, "Paul on Bondage and Freedom," 114–15.
45 Elisabeth Schüssler Fiorenza, "Paul and the Politics of Interpretation," in Horsley, *Paul and Politics*, 54.
46 Wire, *The Corinthian Women Prophets*.
47 Amy-Jill Levine, "Lilies of the Field and Wandering Jews: Biblical Scholarship, Women's Roles, and Social Location," in Ingrid Rosa Kitzberger *Transformative Encounters: Jesus*

and Women Re-viewed, (Leiden: Brill, 2000), 329–52. A version that focuses on Third World women's writings is found in Amy-Jill Levine, "The Disease of Postcolonial New Testament Studies and the Hermeneutics of Healing," *Journal of Feminist Studies in Religion*, 20/1 (2004): 91–9.

48 Judith Plaskow, "Blaming the Jews for the Birth of Patriarchy," *Lilith*, 7 (1980): 11–12, 14–17; and idem, "Anti-Judaism in Feminist Christian Interpretation," in Elisabeth Schüssler Fiorenza (ed.), *Searching the Scriptures*, vol. 1, *A Feminist Introduction.* (New York: Crossroad, 1993), 117–29; Susannah Heschel, "Anti-Judaism in Christian Feminist Theology," *Tikkun*, 5/3 (1990): 25–8, 95–7.

49 Elisabeth Schüssler Fiorenza had earlier characterized the Jesus movement as "renewal or reform movement," but has changed it to an "emancipatory" or "*basileia*" movement, to indicate that the reference point of such emancipation was not Judaism but Roman imperial domination. See "Of Specks, Beams, and Methods: Anti-Judaism and Antifeminism," in idem, *Jesus and the Politics of Interpretation* (New York: Continuum, 2000), 119.

50 Levine, "Lilies of the Field," 331–50.

51 Ibid., 348–9.

52 Kwok Pui-lan, *Chinese Women and Christianity, 1860–1927* (Atlanta: Scholars Press, 1992), 47–51.

53 Homi K. Bhabha, "Of Mimicry and Man: The Ambivalence of Colonial Discourse," in idem, *The Location of Culture* (London: Routledge, 1994), 85–92.

54 Ibid., 89.

55 Elsa Tamez, *Jesus and Courageous Women* (New York: Women's Division, United Methodist Church, 2001), viii.

56 Horsley, *Paul and Empire*, 207–8.

57 Susannah Heschel, "The Image of Judaism in Nineteenth-Century Christian New Testament Scholarship in Germany," in Marvin Perry and Frederick M. *Jewish – Christian Encounters over the Centuries: Symbiosis, Prejudice, Holocaust, Dialogue*, Schweitzer (eds) (New York: Peter Lang, 1994), 234.

58 "Anti-Judaism and Postcolonial Biblical Interpretation," *Journal of Feminist Studies in Religion*, 20/1 (2004): 91–132.

59 Levine, "Lilies of the Field," 350.

60 Ibid.

61 Northrop Frye, *The Great Code: The Bible and Literature* (New York: Harcourt Brace Jovanovich, 1982).

Part II
Empires Old and New

Introduction:
Empires Old and New

R. S. Sugirtharajah

Empire arouses emotions and it is not an easy subject for those biblical critics who aspire to be "objective." Here are four biblical scholars, all from the new imperium – America – but trying, nevertheless, to make sense of empires, both ancient and modern.

The section opens with an extract from Richard Horsley's booklet, *Religion and Empire*. In the booklet, Horsley examines the response to empire in several religions, including Buddhism and Islam, but the extract published here is confined to resistance in ancient Judea. Horsley's contention is that Jewish and Christian histories and literatures originated within a landscape of imperial domination and control. The popular protest movements drew heavily upon traditional religious practices or were patterned after earlier popular protest movements which refused to compromise with imperial demands. However, Horsley's piece ends on a sad note, with a comment on the fate of the once-resistant Christianity, now being co-opted to serve imperial ideology and colonial causes.

Jon Berquist's essay, "Postcolonialism and Imperial Motives for Canonization," considers the early stages of Hebrew Bible canonization influenced by the imperialistic ambitions of the Persian empire. His assertion is that the canon was a politically constructed document for the purpose of advancing imperial ideology, but that the same canon contains postcolonial opportunities and germs of resistance which can be used against the very imperial ideology it sets out to espouse. More significantly, Berquist talks about a moral act of commitment – a commitment which postcolonialism should not lose sight of. Postcolonial biblical criticism should not be satisfied with simply exposing imperial tendencies in canonical texts and deconstructing them, but should go further "to construct interpretations which have decolonizing effects in the contemporary world."

Werner Kelber's essay deals with the question of how oral and written mediums were used as instruments of identity formation, control, and domination by both colonial elites and marginalized groups. The early Christians' use of the written form was constrained by the menacing presence of the Roman empire and their vulnerable position, since their leader had been killed by that empire for his alleged political

stance. Kelber shows how such early Christian writings as Mark, Luke, and the Apocalypse of John competed in the Greco-Roman marketplace of scribal communication and negotiated their different strategies in response. In Mark's case, using the recent history of the life and death of Jesus, the author cautiously presents the kingdom of God as an alternative to all imperial kingdoms. Luke, in the face of Roman supremacy, accommodates the message to the new political realities by portraying Jesus as a social and religious reformer who posed "no threat to the imperial Roman system." The Apocalypse was uncompromising in its condemnation of the Roman world-power, but its anti-Roman rhetoric was camouflaged in a series of symbols and images and set largely in an imaginary universe, inviting the audience to recognize themselves in the ongoing struggle between chaos and order, good and evil.

The section ends with a timely warning against the current imperial tendencies of the Bush administration and its neo-conservative agenda. In the essay entitled, "Desiring War: Apocalypse, Commodity Fetish, and the End of History," Erin Runions identifies two key lexicons in the discourse of the current US administration, of "History" and of "Freedom." History as personified stands as a surrogate for God, and calls the US to its unique and covenantal mission of protecting the world from apocalyptic terror and destruction. The fight against evil is seen as a high calling invested in the US in order to bring the blessings of freedom. This freedom is conjoined with American financial goals and desires. The freedom that is defended by war stands as a shorthand for economic freedom, both at home and abroad. She uncovers the impetus for such an agenda deriving from Christian apocalyptic texts and supported by the reading of a truncated version of Hegel and his interpreter Alexandre Kojéve, as well as borrowing from the end-of-history notions of Francis Fukuyama. Her concern is that the invocation of apocalyptic metaphors is not "benign; the stakes are deadly, both at home and abroad." She ends with a plea that, at a time when America is asserting itself as a new imperial force, those who wish to resist its bellicose stance need to come up with "new metaphors and new philosophical frameworks of resistance."

4

Renewal Movements and Resistance to Empire in Ancient Judea

Richard A. Horsley

The revival of Shiite Islam in Iran provides an analogy that will help us understand the historical origins of what we now call "Judaism" and "Christianity." Christian theologians still project their construct of a unitary, monolithic, but ethnically parochial "religion" called "Judaism" that was succeeded by the more spiritual and universalistic "religion" called "Christianity."[1] The resulting essentialist discourse of "Judaism" among Christians persists both in the field of New Testament studies and in that of Jewish history just as the essentialist discourse of "Islam" persists among Orientalists. The separation of religion from politics, and the historical emergence of Judaism and its spin-off, Christianity, however, did not develop until late antiquity; these institutions are a long-range result of the Romans' use of political and military power to ensure that indigenous peoples' commitment to their traditional way of life did not interfere with their submission to the imperial order.

Until the Roman destruction of Jerusalem and the Temple in 66–70 CE, the situation in ancient Judea under Hellenistic and Roman imperial rule was somewhat analogous to Iran under modern western imperial domination. What modern Westerners usually think of as religion and politics (and economics) were simply inseparable in Judean society in the "second-temple" period (sixth century BCE to first century CE). As in Iran in the late twentieth century, when western imperial powers and/or their client rulers threatened the traditional way of life in Judea, indigenous groups of scribal teachers as well as popular groups mounted intense protests and movements of resistance rooted in a revival of their traditional way of life.

To understand such resistance it is necessary to understand the general structure of the imperial situation in ancient Judea. Following the Babylonian destruction of the

First published in *Religion and Empire: People Power and the Life of the Spirit*. Minneapolis: Fortress Press, 2003, 74–92.

Judean monarchy and Temple in the sixth century BCE, the Persian imperial regime set up a temple-state in Jerusalem (the "second temple") that continued as the imperial instrument of local rule for six centuries, eventually under successive Hellenistic and Roman Empires. Contrary to the standard view that Judea was stable, the successive imperial regimes regularly interfered in affairs in Jerusalem, where rival factions among the high-priestly aristocracy vied for imperial favor. A series of such interventions was perhaps the key factor in touching off the Maccabean Revolt led by the Hasmonean family in the 160s BCE. During the ensuing period of imperial weakness, the upstart Hasmonean regime in Judea aggressively extended its own rule over Idumea to the south and Samaria and Galilee to the north in an imitation of imperial politics.[2]

When the Romans finally took control of the eastern Mediterranean they installed the military strongman Herod over most of Palestine. Just as the Shah was the United States' favored dictator, so Herod the Great became the Emperor Augustus' favored client king. He engineered massive "development" in Palestine, building temples and whole cities (Sebaste and Caesarea) in honor of the emperor, and bestowed lavish gifts upon members of the imperial family and upon cities of the empire, all funded by tax revenues taken from his subjects. The high-priestly families, whom Herod elevated to power and privilege, became the ruling aristocracy in Jerusalem under the authority of the Roman governors during the first century CE, building ever more elaborate mansions in the upper city of Jerusalem.[3] Both the Roman historian Josephus and rabbinic literature give vivid descriptions of just how predatory the priestly and Herodian aristocracy became in its collaboration with the repressive measures taken periodically by the Roman governors.[4]

The realities of imperial domination of the Judean (Israelite) people stood in stark contradiction to the older Israelite tradition to which it claimed to be heir. Although the official scripture of the Jerusalem temple-state (the precursor of the Torah) emphasized materials that provided grounding and legitimation for the Temple and (high-) priestly rule, it also contained early Israelite traditions of their independence under the direct rule of God. Central were the exodus story of God's liberation of the people from bondage to the pharaoh in Egypt and the Mosaic Covenant with their liberating God, which established a people committed to political-economic justice under the direct rule of God, that is, to the exclusion of oppressive human rulers. Among the almost completely nonliterate Israelite village communities subject to the Jerusalem temple-state, the exodus and covenant were understood to be central features of their popular tradition.[5] This early Israelite tradition of the people's independent societal life under the direct rule of God became the basis for persistent resistance and rebellion against imperial rule.

The centrality of such early Israelite traditions in resistance to western imperial rule can be seen most dramatically in the Passover, one of three principal annual festivals in the Judean temple community, celebrating the people's liberation from oppressive foreign rule in Egypt. Although in second-temple times Passover was celebrated in Jerusalem under the oversight of the high-priestly regime, it nevertheless brought to the fore the conflict between the Israelite tradition of independence and the reality of imperial rule. This conflict vividly illustrates the utter inseparability of politics and religion for Judeans under Roman imperial rule.

> When the festival called Passover was at hand . . . a large multitude from all quarters assembled for it. [The Roman governor] Cumanus, fearing that their presence might afford occasion for an uprising, ordered a company of soldiers to take up arms and stand guard in the porticoes of the Temple so as to quell any uprising that might occur. This has in fact been the usual practice of previous procurators of Judea at the festivals.[6]

When the celebrants protested a Roman soldier's lewd gesture, Cumanus unleashed his troops in a violent retaliation typical of Roman rule.[7]

Judeans' insistence on their traditional (Israelite) way of life was far more serious than an occasional outburst of popular unrest. Just as the Muslim "clergy" provided leadership in modern Iran, so the "scribes and Pharisees" often took the lead in anti-imperial protests and other agitation in ancient Judea. To understand the meaning of this behavior, we must appreciate their position in the imperial situation of the ancient Judean temple-state. Since the high priesthood was the creature of empire, the incumbent Judean rulers were beholden to their imperial overlords and generally collaborative. Scribal circles, however, along with ordinary priests, whose very role was to guide the people in maintenance of the sacred traditions and traditional way of life, were always caught in the middle.[8] While they were dependent politically and economically on the priestly aristocracy, they were prepared to lead resistance if their high-priestly patrons collaborated too closely with imperial officials and/or policy. At points of extreme imperial imposition, certain scribal circles even made common cause with the peasantry. The standard modern oversimplification of complex ancient Judean historical realities reduces the most influential scribal groups of the late second-temple period to religious "sects" of "Judaism," presumably in distinction from the "church" of the Temple establishment. Historically, however, these scribal groups can be more appropriately understood as activists in the Judeans' struggle to maintain their traditional way of life against the incursions of western imperial rule. A review of the imperial relations to which the principal groups and movements – the Pharisees, Essenes, "Fourth Philosophy," and *Sicarii* – were responding will clarify their origins and purposes.

The recent revival of Islam and revolution in Iran are particularly helpful models for understanding the emergence of apocalyptic literature and the Maccabean Revolt, which constitute the watershed for subsequent Judean and Galilean movements of renewal and resistance in late second-temple times. Backed by the (Hellenistic) Seleucid imperial regime, the "western"-oriented high-priestly families carried out a Hellenizing reform in the 170s BCE, transforming the Jerusalem temple-state into a Hellenistic city-state. Resistance formed among scribal circles, cultivators and teachers of the people's sacred traditions, and the peasantry, under the leadership of ordinary priests, particularly of the Hasmonean family (see 1–2 Maccabees). A group of the teachers produced visions of God's retaking control of history (Daniel 7–12). God was about to judge the oppressive Seleucid empire and restore "the people of the saints of the Most High" to sovereignty (Dan 7:23–8). That is, justice was finally about to be established in Judean society with its life again directly under the rule of God. Over a period of several years, whether inspired by such visions or not, popular forces fought the imperial armies to a standoff, and regained control of Jerusalem and rededicated the Temple.

Despite the temporary "success" of Judean guerrilla warfare against the Seleucid armies, the basic imperial structure under which Judeans lived did not change. In fact, it was intensified under Roman rule. Yet memory of the temporary liberation helped inspire recurrent movements of resistance and renewal for the next three centuries. Resistance to the Roman Empire mounted by some Judean scribal circles and ordinary priests is analogous to opposition to the Shah and his western imperial backers by members of the Islamic *ulama*. Three of the four groups usually treated as "sects" of "Judaism" originated as movements of resistance to imperial rule or played a significant role in such resistance.

The Essenes – one branch of whom are now identified with the wilderness community at Qumran that left behind the Dead Sea Scrolls – apparently formed in protest against the Hasmonean reversion to imperial rule.[9] Their disillusionment and dissatisfaction with the "wicked" high-priestly rule was so severe that they felt compelled to abandon their previous priestly-scribal positions in society and launch a new exodus and renewed covenant community in the wilderness of Judea.[10] The movement sustained its renewal by withdrawing for several generations. Under Roman rule they became even more adamantly anti-imperial, conceiving of the Romans (the "Kittim") as the embodiment of satanic forces. They even rehearsed ritual warfare in anticipation of the eschatological cosmic battle between the demonic forces of darkness and the Kittim on one side and themselves and the divine forces of light on the other.[11] They also apparently anticipated that in the fulfillment of history, they themselves, having "prepared the way of the Lord in the wilderness" (stated in their Community Rule), would return to a restored temple-state as leaders of a renewed society.

The Pharisees are usually cast in modern religious scholarship either as the legalistic opponents of Jesus or as the precursors of the rabbis who defined "normative Judaism." Historically, however, they were significant mainly as mediators between imperial rule and ongoing Judean attempts to persevere in their traditional way of life. Whatever their own motives, Josephus's accounts suggest that they opposed the Hasmoneans's expansionist practices and their assimilation of Hellenistic, imperial, political culture in their political-religious role as interpreters and adapters of the laws of Moses.[12] Hundreds of Pharisees or Pharisee-like Judeans were crucified as martyrs. As political "realists," however, the Pharisees settled into a patient mediating role, attempting to facilitate the conduct of societal life according to the Torah while serving under Herod and the high-priestly families, who were maintained in their positions of power and privilege by the Romans.

According to the Torah, however, not only did all aspects of Judean life belong under the sole rule and will of God, but (like Allah) God insisted upon sole religious-political-economic sovereignty. This becomes clearly evident in the movement Josephus called the "Fourth Philosophy." (For his Greek readers, Josephus likens these Judean groups to Greek philosophies, the first three being Sadducees, Pharisees, and Essenes.)[13] This new movement, led by a teacher named Judas and a Pharisee named Sadok, organized resistance to payment of the tribute levied by Rome when it imposed direct imperial rule on Judea in 6 CE Josephus explains that they "agreed in all other respects with the views of the Pharisees, except that they have a passion for freedom that is almost unconquerable, since they are convinced that God alone is their leader and master."[14] The pharisaic and scribal leaders of the movement thus

insisted that Judeans could not possibly render tribute to Caesar, since that was tantamount to serving the Roman emperor and Judeans owed exclusive loyalty to God, their sole and direct Lord and Ruler.[15]

We may presume similar motives among the Judean teachers who formed the "Dagger Men" (*Sicarii*; a *sica* is a curved dagger) in the 50s CE. They surreptitiously assassinated collaborative high-priestly figures in the crowds at festival time in Jerusalem. In the summer of 66 they attempted to place themselves at the head of the nascent revolt. Rejected by the popular revolutionary forces in Jerusalem, however, they retreated to the fortress atop Masada on the Dead Sea and finally committed mass suicide there rather than submit to continued Roman rule.[16]

As with the Iranian Shiite *ulama*, for these ancient Judean scribes and Pharisees it was simply impossible to separate political-economic life from religious commitment to a deeply ingrained traditional way of life that refused to compromise with imperial demands. And as with modern Iranians, it was the imperial threat to their way of life that evoked such uncompromising commitment to their God and resistance to imperial incursions.

In contrast to modern Iran and more in accordance with standard theories of revolution, however, it was primarily the ancient Judean (and Galilean) peasantry who periodically mounted serious resistance and revolt against western imperialism. The recurrent popular protests, movements, and revolts constituted far more of a challenge to the Roman imperial order than the more limited and short-lived resistance by scribal-priestly groups. In these popular protests and movements as well, it is virtually impossible to separate politics and religion.

Many of the popular protests of which we have brief accounts clearly were either inseparable from a traditional religious celebration or touched off by a Roman imperial violation of sacred traditions. As mentioned already, protests often occurred at Passover, as part of the celebration of the people's liberation from previous oppressive foreign rule. Large numbers of Judeans carried out a remarkably disciplined, nonviolent demonstration against Pontius Pilate after he sent Roman troops into Jerusalem bearing the traditional Roman army standards featuring representations that violated the covenantal prohibition against images. And when the Emperor Gaius sent a military expedition to erect a statue of himself in the Temple (a representation – of a ruler with claims to divinity!), Galilean peasants mounted a massive strike, refusing to plant their crops, which the Romans and their client rulers depended on for their tax revenues.

Most of the widespread revolts and renewal movements took one of two social forms embedded in Israelite popular tradition.[17] First, in each of the revolts that erupted in every major district of the country at the end of Herod's highly repressive reign and the largest movement in the countryside of Judea in the middle of the great revolt in 66–70, the people acclaimed a king who would lead them. These were all popular messianic movements patterned after the earlier movements in which Saul, the young David, Jeroboam, and Jehu were acclaimed by their followers as messiah/king in order to lead them against the Philistines and other foreign rulers (2 Sam. 2:1–4; 5:1–3; 1 Kgs. 12:20; 2 Kgs. 9:11–13). In the middle of the first century CE a number of prophets such as Theudas and "the Egyptian" each led his followers out into the wilderness or up to the Mount of Olives in anticipation of a new divine action of deliverance. These popular prophetic

movements were clearly patterned after the exodus led by Moses or entry into the promised land led by Joshua.

Both John the Baptist and Jesus of Nazareth belong historically in precisely this context. Judging from the fragments of his preaching and his practice of baptism, John was a popular prophet leading a renewal of the Mosaic covenant. Baptism was the ritual by which one left behind the previous breach of the covenant and committed to the renewed covenant people (Mark 1:2–6; Luke 3:7–9, 16–17). As portrayed in the Gospel of Mark and in the Q speeches, Jesus of Nazareth was leading a renewal of Israel, adapting the popular prophetic "script" of the new Moses-and-Elijah. This renewal featured a new exodus (sea crossings, feedings in the wilderness, healings, exorcism of alien forces), a renewed covenant (Mark 10:1–45; Luke 6:20–49), and a covenant meal (Mark 14:22–28), as well as condemnation of Roman and high-priestly rulers (Mark 5:1–20; 11:14–13:2; Luke 13:28–9, 34–5). Jesus, like John, was not founding a new religion, nor was he merely a religious reformer who merely carried out a "cleansing" of the Temple. Like the other popular prophets, he was leading a renewal of Israel over against its rulers, who were the local representatives of the broader Roman imperial order. The earliest Palestinian communities of the movement Jesus spearheaded, moreover, appear to have followed more or less the same agenda of renewal, as evident in the earliest gospel documents, the story of Jesus in Mark and the Jesus speeches in the Sayings Source Q.[18]

Even the ordinary priests, or at least a large faction of them, joined the adamant resistance to Roman imperial rule as discontent escalated toward revolt in the summer of 66. The priests, particularly the high priests, were always in a delicate position, serving in the political-economic-religious institution of the Temple, which was sponsored by the empire and which served as an instrument of imperial rule. The Romans had charged them with collection of the tribute, payment of which was a violation of the Torah and nonpayment of which was considered tantamount to rebellion by the Romans. After the time of Herod, the official High Priest was appointed (and often deposed) by the Roman governor. And under Augustus the practice had been established of sacrificing on behalf of (apparently not *to*) the people of Rome and Caesar himself.[19]

Nevertheless, in the summer of 66 the priests officiating in Temple services – led by a high-ranking member of the priestly aristocracy, Eleazar, son of the previous high priest, Ananias – declared that they would no longer accept sacrifices from a foreigner, thus rejecting also the sacrifices on behalf of Rome and Caesar.[20] The chief priests, nobles, and most notable Pharisees argued that such sacrifices had always been carried out, which seems likely given the role of the Temple in the imperial order, but the ordinary priests and their leaders, such as Eleazar, surely had Mosaic covenantal tradition on their side.

The prolonged conflict between the Judeans' insistence on pursuing their traditional way of life and Roman imperial domination came to a head in the great revolt of 66–70, which culminated in the destruction of Jerusalem and the Temple by the Romans in their efforts to suppress it. The revolt appears to have been basically a popular insurrection of Judean and Galilean peasants, along with many ordinary Jerusalemites and some regular priests, against their own high-priestly and Herodian rulers as well as the Romans. It seems questionable from Josephus's accounts

whether some of the priestly elite helped lead the revolt or, as Josephus himself admits, pretended to go along in order to regain control of affairs (lest their Roman patrons abandon them).[21] In any case, the point of the Judeans' and Galileans' religious-political-economic commitment is still the same: that God must rule societal life as a whole, even though this was in direct conflict with imperial demands. Even after the Temple was destroyed, and with it the priestly and scribal factions based there, the Judean peasantry again mounted a sustained revolt against Roman rule in 132–5 asserting their independence as subjects only to God.

The Roman conquests of Judea and destruction of the Temple left a powerful impact on the surviving Judeans and Jews of the Diaspora. Blocked in their bid to regain independence under the direct rule of God, Jewish communities now maintained their traditional way of life by means of more passive resistance to the repressive and seductive pressures of Roman imperial rule. It was not until well after the Roman legions devastated Galilee and Judea and destroyed the Temple that the rabbinic circles that shaped later "Judaism" emerged. Some scribes and priests and apparently some Pharisees formed rabbinic circles in Galilee that gradually gained influence in the cities of Galilee and diaspora Jewish communities outside Palestine.[22] They developed distinctive dedication to the written and the oral Torah and the cultivation of Talmudic learning. Not until centuries later, however, did the rabbis manage to gain dominant influence over Jewish communities in general.

Meanwhile, Jewish communities in Palestine and the Diaspora concentrated on communal pursuit of their own way of life insofar as the Roman imperial order allowed, while avoiding actions that might aggravate their imperial rulers. This was far more than religion in the modern western sense. By maintaining certain social and cultural boundaries vis-à-vis the dominant imperial society, they were able to ensure solidarity among their communities. Jewish synagogues were far more than "voluntary associations" that met for worship. They were also the congregations of the local ethnic communities and the form of local self-governance whereby Jewish communities conducted their own socioeconomic life. The "prayer-houses" where they met were community centers as well as sanctuaries for worship. What is usually called "Judaism" has almost always been an ethnic community, a people, as well as a religion, and almost always a people living under the rule of an empire, usually Christian, such as the later Roman Empire, the Holy Roman Empire, the German Reich, and the British empire.

After the Roman crucifixion of Jesus of Nazareth as a rebel leader ("king of the Judeans"), the Israelite renewal movement(s) that he spearheaded among Galileans quickly spread – first among other Israelite peoples such as Judeans, Samaritans, and diaspora Jews. Paul and other diaspora Jews then catalyzed "assemblies" (*ekklesiai*) of the movement among other peoples and cities of the Roman Empire, including Rome itself. Paul even used symbolism central to the Roman emperor cult, such as "the gospel" of the "Lord" who brought "salvation" to the world, as key symbols in his gospel of Jesus Christ as, in effect, an alternative to the Roman emperor. In the divine "mystery" or plan for the true "salvation," God had outwitted the imperial "rulers of this age." Paradoxically, precisely in their crucifixion of the "Lord of Glory," God had begun the final defeat of the imperial powers. Enthroned in heaven, Christ was about to destroy every imperial ruler and power (1 Cor 2:6–8; 15:24–5). The book of Revelation portrayed the Roman Empire as the very embodiment of

dehumanizing and destructive demonic forces. The communities of Christ-believers, however, gradually assimilated to the Roman imperial order, and finally, under Constantine, "Christianity" was established as the imperially sponsored religion. The imperial imagery that Paul had applied to Christ as the anti-imperial Lord was easily transformed back into symbolism that supplied Christian approval and granted legitimacy to the imperial order.

Jesus had led a prophetic movement to renew Israel among Galilean and other villagers, revitalizing the traditional Mosaic covenantal principles of communal mutuality and justice, in resistance to oppressive Roman imperial rule. Within three centuries – and continuing into modern missionary enterprises largely overseen by western European empires – his movement had been utterly transformed into an imperial religion used to control such villagers, often by suppressing or subverting their traditional way of life. The central symbols of imperial Christianity, moreover, were easily transferable to new situations. The English colonies on the eastern seaboard of North America, who understood themselves as God's new Israel in an exodus from oppression in Europe, quickly adopted an identity as the new Rome once they gained their independence. The fusion of these two irreconcilable identities in America's conception of itself is now coming to climactic expression in the upsurge of American imperialism.

It is not clear what is gained by anachronistically projecting the essentialist "religions" of "Judaism" and "Christianity" onto their historical origins in subject peoples' resistance to western imperial domination in movements of renewal of the covenantal Israelite way of life. It is clear, however, what is lost. Blinded by their essentialist assumptions about religion, many modern scholars, as well as contemporary Jews and Christians, are unable to discern and appreciate the historical struggles against imperial domination in which Jewish and Christian histories and literatures originated. Also lost, of course, is the ability to recognize parallels between Jewish and Christian origins and the current struggles of imperially subject peoples to renew their own traditional way of life in the face of persistent western imperial encroachment.

NOTES

All citations of ancient Greek and Latin texts are from Loeb Classical Library editions

1 The standard synthetic and essentialist Christian scholarly concept of "Judaism" constructed in the late nineteenth century can be seen basically unchanged, for example, in Martin Hengel, *Judaism and Hellenism: Studies in Their Encounter in Palestine during the Early Hellenistic Period*, trans. John Bowden (Philadelphia: Fortress Press, 1974), esp. 303–9. A more nuanced but still monolithic picture of "Judaism" is constructed in E. P Sanders, *Judaism: Practice and Belief 63* BCE–*66* CE (Philadelphia: Trinity Press International, 1992).

2 For a detailed reconstruction of this history, see, for example, Jon L. Berquist, *Judaism in Persia's Shadow: A Social and Historical Approach* (Minneapolis: Fortress Press, 1995); Charles E. Carter, *The Emergence of Yehud in the Persian Period: A Social and Demographic Study* (Sheffield: Sheffield Academic Press, 1999); and Richard A. Horsley, *Galilee: History, Politics, People* (Valley Forge: Trinity Press International, 1995).

3 Richard A Horsley, "High Priests and the Politics of Roman Palestine," *Journal for the Study of Judaism*, 17 (1986): 23–55; Horsley, *Galilee*, 132–4; Martin Goodman, *The Ruling Class of Judea: The Origins of the Jewish Revolt against Rome,* AD *66–70* (Cambridge: Cambridge University Press, 1987).

4 Josephus, *Jewish Antiquities* 20. 181, 206–7, 214; *Yerushalmi Pesahim* 57a. See further Richard A. Horsley, *Jesus and the Spiral of Violence: Popular Jewish Resistance in Roman Palestine* (Mineapolis: Fortress Press, 1994), 29–33, 43–9.

5 An exploration of Israelite popular tradition in Galilee and Judea appears in Horsley, *Galilee*, 148–56, and Richard A. Horsley and Jonathan A Draper, *Whoever Hears You Hears Me: Prophets, Performance, and Tradition in Q* (Harrisburg: Trinity Press International, 1999), chs 5, 9, 10, 13.

6 Josephus, *Antiquities* 20. 106–7; cf. Josephus, *War* 2.223–24.

7 Josephus, *War* 2.226. See further Horsley, *Jesus and the Spiral of Violence*, 34–5.

8 See further Richard A. Horsley and Patrick Tiller, "Ben Sira and the Sociology of the Second Temple," in Philip R. Davies and John M. Halligan (eds), *Second Temple Studies III: Studies in Politics, Class and Material Culture*, (Journal for the Study of the Old Testament Supplement Series 340; Sheffield: Sheffield Academic Press, 2002), 74–107.

9 According to the still dominant scholarly reconstruction (see, e.g., Geza Vermes, *The Complete Dead Sea Scrolls in English* (New York: Allen Lane, 1997), 49–66; James C. VanderKam, *The Dead Sea Scrolls Today* (Grand Rapids: Eerdmans, 1994), 99–108; Lawrence H. Schiffman, *Reclaiming the Dead Sea Scrolls: The History of Judaism, the Background of Christianity, the Lost Library of Qumran* (New York: Doubleday, 1995), 84–97.

10 1QS, the "Community Rule" from the Dead Sea Scrolls.

11 1QM, the "War Rule," from the Dead Sea Scrolls.

12 Josephus, *Antiquities* 13.288–98, 372–3, 380.

13 Josephus, *Antiquities* 18.23; *War* 2.118.

14 Josephus, *Antiquities* 18.23.

15 See further Horsley, *Jesus and the Spiral of Violence*, 77–89.

16 Josephus, *War* 2.425, 433–56. Fuller discussion in Richard A. Horsley, "The Sicarii: Ancient Jewish Terrorists," *Journal of Religion*, 59 (1979): 435–58.

17 Documentation and analysis in Richard A. Horsley, "Popular Messianic Movements around the Time of Jesus," *Catholic Biblical Quarterly*, 46 (1984): 471–93; and " 'Like One of the Prophets of Old' ": Two Types of Popular Prophets at the Time of Jesus," *Catholic Biblical Quarterly*, 47 (1985): 435–63.

18 See the fuller analysis and critical discussion in Horsley, *Jesus and the Spiral of Violence*; Richard A. Horsley, *Hearing the Whole Story: The Politics of Plot in Mark's Gospel* (Louisville: Westminster John Knox, 2001); *Jesus and Empire: The Kingdom of God and the New World Disorder* (Minneapolis: Fortress Press, 2003); and Horsley and Draper, *Whoever Hears You Hears Me*.

19 Josephus, *Against Apion* 2.75–7; *War* 2.197; Philo, *On the Embassy to Gaius* 157.

20 Josephus, *War* 2.409–17.

21 So Goodman, *Ruling Class of Judea*.

22 See further Lee I. Levine, *The Rabbinic Class of Palestine in Late Antiquity* (New York: Jewish Theological Seminary of America, 1989), and Shaye J. D. Cohen, "The Place of the Rabbi in Jewish Society of the Second Century," in Lee I. Levine (ed.), *The Galilee in Late Antiquity*, (New York: Jewish Theological Seminary of America, 1992), 157–73.

5

Postcolonialism and Imperial Motives for Canonization

Jon L. Berquist

Postcolonial discourse enables interpreters to expose colonial realities and to direct our gaze upon the imperializing practices involved in the creation of a colony. Without this attachment to specific colonial-imperial relations, postcolonialist theory becomes utopic. Postcolonialism, just like the structures of the colony itself, cannot come into existence without the empire. Of course, the colonized peoples existed prior to the colonization, and they may have organized themselves in any of a number of social forms, but they were not a colony before the imperial intrusion. In order to explore the benefits of postcolonial discourse, I wish to examine the specific colonization of Yehud, the area around Jerusalem, in relation with the Persian Empire that created and named this colony. I will first trace the lines of imperial power between Persia and Yehud, in order to sketch the shape of Yehud's colonial form, with some attention to the ideological tools of imperialization. Because the notions of imperialization and colonization cross between postcolonial theory and sociological analysis, they allow opportunities for theoretical parallax and the chance for a more multidimensional understanding. I wish to explore the ways in which postcolonial discourse can benefit the understanding of colonial Yehud and its nascent canon. My goal is to describe the relationship of colonizing forces to the canon (as it was developed within the period of the Persian Empire). In what sense is the Yehudite canon a colonial and colonizing literature, and/or in what sense is it a postcolonial document? I will argue that the canon is strangely both.

Sociology and Colonial Yehud

Study of Persian-period Yehud or Second Temple Judaism usually commences with a quick refresher on its background (Berquist, 1995a:3–19). If the retelling of

First published in *Semia*, 75 (1996): 15–36.

Jerusalem's history/narrative does not start even earlier, it at least includes Judah's monarchy, its Babylonian defeat and captivity, Persia's conquest of Babylonia and the subsequent inheriting of the areas formerly under Babylonian rule, and the restoration of Judah as a colony within the Persian Empire. Thus the history becomes a narrative of Judah as nation, as exiles, and as restored community. The focus on imperialization, however, redirects the gaze away from Judah. Instead, our travel must begin in the Persian Empire, not in one of its small western provinces.

Persia's imperial conquest of Babylonia is usually assigned the date of 539/538 BCE, although their competition had already lasted several years while Persia gradually assumed greater influence over Babylonia's previous territories and holdings. Persian power over the area of Mesopotamia entered into a relatively uncontested period at the same time that its imperial domination manifested itself; the two processes are not distinct. By 539, when modern historiography claims that Persia "became" the ruling "world" empire, it had already begun its imperializing practices. This notion of imperialization provides a starting point for sociological investigation, which can produce a description of the social process that together make up the imperialization. But the interpreter working with sociological analysis must exercise due caution, for sociology is not a unified discipline. Some forms of sociology, especially theories connected to the writings of Marx, prove very congenial to postcolonial theorists; in fact, much postcolonial theory to date is visibly indebted to Marxist sociology. On the other hand, other sociologies are less directly helpful. The range of functionalist and anthropological approaches may be quite useful in the *description* of a colonial situation's social relations, but their frequent desire to be "value neutral" belies a deep commitment to social stability. These functionalist paradigms are still worth postcolonialists' consideration, but only insofar as interpreters are aware of the methods' ideological investments.

Social theorists have described imperialism as a social process involving the asymmetrical distribution of resources and power to create a centralized imperial core and a number of peripheral colonies that serve to support and finance the imperial power and expansion. Functionalist sociological discourse defines an empire as a large-scale social unit that extracts resources (including labor) from other social units, the colonies. Thus, an empire must always be in relationship with one or more colonies. An empire is not a static social unit, or a category that a social unit attains once it reaches a certain size and power as compared to its neighbors, or once its military defeats another empire. In this sense, it is more correct (or at least more advantageous) to discuss the process of imperialization than the social unit of the empire, since the empire exists only insofar as it *continues* to extract resources.

Empires construct multiple modes of extraction. Conquest is a straightforward example of resource extraction. When an empire defeats the people of a region and takes a bounty of food, products, or humans, it performs an essential task of imperialization. But within the larger context of modes of extraction, conquest is a relatively clumsy affair. Military solutions are notoriously expensive. The expansion of an area shrinks the proportion of the area that is on the periphery; thus the empire's force becomes spread over a greater area and does not increase fast enough to cover the expanded area. Logistically, larger empires have greater problems with funding the movement, feeding, and provisioning of ever-larger armies. A further

problem is that empires often conquer wealthier areas first, and so further expansion by conquest is a matter of diminishing returns (especially in proportion to the imperial wealth). Worse yet, large-scale military endeavors tend to decrease the labor supply available for other economically productive activities, and so empires must consider conquest to be an inefficient mode of extraction, especially over time as the geographic size of the empire grows.

Empires must therefore turn to other sources of extraction. Methods such as taxation are slower and more subtle than conquest, but no less imperialistic. In this environment, the empire creates colonies, that is, defined social units administered by the empire and given the specific task of sending money, goods, and/or services to the imperial core. Different forms of colonialism may be distinguished based on the rate of extraction and the ability of the colony to maintain that level of pay-out. The empire may extract a high amount, leading to a decreasing colonial ability to survive. Alternately, the empire may extract little, allowing the colony some modicum of self-control as well as sufficient resources to attain partial autonomy and to grow; the empire then gains over a long span of time as a result of the increased resources within the colony that the empire can extract. The empire may use its army along with other more bureaucratic measures to intensify local production in order to increase extraction. In these and many other ways, as well as in differing combinations of these modes over time and across geography, imperialization means the empire's removal of resources from colonies.

The Persian Empire monopolized the physical resources of a large geographic area over more than two centuries. As such, it was a highly successful empire that extracted a great deal of wealth and resources from its colonies through a variety of strategies. After its first half-century, it experienced only small and temporary success at conquest, and so it relied on other modes of extraction. Darius, the third emperor, reigned from 522 to 486 BCE, and in his time the empire made important shifts from conquest extraction to other forms more suited to long-term imperialization. Although Darius participated in military endeavors, he is remembered more for his innovations in social organization and legal administration.

Darius's involvement with Yehud included the appointment of governors, some of whose names the Hebrew Bible has preserved. During this time, the empire funded the construction of a temple in Jerusalem to function not only as a religious site but also as a political administrative site and perhaps even as a storehouse for goods to be delivered to the empire. Darius invested resources in Yehud in order to maintain Yehud as a colony for long-term extraction, not only for short-term imperial benefit. Thus, the effects of imperialization and colonization occur not only on the materialist, infrastructural, economic level; there are also important effects in social structure and in the ideological superstructure of the society. Yehud was organized as a colony, experiencing a certain level of independence but still subject to strict imperial controls. The goal of the colonial administration was to maintain the imperial extraction and to reproduce the conditions of imperialization. In other words, the local governor and his administration not only had to pay taxes and tribute to Persia on a set schedule, but they also had to control the Yehudites and their ideology so that they saw the benefit of remaining loyal colonials of the Persian Empire. I have argued elsewhere about the specific conditions that this imperialization produced within Yehud (1995a, 1995c).

One must see the ideological production of Yehud within this context. Although I wish to maintain the social and materialist definition of imperialization as a process of resource extraction, it is vital to recognize the ideological ramifications of such a system. This is the move that functionalist sociology fails to make. Christopher Hampton describes ideology, from a Marxist standpoint, as "a justifying veil for the repressive process by which the system enforces the submission of majorities into acquiescence and conformity with minority will" (Hampton: 3; cp. Miller: 63). In a colonial setting, this refers to the ideology expressed by the imperialists and other Persian agents while they were in the midst of and outnumbered by the natives whose society was being made into a colony. Persia constituted Yehud as a colony; that is, as a social unit the extraction of resources from which the empire wished to maintain over multiple generations. Keeping Yehud as a functioning colony required, in a sense, its continual recolonization. With each new birth, the empire gained a new worker if and only if the colony, on the empire's behalf, socialized the youngster into a colonial. This process required a complex set of social institutions to maintain and reinforce the ideology of colonialism through measures of "domination, accommodation and resistance" (Hodge: 203; cp. Gledhill: 70–1; Memmi: 91).

Persia's imperial activity involved a variety of ideologically colonizing features. At a minimum, a list of Persian strategies should include the common language of Imperial Aramaic (Memmi: 106–7), the construction of provincial bureaucracies, the appointment of Persians to roles within colonial governmental structures, military control of vast regions, taxation and other redistribution of resources, conscription of various persons into imperial service (whether at local levels or within the imperial core), and the ideologies of race and ethnicity within the empire (Sowell: 373). Social processes and ideologies merged to produce the phenomenon of overdetermination, by which the empire provides multiple causations for each effect on the colonized society (Ricoeur). Part of the (re)production of the colony involved Persia's imperial creation and imposition of official documents, legal and otherwise. In this context, it is not surprising that the Emperor Darius was remembered as a law-giver. During his administration, the empire encouraged and required its provinces and colonies to develop written documents that explained each colony's past history and current legal traditions, along with cultic practices. In each region, this was proclaimed as the King's Law – the emperor's own statement of imperial goals in each social unit's own language and custom (Berquist, 1995a:110–12; Dandamaev and Lukonin: 116–18). The imperial administration in Darius's time appears uninterested in standardizing worship throughout the empire, or introducing a single language or coinage system, or adjusting colonial customs to match imperial dress or pottery. Instead, Darius allowed each colony to establish its own legal system, its own history, and its own traditions. Of course, these documents were required to pass imperial review, at least. One could reason a high probability that the documents were written with the assistance of imperial scribes.

Imperial Uses of Ideology

Darius's imperial administration did the same in Yehud as in other regions of the empire; that is, the empire published documents in Yehud, containing laws and

narrative material, known as the King's Law, consisting of previous local traditions, with an unknown amount of imperial censorship, editing, or fabrication. Current evidence leaves this assertion both unprovable and unfalsifiable, but it would parallel the empire's known activity in other areas. A Persian publication of Yehudite traditions in written form, whether during Darius's rule or a subsequent time with the same imperial conditions, would be consistent with several other historical realities: the reference to the King's Law in extant Hebrew Bible texts (Ezra 7:26), the emphasis on public proclamation of the law (Deut 4:44–5:1; Josh 24:1–28; Neh 8:1–18), and the use of Aramaic similar to the imperial language in some texts (Gen 31:47; Jer 10:11; Dan 2:4–7:28; and Ezra 4:8–68, 7:12–16), as well as the perhaps too obvious reality of the existence of a large body of literature from the Yehudite community and its successors. The literature now extant must have derived from some time during the Persian or Hellenistic periods (Davies: 94–133). If there was a large amount of literature available before 539 BCE, it probably was not complete at that point and thus would undergo at least one major redaction, which may well have been in this middle period of the Persian Empire. On the other hand, there are parts of the current canon that postdate the Maccabean era. The identification of these passages as Maccabean or later in date requires the supposition that the surrounding material was unlike it, and therefore earlier. In any case, it is difficult to imagine the entire composition of the Hebrew Bible in Hebrew and Aramaic at a time during or later than the second or first centuries BCE, when the use of Greek had become widespread in the Jewish communities. It is thus more reasonable to think of any Maccabean materials as additions to a previously recognized body of literature.

Such a body of literature would consist of narrative material explaining the roots of the Yehudite community and justifying its status as a colony, as well as legal material that explained how the community should function. Albert Memmi notes that imperialists construct an image of the colonized, and they use this image as justification for their own colonizing activity. "More surprising, more harmful perhaps, is the echo that [this image] excites in the colonized himself. Constantly confronted with this image of himself, set forth and imposed on all institutions and in every human contact, how could the colonized help reacting to his portrait?" (87). This is only a hint about what such a fifth-century canon (or pre-canon) would include, but it is interesting that such a description would rule out hardly anything in the current canon, and that a body of literature corresponding to the Primary History (Genesis–2 Kings) and including the Latter Prophets (Isaiah–Malachi) could function quite well as imperial ideology in the Persian period.

The dating of all texts from the Hebrew Bible is under debate, but the date of first composition is not the issue at present. If there was material considered to be canonical in monarchic or exilic times, this literature continued its transmission through the Persian period and might have been the core of the imperially propagated canon. Whether the empire fabricated texts or slavishly followed older traditions, the fact of their publication and official imperial status remains unchanged. Certainly the Persian Empire did not publish the Hebrew Bible in its current form; there were texts added later. The question of what material was available in the fifth century BCE and what was a later addition is not at stake here. Even if none of the canonical literature existed in the fifth century and was entirely the production of, for instance, Hellenistic historians, the cultural milieu of Helleniza-

tion would present a number of social forces quite parallel to the Persian ideology of imperialization.

What would be the function and characteristics of the Persian imperial promulgation of some early canon for Yehud? First of all, this canon would not have been religiously motivated. It was a politically constructed document for the purposes of advancing an imperializing ideology. But that does not mean that it was antireligious, or even neutral. The connection with family rituals and religion as a function of priests more than kings reflects the colonizing attitudes of the empire (Memmi: 100). In fact, the construction of religion may well have been one of the chief functions of the imperialist canon. Memmi notes:

> With its institutional network, its collective and periodic holidays, religion constitutes another refuge value, both for the individual and for the group. For the individual, it is one of the rare paths of retreat; for the group, it is one of the rare manifestations which can protect its original existence. Since colonized society does not possess national structures and cannot conceive of a historical future for itself, it must be content with the passive sluggishness of the present. (Memmi: 101)

The ideology of the empire must have depended for some of its authority upon a base within the previously existing beliefs of the populace. The canon was, after all, the story of Yehud's history as Israel, not the story of Persian domination. It was not a canon to replace a history or to displace an established religion by establishing a new one. The canon gave expression to the understandings already present while at the same time modifying those understandings. The new literary context could accomplish much of this modification. The Persian-appointed governors and scribes produced the document and pronounced it from the midst of the imperially-funded temple. That act in itself blurred many of the distinctions between old and new, between religion and politics. To believe in this past was to know why Israel did not have its own king, and why it was right to worship at the Jerusalem temple, the proceeds from which supported the Persian Empire. The imposition of canon occurred within a wider context of social and cultural change as the empire intruded to extract; canon is thus contemporaneous with a moment of economic and political force and violence.

Furthermore, the nascent canon had to involve familiar aspects. The populace had to grant authority to the canon in order for its ideology to be effective; it is difficult to imagine an effective and accepted canon that was an entire fabrication, altogether new, to the inhabitants of Yehud, both immigrants and natives. The canon connects the great tradition and the local tradition (Wolf). The empire was constructing a great tradition, in which subject peoples had lost legitimate claim upon their lands and yet still had a vital legal tradition to cast them as law-abiding citizens of the new empire. At the same time, Yehud had local traditions of various ages, which were woven together in such a way as to emphasize the importance of keeping the law and recognizing the imperial rationale for the loss of the land.

A canon itself speaks to these very issues. By its nature, a canon – even one that is preliminary by our later standards of the "full" canon – creates a set of limits and boundaries. Canons obscure other literature through their constant and already self-falsifying claim to be the only text. A canon is a space defined from outside

(*d'hors-texte, à la* Derrida) by the canonizers (Blanchot). As written word, it is a fixed and limited space; it is a ruly space, ruled from within by the logic of its own organization and ruled from without by the power that constitutes the literature as a published piece.

Canon may attempt to delineate itself as text, but in the act of doing so it fails; it is a text of self-contradictory assertion. Although it strives to be determinate, fixed, foundational, and stable, its existence as text denies this; the canonical text is a result of power and cannot exist without the continual application of that power. Even as is the case with any text, its act of constituting itself begins its process of self-destabilizing. Yet it continues to claim its univocality by its status as "a" text. The reference to this literature as the King's Law thus summarizes and presents both of these aspects; canon is a function of imperial power and is inherently orderly (at the same time that it is internally incoherent, because it is *text*). In a sense, Persia colonized the prior traditions of the Yehudites, making them controllable and exploitable. Persia claimed itself as the unwritten subject of the texts, infusing a new metanarrative into the text and turning the texts themselves into objects, written items that could be used and enforced (Blanchot: 202).

This canon contained legal materials. For the Yehudite community, these laws stated basic principles of social organization, such as the Decalogue, the incest and food laws, and the hierarchical arrangement of society under legitimate kings. In addition, the law states the conditions under which the earlier Israelites would lose their land, and the narrative materials in the Primary History document the fulfillment of these conditions and the subsequent removal of Judah's elites from the land. Robert Hodge points out the social connectedness of such narrative trajectories: "From this follows a basic premise for the social analysis of narrative: the social categories that organize the levels of narrative must first be understood in relation to the dominant categories and syntagmatic forms of social life, as these operate through the semiosic context of specific narratives" (175). If this nascent canon operated as Persian imperial ideology, the implications are clear. Israel and Judah lost their land by their own deeds, their own God removed them from the land and placed them under care of another, and now the other (about whom the historical texts are silent) rightfully rules. The prophets are even clearer about this ideological assertion that the Yehudites deserve their loss of land, even though a "remnant" will attain a modicum of control and power. Especially in texts such as Deutero-Isaiah, the Persian imperializing ideology is unmistakable: Cyrus is the messiah, the anointed one with God-given authority to rule over Yehud (Isa 44:24–45:8). This theological justification for political reality depicts Yehud as colony. The texts legitimate, authorize, and perpetuate the ideology of the colonized.

Refocusing Postcolonialism

The above analysis of the role of ideology and textual formation in imperial domination has been informed by sociology, but has not yet moved far beyond a functionalist paradigm. By failing to consider the values of imperialism, colonization, and oppression involved, this functionalist sociological perspective has obscured much. What, then, can postcolonialist theory add to this discussion? Or better, how does

postcolonialism refocus the lens of interpretation to make new (in)sights visible? The variety of theories sharing the moniker of postcolonialism only complicates these questions, but the newness and fecundity of postcolonial theories argues for the embracing of a certain eclecticism. Postcolonialism can sharpen the analysis of Yehud's colonial situation in at least three ways: it can help to show the ways in which the empire dominates, it can help to show the colonizing functions of colonial life, and it can add an ideological emphasis that functionalist sociology misses.

First, postcolonialism emphasizes the imperial modes of domination. By casting light upon the colonizer–colonized relationship, it illuminates certain features of the colony. Postcolonial studies remove the supposed neutrality in which some functionalist sociology wraps itself. Within the postcolonial frame, one cannot consider Persia to be just an example of a large bureaucratic empire, analyzable as an isolated unit, nor can the interpreter take a simply functionalist sociological view of the imperialism's transfer of goods and resources. "Neither imperialism nor colonialism is a simple act of accumulation and acquisition. Both are supported and perhaps even impelled by impressive ideological formations that include notions that certain territories and people *require* and beseech domination, as well as forms of knowledge affiliated with domination" (Said: 9). One must constantly focus on the Persian Empire's modes of extraction; the colonies will be central to this analysis, as will the colonizing ideologies employed by the empire and its servants. Functionalist and Marxist sociologies alike may focus too much on the activity within a single economic generation, but postcolonialism must always focus on the ways in which the populace becomes the colonized, to reproduce the economic relationships of extraction and oppression over multiple generations. "Ideology creates the type of subjects suitable to be 'supports' of social relations and inserts people into places predefined by the structures of social formation" (Miller, Rowland, and Tilley: 9).

Likewise, one cannot simply concentrate on "postexilic Judah" or some similar category; the colonial experience will be crucial to everything that occurs within Yehud. This flies in the face of much biblical scholarship that has tried to explain postexilic religion only in terms of Judean experience, without recognizing the massive economic, military, social, and ideological forces brought to bear on every aspect of Yehudite life (Berquist, 1995a: 3–12).

This is postcolonialism's second great advance, and if taken seriously it would have an enormous impact upon Second Temple studies. The very titling of the period in terms of the "Second Temple" appears remarkably naive and obscurantist from this perspective, another example of the supposed neutrality of standard scholarship that results in missing the point of the object of study. The "Second Temple" terminology can lead interpreters to think that Judah controlled at least its religious development. A phrase such as "colonial Yehud" reflects a situation in which the people of the colony could not even name themselves without the name passing through the imperial filters.

Third, postcolonialist theory consistently concentrates on the conflicts that occur within the ideological space of the colony. Colonies are continually contested sites in every sense. Although sociology at its best provides as much attention to ideology as to economic and social realities, most sociological study has fallen short in this regard, and postcolonialism is a welcome addition. No longer can one speak of a textual ideology that is stable, for they are all already contested.

As an example of the ways that postcolonial discourse can improve the analysis of Yehud, consider the notion of empire as teacher. Jerry Phillips has examined the tendency of imperial cultures to understand their relationship to their colonized populations as a mode of instruction. In other words, the empire seeks to educate the "barbaric" colonies in order to "civilize" them.

> In its classic formulation the moment of imperialism is also the moment of education. Imperialism – a system of economic, political, and cultural force that disavows borders in order to extract desirable resources and exploit an alien people – has never strayed far from a field of pedagogical imperatives, or what might be called an ideology of instruction. (Phillips: 26)

Part of this instructional ideology is the assertion that there is a standard of education (Phillips: 34). This assumes that culture – defined as what the imperial core has that the colonial periphery lacks – is a script, a definable something, often a narrative (or a meta-narrative). One can see the Persian imperialist narrative (the "great tradition"), written upon the mountains for all to see, in the Behistun inscription. Depicting that the representatives of each colony approach Darius bowed, this carving shows the narrative in pictorial form. The inscription also offers the narrative in writing for those wishing the details (Kent: 107–8, 116–34).

Within the context of this concept of imperial education, Darius's creation of local canons comes even more sharply into focus. The colonies were not able to rule themselves; the local narratives prove that themselves, or at least they do within the redaction that the empire provides. Instead, the colonies require the civilization of the empire for their own protection. Perhaps this explains some of the fascination with Egypt within the canonical texts, since Egypt was Persia's chief rival on its western borders for the early part of the Persian Empire. Yehud thus is taught to fix its gaze upon Egypt, the great oppressor who remains a constant threat, morally if not militarily. By gazing upon Egypt with animosity, the text refocuses Yehudite social vision and obscures the domination that Persia plays in the present.

But the education of Yehud goes further. Yehud learns that it is inadequate by itself, that it needs its God's protection, and that God has given them into Persia's hand for protection. Persia teaches that God acts through Persian authority, since the Persian emperors are anointed by God for this purpose. God even demands in the law that tithes and offerings be given to the temple built and staffed by the empire. These are things that the Yehudites would not have known by themselves. The empire must educate them into being colonial citizens.

Many traditions of social thought (including functionalism and, in many ways, the Frankfurt school of critical social theory) understand states as rational systems, in which the ruled participate in their subjugation because they believe that the rulers are justified in their hegemony. The effects of ideology are much deeper. The colonized may be unaware of other social systems, or they may believe themselves to be in need of external social control, or they may be disinterested in taking charge of their own political lives. In any of these cases, the imperial-colonial pattern continues because the colonized do not rebel, and the lack of rebellion results from the imperial social and ideological practices that reproduce the imperialist system. The

ideological components of this imperial reproduction tell individuals what exists, what is possible, what is right, and what is wrong (Therborn: 172).

These Marxist treatments of ideology have the value of connecting textual meaning with the social and historical forces of production. Nonetheless, postmodern sensibilities illuminate a problem within this definition of ideology. The existence of a false consciousness assumes the reality of a "true" consciousness; that is, a system of thinking that actually represents reality. Although ideology is a difficult concept to define, and perhaps an impossible one to discuss with immunity from critique, a working definition is necessary. I will use the term "ideology" to refer to patterned human discourse that privileges those persons in power who initiate that discourse. I understand this as closely related to Spivak's treatment:

> At its broadest implications this notion of ideology would undo the oppositions between determinism and free will and between conscious choice and unconscious reflex. Ideology in action is what a group takes to be natural and self-evident, that of which the group, as a group, must deny any historical sedimentation. It is both the condition and the effect of the constitution of the subject (of ideology) as freely willing and consciously choosing in a world that is seen as background. In turn, the subject(s) of ideology are the conditions and effects of the self-identity of the group as a group. It is impossible, of course, to mark off a group as an entity without sharing complicity with its ideological definition. (Spivak: 118)

Canonical scripture can play a highly significant role in the ideology of imperialism, since religion and scripture also communicate the norms, values, and basic assumptions of a society's ruling class. This ideology inspires something beyond profit and extraction. According to Said, it involves "a commitment in constant circulation and recirculation, which, on the one hand, allowed decent men and women to accept the notion that distant territories and their native peoples *should* be subjugated, and, on the other, replenished metropolitan energies so that these decent people could think of the *imperium* as a protracted, almost metaphysical obligation to rule subordinate, inferior, or less advanced peoples" (Said: 10). In the case of Yehud, the Persian Empire's investment in such ideology is clear: the empire would benefit most from an ideology that emphasizes Yehud's inability to govern itself, to rebel against the imperial power, to expand itself beyond its current borders, or to ally itself effectively with other powers.

These insights are the results of a sociologically-informed postcolonial analysis. Such an analysis uses the descriptive powers of functionalism, the comparative value of anthropology (especially social and political anthropologies), the economic explanatory capability of (cultural) materialism, and the ideological insights of Marxism. In this way, postcolonialism combines these different sociological formulations in the service of understanding the empire in order to oppose it.

Implications of (Post)Colonialism

But doesn't postcolonialism add something even more than this? I believe that there is a greater value in postcolonial theory than those to which I have so far alluded, but it requires taking a step back to view the enterprise in a wider context. The goal of

postcolonial study, in this perspective, is to create interpretations that illuminate the colonial and colonizing tendencies of the text's production and subsequent interpretations, while at the same time to suggest contemporary interpretations that have an effect of decolonizing the present world (including the world of biblical scholarship) (Spivak: 205). Gordon Collier describes this work as an ideological (mis)representation of the history, recognizing that there is no point of immaculate perception from which one's views can be objective. "So long as post-colonial analysts remain aware of the fact that they themselves are engaged in fruitful processes of mistranslations, mistranscription and misidentification not dissimilar to those they would expose, then the project's health will be safeguarded by its own antibodies" (Collier: xv). The point of postcolonialism, then, is not to achieve a new objectivity but to infuse the scholarly discourse with a new subjectivity, following a set of values that measure the new enterprise as "fruitful" rather than as imperializing. This understanding of postcolonialist discourse aligns it more closely with ideological criticism than with sociology.

With this concept of postcolonial study, the interpreter begins to search for canonical texts that can be used against the imperializing ideologies of the canon. Since the postcolonialist attitude is located in the interpreter rather than within the text itself (since texts do not have ideologies), this search is fruitful. As an example, I would point to texts in Third Isaiah such as Isaiah 66:1–5, a passage from the Persian imperial period where the interpreter can hear claims of God's displeasure with the temple and its supporters (Berquist, 1995b). Here God speaks (Hear God speak) against the interests of the imperial administration, repulsing them with vile epithets and accusations of evil. Also familiar are texts such as 1 Samuel 8 that argue against the rule of the king by showing that the hierarchies associated with royal or imperial rule will be costly and detrimental to the people.

Of course, the interpreter must be very careful in dealing with such texts from a postcolonial vantage, because it is difficult to hear the words of the colonized in texts subsumed by the colonists. Gareth Griffiths offers an important warning:

> Even when the subaltern appears to "speak" there is a real concern as to whether what we are listening to is really a subaltern voice, or whether the subaltern is being spoken by the subject position they occupy within the larger discursive economy.... In inscribing such acts of resistance the deep fear for the liberal critic is contained in the worry that in the representation of such moments, what is inscribed is not the subaltern's voice but the voice of one's own other. (75)

At the same time, the postcolonial interpreter can also break the bonds of the canon from outside, tracing the lines of power that formed the canon through exclusion, in order to find the texts outside the canon (Spivak: 118–33). Insofar as the canon insists that it is "the" text, the very presence of noncanonical texts begins to unravel the power systems of the canon and its colonizing. Said describes this as an act of postcolonial reading: "As we look back at the cultural archive, we begin to reread it not univocally but *contrapuntally*, with a simultaneous awareness both of the metropolitan history that is narrated and of those other histories against which (and together with which) the dominating discourse acts" (51). With texts such as

these in hand, the interpreter can begin to break open the canon and its imperializing ideology from both within and without the canon itself.

> In the "post-colonial" moment, these transverse, transnational, transcultural movements, which were always inscribed in the history of "colonisation," but carefully overwritten by more binary forms of narrativisation, have, of course, emerged in new forms to disrupt the settled relations of domination and resistance inscribed in other ways of living and telling these stories. (S. Hall: 251)

Postcolonial theory can gain here from postmodernist textual strategies. In a deconstructionist vein, the interpreter proceeds to the heart of the text and finds its inherent brokenness, a brokenheartedness and a heartfelt resistance familiar to postcolonial theorists. The canonical text is not a unified whole; it is not a body of literature at all. Instead, it is an assemblage held together only by the imperialist power that first created it. Although it is targeted against the colonies with an intention to subdue, this can(n)on cannot fire; it is powerless to conquer because of the weakness of its seams resulting from its mode of creation.

To say that the canon is held together only by imperialist power means several things. First, the historical circumstances of the canon's creation occurred only because a historical empire used the canon as part of its ideology of imperialist instruction. Perhaps more importantly for the field of biblical studies, the canon can maintain the impression of a unified whole with a single ideology (or a center, or a single "biblical" or "canonical" theology) *only* by the continuing application of powerful imperializing ideologies. In order for canonical unity to remain, the interpreter must perceive that the canon has "a subject" which then organizes canonical meaning/theology/ideology around itself. The subject of the canon displaces the actual canon. In a sense, if canon has a subject, then it makes the rest of the canon into objects, mere evidence and example of the subject. To state this in postcolonial language: the continuance of the canon requires that contemporary canonical imperialists must impose their own metanarrative upon the canon in such a way that the canon becomes colony, a unit that exists only to be extracted and exploited for the imperialist's benefit. Canon is a function and expression of power, specifically imperial power. The imperial subject of the canon objectifies and colonizes.

I would consider these statements to be offensive accusations of many biblical scholars and their work, if I was able to imagine any of us approaching the text without this imperializing approach, if any of us were void of metanarratives. I realize that I myself am constructing a metanarrative in competition with other imperializing ones, and at that level this interpretation of canon is no different than the imperialists with whose interpretations I disagree. As I have insisted already, the Persian Empire created a canon out of earlier traditions, shaping it in order to fit their own imperialist ideology. Thus the canon was part of the creation of Yehud's colonial identity. The canon bounded the community, but the canon was not a coherent and consistent explication of imperialist desire, for at least two reasons. First, the canon was created as a patchwork of texts, held together by explicit ideological force. Even though the Persian redaction was done so that we can no longer reconstruct "sources" or prove definitively the words of imperial editing, the canon still represents and contains a variety of viewpoints, languages, geographies,

classes, and ideologies. Thus it cannot be considered complete, coherent, or consistent. The second reason that this must be so is more abstract: the impossibility of creating systems (including texts and ideologies) that are both complete and coherent, as shown variously by Gödel and Derrida. The nature of language and even thought is such that complete coherence is impossible. So the canon – no matter what texts it contained in its first or any subsequent formulation – had gaps and differences, just as its producers' society did. In Said's words, "no vision, any more than any social system, has total hegemony over its domain" (186). The canon is a bricolage that presented and presents multiple views and ideologies.

The postcolonial interpreter faces this bricolage with sensitivity to the ideological use of these different texts. First the interpreter must transcend the contemporary imperializing ideologies to allow the text to deconstruct, but then the interpreter is faced with the variety of voices within the text. Again, postcolonialism provides a space in which to choose voices to construct interpretations that may have decolonizing effects in the contemporary world.

But what does this say about the text? It implies the insight already gained that imperialization had created a bifurcated social world that in turn created a fragmented text. The next interpretive step is to imagine the conflicting ancient worlds of the colonizer and the colonized that in/form the text of the canon. Here sociology once more enters into the interpretive fray, offering to describe these conflicting worlds and specifically the social mechanisms that reproduce the difference between the empire and the colony.

Who constructed the canonical texts in colonial Yehud? The empire funded the writing of a self-justifying ideological metanarrative that overlays and attempts to organize the canon. At the same time, the colonials had a repertoire of laws, stories, themes, customs, and genres that were the required raw materials for much of the canon. Therefore, asking whether the empire or the colony had the greater impact on the canon and its ideology is not a helpful question. Those who wrote the texts occupied a peculiar social location, partaking of the world views of colonizer and colonized at the same time. They were the scribes and the officials of Yehud, a class created and supported by the imperial powers and yet involved on a daily basis with the specificity of life in the colony Yehud. They received power from the empire and exercised power over the colony, but at the same time these administrators and scribes received their resources from the people of Yehud and controlled the flow of resources toward the Persian Empire (Berquist, 1995a; Davies). They were a ruling class within the colony, situated along the chasm between colonized and colonizer.

Postcolonial study must be informed by a careful class analysis if it is to succeed at its academic task of describing the effects of colonization or its ethical goal of decolonization in today's world. Even though postcolonial discourse rightly depicts the differences between the colonizer and the colonized as vast, the network of power relations cannot be reduced to such a simple dichotomy. One of the effects of colonization is a splitting of the colonized's population. In Eisenstadt's analysis, the existence of imperial power creates opportunities for the development of a local elite of collaborators and other administrators, just as the existence of colonial resources creates the opportunity for imperial extraction of those resources. Once the colony begins to feel the imperial power used to extract resources, a local elite begins to stratify the colonial social structure in new ways.

This local elite occupies a strange space within the colonial social world. In part, they are the colonized, but they are also active in the process of colonization and the reproduction of imperial/colonial ideology. Within the colony, they are the highest ranking local officials; within the empire, they are the lowest bureaucrats possible. Their position grows not only from the local resources but from the application of imperial power into the colony. The local official serving the empire often experiences the grudging and provisional acceptance of the imperial because "moving up" is, in some ways, the rhetorical goal for all colonials under imperial tutelage (Phillips). Said describes this position of ideological production:

> Moreover, the various struggles for dominance among states, nationalisms, ethnic groups, regions, and cultural entities have conducted and amplified a manipulation of opinion and discourse, a production and consumption of ideological media representations, a simplification and reduction of vast complexities into easy currency, the easier to deploy and exploit them in the interest of state policies. In all of this intellectuals have played an important role, nowhere in my opinion more crucial *and* more compromised than in the overlapping region of experience and culture that is colonialism's legacy where the politics of secular interpretation is carried on for high stakes. (36)

The effects of an empire upon a colony are much the same as the effects of any state upon its localities. To assume otherwise is to construct categories of benign state power *vs.* intrusive imperial power; that is, to privilege the state as a non-oppressive, non-coercive form of political and economic power. States and empires alike rule through the control of local resources, modes of production, and cultural modes of reproduction. In Göran Therborn's words, the exercise of state power is "a process of interventions in a given society effected by a separate institution which concentrates the supreme rule-making, rule-applying, rule-adjudicating, rule-enforcing, and rule-defending functions of that society" (144–5). In the colony of Yehud during the Persian period, this institution of state power was the Persian imperial administration. These statist interventions reproduce not only the social forces of production and the character of the state apparatus, but also the ideological superstructure that justifies the social system. Thus we can expect the Persian Empire to create ideologies that tend to reproduce the empire and to maintain the power of the ruling class. These ideologies are not a separate feature of society, somehow isolated from daily functioning; the imperialist ideology infuses itself throughout the various rules, norms, customs, and habits of the society (Gledhill: 76–8). The mode of reproduction for this ideology runs through the hands of the colonial administrators who formed the canon as an ideological device for perpetuating their privileged place within Yehudite culture and within the Persian Empire. These persons maintain a delicate balance being situated in the non-space between empire and colony. As Memmi vividly expresses the problem, "a man straddling two cultures is rarely well seated, and the colonized does not always find the right pose" (124).

There are further ambiguities imposed upon this social group of colonial administrators and canonizers. Their literary activities subject them to forces barely understood. In the midst of a social context in which they strive to find themselves a place of their own, their literature constructs the social bifurcation of the empire and belies the existence of themselves as authors. Perhaps no one speaks of this loss-of-self in the (non)space of writing as clearly as Maurice Blanchot:

> When to write is to discover the interminable, the writer who enters this region does not leave himself behind in order to approach the universal. He does not move toward a surer world, a finer or better justified world where everything would be ordered according to the clarity of the impartial light of day. He does not discover the admirable language which speaks honorably for all. What speaks in him is the fact that, in one way or another, he is no longer himself; he isn't anyone any more. (28)

This further expands the vastness of ambiguity for the canon and for its ideological creators and patrons. The canon can never be a truly Persian text; it never becomes a truly imperial artifact. Yet at the same time it is not equivalent to the colony; it does not speak the local vision as the locals would themselves voice it. The canon is part of a mediation between colonizer and colonized, but it is a troubled mediation, not a smooth dialectic synthesis. In the final analysis, the canon does not "possess" an ideology. Even though the canon was and still remains a construct of imperial ideological discourse, the canon is neither colonizing nor decolonizing in any essentialist, ontological sense. Human systems of ideological thought cannot inscribe themselves that successfully. Instead of being a paradigm of colonization, the canon can only be seen as a site of contest and conflict. Conflict was present in the original inscription of the canon. Of course, this conflict is not only a function of the contemporary ideological pressures to be colonizing and/or decolonizing.

Is the Canon Postcolonial?

The canon is an example of postcolonial literature, despite its origins within a colony. At one level, we can affirm that the canon is always already postcolonial if interpreters treat it as such, and develop a decolonizing ideology from or with its texts. A historical argument arises at this point. The text itself was created as a bricolage of texts with immediately conflicting views. It was and is a diverse and pluralistic entity that exists in the spaces where the empire withdraws just enough to allow other voices, even if they are voices with imperial overtones. Persia never required the colonies to construct canons in the imperial language; the local vernacular was the right language for this canonical discourse. As the empire tried to bifurcate society, it failed, creating colonial governments as a wedge group between the colonized and the colonial governments as a wedge group between the colonized and the colonizer. Thus the fictions of an absolute empire begin to fall away within the text created by the one group that defies the splitting attempted by the empire.

Of course, to understand the canon as a postcolonial literature must first entail abandoning the absolutizing assertions about the developing canon. No longer can we assert that Judah's religious devotion was the ultimate force within the society; scholars must consciously move beyond notions of theocracy for the postexilic period. It was not the case historically, and the continued insistence on theocracy merely reaffirms the imperializing forces of the interpretive ideology. There was no one concept of God that emerged victorious to control the canon; the canon itself defies all attempts at control, even the attempts that brought the canon into being. Likewise, the fiction of a postexilic restoration must be rejected; there never was a single idea of the days before exile and there not a single or dominant concept of

how Yehud should organize its own social existence after the exile. No one who went into exile "returned," although some of their children and grandchildren moved to Yehud as colonists. These colonists were not following some master plan that they developed as devout followers of the Yehudite God while in exile; there was no master plan, only a colonizing impulse that took many of the same forms as Persian imperialism did in other neighboring areas.

From a postcolonialist perspective, interpretation is not (only) a technical exercise, but a moral act of commitment. The commitments themselves, however, can shape the historical and sociological insights into the reality of Yehud, and can provide more adequate images for how Yehud operated as a colony. At the same time, I desire to resist the notions of postcolonial study that replicate old oppositions and dichotomies simply by revising or reversing them, since there is a danger within postcolonialist theory to embrace an idealism that serves as a thin mask for further imperialization. For a while, these oppositions may be necessary, but the interpreter must move beyond them.

> Reading (and writing) "against the grain" implies that there *is* a grain to work against. This entails the problem of counterdiscourse, which preserves a binary opposition and perpetuates the privileging of one of the poles even as it seeks to complicate and dismantle the basis for discriminatory contrast. (Sharrad: 201)

In other words, the old image of Judah the purified theocracy *vs.* the political powers of the contemporaneous world should not be replaced by either Yehud the colonized *vs.* the imperializing, colonizing behemoth of Persia, nor by Yehud, the sneaky colony of subversion *vs.* the monolithic culture of Persia. The insights of postcolonial study of colonial Yehud should be much more complex than such facile dichotomies as this. As Catherine Hall writes,

> Unpacking imperial histories, grasping the raced and gendered ways in which interconnections and inter-dependencies have been played out, developing a more differentiated notion of power than that which focuses simply on coloniser and colonised, can have emancipatory potential. It is a history which involves recognition and the reworking of memory. A history which shows how fantasised constructions of homogeneous nations are constructed and the other possibilities which are always there. A history which is about difference, not homogeneity. (76)

The postcolonial canon remains a contested, conflicted site, inscribed with multiple layers of ideologically invested interpretation. It remains a place for interpreters' ideologies to work themselves out in textual strategies and in the present world, where colonialisms and decolonizing are still at work.

REFERENCES

Berquist, Jon L. (1995a). *Judaism in Persia's Shadow: A Social and Historical Approach.* Minneapolis: Fortress.

—— (1995b). "Reading Difference in Isaiah 56–66: The Interplay of Literary and Sociological Strategies." *Method and Theory in the Study of Religion*, 7:23–42.

Berquist, Jon L. (1995c). "The Shifting Frontier: The Achaemenid Empire's Treatment of Western Colonies." *Journal of World-Systems Research*, 1.17:1–25.
Blanchot, Maurice (1982). *The Space of Literature*, trans. Ann Smock. Lincoln, NE and London: University of Nebraska Press.
Chambers, Iain, and Lidia Curti (eds) (1996). *The Post-Colonial Question: Common Skies, Divided Horizons*. New York: Routledge.
Collier, Gordon (ed.) (1992). *Us/Them: Translation, Transcription and Identity in Post-Colonial Literary Cultures*. Cross/Cultures: Readings in the Post/Colonial Literatures in English 6. Atlanta: Rodopi.
Collier, Gordon (1992). "Introduction," in Collier (1992), xii–xv.
Dandamaev, Muhammad A. and Vladimir G. Lukonin (1989). *The Culture and Social Institutions of Ancient Iran*. Cambridge: Cambridge University Press.
Davies, Philip R. (1992). "In Search of 'Ancient Israel'." *JSOTS*, 148. Sheffield: Sheffield Academic Press.
Eisenstadt, S. N. (1969). *The Political Systems of Empires: The Rise and Fall of the Historical Bureaucratic Societies*, rev. edn. New York: Free press.
Gledhill, John (1994). *Power and Its Disguises: Anthropological Perspectives on Politics*. Anthropology, Culture and Society. London and Boulder, CO: Pluto.
Griffiths, Gareth (1994). "The Myth of Authenticity: Representation, Discourse and Social Practice," in Tiffin and Lawson (1994), 70–85.
Hall, Catherine (1996). "Histories, Empires and the Post-Colonial Moment," in Chambers and Curti (1996), 65–77.
Hall, Stuart (1996). "When was the 'Post-Colonial'? Thinking at the Limit," in Chambers and Curti (1996), 242–60.
Hampton, Christopher (1990). *The Ideology of the Text*. Buckingham and Philadelphia: Open University Press.
Hodge, Robert (1990). *Literature as Discourse: Textual Strategies in English and History*. Parallax: Re-visions of Culture and Society. Baltimore: The Johns Hopkins University Press.
Kent, Roland G. (1953). *Old Persian: Grammar, Texts, Lexicon*, 2nd edn, rev. American Oriental Series 33. New Haven, CT: American Oriental Society.
Memmi, Albert (1965). *The Colonizer and the Colonized*. New York: Orion.
Miller, Daniel (1989). "The Limits of Dominance," in Miller, Rowland, and Tilley (1989), 63–79.
Miller, Daniel, Michael Rowland, and Christopher Tilley (eds) (1989). *Domination and Resistance*. One World Archaeology 3. London and New York: Routledge.
Miller, Daniel, Michael Rowland, and Christopher Tilley (1989). "Introduction," in Miller, Rowland, and Tilley (1989), 1–26.
Phillips, Jerry (1993). "Educating the Savages: Melville, Bloom, and the Rhetoric of Imperialist Instruction," 25–44 in (ed.) Jonathan White. *Recasting the World: Writing after Colonialism*. Parallax: Revisions of Culture and Society. Baltimore: The Johns Hopkins University Press.
Ricoeur, Paul (1994). "Althusser's Theory of Ideology," in Gregory Elliott (ed.), *Althusser: A Critical Reader.* Oxford: Blackwell, 44–72.
Said, Edward W. (1993). *Culture and Imperialism*. New York: Vintage.
Sharrad, Paul (1994). "Speaking the Unspeakable: London, Cambridge and the Caribbean," in Tiffin and Lawson (1994), 201–17.
Sowell, Thomas (1996). *Migrations and Cultures: A World View*. New York: Basic.
Spivak, Gayatri Chakravorty (1988). *In Other Worlds: Essays in Cultural Politics*. New York: Routledge.
Therborn, Göran (1978). *What Does the Ruling Class Do When It Rules? State Apparatuses and State Power under Feudalism, Capitalism and Socialism*. London: NLB.

Tiffin, Chris, and Alan Lawson (eds) (1994). *De-Scribing Empire: Post-colonialism and Textuality*. London and New York: Routledge.
Wolf, Eric R. (1966). *Peasants*. Foundations of Modern Anthropology. Englewood Cliffs, NJ: Prentice-Hall.

6

Roman Imperialism and Early Christian Scribality

Werner H. Kelber

In the ancient world, including the Mediterranean civilization of late antiquity, the scribal medium was the prerogative of the political and intellectual elite who administered it in the interest of its national, memorial objectives. As a rule, those in positions of power shared a vested interest in advancing the cause of scribality because control over the medium allowed them to govern the public discourse. More often than not, colonial masters in antiquity – and throughout world history – promoted, shaped, and employed literacy as an instrument of imperial domination, even of oppression. Most frequently and influentially, scribality was applied for the purpose of recording the people's stories and history. And in producing and controlling the record of the past, those who were in charge of the scribal medium decisively determined how people would remember the past, how they thought of their identity – past, present and future – and how they acted in accordance with it. In this way, scribality, literacy, identity formation, and cultural memory constituted a syndrome that could well serve the self-legitimating interests of religious-political powers (Assmann).

The upper class's cultivation of the craft of scribality as an instrument of controlling public consciousness, setting the political agenda, and constructing collective memories is only one possible alliance of social power and scribal medium. It by no means exhausts the uses of scribality. In antiquity – and throughout world history – dissenting groups likewise seized upon the scribal medium to construct their identity vis-à-vis dominant power structures. The Jewish community at Khirbet Qumran, living in self-imposed exile on a high plateau at the northwest corner of the Dead Sea, constitutes a case in point. Originating in the priestly power structure of Jerusalem, the community, once settled down in self-imposed exile, took full advantage of its scribal legacy. Fiercely dedicated to scribal culture, the Qumran dissenters pursued the copying and composing of manuscripts largely in the interest

First published in J. Draper, *Orality, Literacy, and Colonialism in Antiquity.* Atlanta: Society of Biblical Literature, 2004, 135–53.

of defining their religious and social identity vis-à-vis both the priestly establishment of Jerusalem and Roman imperialism.

In antiquity, considerations of the media cannot be limited to scribality. Orality, by far the predominant mode of communication and one that is generally more impervious to public control than the scribal medium, needs to be taken into account as well. So also must the oral-scribal interfaces and conflicts that characterize the medium landscape of antiquity. As far as the oral-scribal dynamics are concerned, what comes to mind is the historic struggle between the Pharisees and the Sadducees (Wellhausen; Rivkin; Neusner 1972; Stemberger 1995b). Like the Qumran community, the Pharisees posed a challenge to the priestly establishment of Jerusalem, but unlike Qumran they designed their strategies largely from within the city's power relations. For the most part, they stayed in Jerusalem and worked within the system, so to speak, while developing beliefs and activities that – by implication at least – threatened to erode and displace the Sadducean establishment.

To begin with, the Pharisees were known for their interest in and cultivation of the written word. In that respect, they hardly differed from the Qumran dissenters or even the Sadducees. But there is more to it than meets the eye, for the Pharisees infused the scroll with a sense of sacrality that exalted it to a point where it was viewed as something like a portable temple or even the promised land. When, therefore, in 70 C.E. the center of the temple went up in flames and the Pharisees – along with the Jesus people – turned out to be the principal survivors among the dissenting groups, they were already conditioned to conduct their religious and civic life apart from the temple and in intense devotion to the new center of the sacred texts. In retrospect, therefore, we can see how the Pharisaic cultivation of the written word unwittingly prepared the people for a diasporic existence in the absence of the physical center.

In contrast, and indeed opposition, to the Sadducees, the Pharisees additionally cultivated the spoken word, or the Oral Torah, as they called it. As far as the Sadduccees were concerned, they insisted on the religious validity of a limited body of manuscripts. For the most part it consisted of the Pentateuch with many of the other writings still being undetermined as to their canonical status. The will of God was thus assumed to be incorporated in a number of scrolls that were both identifiable and controllable. In contrast to the Sadducean concept of the chirographically rooted will of Yahweh, the Pharisaic embrace of the Oral Torah implied that divinity was not to be limited to a narrowly confined body of manuscripts. Hence, not only what was written down, but memorable sayings, ethical instructions, and notable stories enjoyed authoritative validity as they were placed on the same footing with a select group of scrolls. From the perspective of the Pharisees, therefore, the Oral Torah signified an ongoing revelation apart from and in addition to the scribal medium. From the perspective of the Sadducees, on the other hand, the privileging of oral tradition violated the Written Torah and, significantly, placed revelation outside of their control. In thus viewing ancient history as media history, we see how the seemingly esoteric quibble over the Oral Torah among Pharisees and Sadducees in effect constituted a power struggle over the control of the media. What was at stake was the nature and scope of revelation that was to govern Israel.

Viewing the ancient media of orality and scribality as instruments of identity formation, control, and domination used both by the elite and by marginalized

groups invites questions about the motives of early Christians in their use of the scribal medium. Ostensibly, early Christianity will have seized upon the scribal medium for purposes of shaping and constructing its identity, consciousness, and history. This is all the more obvious since early Christian appropriation of scribality coincided with a time in ancient Mediterranean, and especially Israelite, history that was marked with a steady oppression by Roman military forces, excessively punitive taxation, growing discontent and recurrent protests, mass crucifixions as political deterrent, and frequent resistance and renewal movements. How did early Christian writers compete with Greco-Roman powers on the marketplace of scribal communication? Specifically, how did they negotiate their message that was politically fraught with danger because Jesus was generally known to have been executed by the Romans on charges that were likely to have been political and, yet, the message by and about him was in the view of many believers designed for public consumption? With these perspectives in mind, this essay will discuss three early Christian documents, the Gospel of Mark, the Gospel of Luke, and the Apocalypse of John, and examine ways in which these three texts entrust their message to the scribal medium in view of Roman imperialism.

The Gospel of Mark: An Alternative to Roman Power

The pivotal metaphor in the Markan narrative is the kingdom of God. Unlike the role it plays in the Fourth Gospel (John 18:36), it is in fact of this world, involving individual and communal life, and constituted to revamp the structure of society as it presently exists. Announced to people, it is intended both to enlist people and to serve them. Undoubtedly, the kingdom does have sociopolitical implications, though it is an entity in the process of actualization whose final objective still remains to be fulfilled. While fermenting the social body by way of confrontation with evil and renewal, it moves irresistibly toward its historical self-realization.

Recently Horsley (2001a) has written on the sociopolitical dimensions of Mark's Gospel and developed its oppositional features to Roman rule. The interpretation given here differs in suggesting that the kingdom's mission in Mark to revalorize society is at most by implication opposed to Rome and careful to disguise any pronounced opposition to Roman imperial power. While established in this world and designed to transform this world, the kingdom is neither identical with nor in explicit opposition to the powers of this world. In fact, what gives it its distinct qualification is that it is God's kingdom (Mark 1:14–15) and hence neither the Herodians' kingdom nor Caesar's kingdom. In and through the person of Jesus, the kingdom of God is presented as the grand alternative to all other imperial hegemonies.

The Gospel's plot is driven by a great urgency for deliverance that in the first part of the narrative is executed by Jesus' extravagant deeds of power. Both his exorcisms and healings involve him in a severe power struggle with spiritual forces who disclose themselves as representatives of the satanic power structure. Mark clearly narrates a confrontation between the kingdom of God and the kingdom of Satan, and the Romans are, with one exception, not identical with the latter. In short, Jesus' battle with Beelzebul is not perceived in terms of a political confrontation.

One may nonetheless ask whether the Gospel's considerable preoccupation with demon possession and its emplotment of a global confrontation with superhuman forces represents on Mark's part a transposition of political-economic pressures onto a spiritual plane. By both personalizing and globalizing the problem of imperial violence, the exorcism stories would draw attention away from direct confrontation with the Roman oppressors while making sure that the violence that was affecting society was decisively challenged at the highest possible level. It is not inconceivable that Mark's preoccupation with healings and especially excorcisms is not unrelated to the violence inflicted by the Roman occupation and on a subliminal level represent a projection of social suffering and pent-up resentments on demonic forces. However, it is doubtful whether an ancient audience was in a position to hear the exorcism stories with what are after all the anthropological and psychological insights of modernity. While on the micro-level Mark's exorcisms and healings function to liberate individuals from physical suffering and to restore them to the fullness of life, they form on the macro-level part of a cosmic strategy to tie up the strong man Satan and to plunder his house (Mark 3:27). It would be difficult to read a political subtext into this part of the narrative.

An exception to this reading of the exorcisms is provided by the story of the exorcism of the Gerasene demoniac (Horsley 2001a:140–1). Of all the exorcisms in Mark's narrative, this one is distinguished by uncommonly violent proportions (Mark 5:1–20). A man possessed by demons has caused such raucousness that "no man could restrain him any more, even with a chain" (5:3). In answer to Jesus' question, he identifies himself as Legion, and upon the man's request the evil spirits enter a herd of two thousand swine, who rush into the sea to be drowned. In this case, it would be difficult not to acknowledge the anti-Roman sentiments. Both the intensity and the oppressiveness of violence, the naming of the demonic forces as Legion (a Roman military designation), their identification with swine (symbol of Gentile uncleanliness from a Jewish perspective), the large and precise number of swine, and, finally, their drowning in the sea add up to an unmistakably political, anti-Roman scenario. "The double meaning (of Legion) is not lost on the audience" (Horsley 2001a:18). On the narrative level the Gerasene demoniac represents Jesus' most massive excorcism; it takes place on Gentile territory and in repudiation of Gentile uncleanliness. Within the geographical coordinates of the Gospel the incident signifies Jesus' opening of new frontiers and a breakthrough toward a Gentile identity (Kelber 1979:30–3). However, the story clearly resonates with the experiences or reminiscences of a society haunted by demonic Roman violence and indulges wishful thinking of seeing the hated Roman "pigs" driven into the sea. The informed hearer may even discern an analogy between the drowning of the demonic oppressors and the paradigmatic drowning of the Egyptian pursuers of the fleeing Israelites in the red sea (Exod 14:26–8), although direct verbal links between the two stories are not discernible. The anti-Roman resentments, however, that are encoded in the exorcism story are recognizable as such only to the informed hearers who have ears to hear. Any overt confrontation with the Roman imperial authorities is carefully avoided.

Prior to his passion proper Jesus' emplotted activity is increasingly focused on the temple (Mark 11–13) and in fact in growing opposition to the central place. Having entered the temple to look at everything only to depart (11:11), Jesus enters a second

time to judge and disqualify the temple by word and by deed (11:12–25). To all appearances, his act of condemnation (11:15–17) is motivated by his zeal for the religious identity of the temple. Exposed as a place of merchants who abuse the sacred place and rob people of their livelihood, the temple is ideally defined as a place of prayer open to members of all nations. The hearers of this story are never informed of the fact that Jesus' temple activities were fraught with political risks, since the temple precinct was the epicenter of power. Any interference at the center of religious and political power was bound to provoke fateful intervention on the part of Sadducean and Roman powers. As long as the Romans were in control over Israel, they kept a watchful eye on the temple, making sure that law and order prevailed according to Roman imperial interests. Mark's Jesus, however, not only departs from the scene of disturbance unchallenged but returns unharmed a third time to the temple – this time for the purpose of teaching, defining and defending his own authority against that of the temple (Mark 11:27–12:40). Following extensive teaching in the temple, he exits for the last time (13:1) and promptly predicts the physical destruction of the holy place (13:2). As far as Mark is concerned, Jesus' active demonstration in the temple and his verbal condemnation are religiously motivated and carry no overt political consequences.

When in his final speech, delivered to four select disciples on the Mount of Olives and in full view of the temple, Jesus informs them of wars, rumors of wars, and national uprisings (13:5–37), he pointedly apprises them of a time of unprecedented suffering (13:19). Regardless whether the speech addresses a situation prior to or after the conflagration of the temple, hearers are bound to associate "the worst time of suffering since God created the world" (13:19) with Israel's historical experience as a colonized people. However, nowhere is Roman aggression directly identified, let alone challenged, and never is God's judgment, or that of the Son of Man, called upon to punish the oppressive rulers. Indeed, the speech stays remarkably clear of judgmental language. Mark's strategy in dealing with the politically explosive issue of war and the unparalleled violence associated with it is to place it into a larger, a cosmic scheme of events. This larger framework entails the rise of fraudulent redeemer figures (13:5–6, 21–2), the proclamation of the gospel to all the nations (13:10), a shortening of the time of tribulation (13:20), cosmic darkness and a heavenly revolution (13:24–5), followed by the epiphany of the Son of Man (13:26) and the redemption of the elect (13:27). By thus integrating the time of tribulation into a providentially devised scheme of cosmic events, a context of meaning is generated that deactivates anti-Roman resentments and refocuses attention from violence to epiphany.

In the passion narrative, the high priests along with the scribes initiate and advance the plot on Jesus' life (14:1, 10–11, 43) and arouse the Jerusalem crowd against him (15:11). The politically explosive issue of the temple incident does come up in the hearing before the high priest, but it is dismissed as false and conflicting testimony (14:57–9). The accusation that brings about the death sentence is blasphemy (14:64), a religious rather than political charge. As far as Jesus' transfer from Jewish to Roman authorities is concerned, the narrator has Pilate surmise that it was motivated by the jealousy of the Jewish establishment (15:10). Pilate, the highest Roman official in charge of the case, remains unconvinced of Jesus' guilt (15:14),

proposes to release him in place of a man of violence (15:6–9), and "wonders" (15:5: *thaumazein*) when Jesus is alive and still "wonders" (15:44: *ethaumazen*) after he is dead. Contrary to his well-founded historical reputation, the Pilate introduced by Mark into the Christian tradition is a man who tragically failed in his attempt to save the life of Jesus.

There is one scene in the passion narrative that seems to bespeak unbridled anti-Roman sentiments: Jesus' cruel mocking and torture by a battalion of soldiers (15:16–20). Clearly, the soldiers do not carry the blessing of the narrator, and Rome is placed in a blatantly negative light. Yet the scene of mocking is fraught with irony intimating that the direct sense is not entirely to be trusted. The soldiers, determined to make a brutal caricature of Jesus, clothe him with a purple cloak, place a crown of thorns on his head, and salute him as "King of the Jews." The rhetoric of their gestures suggests that a royal investiture, or more precisely the reversal of such an accession to power, has been enacted: Jesus is caricatured as king in an act of utter infamy. But the themes of coronation through humiliation and of induction into kingship by way of a crown made of thorns are entirely in keeping with the Markan narration of Jesus' death. For it is the Markan conception that Jesus acceded to royal power by surrendering all earthly power and by submitting himself to the most brutal of executions. Viewed in this light, the mocking scene does not, on a subliminal level, bespeak anti-Roman sentiments after all, for the soldiers who carry out the royal mocking enact the truth in ignorance and infamy.

There is, lastly, the centurion's affirmation made in full view of Jesus' death: "Truly, this man was Son of God" (15:39). Sanctioned by the heavenly voice both at baptism (1:11) and at the transfiguration (9:7), "Son of God" is the confessional designation fully befitting the Markan Jesus. It is the kind of confession the disciples should have made but never did make. As a matter of narrative fact, the Roman official in charge of the execution turns out to be the only human being in the narrative who ever makes the Son-of-God confession. Rome, not Jesus' own disciples, delivers the most appropriate response to Jesus' death.

Mark's representation of Jesus and God's kingdom is such that it studiously evades any direct confrontational engagement with Rome. While Jesus is a revolutionary who turned against the temple, or rather against those in charge of it, his temple activity is thoroughly depoliticized and the political charge dismissed in the trial. Projected as a figure of power, he turns traditional concepts of political power inside out: a successful exorciser, he dies engulfed in cosmic darkness (15:33); a popular performer of miracles, he suffers a nonmiraculous death; appointed in power, he dies abandoned by God in powerlessness (15:34). This inversion of power has the effect of disarming any perceived threat to Roman power. Far from exposing the brutality of the Roman punishment of crucifixion, the reversal of power constellations renders the crucifixion a source of strength and turns the Romans into unwitting executors of redemption. As for the politically imposed violence, past and present, it is reframed in a larger, a cosmic context. By transposing the source of violence into a transhistorical domain, the perspective on colonial violence is vastly broadened. The unprecedented tribulation and the demise of the temple need to be viewed in the larger context of the history of the kingdom of God and its struggle with the demonic forces of evil.

The Gospel of Luke: An Accommodation to Roman Power

Whether Theophilus was a Jew or a Gentile, a Jewish Christian or a Gentile Christian, Luke's formal address to him as *kratiste Theophilo* (Luke 1:3), and the reiteration of the personal address at the outset of Acts (1:1), expresses an authorial interest in introducing "the Way" (Acts 9:2; 19:9, 23; 24:14) to a person of high social ranking. To hold Theophilus's attention and to meet his likely political inclinations, Luke will be disposed to make a case for the compatibility of the new faith with the pro-Roman cultural elite in the Hellenistic world. This does not mean that Luke's often-observed cultural, political apologetic sells out the gospel to the Greco-Roman ruling class. As is well known, no other canonical Gospel shows greater contempt for the rich and more compassion for the poor than Luke (Degenhardt; Johnson). In this Gospel, human nature reveals itself – in part at least – by a person's relation to money and possessions. Assisting the poor has become an article of faith, and enslavement to possessions versus faith in Jesus, which manifests itself in giving alms to the poor, is an elementary conflict experienced by the followers of the "Way." Nor is the theme of the Roman apology the dominant one in Gospel and Acts, but it is a frequent subtext that ever so often surfaces and in the passion narrative and in parts of Acts clearly comes to the fore.

While the infancy Gospel (Luke 1–2) introduces John and Jesus the protagonist in Septuagintal language and with imagery derived from the Hebrew Bible, thus implanting them in a thoroughly Jewish context, it further links them with political figures who loom large on the stage of ancient Mediterranean history. The emperors Augustus and Tiberius, Quirinius the governor of Syria, king Herod and his brother Philip, and Lysanias the ruler of Abilene – to mention only the more important personages – represent the political coordinates of a history in the midst of which John and Jesus are shown to have been operative. The program implied in this impressive stage setting is that the Jesus movement, far from being an insignificant Jewish, messianic sect tucked away in a forgotten corner of the world (Acts 26:26), was from the beginning linked with eminent profiles in power. A revelation to the Gentiles and a glory to Israel (Luke 2:32), the movement had both a claim on the world and a responsibility for it.

In this spirit, John's preaching is expanded by a series of responses to questions addressed to him by the multitudes, tax collectors, and soldiers (Luke 3:10–14). His counsel amounts to a social and professional ethics of compassion and honesty "in which loyalty to the State is implicit" (Conzelmann: 138). John, who in Mark is presented as an apocalyptic figure, is thereby partially changed into a social reformer and advocate of civic responsibilities. In the case of Jesus, his parents' journey to Bethlehem (Luke 2:1–5) serves a threefold purpose. It has Augustus, the most powerful man in the ancient Mediterranean world, issue a decree that sets in motion "a train of events so far reaching as to excel all human might" (Flender: 57). Second, it has the parents abide by a census that was instituted for the purpose of administering Roman taxation. Any Zealotic implication as far as Jesus' birth, upbringing, and mission is concerned is thereby discounted. Finally, the journey to Bethlehem locates his birth "in the city of David a Savior, who is the Messiah, the Lord" (Luke 2:11), thus stipulating Jesus' Davidic messiahship. In sum, Jesus the Messiah in no way poses a threat to the imperial Roman system.

Luke enunciates peace as a recurring motif more than any other canonical Gospel. Mark uses *eirene* once, Matthew four times, John six times, and Luke (Gospel and Acts) twenty times (Morgenthaler: 92). In Luke, both John and Jesus are introduced as messengers of peace (Luke 1:79; 2:14). The angels heralding the messianic birth announce peace on earth (2:14), whereas the disciples accompanying Jesus on his entry into Jerusalem proclaim peace in heaven (19:38). The reality of peace is, therefore, not restricted to the immanent dimension of history. Rather, peace partakes of a dialectical mode of thought and action whereby events in heaven relate to corresponding events on earth, and vice versa (Flender: 37–56). In Jesus' own words, the trouble with Jerusalem is that it failed to recognize the things that make for peace (19:42). The first greeting extended by the Risen One to the disciples in Jerusalem is "Peace be to you" (24:36). Ideally, the early church lives in a state of peace and under the guidance of the Holy Spirit (Acts 9:31). In one of his speeches Peter summarizes the gospel in terms of "peace through Jesus Christ" (Acts 10:36). This Lukan motif of peace will resonate differently with hearers of the Gospel and Acts. For the most part it appears in contexts that have little to do with the cessation of war and strife; it may imply, but does not directly connotate, absence of violence. However, it shows greater affinity with the Jewish notion of *shalom*, which defines peace as a gift from God that restores harmony in the relationship between God and humans. However, an audience versed in Hellenistic culture may sense undercurrents that are reminiscent of the imperial propagation of the *pax Romana*. Peace (*eirene*), savior (*soter*), good news (*euangelion*), and benefactor (*euergetes*) are part of the vocabulary of the imperial cult and liturgy. Imperial births and enthronements are tidings of joy that celebrate the emperor as savior and benefactor under whose governance land and sea will enjoy peace and well-being. But whether the Lukan Jesus, messianic herald of peace, is perceived in fulfilment of the *pax Romana* or in competition with it, he is in either case politically innocent of and immune to the Zealotic gospel of violence.

Yet appeasement of the Roman will to law and order does not fully characterize Lukan strategy. Already in the infancy Gospel, Mary's Magnificat (Luke 1:46–55) challenges positions of power and introduces the revolutionary theme of social reversal. In appealing to God as the one who "has scattered the proud in the imagination of their hearts" (1:51), the Gospel avails itself of decidedly provocative language, and in asserting that God "has put down the mighty [*dynastas*] from their thrones, and exalted those of low degree" (1:52), it is decidedly taking political risks. Statements of this kind carry positively social, even political implications that do not lend themselves easily to a spiritualized interpretation. Only slightly less precarious are Jesus' own words to the effect that among his disciples Gentile power relations ought to be reversed: whereas Gentile kings, who call themselves benefactors, rule over their subjects, among his followers the leader is destined to serve (22:25–6). This does suggest that the social structure enacted by the "benefactors" can only serve as a negative example for those who wish to follow in the "Way." At an earlier point in the Gospel the Lukan Jesus had emphatically denied that his mission was to deliver peace on earth. Instead, he intended to light a fire that would divide households and turn family members against one another (12:51–3). In this instance, peace as cultivation of family structures and values is subverted. As a general rule, imperial powers will not look favorably upon the dissolution of family ties, even

though sayings of this kind are meant for internal, Christian consumption. There is, finally, the tantalizing Lukan episode regarding the two swords (22:35–8). Concluding his farewell speech, Jesus counsels the purchase of a sword and is promptly presented with two. There clearly is an air of violence hovering over the scene. However, the suspension that is building up in this scene is taken up and resolved in the following episode of the arrest (22:47–51). When violence erupts at the arrest and one of Jesus' followers (disciples?) puts the sword to action and cuts off the right ear of the high priest's slave, Jesus interferes and reverses the violence by performing his last healing. An overzealous follower is thereby repudiated, and Zealotism at a pivotal juncture in Jesus' life repudiated. For the most part, language that affronts Roman sensibilities is the exception rather than the rule.

More than the other canonical Gospels Luke has foregrounded Jerusalem and its demise. His narrative relates the military siege and destruction of the city in historically graphic terms: Jerusalem is "surrounded by armies" (Luke 21:20); the "enemies will set up ramparts [around it] and surround [it], and hem [it] in on every side, and crush [it] to the ground" (19:34–5); it will be "trodden down by the Gentiles" (21:24); and people "will fall by the edge of the sword" (21:24). But in spite of a historical awareness of both the military logistics and the human tragedy surrounding the event, the Gospel will issue neither complaint nor criticism concerning Roman brutalities and refrain from holding Roman military and/or political authorities responsible for the indescribable suffering of the people. What is lamented is Jerusalem, not the Romans. The fault, Luke argues, lies with the city and its citizens who habitually killed the prophets (13:34) and missed the appropriate time (*kairos*) of God's visitation (19:44). Additionally, Luke firmly draws a connection between the fate of the city and that of Jesus, a link already affirmed less emphatically by Mark. Notably, Luke abides by the Markan pattern in treating the destruction of city and temple in the context of Jesus' story, not, as required by historical chronology, in the context of his (Luke's) second volume, Acts. Over and above the Q lament (Luke 13:34–5) and Mark's apocalyptic anticipation (Mark 13:14–20 = Luke 21:20–4), Luke introduced two more lament scenes: Jesus' weeping over Jerusalem (Luke 19:41–4) and his grieving over the daughters of Jerusalem (23:27–31). Both scenes are placed in the passion narrative, one at the entry into Jerusalem and one on the way to crucifixion. In his last word prior to his execution Jesus wonders what will happen when the wood is dry if this was being done while it was still green (23:31), thereby linking his own demise with that of the city. Undoubtedly, Luke is in possession of detailed knowledge about Jerusalem's destruction, but his mode of argumentation is of a conventionally religious kind. He will not allow himself to express overt animosity toward the destructiveness of Roman political and military power.

In the passion narrative Luke further develops the *apologia Romana*, already in existence since Mark, into a programmatic theme. He has Jesus' opponents resort to the intensely political issue of Roman taxation in order to bring him to trial (Luke 20:20). When they deliver him to Pilate it is precisely on this charge of having committed a crime against the imperial government: "We found this man perverting our nation, for-bidding us to pay taxes to the emperor, and saying that he himself is the Messiah, a king" (23:2). Kingship, messianism, revolution and Roman taxation constitute the core of the indictment, a potent political charge that is designed to

bring about the death sentence. Luke, although not unaware of Pilate's insensitivity toward ethnic people and religious issues (13:1), nevertheless takes a major step toward promoting the Roman governor into a model Christian. Pilate responds not once, but three times: there was no basis for the charges (23:4), Jesus was not guilty (23:14), and there is, therefore, no judicial ground for granting the requested death sentence (23:22). This is the first time in the Christian tradition that a formal charge of political culpability has been brought against Jesus and that it has been formally dismissed, and dismissed by the principal Roman authority. Henceforth, the *apologia Romana* is firmly entrenched in Christian consciousness.

After Pilate has pronounced Jesus innocent, Luke will not have the latter tortured by Roman soldiers. In Mark, Pilate has Jesus scourged (Mark 15:15) before he turns him over to the soldiers, who in turn subject him to torture. Hence prior to his execution the Markan Jesus twice undergoes physical suffering on the instruction of Roman authorities and by Roman hands. Mark, Matthew, and John all report the so-called mocking by the Roman soldiers. In Luke, however, Roman soldiers verbally abuse and mock Jesus while he suffers on the cross (Luke 23:36), but neither they nor Pilate will subject him to physical torture prior to his execution. Instead, the Gospel projects Jesus' physical abuse by the soldiers backward into the courtyard of the high priest, where "the men who were holding" him subject him to mocking torture (22:63–5). This is a harbinger of things to come in the Christian tradition: the culpability for Jesus' death is increasingly transferred from Roman to Jewish authorities, and eventually to the Jewish people at large. The Gospel's Roman apology reaches its peak with the centurion, the Roman official in charge of the execution, pronouncing Jesus innocent in full view of his death (23:47). In short, as far as Luke is concerned, Jesus' death was a judicial error forced upon the Romans by the Jewish people and authorities of Jerusalem.

As far as Luke's concept of history is concerned, a major rationale for Jesus' birth, mission, and death was the inauguration of an ecumenical movement. However, with one exception Jesus himself refrained from pursuing the Gentile mission. He initiated it in his inaugural sermon at Nazareth (Luke 4:16–30, esp. 25–7), by way of a single, programmatic journey unto Gentile territory (8:26–39), and by his commissioning of the seventy (10:1–12), but the execution of the Gentile mission itself was the work of the early church and for this reason had to be relegated to the second volume, Acts.

Luke's so-called "great omission," the deletion of Mark 6:45–8:26, is a deliberate procedure undertaken in the interest of the theme of the Gentile mission. In Mark this segment corresponds exactly to Jesus' sanctioning of the Gentile mission. Luke deletes this narrative segment not because of lack of interest in the theme but because it is the theme to be treated in Acts.

In view of Luke's sympathy toward Gentile culture and Roman power, the goal and ending of his two-volume work is of particular interest. After Paul, who identifies himself as a Roman citizen by birth (Acts 22:25–9; 23:27) and appeals to the Roman emperor (25:10–12), arrives in Rome, he spends two years in the capital proclaiming the gospel that was meant for the Gentiles without any interference on the part of the authorities (28:16–30). Luke's work, as the construction of all narrative, entails to some extent a plotting backwards from its anticipated ending. This interior retrospectivity (Ong 1977b) implies that both Gospel and Acts are narrated with a view

toward, and from the perspective of, the city of Rome that Paul was to reach at the end of Acts. In different words, Luke constructs both Gospel and Acts from the perspective of a Christianity that had safely arrived and settled in the capital of Rome.

Given the preeminence of the Gentile theme, Luke had to face up to the realities of the Roman Empire. His Roman apologetic arose out of a perceived necessity to devise a modus operandi with the imperial state and is not necessarily an ad hominem construction tailor-made for a particular social setting, conventionally called the Lukan community. Hence in effect, and probably in intention, Luke makes a case for the compatibility of Christianity with Rome. He is keenly aware that his case will be ineffective unless it addresses the controversial issue of Jesus' political culpability. Crucifixion by the Romans made Zealotic criminality, or rather the charge of Zealotic criminality, to be eminently plausible. In the course of his argumentation, Luke, therefore, had to concede that the charge of political criminality was indeed an issue in the case of Jesus and the principal reason for his judicial hearing before Pilate. The Roman declaration of Jesus' innocence constituted the linchpin of Luke's Roman apology. In following Mark, he reinforced his case by introducing a paradoxical twist: it was the Jews who entertained seditious sympathies because they requested the release of Barabbas, a known Zealotic insurrectionist. In the last analysis, therefore, no other than Pilate himself lent support to Zealotism by giving in to Jewish pressure and ordering the release of Barabbas. Admittedly, Jesus was a social and religious reformer, a revolutionary even, but he explicitly rejected the political gospel of violence.

The Apocalypse of John: A Subversion of Roman Power

John's Apocalypse dramatizes a global conflict between the forces of evil plotting destruction and death and those of redemption visualizing order and life. To stage the drama, the narrator operates with a collage of symbols creating a largely imaginative universe of compelling rhetorical persuasiveness. The fierce conflict is principally enacted by the Lamb, one like the Son of Man and the Bride, representing the forces of life, and at the opposite side the city of Babylon, the great Whore and the Beast impersonating the powers of destructiveness. While precise historical references are, we shall see, infrequent in the narrative, poetic language and images predominate. Symbols are used flexibly and at times interchangeably. Only with difficulty can they be reduced to steno-symbols that would require a one-to-one relation of symbol and meaning. For the most part John's Apocalypse employs symbols as tensive figures evoking a wide range of meanings that cannot be exhausted in any one apprehension of meaning (Wheelwright; Perrin: 29–30; Schüssler Fiorenza: 183–6).

The rich legacy of connotations that the symbols carry derives in part from the Jewish tradition, especially the book of Ezekiel, and from the apocalyptic strands of it, and within the apocalyptic tradition above all from the Apocalypse of Daniel. In part, however, the Apocalypse summons symbolic representations that draw on deeper archaic sources. This applies especially to the combat theme that pits the forces of chaos, sterility, and death against those of order, fertility, and life. That theme derived from and resonates with an archaic Near Eastern myth of combat and creation (Gunkel 1895; A. Y. Collins). However, the Apocalypse's collage of symbols

does not arise exclusively from primordial and apocalyptic memorial wellsprings nor exist exclusively in the harmonious configuration of its own interior world. It relates in complex ways to history. Symbols are being invoked in the historical context of readers/hearers, and the symbolic dramatization is to a degree at least shaped from the perspective of and with a view toward the Apocalypse's recipients and their experiences in the present. This is why the collage of symbols can take on life in and for the historical audience/readership. Tapping a deep register and configuring it with a view toward the present, the vastly imaginative narrative reaches out to hearers/readers, inviting them to make sense of their historical experiences in the context of the apocalyptic narration. On this view, John's Apocalypse is neither an aesthetic world closed unto itself and without any social, historical, political parameters nor a poetic world that is limited to a one-to-one translation of its symbols into history. It rather appeals to hearers/readers both as participants in, and victims of, history and as sharers in the memories of ancient myths. In short, the Apocalypse is a poetic narration that mobilizes hearers to explore their historical conflicts in an archetypal, symbolic dramatization of a primal conflict. The latter constitutes a combat of worldwide, indeed cosmic dimensions, parts of which have been set into motion "from the foundation of the world" (Rev 13:8). Insofar as the Apocalypse has globalizing implications, it functions as an explanatory mechanism that projects hearers into the cosmic drama and encourages them to comprehend their present crisis in global dimensions.

When the Apocalypse singles out Babylon as the quintessential rogue city, it taps into resentments that run deep in Jewish, Jewish-Christian consciousness. Ever since the ancient Babylonian Empire had humiliated Judah and destroyed Jerusalem's temple in 587 BCE (2 Kgs 24–25), Babylon had become a proverbial expression of anguish and enragement in the face of foreign, imperial oppression. One of the pivotal features of John's Apocalypse is the fierceness and relentlessness of judgment that it pronounces on Babylon. The six direct references to Babylon are all placed in negative, judgmental contexts (Rev 14:8; 16:19; 17:5; 18:2, 10, 21). Employing the formulaic diction of a dirge or lament modeled on Isaiah (21:9), the Apocalypse announces mournfully the downfall of Babylon, the great city: "Fallen, fallen is Babylon the great!" (Rev 14:8; 18:2). Plagues in the form of "torment and grief," "pestilence and mourning and famine" (18:7–8) will be inflicted upon her. An unprecedented earthquake will split the city of all cities into three (16:18–19), fire will consume her (18:8), and she will become "a dwelling place of demons" (18:2). "Babylon the great" is beyond redemption and doomed to destruction.

The city-destruction rhetoric (Rossing: 62) comprises indictments of prostitution, murder, as well as of arrogant claims to universal power – all directed against the great city of Babylon. The charge of prostitution (*porneia*: Rev 14:8; 17:5; 18:3) is polyvalent and open to interpretations in terms of illicit relations with foreign cities (including sexual promiscuity), participation in imperial cult practices, and/or, we shall see, the advancement of commercial ties that compromised the integrity of the merchants and fed the great city's voracious appetite. There are, moreover, frequent expressions of anguish over the shedding of the blood of saints, prophets, and witnesses of Jesus, and in one instance at the very least these atrocities are attributed to Babylon (18:24). Ruling "as a queen" (18:7), "Babylon, the mighty city" (18:10) indulged herself in the narcissistic illusions and arrogance that is endemic to world

powers (18:7). She has seduced and deceived the nations of the earth and contributed to their downfall (14:8; 18:23). However, her own imminent fall will bring about the collapse of the nations and "the cities of the nations" (16:19; cf. Isa 14:12). Hence, her day of doom will be cause for universal lament on the part of "the kings of the earth" (Rev 18:9–10), who had entertained relations with the glamorous queen, the "mother of whores" (17:5).

A conspicuous feature in the Apocalypse's narration concerns references to economics and commerce, with a special emphasis on issues pertaining to seafaring, navigation, and maritime trade. This is atypical in the rhetorical repertoire of apocalyptic language and for this reason deserves to be viewed as in some sense case-specific (Kraybill). "Clothed in fine linen, in purple and scarlet, adorned with gold, with jewels and with pearls" (Rev 18:16), enchanting Babylon is a city of unprecedented wealth. She is said to entertain a flourishing shipping trade, exporting numerous items and vast quantities of luxury items ranging from gold to the human cargo of slaves (18:11–13). Shipmasters, seafarers and sailors, kings and merchants, "the magnates of the earth" (18:23), such as those who traded and traveled on sea and who gained wealth from Babylon and benefited from her in numerous ways – all of them will be devastated by her demise (18:9, 14–15, 17–19, 23). In focusing on the shipping trade, the Apocalypse targets what tended to be a nerve center in ancient power politics: commerce, shipping, and imperial interests blended together and fed one another. Standing within a Jewish tradition of resistance to oppressive imperialism, the Apocalypse counsels a strategy of commercial noncooperation with corrupt and vainglorious Babylon.

With rare exceptions, the rogue city of Babylon is conventionally interpreted as a figure for imperial Rome. However, that interpretation entails complex hermeneutical configurations. As far as the Apocalypse's dramatized imagery is concerned, we are dealing first and foremost with an intricate symbolic interaction of Babylon, the evil Woman, and the evil Beast. The Woman clothed in luxurious garments and adorned with expensive jewelry is marked as the embodiment of all the impurities on earth. Representing both the wealth and the abominations of Babylon, she carries on her forehead an inscription that reads: "Babylon the great, mother of whores and of earth's abominations" (Rev 17:5). This identification is fully confirmed in nonsymbolic, propositional language: "The woman you saw is Babylon the great city that rules over the kings of the earth" (17:18). There is, moreover, the Beast arising out of the abyss of the sea (13:1) carrying blasphemous names on its head (13:1; 17:3) and uttering "haughty and blasphemous words" (13:5). It will receive homage from the tribes, nations, and peoples of the earth (13: 7–8) although its reign of terror is of limited duration. For forty-two months (13:5) it will exercise its military authority, make war on the saints (13:7), and assault the Lamb (17:14), but its end is destruction as it is conquered by the Lamb (17:14). The scarlet Beast is linked to the evil Woman insofar as she takes her seat on it and, clothed in purple and scarlet, rides on it (17:3–4). Thus, Babylon, the great Whore, and the scarlet Beast are the three principal embodiments of evil. While the symbolic representations alternate between a city, a person, and an animal, their functions and attributes closely interact to the point of blending into one another. All three function as manifestations and agents of inordinate wealth, corruption, idolatry, blasphemy, and universal domination.

To the extent that Rome plays a role in the apocalyptic scenario, she is, therefore, represented not merely by Babylon but by all three principalities of Evil. There are a number of links connecting the symbolic world embodied by Babylon, the great Whore, and the scarlet Beast with imperial Rome. We have already seen that the extensive maritime language falls outside the symbolic world and appears to connect with historical realities current in the world of the author and audience. No city in the ancient Mediterranean fits the Apocalypse's diatribe against seafaring and maritime commerce better than Rome. Ostia, the city's principal port, was the center of a vast commercial network and the destination of countless trade routes. Merchants not only realized a hefty profit from Rome's boundless appetite for ordinary and extraordinary goods but also became dependent on Rome – its economic status, its currency, its cultural needs and tastes, and its political powers. Moreover, the Apocalypse expresses abhorrence of emperor worship (Rev 13:4, 12–17; 16:2; 19:20), raising the specter of links between seamanship and imperial cult practices (Kraybill: 123–32). Numismatic evidence displays the very alliance between commerce, Roman military, pagan gods, and imperial cults that the Apocalypse found deeply objectionable. Indeed, no mercy is held out for those who worship the Beast and its image (14:9–12). From the perspectives of the Apocalypse, all these practices and beliefs centered on the unholy alliance with Babylon/Rome.

This is evident as well from the Beast's deadly focus on the destruction of Jerusalem. It is said that the Beast conquers "the holy" or "the great city," which is the very city "where also their Lord was crucified" (Rev 11:2, 8). The streets of Jerusalem will be soaked in the blood and strewn with the bodies of her victims as a result of the conquest that will last forty-two months (11:2, 7–8; 13:5). The Beast is thereby unmistakably associated with the brutalities of the Roman military might, and the principal conquest with the fall of Jerusalem, the holy city. Clearly alluding to the tragic event of 70 CE, which looms large in the background, the Apocalypse enjoins its hearers/readers to comprehend the struggle with Rome as the reactivation in the present of an old, archaic conflict. The Woman, finally, who rides on the Beast, is also seated on seven mountains (17:9), which is sometimes taken to refer to Rome as the city of the seven hills. In sum, the rogue city, the seductive Woman, and the abominable Beast are symbols with floating and interactive connotations whose core identity, however, is Rome, the paradigmatic city of imperial corruption and idolatry. Once we recognize that the Apocalypse's objection to Rome found expression through the principal trinity of evil representations, not by reference simply to the ancient city of Babylon, the profundity of its anti-Roman sentiments is difficult to overstate.

Given the depth of the Apocalypse's antagonism toward Rome, it may be tempting to view its symbolic language and imagery as a strategy borne out of political considerations. Yet the objective of the apocalyptic scenario, which draws on a rich source of established diction, imagery, and configurations, is ultimately not intelligible as, let alone reducible to, a rhetoric of political prudence. To be sure, Rome is invoked in a complex narrative web of symbols and images and never directly mentioned by name. More than that, it is doubtful whether the Apocalypse intends to invite hearers to decode its world, symbol after symbol and image after image. Indeed, many commentaries are still unduly preoccupied with determining links between the coded symbolic world and historical data, events, and personages,

thereby treating the imagery as steno-symbols rather than as tensive figurations. But rather than translating each item into current history, the Apocalypse invites audiences to project themselves into its world. As hearers involve themselves in the dramatization of the conflict between Babylon, the great Whore, and the abominable Beast versus the heavenly Jerusalem, the Bride, and the Lamb (or one like the Son of Man), they locate their own roles and identities in the scenario. There is a sense, therefore, in which hearers are invited to reorient, to relive even, their present conflict with the world power of Rome. However, the symbols are often plurisignificant, evoking multiple floating and interactive representations. As the heavenly Jerusalem functions as an archetypal ideal, so also does Babylon function as its satanic parody. It does represent Rome, but also more than the human, imperial city. The scarlet Woman is also seated on the waters, which pass for "peoples and multitudes and nations and languages" (Rev 17:15). She does represent Rome, but also more than the human, imperial city of Rome. The Beast is a sea monster, which conjures up archaic, mythological anxieties (11:7; 13:1–10, 18; 15:2; 16:13; 17:7–14). It does represent Rome, but also more than the human, imperial city of Rome. Hence, the symbols not only assist hearers in identifying current events but also open up to a world that encompasses and transcends the present crisis, assisting hearers in recognizing themselves and their conflict as part of an archaic, global confrontation between chaos and order.

Conclusion

We have observed the early Christian appropriation of the scribal medium as an instrument of identity formation. As a marginalized group, the early Christians scribalized their traditions for the purpose of solidifying cultural memory and constructing a sense of history. In the case of Mark, scribality unified the selected memories of the recent past in the interest of identity formation at a decisive juncture in early Christian mnemonic history. Luke created a sense of Jesus' past history from the perspective of the subsequent history of the expansion of the new faith into the Gentile world. The Apocalypse designed a largely imaginary world, vastly expanding the universe of experiences and identifications and summoning its hearers/readers to find identity in it. In all three instances, scribality, cultural memory, and identity formation cooperated in the interest of constructing early Christian self-legitimation. In different ways this self-legitimation was affected by the relations one negotiated with the Roman world power. As a rule, the public medium of scribality had to process this explosive aspect of early Christian identity with utmost discretion. Mark's text of the life and death of Jesus articulated a cautiously couched program of an alternative to Roman power. Luke, while retaining vigorous, social ethics, nonetheless wrote what amounted to a program of acculturation to the new political realities of Roman supremacy. The Apocalypse, finally, articulated an uncompromising condemnation of the world power, but its anti-Roman scenario was judiciously camouflaged in the coded diction and imagery of an apocalyptic dramatization. In this way early Christians prepared the way into the Roman Empire for the message of and about the one who was crucified as a criminal by Roman law and authority.

REFERENCES

Assmann, Jan (1992). *Das kulturelle Gedächtnis: Schrift, Erinnerung und politische Identität in frühen Hochkulturen*. Munich: Beck.
Collins, Adela Yarbro (1976). *The Combat Myth in the Book of Revelation*. HDR, 9. Chico, Calif.: Scholars Press.
Conzelmann, Hans (1961). *The Theology of St. Luke*, trans. Geoffrey Buswell. New York: Harper & Row.
Degenhardt, Hans-Joachim (1965). *Lukas, Evangelist der Armen*. Stuttgart: Verlag Katholisches Bibelwerk.
Flender, Helmut (1967). *St. Luke: Theologian of Redemptive History*, trans. Ilse and Reginald Fuller. Philadelphia: Fortress.
Gunkel, Hermann (1895). *Schöpfung und Chaos in Urzeit und Endzeit: Eine religionsgeschichtliche Untersuchung über Gen 1 und Ap Joh 12*. Göttingen: Vandenhoeck & Ruprecht.
Horsley, Richard A. (2001a). *Hearing the Whole Story: The Politics of Plot in Mark's Gospel*. Louisville: Westminster John Knox.
Johnson, Luke T. (1977). *The Literary Function of Possessions in Luke-Acts*. SBLDS, 39. Missoula, Mont.: Scholars Press.
Kelber, Werner H. (1979). *Mark's Story of Jesus*. Philadelphia: Fortress.
Kraybill, J. Nelson (1996). *Imperial Cult and Commerce in John's Apocalypse*. JSNTSup, 132. Sheffield: Sheffield Academic Press.
Morgenthaler, Robert (1985). *Statistik des Neutestamentlichen Wortschatzes*. Zurich: Gotthelf-Verlag.
Neusner, Jacob (1972). *From Politics to Piety: The Emergence of Pharisaic Judaism*. Englewood Cliffs, NJ: Prentice Hall.
Ong, Walter J. (1977b). "Maranatha: Death and Life in the Text of the Book," in *Interfaces of the Word: Studies in the Evolution of Consciousness and Culture*. Ithaca, NY: Cornell University Press, 230–71.
Perrin, Norman (1976). *Jesus and the Language of the Kingdom: Symbol and Metaphor in New Testament Interpretation*. Philadelphia: Fortress.
Rivkin, Ellis (1978). *A Hidden Revolution*. Nashville: Abingdon.
Schüssler Fiorenza, Elisabeth (1998). *The Book of Revelation: Justice and Judgment*. Minneapolis: Fortress.
Stemberger, Günter (1995b). *Jewish Contemporaries of Jesus: Pharisees, Sadducees, Essenes*, trans. Allan W. Mahnke. Minneapolis: Fortress.
Wellhausen, Julius (2001). *The Pharisees and the Sadducees: An Examination of Internal Jewish History*, trans. Mark E. Biddle. Macon, Ga.: Mercer University Press.
Wheelwright, Philip E. (1962). *Metaphor and Reality*. Bloomington: Indiana University Press.

7

Desiring War: Apocalypse, Commodity Fetish, and the End of History

Erin Runions

This paper argues that the repeated buzzwords "history" and "freedom" in official documents of the Bush administration work to conflate religious and economic desire as a means of motivating war. Bush's apocalyptically inflected invocation of a personified "History", who calls the US to defend and advance freedom, also betrays a philosophical underpinning that is illuminated through Francis Fukuyama's explication of the "end of history". This exploration of the religio-philosophical framework for Bush's public discourse pays attention to the ways in which it mirrors Fukuyama's ultimately neoconservative, Nietzchean reading of Kojève, in which the Hegelian fight unto death is never quite resolved.

Introduction

This paper is part of a larger project that seeks to find new metaphors for resisting imperialism that do not simply repeat a violent apocalyptic longing for the destruction of evil. It also comes out of a conviction that the left – marxist, anarchist, and even democrat – must begin to engage religious arguments at some level, even if they are predisposed otherwise. The right has been smart in its long term planning and in its use of religious, philosophical and co-opted leftist rhetoric (Parenti 2003), especially apocalyptic and utopian rhetoric. As some political theorists have argued, it is time for the left to take a more comprehensive view intellectually and strategically in order to counter such rhetoric in the long term.[1]

As a first step in this project, then, I look at the convergence of religion and philosophy in the discourse favored by George W. Bush, in which personified "history" calls the US to guard "freedom" for the world in the face of looming terror. I suggest that by tapping into both a Christian heritage of apocalypse and a

First published in *The Bible and Critical Theory*, 1/1 (2004).

truncated version of the philosophy of Hegel and Kojève, this discourse allies religious desire for the end of history with desire for economic freedom, in order to further the US practice of generating war and the interests served by war.[2] The conflation of religious and economic desire points to an underlying philosophy that values the Hegelian *struggle* for recognition, rather than its resolution. In my view, it is vital to dissect such rhetoric because it will undoubtedly resurface, as do political figures (and their progeny).

Cosmic origins and ends for military action

Before looking more carefully at how the rhetoric of history and freedom is used by the Bush administration, let me first indicate how I read the larger apocalyptic framework into which it taps. As I will suggest below, through an apocalyptic framework, military conflict is given cosmic-dressed-as-secular origins (the call of history) and utopic ends (freedom).

The position taken by the Bush administration with respect to the rest of the world clearly falls within the tradition of covenantal, messianic chosenness by God, which, as I've argued more thoroughly elsewhere, is both a covenantal and apocalyptic discourse (Runions 2004). Throughout Bush's rhetoric, the nation is chosen to use its military strength in the role of ensuring freedom for the rest of humanity.[3] The rhetoric recalls the longstanding tradition of manifest destiny in US nationalism that, as Stephanson argues, "constitut[es] itself not only as prophetic but also universal" (Stephanson 1995: xiii).

The cosmic duty of the chosen nation, as the fight with terror suggests, is a battle with evil itself, won through constant surveillance and vigilance. The language used by Bush, of shadowy networks of terrorists in their caves and hiding places, evokes the image of lurking evil, threatening the nation at every turn. The evil terrorists are those who (like Satan, presumably) "seek to master the minds and souls of others" (Bush 2002d). In the call to root out "hidden evil" and "mad ambition" (Bush 2002e), a rhetoric continually demanding surveillance is assimilated to a long standing religious heritage of spiritual surveillance.[4] This heritage continues, as US officials scrutinise those within and without the nation's borders for any sign of affiliation with "evil."

The apocalyptic framing is not subtle in any way, but, perhaps as a weak attempt to broaden the target audience, it is also translated into the secular language of history and freedom. To give one example among many, in the speech on the first anniversary of 9.11 Bush said, "I believe there is a reason that *history* has matched this nation with this time. We fight, not to impose our will, but to defend ourselves and the blessings of *freedom*" (Bush 2002d, emphasis mine). "History" stands as a personified, and apparently atemporal, figure; it stands outside of any temporal or chronological understanding of human life that usually comes under the rubric of history. It is removed from the regular sphere of human activity, in order to act as some kind of higher authority. "History" seems to be a thinly veiled, secular substitution for "God",[5] who chooses and calls the US to its unique, covenantal, and universal mission of protecting the world against apocalyptic terror and destruction.

Compliance with history's calling is promised to result in a future of freedom ("the future belongs to the free" – Bush 2002b), in which peace and justice abound: "History has called our nation into action. History has placed a great challenge before us: Will America – with our unique position and power – blink in the face of terror, or will we lead to a freer, more civilized world? There is only one answer: This great country will lead the world to safety, security, peace and freedom" (Bush 2002c). The language co-opts the audience into support for the "one answer" for the future: freedom. At the same time, though rather humorous in the attempt to describe fortitude (not blinking), it signals the importance of surveillance (eyes wide open) in the strategy to promote freedom.

Freedom must not only be defended, it must also be advanced through military power, because it is the ultimate goal and the fulfilment of humanity's potential:

> The advance of freedom is the calling of our time; it is the calling of our country... America has put our power at the service of principle. We believe that liberty is the design of nature; we believe that liberty is the direction of history. We believe that human fulfillment and excellence come in the responsible exercise of liberty. And we believe that freedom – the freedom we prize – is not for us alone, it is the right and the capacity of all mankind [sic] (Bush 2003b).

Pre-emptive military action is framed as merely the responsible exercise of one nation in the principled service of others. Bush's speeches are filled with similar statements, based on his belief that "freedom is the deepest need of every human soul" (Bush 2004b). In his view, freedom will fill humans' most fundamental desires, those based on spiritual need. Precisely because of freedom's "universal" and "spiritual" nature, history's call to ensure its victory must be heeded. The point is that to ensure freedom evil must be *fought*, and that fighting is a sign of spiritual resolve and fortitude: "America has entered a great struggle that tests our strength, and even more our resolve... we have made a sacred promise to ourselves and to the world: we will not relent until justice is done and our nation is secure" (Bush 2002d; see also Bush 2002a and Bush 2002c). Thus, using an apocalyptic framework, actual material military conflict is given spiritual resonance. The language works not only on the level of giving sacred import to the nation's military endeavours, but it also interpellates individuals – insofar as they believe in good and evil – into supporting the conflict. Especially in a cultural environment shaped by Manichean stories in film, who in their right mind would take a stand for evil?[6]

Freedom as Commodity Fetish

History's call to freedom does more than just authorise war as a high calling though. The war for freedom facilitates and reflects material desires, processes of production, and the exchange of commodities. Religious desire strengthens economic desire. As I will show below, the exchange of commodities demanded by American access to markets is projected onto the exchange between the cosmic figures of history and freedom. Together history and freedom substitute for, and perhaps also make real, the desire for access to the US's "responsibly limited" resources. Freedom

is the central figure here. History merely confirms the gravity and truth of the matter. Freedom to contribute to the American economy and to adopt American values is related to a desire for resources, thus it must be both defended and advanced.

Bush's rhetoric of defending/advancing freedom (i.e., war in the name of history) is often tangentially related to questions of domestic economy. The sacred fight for freedom becomes conjoined with Americans' financial goals and desires, notably for jobs, access to education, home ownership and more access to earnings through tax reductions. A striking example of the connection between the call to war and Americans' material desires comes in the speech "President Calls on Senate to Pass American Dream Downpayment Act" (Bush 2003a). The speech, ostensibly about affordable home ownership, begins with a statement invoking desire: "People in this country ought to be able to work hard and dream big, and realize their dreams." Then, after aligning the administration's many attempts to meet the challenge to the economy with its efforts to "answer" the threat to security, the second half of the speech validates the war on terror and pre-emptive strikes.[7] By virtue of juxtaposing external security threats with internal economic desires (and worries about meeting those desires), the speech implies that the two realms are interdependent.[8] Thus, the freedom that must be defended by war stands in, as a sort of shorthand, for a desired set of material wants that must be advanced (the American dream). One must have a job, a house, and lowered taxes, if one is to be really free. At the same time, the very idea of freedom (or loss thereof) generates those desires.

In terms of foreign affairs, freedom is related to the success of a society. In Bush's discussion of freedom in Iraq and the Middle East (Bush 2003b) – one of his longer meditations on the nature of freedom, to which I will return presently – he states, "The prosperity, social vitality and technological progress of a people are directly determined by the extent of their liberty. Freedom honors and unleashes human creativity – and creativity determines the strength and wealth of nations." Here, desire for wealth, creativity and technology are ascribed to nations of the Middle East and projected onto a screen called freedom. By contrast, the actual "freedom deficit" in the Middle East is said to have negative effects, such as poverty and lack of women's rights.[9] But such lack of personal liberties is the result of economic policy (who knew Bush was such a Marxist?): "These are not the failures of a culture or a religion. These are the failures of political and economic doctrines" (Bush 2003b). Thus, economic freedom (unhindered by "governments [that] still cling to the old habits of central control") is understood as the prerequisite for social and religious freedom. The fight for freedom is, therefore, a fight for a political and economic doctrine that does away with centralized control, in favor of privatized economies, from which will follow other forms of freedom.[10]

Elsewhere, this economic doctrine, applied to international relations, is called "free and fair trade" (Bush 2004a). In the 2002 *National Security Strategy*, free trade is defined as a "moral pillar" which dictates the economic pillar of being able to buy *and sell* what one makes; it is "real freedom, the freedom for a person – or a nation – to make a living" (White House 2002: 18).[11] Importantly, then, one of the main goals of free and fair trade is "to open up new markets for America's entrepreneurs and manufacturers and farmers" (Bush 2004a).[12] So it would seem that economic freedom in other countries includes being open to the American market. Clearly, then, freedom is tied to the American economy, both at home and abroad.

Not only is the fight for freedom invoked to stimulate material desires and ensure the free flow of commodities, but it also regulates and limits that flow. So for instance, in the "Compassionate Conservatism" speech (Bush 2002b), the war on terror (Afghanistan) is used to set up the argument to limit welfare at the domestic level and aid contributions on the international level. This particular speech makes a fascinating argument in which freedom is set up as a particularly American value that can be, and is, *exchanged* for work, money or conformity with other American dictates. Early on in the speech, the audience is interpellated, once again, by the call from history to defend and advance freedom. However, the war on Afghanistan is not simply proclaimed as a war against "tyranny and terror and lawless violence" for all humanity; it is also seen as a war for American values: "Whenever America fights for the security of our country, we also fight for the values of our country." This statement begins a transition from speaking about the war to the main subject matter of the speech, the compassionate conservatism that will lead to the realization of American values and ideals, summed up in the four freedoms. Freedom from poverty is considered a particularly American value.

Such freedom, however, is not to be accomplished through free money, such as welfare or international aid, but rather it is to come as a result of an exchange.[13] On the domestic front, freedom from poverty can be obtained through "work [i.e. workfare] and community and responsibility and the *values that often come from faith*" (Bush 2002b, emphasis mine), with mention of incentives for charitable giving. Thus freedom, at least freedom from poverty, is not "God Almighty's gift to each and every person in the world" (Bush 2003a) as proclaimed a year and a half later, perhaps as a corrective to this earlier speech; it is rather a matter of exchange. The same thing is said on the international front. Nations receiving aid are expected to "end corruption, *to open their markets*, to respect human rights, and to adhere to the rule of law" (Bush 2002b, emphasis mine). Monetary aid that will bring freedom from poverty is only given in exchange for conformity to American demands, including the demand to buy American products, and the demand to follow an American standard of law[14] and behavior.

Here in some ways, freedom acts as a commodity, but one elevated above others as a "universal value." It can be exchanged for labor (workfare, labor forces of foreign markets), money (charitable giving, sales to foreign markets), and American values (faith-based, rights-based, law-based). As a universal value, it acts something like the way Marx describes gold. For Marx, gold is a standard form used to mark the exchange-value of commodities, that is, the labor time they represent. It "acts as a universal measure of value" (Marx 1977: 188). It is, however, a purely imaginary expression of value: "it does not require the tiniest particle of real gold to give a valuation in gold of millions of pounds' worth of commodities" (p. 190). Like gold, freedom, in Bush's discourse, marks the value of labor and can also be exchanged for money (non-gold currency). And like gold, as a universal value against which other things are measured, freedom does not really have to exist anywhere. Because the US can influence market conditions through threat of military force, it can demand freedom without having to have the tiniest little bit of it. This is perhaps why the US can proclaim itself as the model of freedom and can, without ever being called to account for duplicity, make such statements as, "Successful societies limit the power of the state and power of the military... Successful societies protect freedom with

the consistent and impartial rule of law, instead of selecting applying [sic]... Successful societies allow room... for political parties and labor unions and independent newspapers and broadcast media" (Bush 2003b). By this definition, the US can hardly be a successful society, but it does not matter, since freedom is an imaginary value of exchange.

But freedom is even more evasive than gold, because it exists on a cosmic level. It is called into being by history, thus elevating the banal but bloody enforcement of commodity exchange to the level of the immaterial, where it cannot be grasped (nor critiqued). It seems that in late-stage capitalism the commodity fetish has come almost full circle: now the relation between things is projected back onto personified cosmic figures. Perhaps the analogy that Marx makes between the commodity fetish and the "misty realm of religion" has become more than just analogy: the items to be exchanged through markets opened to Americans "appear as autonomous figures endowed with a life of their own, which enter into relations both with each other and with the human race" (Marx 1977: 165).[15] In this cosmic configuration, elevated religious desire and economic desire converge. As fetish, this cosmic relationship substitutes, and perhaps also creates (material) desires (Freud 1953: 20, Freud 1961). As fetish, it mediates those desires and directs their fulfillment (through proper avenues of work and values). As fetish, it regulates and limits certain sets of human relations within the United States and between the United States and other nations.

Desire at the End of History

Plainly, in this discourse, the United States is positioned as capable of leading or prodding the world to freedom. Because it has achieved this imaginary ideal freedom, it overflows with it. It provides means to the fulfillment of all desire. Perhaps this is why Bush has such access to the voice of "history": he and his nation have arrived at the ultimate goal of history, they have reached the end of history, they have crossed to the other side where they can comfortably sit and chat with the all-knowing "history".

The rhetoric is remarkably like that found in Francis Fukuyama's bestseller of the early nineties, *The End of History and the Last Man* (Fukuyama 1992). As I will argue below, the similarity is not merely coincidental; indeed, Fukuyama's book can be read as an indicator of the kind of philosophical subtext on desire and war that might be at work in Bush's rhetoric. Fukuyama's work has generally been understood as proclamation of the triumph of US liberal democracy at the end of history. In a succinct statement found in his earlier essay, "The End of History?", Fukuyama claims that "What we may be witnessing is not just the end of the Cold War, or the passing of a particular period of postwar history, but the end of history as such: that is, the end point of mankind's ideological evolution and the universalization of Western liberal democracy as the final form of human government" (Fukuyama 1989: 4). With the death of communism, Fukuyama argues, all major contradictions have been resolved; it is now simply a matter of waiting for the rest of the world to come into the fold. This view seems to proclaim the victory of global capitalism.

It is in no way surprising that the rhetoric of the present administration should resemble the work of Fukuyama, given that he is a signatory in the statement of principles for The Project for the New American Century[16] (the same think tank that produced the position paper for the Bush administration's military strategy, *Rebuilding America's Defenses: Strategy, Forces and Resources for a New Century* in 2000[17]). Not surprisingly, then, the beginning of the 2002 *National Security Strategy* sounds very much like Fukuyama's proclamation of the end of history:

> The great struggles of the twentieth century between liberty and totalitarianism ended with a decisive victory for the forces of freedom – and a single sustainable model for national success: freedom, democracy and free enterprise . . . For most of the twentieth century, the world was divided by a great struggle over ideas: destructive totalitarian visions versus freedom and equality. That great struggle is over. The militant visions of class, nation, and race which promised utopia and delivered misery have been defeated and discredited . . . We will work to translate this moment of influence into decades of peace, prosperity, and liberty . . . Our goals on the path to progress are clear: political and economic freedom, peaceful relations with other states, and respect for human dignity. (White House 2002: i, 1)

Here, the US stands at the end of history, welcoming and encouraging others also to heed the call of history to step over to the other side, to the realm of neoliberal capitalism.

Though Fukuyama's text has been soundly critiqued in many quarters,[18] it is still worth returning to this text to see how it might illuminate the philosophical presuppositions of the present Republican configuration. The concept of the end of history that he evaluates in the book is one hinted at by Hegel and elaborated on by his influential twentieth-century interpreter, Alexandre Kojève, in his lectures on *The Phenomenology of Spirit*. While Hegel's philosophical system described the dialectic movement of history toward its ultimate goal,[19] Kojève cryptically suggests that the end of history had been reached. Fukuyama frequently comes back to one of Kojève's footnotes, which says, "I was led to conclude from this that the 'American way of life' was the type of life specific to the post-historical period, the actual presence of the United States in the World prefiguring the 'eternal present' future of all humanity" (Kojève 1969: 161)[20] In concurring with Kojève's assessment of the US, Fukuyama is, therefore, generally heralded as a Hegelian/Kojèvian prophet of a particularly American neoliberalism.

Fukuyama might also be considered an apocalyptic prophet. It is worth noting that Hegel's contention that history moves toward an ultimate goal has strong apocalyptic overtones, though sublimated into a philosophical framework.[21] So Fukuyama, interpreting Kojève/Hegel, applies an apocalyptic philosophy to an analysis of an economic system. In so doing, he brings together two powerful desires – religious desire for the end and neoliberal desire for unhindered access to goods and markets. As argued above, these are the desires at work in the cosmic relationship between freedom and history in Bush's rhetoric. (Perhaps not surprisingly, one of Kojève's most influential contributions to the Hegelian project was an elaboration of the role of desire in the dialectic, as is taken up most clearly in the work of Lacan). Assuming that there is something of Fukuyama, and therefore also

of Kojève, in the Bush administration's rhetoric, one might look to Kojève to clarify the philosophical stakes behind the rhetoric that both makes use of and produces religious and economic desire.

The relationship between freedom and history in Bush's rhetoric can be read productively with Kojève's discussion of desire in the dialectical progression of history. For Kojève, interpreting Hegel, time (i.e., historical time) progresses toward an end. But it is a dialectical movement from the future, through the past, to the present, by means of desire. Desire (e.g., desire for freedom) is directed toward an absent future, and thus it is "directed toward an entity that does not exist and has not existed in the real natural world" (Kojève 1969: 134). As such, it is a desire for something other than what is; the present must, therefore, be negated, in order for desire to be fulfilled. As soon as the present is negated, it moves into the realm of the past. The past is, therefore, formed negatively. So in this dialectical movement, says Kojève, desire for the future must negate, even annihilate, a past (pp. 135–8).

In a footnote, Kojève reflects on what makes something a "historic" moment in the present; it is both the impulse *and the ability* to do away with the present, based on past evidence (i.e., memory). He gives the example of Caesar's decision to aim for world domination (the future) in a moment of peace (the present). Caesar's decision is historic only because he is able to enter into the dialectic of time on the basis of *past* abilities to fight and win wars. Thus, in true dialectical fashion, something of what has been negated (the past) must be preserved and carried over into the new present. In other words, the past is not completely annihilated, it cannot be forgotten entirely. The memory of past success is necessary to the creation of the "historic" moment. What is lost or forgotten in the process of negation, however, is any lack of the desired end (here, domination) in the present-becoming-past. What is remembered is only past evidence of having been able to make others conform to one's desire.

Within this logic it would not be surprising to find that a political discourse positioned to evoke ideological and religious desire (for freedom, ideological dominance and the end of history), as well as economic desire (for the American dream and concomitant markets open to American buying and selling), would constantly have both to negate and to affirm the past. This perhaps explains how the Bush administration can continue its triumphal bellicosity amidst constant accusation and scandal. The Kojèvian dialectic shows that "history" can only come into view, can only make its call, by immediately forgetting that there never really was any freedom in the past and by triumphantly remembering the past successes of coercion.

However, the attempt to evoke the desire for freedom *at the end of history* does not quite fit into this philosophical framework. For Kojève, the end of history also marks the end of the dialectic, and therefore, presumably, the end of desire. The function of freedom as commodity fetish, however, shows that desire, both economic and apocalyptic, is a requisite part of capitalist exchange. In a Kojèvian framework, where desire is intimately related to the dialectical progression of history, the end of history would have to entail the end of desire, and therefore of capitalism. According to this line of reasoning, then, the freedom that Bush proclaims – economic freedom desired by all people – can only be the beginning of one more stage in the dialectic.

The Fight unto Death

The fact that a secularized form of religious desire stands in for economic desire in Bush's efforts to secure new markets indicates that, even if unconsciously, his speechwriters do not concur with the contention that the United States' version of liberal democracy marks the end of history, as proposed by Kojève. I would like to look at a point in Bush's public discourse that appears more consciously to contest both the Hegelian/Kojèvian framework in which the dialectic is finally resolved, and the notion that the United States holds freedom out to other nations so that they too can enter into the heavenly realm of the end of history. In the speech on freedom in Iraq and the Middle East, Bush (2003b) again stresses the need to fight for freedom, but he does so in a way that breaks with an understanding that freedom marks the final point in history. In the speech, Bush reminds his audience that "liberty, if not defended, can be lost." He further asserts, in a startlingly philosophical statement, that "the success of *freedom is not determined by some dialectic of history*" (emphasis mine). Instead, freedom is "by definition" determined by "our willingness to sacrifice for liberty." Now given the usual articulacy of the President, one cannot assume that "dialectic" is a word well known to him; nor can one assume it to be part of the colloquial language of his general public. This line cannot, therefore, be read as a casual mistake, or a throwaway line. It is only intelligible if it is understood as a philosophical contention on the part of his speechwriters that freedom does not come through the resolution of the dialectic. The argument of the speech seems to be that any loss of freedom cannot be understood as part of a natural progression through negation to something higher. But what is at stake here in replacing the logic of dialectic with the logic of sacrifice? The stakes seem to have gone up: now it is human life that must be exchanged for freedom. But why? Are Bush's advisors and speechwriters not, like Fukuyama, neo-Hegelian? What precisely is the philosophical contention?

I would suggest that this line marks the philosophical break that the Bush administration makes with neoliberalism, by way of a neoconservative Nietzschean corrective to Kojève.[22] Where neoliberalism understands free trade as a sort of liberal world contract, sufficient to bring about the desired capitalist end of free trade (through globalization, multilateralism, and, of course, quiet military coercion), neoconservatism eschews liberal values of equality and mutual exchange and attempts to re-establish an environment in which a desire to be recognised by others (through imperialism, unilateralism, and overt and celebrated military coercion) can lead to self improvement and excellence (Fukuyama 1992: 304). The philosophical bases for this rupture are outlined in Fukuyama's *End of History and the Last Man*.

For Fukuyama, what is meant by the dialectic is the famous struggle for recognition between master and slave. The question he pursues in the book, posed by Kojève's interpretation of Hegel's master–slave dialectic, is whether or not liberal democracy at the end of history arrives at the mutual recognition attending the resolution of the master–slave dialectic. Fukuyama concludes that liberal democracy's valorisation of universal recognition, or equal rights, does indeed mark the resolution of the master– slave dialectic. His central question, however, is whether such a state of universal recognition would be satisfying. He contends, with Hegel

and Kojève, that the desire for recognition is central to human experience, but he asks "whether liberal democracy adequately satisfies the desire for recognition" (Fukuyama 1992: 289).

Fukuyama does not answer the question of whether liberal democracy is satisfying in the affirmative, but rather presents a critique of universal recognition that is consistent with neoconservative thought. It is well known that Fukuyama trained with Allan Bloom, a disciple of the neoconservative intellectual historian Leo Strauss,[23] but commentators do not usually detail the influence of neoconservatism in Fukuyama's reflection on Kojève.[24] Derrida, for instance, reminds his readers that Fukuyama's book is written in the Straussian tradition, though exploited as "the finest ideological showcase of victorious capitalism in a liberal democracy." In spite of this heritage, says Derrida, the text is ambivalent, "suspensive to the point of indecision," especially in its concluding discussion of responses from the Right and from the Left to the proposition that the US version of liberal democracy marks the end of history (Derrida 1994: 56).[25] I would contend that Fukuyama is not indecisive in the least; rather, he strongly favors the response from the Right. Following a rightist reading of Nietzsche, he asks, "Is recognition that can be universalized worth having in the first place?" (Fukuyama 1992: 301). Indeed, it appears that the central contention of Fukuyama's book is to affirm the right-wing critique of the end of history. Of his two critiques of universal recognition – one propounded by Marx, suggesting that universal recognition has not actually been reached within capitalism, and one offered by Nietzsche – he prefers the latter, which he calls a "more powerful criticism of universal recognition" (p. xxii) arising from the "more profound pole of criticism [of Hegel]" (p. 300).

The "powerful critique" that Nietzsche contributes to Fukuyama's argument is the understanding that because recognition is trivialized within democracy, at the end of history, the "last man" ends up in the same place as the slave in Hegel's master–slave dialectic. Without the struggle for recognition, society degenerates. The last man is complacent and unable to deal with real moral issues, a man without a chest (Fukuyama 1992: 7). The structure of Fukuyama's argument is remarkably similar to that of his teacher, Allan Bloom, in the introduction to the English translation of Kojève's lectures on Hegel:[26]

> But looking around us, Kojève, like every other penetrating observer, sees that the completion of the human task may very well coincide with the decay of humanity, the rebarbarization or even reanimalization of man.... After reading it, one wonders whether the citizen of the universal homogeneous state is not identical to Nietzsche's Last Man... We are led to a confrontation between Hegel and Nietzsche and perhaps, even further, toward a reconsideration of the classical philosophy of Plato and Aristotle, who rejected historicism. (Bloom 1969: xii)[27]

Bloom wonders, perhaps, because Strauss says as much in *On Tyranny*, in his reply to Kojève's comments on his reading of Xenophon's *Hiero*. Strauss writes, "The state through which man is said to become reasonably satisfied is, then, the state in which the basis of man's humanity withers away, or in which man loses his humanity. It is the state of Nietzsche's 'last man'... If the universal and homogeneous state is the goal of History, History is absolutely 'tragic' " (Strauss 1968: 223).

Fukuyama reflects such a reading of Nietzsche when he asks, "If everyone was fully content merely by virtue of having rights in a democratic society, with no further aspirations beyond citizenship, would we not in fact find them worthy of contempt?" He further states:

> A civilization . . . that fanatically seeks to eliminate every manifestation of unequal recognition will quickly run into limits imposed by nature itself. We stand at the close of a period in which communism sought to use state power to eliminate economic inequality, and in doing so undercut the basis of modern economic life. If tomorrow's isothymotic passions [desiring equal recognition (1992: 182)] try to outlaw differences between the ugly and beautiful, or pretend that a person with no legs is not just the spiritual but the physical equal of someone whole in body, then the argument will in the fullness of time become self-refuting, just as communism was. (Fukuyama 1992: 314).

In other words, a liberal democracy that settles for equal recognition will be doomed to the same fate as communism. Clearly then, Fukuyama follows the neoconservative tradition of reading Kojève. But what solutions does he propose?

After outlining the degeneracy of the end of history, Fukuyama accepts a number of what he calls Nietzsche's "acute psychological observations", including "the way in which struggle and risk are constituent parts of the human soul, [and] the relationship between the desire to be greater than others and the possibility of personal excellence and self-overcoming" (Fukuyama 1992: 313). This striving for superiority is "necessary for the creation of anything else worth having in life" (p. 302). In other words, the fight for recognition, the fight for superiority is for Fukuyama, after Nietzsche, central to success, even, in "some degree . . . a necessary precondition for life itself" (p. 315).

Fukuyama's Nietzsche is grafted onto Kojève's understanding of the movement of dialectic as combative. Any real desire, Kojève argues, is desire for social recognition, which engenders the fight unto death. In fact, for Kojève, "desire *is realized* by the action of the fight to death for pure prestige. And this fight is realized by the victory of the master over the slave, and by the latter's work in the Master's service" (Kojève 1969: 144). Desire is, of its nature, bellicose. Of course, the work of the slave in *satisfying* the master's desire is for Kojève what eventually brings about the resolution of the dialectic, but Fukuyama seems to want to interrupt the process, in order to restart the dialectic, and to restart history (Fukuyama 1992: 334).

Fukuyama does not want to give up on liberal democracy, he says. He argues that a liberal democracy will find ways to accommodate the "natural" strivings for superiority that will necessarily emerge.[28] People "will want to risk their lives even if the international state system has succeeded in abolishing the possibility of war" (Fukuyama 1992: 314). Fortunately, says Fukuyama, liberal democracies provide a great deal of internal room for these strivings, including entrepreneurship and sports (pp. 315, 319). However, even these avenues may not be sufficient to satisfy some people's longing for recognition:

> One suspects that some people will not be satisfied until they prove themselves by that very act that constituted their humanness at the beginning of history: they will want to risk their lives in a violent battle, and thereby prove beyond any shadow of a doubt

> to themselves and to their fellows *that they are free*. They will deliberately *seek discomfort and sacrifice*, because the pain will be the only way they have of proving definitively that they can think well of themselves, that they remain human beings . . . A liberal democracy that could fight a short and decisive war every generation or so to defend its own liberty and independence would be far healthier and more satisfied than one that experienced nothing but continuous peace. (Fukuyama: 1992: 329)

In short, only the risk of war can fulfill the striving for superiority that is prerequisite for excellence, and even, for life itself. He also argues that it is in this arena that politicians can gain recognition where otherwise they might not. Thus, "America's 1991 war in the Persian Gulf indicates that a politician like George Bush, inconsistent and constrained on the domestic issues, can nonetheless create new realities on the world stage" (Fukuyama 1992: 318). In short, a leader can lead a country beyond itself into new realities that change the world, by demanding recognition that will inaugurate the fight unto death.

Restarting History

Bush-the-Younger's statement that freedom is not the result of the dialectic of history is consistent with this view. Freedom is *not* that which waits for the world at the end of history, for if it were, it would mark both the resolution of the dialectic and the end of capitalist desire. By contrast, freedom, in the terms in which it is defined by Bush's rhetoric, is the epitome of capitalist desire. Held out as a universal value, it can be read both as a demand for recognition and as a demand for war. It is not the resolution of the dialectic, but rather that which will generate the never quite resolvable dialectic, understood as the continual fight unto death and the ascendancy of the master.

What then can we say about Bush's demand for "our willingness to sacrifice for liberty" (Bush 2003b)?[29] Is it the reassertion of a Christian philosophy over and against a neoconservative Nietzschean philosophy, marking a conflict between Bush's evangelical speechwriter Mike Gerson, and other members of the Bush administration? Perhaps, but it also marks an awareness that a nation cannot gain recognition on the international front without some loss of life. Yet whose life? Whose sacrifice? Clearly, neither Bush nor members of his administration will sacrifice their lives.

Fukuyama conflates the term "sacrifice" with risk; it is that which will assure people that they are more than merely citizens of a democracy, that they are in fact human. But there is something somewhat disingenuous about substituting sacrifice for risk. Within the Hegelian/Kojèvian framework, sacrifice signifies the slave's recognition of, and consequent submission to, the master. Within a Nietzschean framework, sacrifice is the outworking of a slave mentality; it is not, therefore, to be admired. What can be said, then, about the demand that others sacrifice in the name of freedom (freedom to own houses, to have jobs, to go to school)? It seems to me that the demand for sacrifice is, as a demand for recognition of leadership, a request by the nation's leaders for their electorates to recognise that that freedom is theirs to offer. By granting recognition, the population submits. More broadly, it may be a

demand that begins the fight unto death between the ruling class and the citizenry, culminating in a reified class division, in the separation of masters from slaves. Here economic desire, religious desire, and desire for recognition become one and the same: these are desires that can only result in the fight unto death.

In conclusion, it appears that the use of apocalyptic metaphors to motivate economic ends is not benign; the stakes are deadly, both at home and abroad. Moreover, it appears that war, for this administration, is not simply a means to an end; rather, it is the beginning of a new imperialist history. Those interested in strategising against perma-war may wish to consider the bellicose stance of the present administration as a philosophical program rather than as a shocking outbreak of fascistic lunacy. It is my hope that such strategising will take seriously the convergences of religious and economic desire and work to find new metaphors and new philosophical frameworks for resistance.

NOTES

1 Christian Parenti (2003) argues that the Austrian economist F. A. Hayek helped strategize "the modern political right's 'war of ideas.' " Hayek's vision included long range planning (as opposed to engagement in "day-to-day political fights"), and the co-optation of socialist use of utopia as a political motivator. In Parenti's words, "Hayek invites us to reconsider the role of ideas and the long-term timeframe of their impact." Neta Crawford also underlines the importance of 'building the new world conceptually', in her steps to finding a way out of the logic of American empire (Crawford, 2004), 7–8.

2 For an excellent and illuminating analysis of the sustained US drive for empire – embedded in its foreign policy from the beginning of the twentieth century until the present – see Bacevich (2002).

3 For instance, the September 2002 *National Security Strategy* – that major policy paper for the Bush administration known best for advocating "pre-emptive strikes" – claims that the duty of the United States is to "defend liberty and justice because these principles are right and true for all people everywhere" (White House, 2002), 2. The task of policing a "universal" law in the world is consistently framed in the discourse as a divine calling. The chosenness of the US has become so aggrandised in this administration's rhetoric, that in his speech on the first anniversary of 9.11, Bush famously made the same claim about the US that the writer of John's gospel makes about Christ: "America is the hope of all mankind... That hope lights our way. And the light shines in the darkness. And the darkness will not overcome it" (Bush, 2002d). For further analysis of the logic of this citation, see Castelli (2005).

4 As Edward Ingebretsen has pointed out in his work on the apocalyptic roots of American culture, the fear of hidden evil has been part of American life since the time of the first settlers. Early Americans, Ingebretsen argues, were constantly reminded that hell and all forms of evil threatened to intrude at any moment, and of individual susceptibility to entertaining evil. A most terrifying aspect of evil was its ability to creep into the lives of individuals or their neighbors; thus constant guard was kept against it. Interior scrutiny formed good citizens, whose good behavior banished evil and fear (Ingebretsen, 1996), 21–8.

5 As Elizabeth Castelli (2005) has observed, in the 9.11 anniversary speech, history actually converges with God, who is also said to have given "us" the duty and privilege of "defending America and our freedom." Castelli's observation can be extended to the rest of the discourses produced by the Bush administration.

6 See Murphy (2003) for a discussion of Bush's discourse as epideictic rhetoric (i.e., "appeals that unify the community and amplify its virtues") as opposed to the more common deliberative rhetoric of politicians, (i.e., "arguments to justify the expediency or practicality of an action" (p. 609)).

7 "We are in a new kind of war and it requires a new kind of strategy. We will not wait for further attacks; we will not hope for the best. We will strike our enemies before they can strike us again" (Bush, 2003a).

8 A similar connection between the war for freedom and the economy at home is made in the 2004 State of the Union Address. The apocalyptic justification for the war with which the speech begins ("we refuse to live in the shadow of this ultimate danger" (Bush, 2004a)) is followed by the statement that "adversity has also revealed the fundamental strengths of the American economy." These strengths, which appear mainly to be deficits, Bush details by listing his accomplishments and future plans for tax reductions, job creation, and access to education and health care.

9 For an analysis of the question of women's rights as it relates to the apocalyptic discourse of the Bush administration, see Runions (2004).

10 For a discussion of the limits and contradictions in Bush's understanding of freedom and decentralized government, see Singer (2004), 63–89.

11 For analysis of this citation, see Crawford (2004), 5. For an analysis of the trade barriers that Bush has put in place, in spite of his discourse valorizing free trade, see Singer (2004), 126–32.

12 For a history and analysis of the US "strategy of openness," see Bacevich (2002).

13 For a discussion of Bush's decisions on humanitarian aid, with a focus on AIDS aid, see Singer (2004), 119–26.

14 One must also assume that adherence to the rule of law is adherence to law as defined by the US, since it openly denies recognition of other legal bodies, such as the International Criminal Court: "Americans are not impaired by the potential for investigations, inquiry, or prosecution by the International Criminal Court, whose jurisdiction does not extend to Americans and which we do not accept" (White House, 2002), 31.

15 Space does not permit an engagement of Jacques Derrida's gloss of Marx's analogy between commodity fetish and religion as "idealization, autonomization and automatization, dematerialization and spectral incorporation, mourning work coextensive with all work, and so forth" (Derrida, 1994), 166; it may be important at some point to think about the cosmic figure "freedom" in the Bush discourse as it relates to the mourning produced in the work of war. Derrida considers this "return of the religious" in Marx to be symptomatic of a quasi-transcendental messianic structure of experience ("that irreducible movement of the historical opening to the future"), through which he wishes to reclaim the revolutionary potential of Marx (1977) 167–9. For further elaboration of this point, see his response to the critics of *Specters of Marx* in Sprinker (1999), 250–6. I would, at a later date, like to explore Derrida's messianic without the messianism with respect to the problem of apocalyptic language in public discourse.

16 According to his own home page (http://www.sais-jhu.edu/fukuyama/biograph), Fukuyama has been involved in producing Republican ideology and foreign policy since the 1980s. He served on staff for the State Department during the Reagan administration (1981–2, 1989) and worked for the RAND Corporation for much of the eighties and some of the nineties. He is also a signatory in the Project for the New American Century's letter of support for the war on terror: <*http://www.newamericancentury.org/Bushletter.htm*>.

17 Project for the new American Century. *Rebuilding America's Defenses: Strategy, Forces and Resources for a New Century* (Washington DC: Project for the New American Century, 2000): <*http://www.newamericancentury.org/RebuildingAmericasDefenses.pdf*>.

18 For an excellent account of the intellectual history behind the proclamation of the end of history, and a critique of Fukuyama's optimism about capitalist democracy, see Anderson (1992), 279–375.

19 Anderson points out that Hegel nowhere directly posits the *end* of history, though his work strongly moves in that direction (Anderson, 1992), 285–94.

20 Fukuyama seems to ignore Kojève's two following statements: one, that "Man's return to animality appeared no longer as a possibility that was yet to come, but as a certainty that was already present," and two, that he later changed his mind on the point that the US has reached the end of history. For a discussion of the humor of this passage, and a re-reading of it, see Derrida (1994), 71–5.

21 For a reading of Hegel's apocalypticism, see Altizer (2000). For an analysis of the particularly Christian reading of Hegel in *The End of History and the Last Man* (Fukuyama, 1992) see Derrida (1994), 60–1. Derrida also underscores the biblical figures of gospel and promised land found there (pp. 56–8).

22 There has been a great deal of discussion about the neoconservative influence on the Bush administration. For a sampling of the numerous analyses of the effect of neoconservatism on the Bush administration see Carr (2003), Hagan (2003), Milbank (2002), Singer (2004), Tanenhaus (2003); for critiques of such analyses as conspiracy theories (and warnings of the anti-Semitism of some critics of neoconservatism) see Lieber (2003); for an insider's description of neoconservatism see Kristol (2003).

23 For Strauss's influence on neconservatism see Drury (1988), Rozen (2003), Singer (2004); for an insider's perspective on the influence of Strauss see Berkowitz (2003); for Strauss's love of Nietzsche as a strong critic of modernity see Drury (1988), 170–81.

24 Drury points out that Fukuyama must be read as a neoconservative, even though his work was "received as a manifestation of American triumphalism" (Drury, 2004) 180, n. 24.

25 Anderson also calls Fukuyama "deeply equivocal" on this point (Anderson, 1992), 344.

26 A complicating factor in this genealogy is the friendship between Strauss and Kojève. As a protégée of Strauss, Bloom also studied with Kojève. Their philosophical differences show up most clearly in the exchange between Kojève and Strauss in *On Tyranny* (Strauss, 1968). For analysis of these personal and philosophical relationships, see Drury (1994).

27 A return to classical philosophy is, of course, one of the trademarks of neoconservative thought (see Drury, 1988). For an exposition and analysis of the effect of Fukuyama's reading of Hegel through Plato, see Anderson (1992), 50.

28 The focus on nature betrays a Straussian desire to return to "natural" hierarchies, over and against rights-based equalities; see *Natural Right and History* by Strauss (1953). Of interest to biblical scholars, Strauss opens this text with two epigraphs from the Hebrew Bible that would bear some analysis.

29 The demand for sacrifice seems to increase as the war in Iraq goes on. Bush's press conference on April 13, 2004, attests to an increase in the rhetoric of sacrifice (Bush, 2004b).

REFERENCES

Altizer, Thomas J. J. (2000). "Modern Thought and Apocalypticism." in Stein, Stephen J. (ed.), *Encyclopedia of Apocalypticism*, Vol. 3, *Apocalypticism in the Modern Period and the Contemporary Age*. New York: Continuum.

Anderson, Perry (1992). *A Zone of Engagement*. London: Verso.

Bacevich, Andrew J. (2002). *American Empire: The Realities and Consequences of U.S. Diplomacy*. Cambridge, Mass.: Harvard University Press.

Berkowitz, Peter (2003). "What Hath Strauss Wrought: Misreading a Political Philosopher." *The Weekly Standard*, 8/37. Available from: <http://www.weeklystandard.com/Content/Public/Articles/000/000/002/717acusr.asp>.

Bloom, Allan (1969). "Introduction," in Allan, Bloom (ed.), trans. James H. Nichols Jr., *Introduction to the Reading of Hegel: Lectures on the Phenomenology of Spirit*, assembled by Raymond Queneau. Ithaca, NY: Cornell University Press.

Bush, George W. (2002a). "President Delivers State of the Union Address" [Internet]. Washington, DC: The White House; released online 29 January 2002. Available from: <http://www.whitehouse.gov/news/releases/2002/01/20020129-11.html>.

—— (2002b). "President Promotes Compassionate Conservatism" [Internet]. San Jose, Calif.: The White House; released online 30 April 2002. Available from: <http://www.whitehouse.gov/news/releases/2002/04/20020430-5.html>.

—— (2002c). "Remarks by the President in address to the nation" [Internet]. Washington, DC: The White House; released online 6 June 2002. Available from: <http://www.whitehouse.gov/news/releases/2002/06/20020606-8.html>.

—— (2002d). "President's Remarks to the Nation" [Internet]. Ellis Island, NY: The White House; released online 11 September 2002. Available from: <http://www.whitehouse.gov/news/releases/2002/09/20020911-3.html>.

—— (2002e). "Remarks by the President in Address to the United Nations General Assembly" [Internet]. New York, NY: The White House; released online 12 September 2002: <http://www.whitehouse.gov/news/releases/2002/09/20020912-1.html>.

—— (2003a). "President Calls on Senate to Pass American Dream Downpayment Act" [Internet]. Dinuba, Calif.: The White House; released online 15 October 2003. Available from: <http://www.whitehouse.gov/news/releases/2003/10/20031015-10.html>.

—— (2003b). "President Bush discusses freedom in Iraq and Middle East" [Internet]. Washington, DC: The White House; released online 6 November 2003. Available from: <http://www.whitehouse.gov/news/releases/2003/11/20031106-2.html>.

—— (2004a). "State of the Union Address" [Internet]. Washington, DC: The White House; released online 20 January 2004. Available from: <http://www.whitehouse.gov/news/releases/2004/01/20040120-7.html>.

—— (2004b). "President Addresses the Nation in Prime Time Press Conference" [Internet]. Washington, DC: 13 April 2004. Available from: <http://www.whitehouse.gov/news/releases/2004/04/20040413-20.html>.

Carr, David (2003). "White House Listens when Weekly Speaks." *The New York Times*: March, E1.

Castelli, Elizabeth (2005). "Globalization, Transnational Feminisms, and the future of Biblical Critique," in K. Wicker, Musa, Dube, and Althea, Spencer-Miller (ed.), *Feminist New Testament Studies: Global and Future Perspectives*. New York: Palgrave.

Crawford, Neta (2004). "U.S. Foreign Policy Post-September 11: Some Notes for the Barnard Conference: Why?", *Scholar and Feminist Online*, 2/2. Available from: <http://www.barnard.edu/sfonline/reverb/crawfor6.htm>.

Derrida, Jacques (1994). *Specters of Marx: The State of the Debt, the Work of Mourning, and the New International*. New York: Routledge.

Drury, Shadia (1988). *The Political Ideas of Leo Strauss*. New York: St Martin's Press.

—— (1994). *Alexandre Kojève: The Roots of Postmodern Politics*. New York: St Martin's Press.

—— (2004). *Terror and Civilization: Christianity, Politics and the Western Psyche*. New York: Palgrave MacMillan.

Freud, Sigmund (1953). "Three Essays on the Theory of Sexuality." in James Strachey (trans.), *The Standard Edition of the Complete Psychological Works of Sigmund Freud*. London: Hogarth, 125–248.

Freud, Sigmund (1961). "Fetishism," in James Strachey (trans.), *The Standard Edition of the Complete Works of Sigmund Freud*, vol. 21. London: Hogarth, 149–57.

Fukuyama, Francis (1989). "The End of History?", *National Interest*, summer, 16:3–18.

—— (1992). *The End of History and the Last Man*. New York: Free Press.

Hagan, Joe (2003). "President Bush's Neoconservatives were Spawned Right Here in NYC, New Home of the Right-wing Gloat." *The New York Observer*, April: 1.

Ingebretsen, Edward J. (1996). *Maps of Heaven, Maps of Hell: Religious Terror as Memory from the Puritans to Stephen King*. Armonk, NY: ME Sharpe.

Kojève, Alexandre (1969). *Introduction to the Reading of Hegel: Lectures on the Phenomenology of Spirit*, assembled by Raymond Queneau, trans. James H. Nichols, Jr. Ithaca, NY: Cornell University Press.

Kristol, Irving (2003). "The Neoconservative Persuasion: What It Was, and What It Is." *The Weekly Standard*, August, 8/47. Available from: <http://www.weeklystandard.com/Content/Public/Articles/000/000/003/000tzmlw.asp>.

Lieber, Robert J. (2003). "The Neoconservative-Conspiracy Theory: Pure Myth." *The Chronicle of Higher Education*, May: 14.

Marx, Karl (1977). *Capital*, trans. Ben Fowkes vol. 1. New York: Random House.

Milbank, Dana (2002). "Who's Pulling the Foreign Policy Strings?". *The Washington Post*, May:A19.

Murphy, John M. (2003). " 'Our Mission and Our Moment': George W Bush and September 11th." *Rhetoric and Public Affairs*, 6/4:607–32.

Parenti, Christian (2003). "Winning the War of Ideas." *In These Times*, 27/6. Available from: <http://inthesetimes.com/comments.php?id=399_0_1_0_M>.

Rozen, Laura (2003). "Con Tract: The Theory behind Neocon Self-deception." *The Washington Monthly*, October: Available from: <http://www.washingtonmonthly.com/features/2003/0310.rozen.html>.

Runions, Erin (2004). "Biblical Promise and Threat in U.S. Imperialist Rhetoric, Before and After September 11, 2001." *The Scholar and Feminist Online*, 2/2. Available from: <http://www.barnard.edu/sfonline/reverb/runions1.htm>.

Singer, Peter (2004). *The President of Good and Evil: The Ethics of George W Bush*. New York: Dutton.

Sprinker, Michael (ed.), (1999). *Ghostly Demarcations: A Seminar on Jacques Derrida's Specters of Marx*. London: Verso.

Stephanson, Anders (1995). *Manifest Destiny: American Expansionism and the Empire of Right*. New York: Hill and Wang.

Strauss, Leo (1953). *Nature Right and History*. Chicago, Ill: University of Chicago Press.

—— (1968). *On Tyranny: Revised and Enlarged*. Ithaca, NY: Cornell University Press.

Tanenhaus, Sam (2003). "So Right, They're Wrong? The NeoCons who Pull George W Bush's Strings." *Vanity Fair*, 515:114.

White House (2002). *The National Security Strategy of the United States*. Washington, DC: Government Printing Office. Available from: <http://www.whitehouse.gov/nsc/nss.pdf>.

Part III
Empire and Exegesis

INTRODUCTION: Empire and Exegesis

R. S. Sugirtharajah

This section brings together alternative and counter-readings of biblical texts which, like other resistance readings, complicate and fracture the received interpretation and refuse to adopt a simple and single reflection on reality. This is an important advance, though it has its limitations. While postcolonial criticism outside the discipline of biblical studies is significantly energized by poststructuralism, psychoanalysis, and Marxism, biblical scholarship still operates, as demonstrated by these essays, within the framework of a hermeneutics of suspicion.

The section opens with Itumeleng Mosala's essay, "The Implications of the Text of Esther for African Women's Struggle for Liberation in South Africa." Although this essay was written at the height of apartheid, and long before the advent of postcolonialism, it is included because it raises issues which postcolonialism later came to espouse. Namely, it places the biblical books in the heart of the empire, in this case the Persian; it exposes imperial extravagance; it exposes the sacrifice of women's rights in the cause of national struggle; and it is totally silent about the plight of the subalterns.

Laura Donaldson revisits the story of Ruth and undertakes a fascinating reading as a Cherokee woman. She tries to reposition Ruth in the light of the specific cultural and historical predicament of American Indian women. In doing this, she dismantles the dominant readings which have made Ruth an exemplary convert/assimilator. In the process, Donaldson discovers another often under-exegeted indigene character in the text – Orpah, the sister-in-law of Ruth, who returned to her mother's house. Donaldson's contention is that it is Orpah who engenders hope and provides an emancipatory vision for Cherokee woman because it was she who embraced her own clan and cultural traditions.

Philip Chia's essay, "On Naming the Subject: Postcolonial Reading of Daniel 1," finds analogies for the experience of the citizens of Hong Kong under colonial rule in experiences described in the Book of Daniel. In his view, a fourfold strategy is advocated in the text. These – segregation, language, education, and naming – are replayed in the situation in colonial Hong Kong. An agonizing feature is the search for identity and the naming of oneself as the subject or object of the colonizer. The

renaming of Daniel and his friends with Chaldean names is an act of colonization. This is a double bind in the sense that it simultaneously affirms and downgrades them. The experience of Daniel is "too much of an experience of the colonized."

Kari Latvus's essay confronts two empires: one biblical, the Assyrian; and the other modern, the Russian. Latvus notes a strong influence of Babylonian colonial intentions in 2 Kings 24–5, which describes how Judah was fragmented, dispersed, and exposed to a multicultural Orient as a result of the imperial adventures of the Assyrians. In examining the narrative, Latvus advocates the need to decolonize the image of Yahweh, who was once seen as the champion of the poor and source of all life but is now presented as an ally of the colonial power. He also brings to attention how the narrative focuses on maintaining good relations between the ruler and the ruled, promoting the imperial virtues of subordination and loyalty, and renouncing rebellion. Latvus's piece is not a simple exercise in historical reading but a hermeneutical enterprise which sees a parallel between what happened in ancient Israel, and Finland's position with regard to the Russian empire when the people of Finland were forced to preserve cordial relations with the superpower.

Musa Dube's "Rahab Says Hello to Judith: A Decolonizing Feminist Reading" is a contrapuntal reading of two key leading women characters in the Hebrew scriptures. Both Judith and Rahab are presented from a patriarchal perspective and with an imperial agenda in mind. In Musa's view, the character of Judith is reified and restricted. Though she was a champion of anti-imperialism, her opposition to patriarchy is somewhat limited. Postcolonial feminist reading should go beyond the limited crumbs that fall from the table of the patriarchal and imperialist biblical narratives, and search for a wider scriptural understanding which will take into account what Musa calls the oral-Spirit framework, a space to speak new words of justice and liberation. Mosala's Esther and Dube's Judith serve as reminders that women's questions should not be relegated to the margins in the noble cause of achieving national liberation.

Tat-siong Benny Liew's "Tyranny, Boundary and Might: Colonial Mimicry in Mark's Gospel" takes a different turn on Mark. A Hong Kong Chinese, now working in North America, his reading of Mark is energized by his diasporic consciousness, which is sensitive to colonialization and refuses to idealize. Without denying the anti-colonial and liberationist streak embedded in Mark, which was celebrated by the earlier liberation readings, Benny's assertion is that Mark duplicates and internalizes colonial ideology and engages in colonial mimicry. Alarmingly, in Mark, authority is about following orders and commands and the power to wipe out those who do not comply. In other words, Mark occupies an ambivalent and variegated terrain.

Stephen Moore's essay, "Mark and Empire: 'Zealot' and 'Postcolonial' Readings," further explores the irresolute nature of Mark's gospel vis-à-vis the Roman empire. His contention is that the gospel lacks the explicit hostility found in the Book of Revelation. In reifying the figure of Jesus and investing him with absolute authority, Moore wonders whether Mark was replicating imperial ideology by simply substituting Jesus for Caesar, and the empire of God for the empire of Caesar. In his reading, Moore finds that Mark's attitude to Rome is infused with simultaneous enchantment and repulsion. While discovering a deep tension, especially in the apocalyptic section of the gospel, Moore recovers in the story of the Widow's

mite, a voluntary self-disinvestment, an "act of epiphanic extravagance whose immeasurable immoderation thrusts it outside every conventional circle of economic exchange."

Mary Huie-Jolly's essay is an example of how colonial practices produce an idiosyncratic reading. She describes how certain Maoris converted by missionaries, in response to colonial rule which threatened their way of life and annexed their ancestral lands, began to identify themselves with the biblical Jews and to "leave the way of the Son." It was the Johannine Christology depicted in John 5, with its exalted claims for the Son as equal to God and presenting the Jews as the marginal community, which provided the Maoris with an impetus to turn away from the Christianizing efforts of the missionaries. Huie-Jolly makes it clear that, although there is no direct connection between the Johannine and Maori contexts, the claims made for the Son and reinforced in the Churches' creeds prompted the Maoris to identify themselves with the biblical Jews. The identification of their plight with that of the Hebrews of old is another example of how victims of colonialism from non-Semitic cultures saw reflections of their own experience portrayed in the lives of the biblical Jews. Such an identification enabled them to regain self-esteem and redefine themselves in the face of the missionary onslaught.

Mayra Rivera, in her article, "God at the Crossroads: A Postcolonial Reading of Sophia," excavates the divine figure of Sophia, whose origin, identity, and status are enmeshed in scholarly debates which are marked by denial of her true potency. Rivera rehabilitates Sophia as a living hybrid, distinctly foreign and female, manifesting at a crossroads with misfits, mongrels, and mulattos, unsettling assumptions and at the same time opening an avenue for a new hermeneutics of divine wisdom.

None of these re-readings should lull us into believing that the Bible was a counter-imperial document. One should not forget that the same document was used to sanction war, colonialism, annihilation of cultures, annexation of lands, racism, and imperial intentions.

8

The Implications of the Text of Esther for African Women's Struggle for Liberation in South Africa

Itumeleng J. Mosala

Introduction

There exists a great deal of confusion concerning what exactly is meant by Liberation Theology. In part, the confusion relates to the use of terms, and in two different ways. First, there is the failure to distinguish between Liberation Theology and Theology of Liberation. Liberation Theology refers to the Latin American form of the Theology of Liberation. It is associated with the names of activist scholars such as Segundo, Gutiérrez, Assmann, Bonino, etc. By contrast, the term Theology of Liberation is generic and denotes a movement of Third World people involved in a struggle to break the chains of cultural-religious imperialism that help to perpetuate their political and economic exploitation.

The second form of the terminological confusion is conceptual, involving a discourse imperialism of a certain kind. At first sight, there may seem to be no distinction between this form of terminological confusion and the first. There is here a tendency to refer to all Third World theologies of the poor and oppressed peoples as Liberation Theologies, thus subsuming them under the Latin American version of the Theology of Liberation. This mistake is made mostly, though by no means exclusively, by white radical people who identify culturally more with the European descendants of Latin America than with Third World people. Cornel West raises the question of the political implications of this cultural preference of the political Left when he writes:

> For oppressed colored [black] peoples, the central problem is not only repressive capitalist regimes, but also oppressive European civilizing attitudes. And even Marxists who reject oppressive capitalist regimes often display oppressive European civilizing

First published in *Semia*, 59 (1992): 129–37.

> attitudes toward colored peoples. In this sense, such Marxists, though rightly critical of capitalism, remain captives of the worst of European culture. (1981: 256)

In addition to the confusion of terms, it is not being extreme to suspect a good deal of ideological distortion, that is, a deliberate misunderstanding that seeks to make a mockery of or to obscure things, in the face of which a simple apology for the Theology of Liberation would be grossly inappropriate. This is so not only because this theology has been in existence for so long that it is now an inescapable reality, but also because so many significant strides have already been made in developing it. In the case of South Africa, black theologians have been at work for more than a decade now wrestling with many issues of the nature, the method, the specific form, the epistemology, the sources and the goals of the Black Theology of Liberation. More recently, the question of the Black Feminist Theology of Liberation has emerged as a high priority on the agenda of Black Theology.

For the reason, therefore, of wanting to get on with business of *doing* Black Theology as opposed to simply *apologizing* for it, as well as for the reason of giving priority to a Black Feminist theological discourse, I have chosen to address the topic of the implications of Esther for African women's struggle for liberation in South Africa.

Reading the Bible in South Africa

That the Bible is a thoroughly political document is eloquently attested to by its role in the Apartheid system in South Africa. No other political or ideological system in the modern world that I know of derives itself so directly from the Bible as the ideology of Apartheid. The superiority of white people over black people, for example, is premised on the divine privileging of the Israelites over the Canaanites in the conquest texts of the Old Testament.

For this reason, in South Africa, all manner of theological sophistry has been produced by way of countering this embarrassing use of the Bible. The dominant opposition discourse against this way of using the Bible has been the liberal humanist one. The key characteristic of this oppositional perspective has not been its fundamental disapproval of the conquest texts of the Old Testament. Rather, this model concurs with the conservative model in its approval of the conquest texts, but disagrees with the Apartheid ideologues' interpretation of them.

Thus in effect a biblical hermeneutics of textual or authorial collusion/collaboration, rather than one of struggle or revolt, dominated the debate concerning the reading of the Bible. Increasingly, therefore, biblical appropriation in South Africa became alienating to Blacks as their reality constantly contradicted their supposed inclusion in the biblically-based love of God.

Consequently, the struggle of the 1960s, which led to the exile, imprisonment and banishment of many Blacks and their organizations, notwithstanding God's love for them witnessed to in the Bible, produced a crisis in black people's self-insertion in the story of the Bible. The rise of Black Theology, which, like its counterpart – Liberation Theology – in Latin American, grounded itself in the liberation stories of the Bible, signified black people's discursive attempt to deal with this crisis. This new

reading of the Bible by black people themselves in the light of the struggle for liberation would attempt to argue that liberation and not conquest or oppression was the key message of the Bible.

Black Theology and Liberation Theology's biblical hermeneutics was a product of a crisis situation and not of a revolt on the part of the readers. In South Africa it was not until the post-1976 period, when black people seem to have looked death in the face and come to terms with it in their struggle against the forces of Apartheid, that revolutionary reading practice became an integral part of the social insurgency of the black masses and a necessity of the organic location of its subjects in the context of that insurgency.

The new and developing biblical hermeneutics of liberation differs from the liberal humanist tradition in that it represents a theoretical and not simply a moral mutation from ruling class hermeneutics. Such new reading of the Bible, particularly in the context of South Africa, would concur with Terry Eagleton when he says, in support of what in literary criticism has come to be know as the "Revolt of the Reader" movement:

> That readers should be forcibly subjected to textual authority is disturbing enough; that they should be insultingly invited to hug their chains, merge into empathetic harmony with their oppressors to the point where they befuddledly cease to recognize whether they are subject or object, worker, boss, or product is surely the ultimate opiate. (1986: 182)

A study of Esther's relevance for African women's liberation struggle will need to take into account the tradition of the revolt of the reader that is becoming part of Black Theology's liberation praxis. Not only will this hermeneutics refuse to submit to the chains imposed on it by the biblical exegetes of Apartheid, or those of the liberal humanist tradition including its black and liberation theology versions, but it will contend against the "regimes of truth" (West 1985: 120) of these traditions as they manifest themselves in the text of the Bible itself.

The Biblical Scholarship of Esther

Most studies of the book of Esther are preoccupied with questions of its religiosity, canonical status, historicity and purpose. The problem with these studies is not that they address themselves to these questions but that they rely heavily on the text itself not only for information but also for the theoretical frameworks with which the text must be interpreted. Thus most works simply retell the story, assess the obvious irreligiosity of the text and confirm the book's own confession of its purpose.

Traditional scholarship does, however, raise crucial issues which a biblical hermeneutics of liberation cannot ignore. Norman Gottwald, for instance, addresses the question of the plot of the story, "replete with dramatic reversals" (561) which it is important to note in order to understand the rhetorical devices employed by the dominant ideology of the text. It is also crucial to observe concerning the historicity of the book that:

> The archaic placement of the story in the Persian court is accomplished with considerable knowledge of its inner workings and customs, but there are so many historical inaccuracies and improbabilities that the work cannot be taken at face value. The story may draw on memories of conflicts over Persian policies toward the Jews in which the Jews serving in the imperial court were involved, but the actual setting of the narrator is in the Maccabean-Hasmonean era. This is indicated by several lines of evidence: the intensity and bitterness of the Jewish–Gentile conflicts in the book which are pictured as "fights to the finish," the lack of external references to the book until late Hellenistic times, and the very late appearance of Purim as recognized Jewish festival. (Gottwald: 562)

Historical-critical scholarship provides these insights which cannot be ignored by newer exegetical and hermeneutical methods. It must be noted, however, that traditional scholarship consistently fails to draw the ideological implications of its historical and literary studies. This is because it is often in ideological collusion with the text. A criticism that sets itself the task of serving the cause of human liberation must overcome this limitation. For as Eagleton rightly argues:

> The task of criticism . . . is not to situate itself within the same space as the text, allowing it to speak or completing what it necessarily leaves unsaid. On the contrary, its function is to install itself in the very incompleteness of the work in order to *theorise* it – to explain the ideological necessity of those "not-saids" which constitute the very principle of its identity. Its object is the unconsciousness of the work – that of which it is not, and cannot be, aware. (1976: 89)

African Women's Struggle for Liberation

The hermeneutical weapons of struggle of African women must of necessity issue out of the specificity of their praxis within what Cornel West calls the process of "critical negation, wise preservation, and insurgent transformation of the black lineage which protects the earth and projects a better world" (1985: 124).

In the South African situation black women's struggle takes at once the form of a gender, national, and class struggle. The oppression and exploitation of black women operates at all those levels. What is more, these dimensions of African women's struggle span different historical periods and social systems each of which has inflected this struggle in particular ways.

Contemporary African women are products of pre-capitalist semi-feudal, colonial and settler-colonial monopoly capitalist racist social systems, on the one hand, as well as of heroic anti-sexist, anti-colonial, anti-racist and anti-capitalist struggles in South Africa, on the other hand. At different times and in different ways aspects of these processes and struggles were dominant or subservient in determining who African women were and how they would wage their struggle.

Thus, given this complex nature of African women's struggle, a biblical hermeneutics arising out of such a struggle can hardly be simplistic. It is rather akin to the program that West suggests for revolutionary black intellectuals. He writes:

> The new "regime of truth" to be pioneered by black thinkers is neither a hermetic discourse (or set of discourses), which safeguards mediocre black intellectual produc-

> tion, nor the latest fashion of black writing, which is often motivated by the desire to parade for the white bourgeois intellectual establishment. Rather it is inseparable from the emergence of new cultural forms which prefigure (and point toward) a post-Western civilization. (1985: 122)

A hermeneutics of liberation which is envisaged for an African women's struggle will be at once a human, African and feminist hermeneutics of liberation; it will be *polemical* in the sense of being critical of the history, the devices, the culture, the ideologies and agendas of both the text and itself; it will be *appropriative* of the resources and victories inscribed in the biblical text as well as its own contemporary text; it will be *projective* in that its task is performed in the service of a transformed and liberated social order (for these terms, see Eagleton 1981: 113).

Reading the Text of Esther

A Feudal-Tributary Text. The social formation implied by the text of Esther is clearly a kind of feudal or tributary system. Chapter 1 describes the social and political topography in the Persian Empire which patently presupposes the tributary mode of production; a hierarchical political structure with the monarch – *melek* – at the head of the royal ruling class, followed by the chiefs and governors (*śārîm*) still within the ruling nobility (vv. 1–3); then follow the non-royal ruling class factions, some of whom may be properly designated middle class, the influential sector – probably by virtue of its property ownership – advisors and people of high office (*gĕdôlîm, ḥăkāmîm* and *yōsĕbîm*, vv. 5, 13–14). The Queen (*malkâ*) is of course a member of the royal nobility, but even in a fairly straightforward descriptive text like chapter 1 her insertion into the ruling class is gender-structured (vv. 10–11), in that mention of her necessitates the royal summoning of seven eunuchs, symbolizing the private property character of the sexuality of the king's wife. In fact, the fundamental problematic of this chapter as indeed of the whole text of Esther is the *gender structuring of politics*.

The feudal social relations of the Persian Empire as articulated in this text reflect two forms of oppression and exploitation. The one form is present by its absence; it is represented by the "not-said" of the text. This form of oppression is signified in the verses of chapter 1 that describe the use to which the surplus production of the economy was put. In typical feudal and tributary fashion, surplus was squandered on non-productive luxury goods and a luxurious life-style among the ruling classes. None of it was invested in productive activities or technologies in order to enable development to take place. More importantly, verses 5–9, which describe this wasteful expenditure of the economic products, simultaneously function to obscure the social relations of production on which this consumptionist practice is premised. It mystifies the fact that behind these luxurious goods and extravaganza lie exploited, oppressed and dispossessed peasants, serfs, and sub-classes. This text, which is otherwise excellent in its provision of socio-economic data, is eloquent by its silence on the conditions and struggles of the non-kings, non-office holders, non-chiefs, non-governors and non-queens in the Persian empire.

The second form of oppression is patriarchy. This specific kind of oppression is an inherent part of the structure of feudal society. This central thrust of the book begins, in chapter 1, with the question of the anti-patriarchal revolt of Queen Vashti. The text's agenda is spun around the view, generated by the text itself and representing its dominant ideology, that the audacity of one woman unleashed the political possibilities reflected approvingly in the rest of the book. All this, however, is located in and refracted through a feudal social-structural arrangement, producing a thoroughly feudal text.

African women, who are themselves products and victims of past feudal legacies and are presently historical subjects in the context of transformed but pervasive tributary/feudal practices under capitalism, understand the specificity of this form of oppression. Further, they recognize that this oppression cannot simply be subsumed under other kinds of oppression such as capitalist or colonial oppression. For this reason the revolt of Queen Vashti represents a form of struggle with which an African biblical feminist hermeneutic of liberation must identify. It does not accept the implicit condemnation of Vashti by the text, and eschews the technique whereby her revolt is used as a reason for the rise of an apparently more acceptable queen. This identification is possible only on the basis of a biblical hermeneutics of struggle.

A survival text. The book of Esther builds its story around the memory of very difficult times under colonial exile. The specific lesson it seeks to draw attention to revolves around the struggle for survival. In particular, two forms of survival are accented in this story: cultural and national survival. Needless to say, these two types of survival are inseparable, though not identical.

The material conditions of the practice of survival presupposed by the text are political powerlessness, economic exploitation, cultural and national alienation. The text proposes its own solution. It suggests a pure survival strategy, which is not underpinned by any liberative political ideology. According to this solution Esther gets incorporated into the feudal haven of the King, Mordecai is appointed an administrator in the colonial political machinery and later an even higher honor is given him. Through the cooperation of these two figures the rest of the oppressed Jewish community manage to survive the odds against them, and in fact find themselves in a position where they outpace the Persians at their own game.

The price that the oppressed pay for this turn of events favorable for them is at least two-fold. Firstly, the oppressed must be seen to have bought heavily into the dominant ideology in order that their survival struggle should find approval. In chapter 9 this ideological capitulation is expressed in three terse but powerful repetitious statements: v. 10, "However, there was no looting"; v. 15, "But again, they did no looting"; v. 16, "But they did no looting." This principle of upholding the sanctity of property over the life of people is well known as part of ruling-class ideology. The final chapter of the book of Esther exposes the politics of this ideology when it summarizes the thrust of its discourse:

> King Xerxes imposed forced labor on the people of the coastal regions of his empire as well as on those of the interior.... Mordecai the Jew was second in rank only to King Xerxes himself. He was honored and well-liked by his fellow-Jews. He worked for the good of his people and for the security of all their descendants. (10:1, 3)

Secondly, in this book the survival of the group is achieved first and foremost by the alienation of Esther's gender-power and its integration into the patriarchal structures of feudalism.

A patriarchal text. More than being a feudal and survival discourse, the book of Esther is a patriarchal text. There are at least three objections that a biblical hermeneutics of liberation must raise against it. These three are related to each other and to the questions raised in relation to the text's feudal and survival character.

Firstly, the text's choice of a female character to achieve what are basically patriarchal ends is objectionable. The fact that the story is woven around Esther does not make her the heroine. The hero of the story is Mordecai who needless to say gives nothing of himself for what he gets. Esther struggles, but Mordecai reaps the fruit of the struggle. African women who work within liberation movements and other groups will be very familiar with these kinds of dynamics. A truly liberative biblical hermeneutics will struggle against this tendency.

Secondly, the book of Esther sacrifices gender struggles to national struggles. In the name of the struggle for the national survival of the Jewish people it disprivileges the question of gender oppression and exploitation. The matter of the subsumption of some struggles under others is a serious issue of discourse imperialism. In the book of Esther this problem is especially unacceptable given the purely nationalist character of the national struggle. The Maccabean-Hasmonean revolution which probably underlies the nationalist struggle of the text of Esther is known to have replaced Greek Hellenism with Jewish Hellenism.

Thirdly, the discourse of Esther suppresses class issues, including the class character of cultural practices. The feast of Purim, for example, which represents the principal cultural benefit of the Esther revolution, is not located in class terms in such a way that proper ideological choices can be made about it. In this it is very much like many cultural practices that seem inherently autocratic in the demands they place on their people.

Conclusion

This essay has tried to take seriously Elisabeth Schüssler Fiorenza's critique of what she calls the biblical "hermeneutics of consent" (15 and *passim*). In taking this critique seriously it has argued for the need for a cultural-materialist biblical hermeneutics of struggle. Such a hermeneutics will raise questions of the material, ideological and cultural conditions of production of the text. It is argued here that it is only when such questions are raised that the political issues affecting nations, women, races, age groups, and classes will receive proper treatment in the interpretation of the Bible.

The conviction that I have articulated elsewhere must be reiterated here, namely, that oppressed communities must liberate the Bible so that the Bible can liberate them. An oppressed Bible oppresses and a liberated Bible liberates (Mosala: 193).

REFERENCES

Eagleton, Terry (1976). *Criticism and Ideology: A Study in Marxist Literary Theory.* London: NLB.
—— 1981. *Walter Benjamin: or Towards a Revolutionary Criticism.* London: Verso.
—— 1986. *Against the Grain: Essays 1975–1985.* London: Verso.
Gottwald, Norman (1985). *The Hebrew Bible: A Socio-Literary Introduction.* Philadelphia: Fortress.
Mosala, Itumeleng J. (1989). *Biblical Hermeneutics and Black Theology in South Africa.* Grand Rapids: Eerdmans.
Schüssler Fiorenza, Elisabeth (1984). *Bread Not Stone.* Boston: Beacon.
West, Cornel (1981). "The North American Blacks," in S. Torres and J. Eagleson (eds), *The Challenge of Basic Christian Communities: Papers from the International Ecumenical Congress of Theology, February 20–March 2, 1980, São Paulo Brazil.* Maryknoll, NY: Orbis, 255–7.
—— (1985). "The Dilemma of the Black Intellectual." *Cultural Critique*, 7: 109–24.

9

Rahab Says Hello to Judith: A Decolonizing Feminist Reading

Musa W. Dube

Rahab, clad in her prostitute attire, is on her way from seeing the spies off, soon after she had misdirected the soldiers of Jericho. Judith, in her tiara and with her servant, is hurriedly walking back to Bethulia, carrying the heavy and bloody head of Holofernes, the army general. The two women unexpectedly bump into each other. For a moment, they stand face to face in silence. Under the moonlight, Judith catches a momentary glimpse of Rahab's naughty and brief smile. Judith smiles back nervously. In that split of a second, both women are startled to see the self reflected in the other's face. As Judith turns and walks slowly away, Rahab says, "Hello, Judith!"

Postcolonial Feminist Communities and Spaces of Reading

Postcolonial feminist readers in biblical studies are part of the communities that struggle for liberation in the Two-Thirds World and elsewhere. The struggle for liberation of postcolonial feminist readers is located within the framework of resisting global and national structures of oppression – be they politically, economically, socially, or culturally based. Since gender oppression pervades all sectors of life, postcolonial feminist readers add gender analysis to the struggle of Two-Thirds World communities of resistance to ensure that national and international efforts of establishing justice do not sideline gender justice. Postcolonial feminists thus ask how various forms of national oppression affect women and men, how international forms of oppression affect men and women, how gender oppression functions with other forms of oppression such as class, race, ethnicity, age, and sexual orientation. They also propose various ways of reading that will chart social justice and that take on gender justice in national and international relations.

First published in Fernando Segovia, *Toward a New Heaven and a New Earth*. Maryknoll, Ky.: Orbis Books, 2003, 54–72.

Insofar as biblical texts are concerned, postcolonial feminist struggles for liberation function within communities of faith that embrace these texts as normative and where these texts are read side by side with other normative traditions, be they religious or not, be they written or not. Postcolonial feminist readers of biblical texts and other "World" texts are, therefore, working with those communities of faith that seek liberation and justice. Within the academy, this includes being in solidarity with other feminist and liberation theologians of various backgrounds. Yet postcolonial feminist readers not only dialogue with feminist and liberation theologians in the biblical guild; they also challenge Western feminists to extend the horizons of their liberation discourse to acknowledge the postcolonial condition of our world,[1] and they challenge Two-Thirds World liberation theologians to add the search for gender justice in liberation rhetoric.[2] Postcolonial feminist readers find their impetus within these various settings and communities of readers for liberation. It is within these spaces of those who are searching earnestly for liberation that postcolonial feminist discourse has hope for planting seeds for a better future, a better world.

My postcolonial feminist hermeneutics is historically based and informed by African Independent Churches (AICs) communities of faith and struggle.[3] These are churches that began as protest movements against colonial oppression and exclusion. The AICs were founded by an African woman.[4] Women in the AICs articulated their faith by seeing themselves as part of the national struggle for liberation, the struggle against colonial oppression. They saw themselves as belonging to the Christian and African faith. They did not feel inadequate for full involvement in searching for just national and international relationships, nor did they regard African religions as pagan traditions. AICs women lit the torch for me as well as for other African women theologians and biblical scholars. By their practices they began to open a political space and to build communities of resistance within which women could seek national and international justice without sacrificing the feminist search for gender justice.

Within this space of faith and political commitment to the struggle for liberation, postcolonial feminist readers of African background/s seek to establish how biblical texts depict international relations: Do they provide us with any paradigm for relations of liberating interdependence in economic, political, and cultural spheres? Or do they provide for oppressive relations, and, if so, how can our reading practices transform them into liberating texts? We ask how biblical texts depict gender relations: Do they endorse gender oppression, or do they provide us with any paradigm of gender justice in economic, political, cultural, and social spheres? We ask how biblical texts interact with our indigenous texts/beliefs: Do they provide for oppression, liberation, or both in all spheres of life and for both genders? In short, postcolonial feminist readers of various background/s are located within the liberation communities of the Two-Thirds World by insisting that gender justice must permeate all our plans and projects of liberation.

It is on these grounds that, in my postcolonial feminist strategy of reading the Bible, I pose questions such as the following:[5]

- Does this text have a clear stance against the political imperialism of its time?
- How does imperialism affect men and women of ancient and present times?

- Does this text encourage travel to distant and inhabited lands? If so, how does it justify itself? Who travels and why? To which side of the text am I journeying as a reader?
- How does this text construct difference: Are there dialogue and mutual interdependence or condemnation of all that is foreign?
- Does this text employ gender representations to construct relationships of subordination and domination? If so, which side am I reading from: the colonizer, the colonized, or the collaborator? If I concentrate on patriarchal analysis of the text, does this translate to a decolonizing act?
- How can one reread this text for relationships of liberating interdependence between genders, and among races and other social categories of our worlds?

Such questions shall inform my postcolonial feminist reading of Judith, as I proceed to interrogate the manifestation of the forces of patriarchy and imperialism in the text, how the text uses the female body, the characters and readers of the text, and ways of reading that promote the human rights of all and the dignity of all creation. The study will be divided into four parts. First, I focus on the early chapters of Judith, highlighting imperial oppression in the text and how such oppression affects women and men, including how it works with patriarchy. Second, I interrogate the use of gender to articulate positions of subordination and domination in Judith. Third, I examine the character of Judith herself by asking whether she resists both imperialism and patriarchy. Finally, I bring together the characters of Judith and Rahab for purposes of comparison. I conclude the study by searching for liberating strands in Judith.

Establishing the Imperial Setting and Context in the Text

In my postcolonial feminist reading of the text, establishing the presence of imperialism is important. This approach underlines imperialism and its manifestation of colonialism as a form of oppression in international relations of both the past and today. Imperialism/colonialism is thus a subject of attention because it oppresses both women and men, but above all because it subjects women and other marginalized groups to multiple forms of oppression by working with national patriarchal forms of oppression and the imported forms of patriarchy.

In the book of Judith, one needs no special pleading to highlight imperialism in the text and its effects on women and men in colonized and targeted colonies. The book begins by painting a vivid setting of the imperial powers of oppression: "It was the twelfth year of the reign of Nebuchadnezzar, who ruled over the Assyrians" (1:1). The reigning emperor is at war with Arphaxad and calls for assistance from Persia to Ethopia. Those who resist are subject to his military might. Nebuchadnezzar sends his general, Holofernes, with the following message, "Thus says the Great King, the lord of the whole earth. . . . March out against all the land to the west . . . for I am coming against them . . . and will cover the whole face of the earth. . . . You shall go and seize all their territories for me in advance" (2:5–10). The latter instruction identifies Nebuchadnezzar as a colonialist proper – that is, his imperialism includes taking possession of foreign geographical areas. Nebuchadnezzar further swears by

his own power to accomplish his plan: "For as I live," he says, "and by the power of my kingdom, what I have spoken I will accomplish" (2:12). With these instructions, Holofernes "set out . . . to cover the whole face of the earth" (2:19). He "ravaged," "plundered," "surrounded," "destroyed," "burned" tents, towns, cities, and lands; he "seized territory" and "killed everyone who resisted him" (2:21–7). So great was his imperial military power and so ruthless was his destruction that many targeted nations realized that their destruction was inevitable if they resisted. They thus sent messengers of peace and surrendered themselves and their belongings to the imperial power (3:1–7).

Imperial presence is attested in this narrative also by the amount of traveling, the type of travelers, and the impact of such traveling on those who are visited. The text gives us a vivid image of Holofernes and his army as powerful travelers. They travel with the power of the sender, Nebuchadnezzar. They are so powerful that they can enter foreign and autonomous nations and dispossess the inhabitants of their political, cultural, and economic power (2:21–7). They inspire terror (2:28; 4:2) and seemingly execute death randomly on their targeted victims (2:23–7). These powerful travelers are notably male. Yet there are other travelers in this narrative, including powerless travelers, who travel to meet and welcome Holofernes (3:1–7); those who will be dispossessed (2:9); Judith and her servant, who take on the ticket of deceit to trick the powerful (chaps. 10–13).

As readers, we are somehow travelers along with the characters of the narrative. Which kind of travelers are we?[6] Which kind of travelers do we wish to be? Are we the empire of Nebuchadnezzar reaching out? Are we the powerful army that covers the whole face of the earth? Are we the powerless nations that come to lie prostrate before the powerful to surrender all their human rights? Are we Judith, the powerless heroine, who takes it upon herself to resist the power of Holofernes? If we travel with Judith to the camp, is it because we want to kill Holofernes because he represents imperialism or because he is a man who represents patriarchal power, or both? This is a question well worth pondering. Further, in our current days of global mobilization, marked by pronounced power disparities, which side of power do we travel as feminist biblical readers? Perhaps we wish to mark new and different routes – how different are they?

Indeed, the journeys of Holofernes bring him and his army to Israel, a nation that decides to resist this ruthless power. By their resistance the nation of Israel marked itself for death, for Nebuchadnezzar had so commanded (2:11). Their towns are besieged – among them, Bethulia, where the main character of the book, Judith, resides.

Historicity of the imperial setting of Judith

In his reading of the book of Judith, André LaCocque notes that the book is replete with "intentional historical and geographical blunders" and that "it accumulates deliberate anachronisms."[7] Studies of the book of Judith find that the narrative interweaves different historical events, places, and people without observing their correct date and setting. The narrative also creates new places and characters that cannot be identified with any historical persons or events. For example, Nebuchadnezzar was not a ruler of Assyria and did not rule from Nineveh; he was an earlier emperor based in Babylon, who sacked Israel and forced people into exile in the year

587 BCE (2 Kgs. 24–5). Moreover, the emperors of Babylon, Assyria, and Persia never requested to be worshiped until Alexandrian imperial times and Ptolemy V; Holofernes and Bagoas are historically identified as Persian rather than Assyrian or Babylonian; places such as Put and Lud (2:23), Geba (3:10), Kona, Belmain, Choba, and Aesora (4:4), and Bethulia (4:6), among others, cannot be located.

The question, however, is: What does the narrative communicate by interweaving different events, places, persons, and times? By equating the Babylonian emperor Nebuchadnezzar with the Assyrian Empire, by equating the imperial worship of Alexandrian times (Ptolemy V) with Nebuchadnezzar, and by identifying Persian military figures with the Assyrian Empire – all centuries apart – the narrative dramatizes the perversity of imperialism in ancient times. It underlines the imperial setting in the biblical text as a whole, thereby forcing the readers to ponder this form of oppression in our current world and to realize that one's deeds can easily identify one with emperors regardless of the place where or when one lives.

Further, the characterization of Nebuchadnezzar and the acts of Holofernes vividly underline imperialism as an oppressive institution. Nebuchadnezzar is supposedly angry with the "whole region"; he plans to take revenge "on the whole territory" and to "kill . . . all the inhabitants," "every one" in numerous foreign nations (1:12). People have been marked for either subjugation or death. When he gives his instructions to Holofernes, Nebuchadnezzar describes himself as "the lord of the whole earth" (2:5). His troops, he says, should march against "all the land" (2:6), "cover the whole face of the earth" (2:7), and "lead them away captive to the ends of the whole earth" (2:9). Holofernes, his general, has been instructed to "seize all their territory for [him]" (2:10) and to commit to the sword all who resist. In these phrases the imperial setting of Judith is graphically conveyed, for the narrative spells out that Nebuchadnezzar grants himself "unlimited" access to other nations and their resources. René Maunier correctly notes: "This is the conception of Empire . . . to know no bounds."[8] Thus, Nebuchadnezzar, on the basis of military muscle, appropriates for himself the right to enter all nations, to dispossess all women and men, and to kill those who resist. The texts demonstrate that he knows no boundary.

Glory, gold, and God

On first reading, Nebuchadnezzar's military expeditions seem to be senseless acts of seeking military glory. He is allegedly moved by anger and revenge (2:6–7), yet it quickly becomes clear that imperialism has an economic (gold) and a cultural side. For example, Holofernes is instructed to "seize all their territory" (2:10) for the emperor. The territory of a nation not only constitutes a physical piece of land but also contains the economic and cultural resources of a people. Those who are subjugated and stripped of territory lose political as well as economic and cultural power, as is vividly demonstrated by those who choose to surrender in 3:1–8:

> We the servants of Nebuchadnezzar, the Great King, lie prostrate before you. Do with us whatever you will. See, our buildings and *all* our land and *all* our wheat fields and our flocks and herds and *all* our encampments lie before you; do with them as you please. Our towns and their inhabitants are also your slaves; come and deal with them

> as you see fit . . . and *all* in the countryside welcomed him with garlands and dances and tambourines. Yet he demolished *all* their shrines and cut down their sacred groves; for he had been commissioned to destroy *all* the gods of the land, so that all nations should worship Nebuchadnezzar alone, and that *all* their dialects and tribes should call upon him as a god. (Emphasis mine.)

This passage shows that imperial projects are propelled not so much by the simple desire of showing military power but rather by economic forces. This is the "gold" face of imperialism. Nebuchadnezzar possesses everything they had – lands, people, property.

This is often accompanied by what some have characterized as the "God" factor of imperial claims. Thus, the narrative depicts Holofernes as destroying the religious/cultural symbols of his victims in order to install the religion of the colonizer. For imperialism, this is an integral strategy of subjugation. Imperialism must take control of both the land and the minds of the subjugated by suppressing the local religious.[9] This is so because, if the religious/cultural symbols of the subjugated are left intact, they can serve as a potential weapon of resistance. Faith could then become a space for national unity and autonomy against the colonizer.

In sum, in the Book of Judith imperial oppression is depicted as using the following strategies of conquest: military might (2:21–27), intimidation (2:28; 4:2), exile (1:9), dispossession and cultural assimilation (3:1–8). While these form the three G's – God, Gold, and Glory – that often propel imperial projects, there is a fourth "G" to be found in such projects as well, namely, gender, which tends to be neglected in studies of imperialism. From the point of view of feminism, the reader should ask such questions as the following: What happens to women in these dispossessed nations, given that under "normal" circumstances they are more often than not denied access to economic resources by patriarchal structures? What happens to their cultural status, given that they are "usually" at the lowest rung of power? What is the situation of women in the colonizing nations? How is the female body used in colonial contexts and rhetoric? Such questions I should like to address by interrogating the text of Judith 1–7 concerning women in the colonized and colonizing nations.

God, Gold, Glory, and Gender

It is a feminist tradition in biblical studies to focus on passages that feature women, as attested by our current women/feminist commentaries. Even the choice to focus on the Book of Judith in this article reflects this trend. No doubt the method has furthered the feminist struggle by highlighting women as both victims and agents of liberation in the text, but the approach seems to imply that passages that do not feature women characters are less important to the feminist search for justice. The approach seems to neglect the fact that gender constructions pervade all social spheres of life. Following the tradition of interpretations that focus on women characters, most feminist readers of Judith in the academy tend to concentrate on Judith herself and her position in relation to her subversion or endorsement of patriarchy. When they do touch on the first part of the book, chaps. 1–7, it is either in passing or in preparation for a study of

the character Judith in chaps. 8–16, as a figure who seemingly refuses to fit easily into the patriarchal categories of social interaction.

Given this feminist tradition of focusing on women characters in the text, some readers/listeners may rightfully ask what is feminist about the reading I am proposing. I would answer that my reading attempts to expose some of the colors of imperial oppression. This is a precaution that serves to call a feminist reader to read not as a colonizing agent but as a decolonizing partner, in search of liberation. The reader/listener may further ask if it is not better to see the violence that characterizes the first part of Judith as patriarchy rather than imperialism, with imperialism as but a manifestation of patriarchy. Undoubtedly, Nebuchadnezzar and his armies are all male and definitely come from patriarchal nations. But so are his victims – they are also patriarchal, but they are not necessarily imperial nations. While we could risk generalizing that all societies are patriarchal, we cannot say that all societies are imperial. My postcolonial feminist approach, therefore, seeks to underline the need to understand the imperial/colonial powers of oppression. It seeks to show that these are independent forces of oppression. Although such forces often work in tandem with patriarchy, the two are not identical. They overlap on many fronts and work through various forms of oppression, such as race, ethnicity, class, and gender. Yet it is important to acknowledge that, while patriarchy oppresses women and some men of marginalized categories, imperialism oppresses all its subjects, including upper-class men.

In giving a feminist reading of Judith 1–7 – chapters that deal primarily with the military attacks and advances of Holofernes and the plunder and surrender of many foreign nations – my postcolonial feminist reading seeks to highlight all forms of oppression, including the fourth "G" of the imperial/colonial project, gender. To this purpose, I pose the following questions:

- What is the role of women in these imperial acts?
- How does patriarchy work together with imperialism?
- How are women affected in the colonizing and the colonized nations?
- What would be a feminist alternative to international relations as opposed to the one provided by the text?

The text makes clear that, in the colonizing nation of Assyria, the leadership is in the hands of Nebudchanezzar, Holofernes, and Bagoas. Similarly, in the colonized/targeted nations, leadership is in the hands of men: King Arphaxad, Uzziah, Chabris, Charmis, and Joakim, the high priest, who is both a political and a religious leader of Israel. In short, patriarchy is found in both colonizing and colonized nations. Women are clearly marginalized from public positions of leadership on both sides because of patriarchal structures. But are they equally oppressed in imperial settings and contexts? I should like to examine this question briefly by investigating colonized and colonizing women as they appear in the text.

Colonized women

Colonized women are not only subjugated to the patriarchy of their lands but also are marked for death, dispossession, and exile, together with the men of such lands. Imperialism oppresses both men and women, even those of high status. This is

graphically demonstrated in 4:9–12, when the nation of Israel chooses to resist the impending imperial power:

> And *every man* of Israel cried out to God with great fervor, and they humbled themselves with much fasting. They and their wives and their children and their cattle and every resident alien and hired laborer and purchased slave – they *all* put sackcloth around their waists. And *all the Israelite* men, women, and children living at Jerusalem prostrated themselves before the temple and put ashes on their heads and spread out their sackcloth before the Lord. They even draped the altar with sackcloth and *cried out in unison*, praying fervently to the God of Israel not to allow their infants to be carried off and their wives to be taken as booty, and the towns they had inherited to be destroyed, and the sanctuary to be profaned and desecrated to the malicious joy of the Gentiles. (Emphasis mine.)

The passage shows clearly that imperialism affects all, regardless of gender, class, or age. It also makes it clear that, in the resistance against imperialism, the colonized women stand together with the colonized men in the fight. Their lives, land, property – everything – are at stake. A colonized people thus manages to file away temporarily their social differences in the face of imminent political, economic, cultural, and (very possibly) physical death.

This overlooking of social categories in imperial settings is seen also in 7:23–5:

> Then *all the people*, the young men, the women, and the children, gathered around Uzziah and the rulers of the town and cried out with a loud voice, and said before all the elders, "Let God judge between you and us! You have done us great injury in not making peace with the Assyrians. For now we have no one to help us; God has sold us into their hands, to be strewn before them in thirst and exhaustion." (Emphasis mine.)

Double/multiple oppressions

Yet one gleans from the passage that colonized women may be subjugated to the patriarchal power of the attacking nation, "captured" and "carried off" as booty – to become servants of the capturers, slaves, concubines, or wives of the slayers of their own people. One also learns that, despite this united form of resistance against the colonial power, the patriarchy of the subjugated nation remains alive. Israelite men are still put first, underlining their superiority. Israelite women are referred to as "their wives," while no such possessive pronoun is tagged onto the men of Israel with reference to their spouses. In fact, the latter part of this prayer is quite telling: the concern for "their wives" in particular suggests that in this "unison" cry it is really the men of Israel who are praying.

Class differences remain rife during the struggles against colonialism. For example, there were still foreign laborers, servants, and slaves. Indeed, they cry together with the men of Israel, but they occupy the lower classes. Israel, like many colonized nations fighting for liberation, has not eliminated oppressive class, age, and gender categories among its own people. It follows, then, that, should the struggle for independence come to an end, things will be back to their "normal" situation: males will be males; females will be females; slaves will be slaves; foreign workers will be foreign workers; and children will be children. In short, all members

of society will be expected to resume their designated social space. In fact, this back-to-"normal" movement after the liberation struggle is perhaps demonstrated by Judith, who, despite her outstanding national contribution through her wisdom and courage, is not invited to assume leadership but is offered marriage proposals by her own countrymen. Moreover, the outspoken Judith, the one who had summoned rulers and elders to her presence and had criticized their decisions, insists no more on public leadership.

Colonizing Women

Colonizing women are conspicuous by their absence in the Book of Judith. I can only imagine them – that they suffer from anxiety as they wait indefinitely for their spouses, brothers, and fathers to return from the emperor's war. Yet they do not resist Nebuchadnezzar and Holofernes, as we see the colonized women of Israel move to resist their leaders (7:23–25). The silence of colonizing women betrays some degree of consent, some degree of security. They share in the booty brought by their men. They share in the glory. They are sheltered. This is attested not only by their lack of protest but also by the fact that, unlike the Israelite men who cry that "their wives" will be carried away (4:12), the Assyrian men in the army do not harbor such fears. They do not mourn that "their wives and children" will be killed or taken captive; they have "some" degree of security – until that time, perhaps, when their army is slaughtered by the Israelites (15:1–7). We can then imagine numerous widows of the empire, who may find survival in a colonizing but patriarchal nation difficult. They may be honored or neglected; they may remarry or turn to other means of survival.

Decolonizing Feminisms

The analysis of chaps. 1–7 leads to a number of conclusions regarding the relation of feminism to imperialism. First, a feminist reader who collapses imperialism into patriarchy is likely to overlook that women in colonized and colonizing nations are not equally oppressed. The colonized woman's oppression is greater, and the colonizing woman has a hand in this. Second, in colonized settings both men and women of different social categories are oppressed, and a joint front of resistance against imperialism is assumed. Social status is temporarily overlooked, but easily resuscitated once imperialism is no longer a factor to contend with. Third, feminist readers who do not distinguish between patriarchy and imperialism as two forms of oppression that overlap and use a number of similar categories of oppression are likely to read in collaboration with imperialism or even as a colonizer by failing to point out that imperialism – the act of some aggressive nations which impose their power by dispossessing some less aggressive nations from economic, political, and cultural autonomy – is a gross violation of human rights, one that should not be condoned by feminist readers in their search for a just world.

What, then, is a postcolonial feminist alternative? Can one find this alternative in the text? While my answer to this question will be clearer toward the end of this study, my analysis already suggests that, given the pervasiveness of imperialism from ancient to current times (today it manifests itself as globalization) and given its impact on the lives of women and men, feminist readers seeking a just world should

also become decolonizing readers in their liberation hermeneutics. Feminists can become decolonizing readers by ensuring that they do not bracket imperial oppression in texts but rather identify it as a force of oppression that must be resisted and for which other ways of relating must be sought.

Thus far, my reading has focused on highlighting the imperial setting in the narrative of Judith, how imperialism affects women of different classes (colonized and colonizing, low and high), and how imperialism differs from patriarchy. At this point, I turn to Judith herself in order to further scrutinize these factors. In particular, my question regarding chaps. 8–16 is: Can the character of Judith serve as a decolonizing feminist figure – one who resists both forms of oppression, patriarchy and imperialism, in her struggle for liberation? Does she offer us a model of liberating interdependence? Is she an ideal feminist model of liberation in a postcolonial world, or is Judith a case of the use of female bodies in colonial contexts to articulate a discourse of suppression and resistance?

Judith: "You are the Great Pride of Our Nation" (15:9)

The Israelites have decided to resist the armies of Holofernes. This, the readers know, means that they will be killed (2:11). The huge Assyrian army has besieged them. Bethulia has been cut off from its water supplies. The thirst of men, women, and children intensifies as each day passes by. Resistance begins to wear off. So the people come to the leaders, Uzziah and the elders, and protest, "For it would be better for us to be captured by them. We shall indeed become slaves, but our lives will be spared, and we shall not witness our little ones dying before our eyes, and our wives and children drawing their last breath" (7:27). The leaders of Bethulia, witnessing this great distress, decide to strike a compromise with the people: if the Lord does not act and save them within five days, then they will let them willingly surrender themselves to the Assyrian army (7:30). Judith hears of this resolution. She sends her servant to "summon Uzziah and Chabris and Charmis, the elders of her town" (8:10). She openly protests against their decision saying, "Who are you to put God to the test today... for God is not like a human being, to be threatened, or like a mere mortal, to be won over by pleading" (8:11–17). From this point on, the narrative will focus, almost exclusively, on Judith until the end, describing her beauty, her wisdom, her piety, and showing how she successfully saved her nation from the armies of Holofernes.

Judith as a decolonizing woman

The character of Judith is introduced to us in an intensely imperialized context, a setting that required nations and individuals to surrender to imperialism or die. She comes in at a point when the people of Bethulia are contemplating surrender to the imperial powers to avoid dying of thirst and exhaustion. Judith enters as a champion in resisting imperialism. First, she uses as a weapon the religious beliefs of her people. She argues that they have no right to put God to the test, that only God has a right to test them and that God will deliver them in God's own time or even destroy them. She recommends continued prayer as they await

deliverance. Second, when Uzziah insists that he cannot revoke his own limit of five days, Judith decides to take it upon herself to confront the imperial forces oppressing her nation.

For this undisclosed plan she asks that the gate be opened for her and her maid. In preparation, Judith enters into prayer by covering her head with ashes, putting on sackcloth and crying out with a loud voice,

> For your strength does not depend on numbers, nor your might on the powerful. But you are the God of the lowly, helper of the oppressed, upholder of the weak, protector of the forsaken, savior of those without hope. Please, please, God of my father, God of the heritage of Israel, Lord of heaven and earth, Creator of the waters, King of all your creation, hear my prayer! Make my deceitful words bring wound and bruise on those who have planned cruel things against your covenant, and against your sacred house, and against Mount Zion, and against the house your children possess. (9:11–13)

At the end of her prayer, Judith prepares to go to Holofernes by changing her attire, from sackcloth and widowhood clothes to festive clothes. Judith reportedly "made herself very beautiful, to entice the eyes of all the men who might see her" (10:4). Then, with her food and utensils packed, she and her maid went out of the gate and to Holofernes' military camp. Judith is brought to Holofernes, and, as the text never fails to inform the reader, all the men are stunned by her beauty (10:7, 14, 19, 23), as is Holofernes (11:23), who then plans to seduce her by inviting her to a banquet (12:10). During the feast, Holofernes drinks too much (12:20). Judith reaches for his head, cuts it off, and returns to Bethulia (13:6–11). Without leadership, the Assyrian army is easily put to rest (15:7). Bethulia, Judea, Jerusalem – the whole of Israel is saved!

The high priest, Joakim, and the elders from Jerusalem come to see Judith. They proceed to bless her, "You are the glory of Jerusalem, you are the great boast of Israel, you are the great pride of our nation! You have done all this with your own hand; you have done great good to Israel, and God is well pleased with it. May the almighty Lord bless you forever!" The people respond, "Amen" (15:10). The narrative continues, "All the women of Israel gathered to see her, and blessed her, and some of them performed a dance in her honor" (15:12). In response, Judith stands up and goes "before all people in the dance, leading all the women, while all the men of Israel followed" (15:13). She sings a song of thanksgiving and praise, and all the people join in. In the song she tells how the Lord delivered Israel "by the hand of a woman" (16:5). She fully discloses to all assembled the deceitful plan that brought down Holofernes and his army (16:5–10). The celebration moves to Jerusalem, where it continues for three months, before everyone returns to their respective towns.

As a woman, Judith demonstrates unwavering anger against imperialist structures that have condemned her people and her land to gross injustice, facing either the surrender of all human dignity or death. While she is no commander of massive armies but a widow who holds no particular social power, save for her impeccable reputation of wisdom, beauty, and piety, Judith will not condone the injustice of imperialism, the arrogance of such a powerful nation as Assyria. Rather, she calls

upon "the God of the lowly, helper of the oppressed, upholder of the weak" (9:11). The reader particularly notes that the whole town is on the brink of collaboration with imperialist powers, but Judith insists that they cannot condone this oppression. They must resist imperialism, even if God chooses not to protect them; they must not collaborate, even if God chooses to destroy them before their enemies. She backs her words with actions until that time when she brings the head of Holofernes home. She leads the whole nation in a song of liberation. Judith has done it. She has saved her nation from dispossession, dehumanization, and death.

As a decolonizing woman, Judith has a lot to offer the feminist discourse of liberation in biblical studies. Judith is a woman we need in our feminist discourse, for she summons us to resist imperialism and its collaborators in our own worlds. Dancing to the song of Judith, we must recognize imperialism as a completely unacceptable institution, one that needs our absolute resistance. The crucial question now is: Does Judith resist patriarchy with the same energy?

Judith as a depatriarchalizing figure

We meet Judith in a city and nation ruled by men. Yet she demonstrates significant forms of power and leadership in her own way. First, she is a widow of property: she lives in her own estate, has a maid who runs her estate (8:10), is given property (16:18–19), and distributes property (16:24). Judith's wisdom is widely acknowledged by Israelites and outsiders (9:29; 11:8). She summons rulers to her presence, and they obey (8:10); she makes independent plans, refuses to disclose them, and the leaders obey (8:34); she demonstrates a courage not associated with women in patriarchal socialization by going to the military camp of Holofernes and bringing his head back with her (13:1–9). Her contribution is publicly recognized, and she is openly praised and honored (15:8–10). Judith tops it all when she leads women and men in a song saying, "But the Lord Almighty has foiled them by the hand of a woman" (16:5). This song seemingly makes mockery of the fears of Israelite men, who were concerned that "their wives" would be carried away, by showing that these wives of theirs are not as helpless as they might seem. Judith seems to demonstrate that women can defend themselves.

At this point, however, when I expect Judith to take the struggle further, to insist on showing her leadership skills within the institutions of her nation and to show that God does not discriminate against women even in peaceful times, she withdraws from the public sphere to the silence and privacy of her home. This is particularly emphasized in the book's last verses:

> After this they all returned home to their own inheritances. Judith went to Bethulia, and remained on her estate. For the rest of her life she was honored throughout the whole country. Many desired to marry her, but she gave herself to no man all the days of her life after her husband Manasseh died and was gathered to his people. She became more and more famous, and grew old in her husband's house. She set her maid free. She died in Bethulia, and they buried her in the cave of her husband Manasseh. . . . Before she died, she distributed her property to all those who were next of kin to her husband, and to her own kindred. No one ever again spread terror among the Israelites during the lifetime of Judith, or for a long time after her death. (16:21–5)

First of all, these verses underline that Judith's identity is inseparably tied to that of her late husband, Manasseh. Second, they dissociate her from the ownership of property: she gives the goods from Holofernes to the temple and distributes all her property among her relatives. Finally, she is buried together in the same cave with Manasseh. Indeed, while the text states that she was honored and famous, the only evidence given in this regard is that "many desired to marry her" (16:22). Although she rejects their offers, one notes that she is not without a man in her life – she is with Manasseh.

A feminist reader thus realizes that Judith may have offered public resistance against collaboration with imperialism, but she makes no such challenge against patriarchy. Rather, she works with and within its framework. For instance, Judith does not question the "male only" leadership of her city and country, although her wisdom and courage surpass those of many men. Priests, elders, and high priests are all male and remain so. Further, while acknowledging her wisdom and courage (8:28–9), the public leaders of Israel make no effort to invite her to assume public leadership, despite the fact that she has ably demonstrated her powers of leadership. The Judith who seemed to hold a sharply subversive weapon against patriarchal claims ends up by withdrawing from the public space to the private. She is buried in the grave of her husband!

"The Lord Almighty has foiled them by the hand of a woman" (16:5)

Judith is, undeniably, a heroine of the national struggle against imperialism. Yet she makes little or no effort to display the same fearless anger toward patriarchy. Rather, Judith – this incredibly beautiful woman who leaves all men gasping, who has the brains to match her looks, and who possesses impeccable piety on top of it all – returns to "normal" life after the struggle for independence. If we consider the fact that this narrative was most probably written by a male author, then our dear Judith closely resembles those Two-Thirds World women who participated in the wars of liberation but who were discouraged from waging the feminist struggle for liberation. To me, this characterization of Judith closely parallels the strategy of "first things first" in the African context of liberation wars.[10] The statement, "But the Lord Almighty has foiled them by the hand of a woman," is thus not necessarily a song of a woman celebrating womanpower; it is rather a patriarchal song of Israelites, directed to the defeated men on the other side of the city. We need to ask, therefore, how is the body of Judith used in this story?

This brings me to the last question, which concerns reading texts that use gendered images to articulate positions of subordination and subjugation. The major question here is, does the narrative of Judith use gendered images to articulate a discourse of subordination? If so, can we employ such metaphoric and representative women characters for feminist purposes of liberation? And what are the dangers of claiming such images for feminist purposes? These questions take us back to the nocturnal encounter of Rahab and Judith outside the city gates, described at the opening of this article. What did Rahab and Judith see in each other's eyes, when they bumped into each other outside the city hall?

Rahab and Judith: Phantoms of Power Struggles in Imperial Settings

The narrative characterizes Judith as a very attractive woman, to a point where a reader needs to make an effort to avoid falling for Judith's extraordinary beauty and to see her as a phantom of patriarchal power struggles in imperial settings. I would admit, however, that Judith apparently not only enticed all men who saw her but also attracted women – many contemporary feminist readers seem to fall for her, claiming her as a feminist heroine. But if and when we try not to let her beauty blind us, then we find her quite close to Rahab, the sex worker of Jericho. Both women, I would insist, are patriarchal constructions of land possession rhetoric at critical moments of imperial attack. A brief look at Rahab, whom I regard as Judith's counterpart, is in order at this point, in order to understand the significance of their similarities and differences.

Rahab comes much earlier in the history of Israel (Josh. 2). When the Israelites cross the Jordan to take possession of the land that God promised them, they come to Jericho. Joshua sends two spies to investigate the land and report back to him. The two spies come to Jericho. They enter the house of a sex worker, Rahab, and spend the night there. The people of Jericho hear about the spies in Rahab's house and come searching at her door, but she hides them and misleads the soldiers of her own city, saying that the men have already departed. Rahab, however, uses this moment to negotiate for her own safety and that of her family, saying to the two spies:

> I know that the Lord has given you the land, and that dread of you has fallen on us, and that all the inhabitants melt in fear before you. For we have heard how the Lord dried up the water of the Red Sea before you when you came out of Egypt, and what you did to the two kings of the Amorites that were beyond the Jordan, to Sihon and Og, whom you utterly destroyed. As soon as we heard it, our hearts melted, and there was no courage left in us because of you. The Lord your God is indeed God in heaven above and on earth below. Now then, since I have dealt kindly with you, swear to me by the Lord that you in turn will deal kindly with my family. Give me a sign of good faith.... (Josh. 2:9–12)

The men said to her, "Our life for yours!" (2:14). The spies return to their camp and report, "Truly the Lord has given all the land into our hands; moreover all the inhabitants of the land melt in fear before us" (2:24). The spies, it should be noted, never explored Jericho, save the body of Rahab, the sex worker. Rahab is Jericho.

Jericho is then besieged by the Israelites. They march around the city for seven days, with armed men in front followed by priests carrying the ark of the covenant. Each night they retreat to a camp. On the seventh day, Joshua commands them, "Shout! For the Lord has given you the city" (6:16). They shout and the walls of Jericho fall. The armed men then destroy "all in the city, both men and women, young and old, oxen, sheep and donkeys" (6:21). Rahab and her family are saved. They burned the city, but "the silver and gold, and the vessels of bronze and iron, they put into the treasury of the house of the Lord" (6:24). "But Rahab the prostitute, with her family and all who belonged to her, Joshua spared. Her family has lived in Israel ever since..." (6:25).

In my short reconstruction at the beginning, Judith and Rahab bump into each other outside the city, and "both women are startled to see the self reflected in the other's face." What are the similarities between these women? Both of these women represent their lands – the fate that shall befall their lands in the face an imperial threat. Their characters are therefore allegorical stories that foreshadow how the prevailing imperial power struggles shall unfold. Thus, the features of each woman are quite significant, insofar as they tell us about each land/city/nation. Rahab here thus reads well as Canaan/Jericho, while Judith is Israel/Bethulia. The fate of their lands is what distinguishes each character, foreshadowing whether the land shall be taken or not taken by the invading foreign power.

Thus, we encounter Rahab as a sex worker – a woman who can be taken by any man who desires her. She bears porous boundaries. She is a woman/land that can exchange hands from one man to another, a woman who owes no allegiance to any man, save the one who is ready to pay for her services. As a representative of Canaan/Jericho, Rahab entrusts herself to the invading power, the Israelite spies, and betrays her own people, whom she judges too weak to withstand the invading power. What happens to Jericho after this encounter is consistent with the character of Rahab: Jericho is entered and taken.

Similarly, we encounter Judith as Israel/Bethulia. Her character is the story of what Bethulia shall become in the face of imperial invasion. Judith is a chaste widow of impeccable beauty and piety. Her social status as a widow implies that she can be wooed and won by any man who wishes to try. But, no, Judith has had one man and she will not have another. She is committed to Manasseh and will remain so until her death, when she will join her husband even in death. Physically, Judith is also a very beautiful and attractive woman, desired by all men who see her, but in her appetites there are no excesses, for either food or sex. She is a pure widow, whose eating habits and sexual passions are strictly controlled. Will the invading power/Holofernes have Judith/Israel/Bethulia? No, it will not. Judith/Bethulia will be desired, and it will look as if she is available or accessible, but, no, she will not be taken. The story of the invasion of Bethulia follows accordingly.

The difference between Rahab and Judith is clear: the former represents collaboration with imperialism, while the latter stands for resistance, yet both narratives are Israelite. Accordingly, in Rahab's story Israel is the invader, projecting Canaan/Jericho as a sex worker who can be taken; in Judith's story Israel is the invaded, projecting a woman who is desired but who cannot be taken. In both cases, however, the story of the desired land is identified with a woman, whether loose (Rahab/Jericho) or pure (Judith/Bethulia). These women characters are presented from a patriarchal perspective as ways of articulating imperial agendas. Can they be read for feminist liberation purposes?

Liberation Strands in Judith

To read Judith as a feminist text of liberation, it is necessary to acknowledge fully that "the master's tools can never dismantle his house."[11] Within this cautionary framework of suspicion, one will do well to see Judith as an embodiment of both patriarchal and imperial power struggles. If she can be rescued and brought to the

services of women's liberation, then readers will do well to read as "decolonizing feminists." Such a biblical hermeneutics of liberation must seek to resist both the imperial and the patriarchal manifestation of oppression in texts and in real life. Within this cautionary framework of suspicion, Judith can certainly serve as a reminder to Western feminists of the need to be committed to fight against imperialism. For feminist/women/womanist readers from the Two-Thirds World, Judith serves as a good reminder that "the women's question should not be relegated to the days after the revolution" anymore.[12]

The story, however, does not make Judith a model who fully embraces both the struggle against patriarchal oppression and the struggle against imperial oppression, along with other accompanying categories of oppression, such as race, ethnicity, class, and age. When it comes to reading the available scriptures of the world, feminists of various backgrounds will have to remember, as I have argued in another context, that,

> While the patriarchal, imperialist and many other oppressive aspects of various world scriptures are being addressed; while the suppressed scriptures of the colonized and women from multiple traditions are being restored and re-interpreted, the various feminist theological discourses must also enter and operate from the arena of oral-Spirit aggressively.... The oral-Spirit framework can be a creative space, where women articulate their own sacred, life-affirming and liberating words of wisdom. In the feminist oral-Spirit space, responsible creativity that involves attentive listening to many oppressed voices and empathy; active prophecy that speaks against oppression and seeks liberation; and intent praying that seeks partnership with the divine, can begin to hear, speak and write new words of life and justice.[13]

In short, while a decolonizing feminist biblical hermeneutics must critique both patriarchy and imperialism in the available world scriptures, it also needs to liberate itself from the bondage of patriarchal and imperial texts whose liberative power comes as crumbs that fall from the master's table. Instead, feminists of various backgrounds need to embody God's Spirit, to enter a new space, to speak new words, and to speak into existence a new world of justice and liberation to all the members of the earth community.[14]

NOTES

1 Kwok Pui-lan, "Reflections on Women's Sacred Scriptures," (eds.) Kwok Pui-lan and E. Schüssler Fiorenza, in *Women's Sacred Scriptures, Concilium* 1998/3 (Maryknoll, NY: Orbis Books, 1998), 109–12; and M. W. Dube, "Toward a Postcolonial Feminist Interpretation of the Bible," in K. Doob Sakenfeld, S. Ringe, and P.A. Bird (eds), *Reading the Bible as Women: Perspectives from Africa, Asia and Latin America, Semeia*, 78 (Decatur, Ga.: Society of Biblical Literature, 1997), 11–26.

2 T. S. Maluleke, "Half a Century of African Christian Theologies: Elements of the Emerging Agenda for the 21st Century," *Journal of Theology for Southern Africa*, 99 (1997): 20–3.

3 M. W. Dube, "Readings of *Semoya*: Botswana Women's Interpretations of Matt. 15:21–28," in G. West and M. W. Dube (eds) "*Reading With*": *An Exploration of the Interface between Critical and Ordinary Readings of the Bible: African Overtures, Semeia*, 73 (Decatur, Ga.: Society of Biblical Literature, 1996), 112–14.

4 M. L. Daneel, *The Quest for Belonging: Introduction to a Study of African Independent Churches* (Gweru: Mambo Press, 1987), 46–59.
5 M. W. Dube, *Postcolonial Feminist Interpretation of the Bible* (St. Louis: Chalice Press, 2000), 129.
6 M. W. Dube, "*Batswakwa*: Which Traveller are You (John 1:1–18)?" *Journal of Theology for Southern Africa*, 108 (2000): 150–2.
7 A. LaCocque, *The Feminine Unconventional: Four Subversive Figures in Israel Traditions* (Minneapolis: Fortress Press, 1990), 31.
8 R. Maunier, *The Sociology of Colonies*, 2 vols, ed. and trans. E. O. Lorimer (London: Routledge & Kegan Paul, 1948), 1:19.
9 M. W. Dube, "Consuming a Colonial Cultural Bomb: Translating Badimo into Demons in the Setswana Bible (Matthew 8.28–34; 15.22; 10.8)," *Journal for the Study of New Testament*, 73 (1999): 33–6.
10 Dube, *Postcolonial Feminist Interpretation of the Bible*, 112–14.
11 A. Lorde, *Sister Outsider: Essays and Speeches* (Trumansburg, NY: The Crossing Press, 1984), 110–13.
12 N. Tohidi, "Gender and Islamic Fundamentalism: Feminist Politics in Iran," in C.T. Mohanty, A. Russo, and L. Torres *Third World Women and Politics of Feminism* (Bloomington: Indiana University Press, 1991), 260.
13 M. S. Dube, "Scripture, Feminism and Postcolonial Contexts," in *Women's Sacred Scriptures*, ed. Kwok Pui-lan and E. Schüssler Fiorenza, 52–3.
14 Dube, *Postcolonial Feminist Interpretation of the Bible*, 115–17.

10

The Sign of Orpah: Reading Ruth through Native Eyes

Laura E. Donaldson

Prologue: Reading in the Contact Zone

This was no party
how the house was shaking.
They were trying
to nibble my bones, gnaw
my tribal tongue.
They took turns
pretending they had the power
to disembowel my soul
and force me to give them
my face to wear
for Halloween.
They like to play
that I want to change,
that I don't mind ending myself
in their holy book.
They think they can just twist till the blood has drained
and I am as white
and delightsome
as can be.

Wendy Rose, "The Mormons Next Door"[1]

The act of reading the Bible has been fraught with difficulty and contradiction for indigenous peoples. On the one hand, the translation of God's Book into Native vernacular comes with a high price: the forcing of oral tongues into static alphabets and its context of a colonizing Christianity. All too often, biblical reading has

First published in R. S. Sugirtharajah, *Vernacular Hermeneutics*. Sheffield: Sheffield Academic Press, 1999, 20–36.

produced traumatic disruptions within Native societies and facilitated what we now call culturecide. On the other hand, this depressingly long history of victimization should not obscure the ways in which Native peoples have actively resisted deracinating processes by reading the Bible on their own terms.[2] As Rigoberta Menchú (Quiché Mayan) notes in her moving *testimonio, I, Rigoberta Menchú*:

> We accept these Biblical forefathers as if they were our own ancestors, while still keeping within our own culture and our own customs... For instance the Bible tells us that there were kings who beat Christ. We drew a parallel with our king, Tecún Umán, who was defeated and persecuted by the Spaniards, and we take that as our own reality.[3]

Whether Menchú and the Quiché Mayan people scan a printed page or learn the stories by heart, they claim the Bible's "reality" as their own and thus exceed the bounds of imperial exegesis. A vivid example of this dynamic emerges from the way Menchú and other women of her community learned to negotiate the biblical narratives of liberation.

As Menchú remarks, the Quiché began their reading process by searching the scripture for stories representing "each one of us." While the men of Chimel village adopted Moses and the Exodus as their paradigm text of liberation, the women preferred the tale of Judith, who "fought very hard for her people and made many attacks against the king they had then, until she finally had his head."[4] Here, the distinct hermeneutic tradition of Mayan women begins to emerge – one that does not indoctrinate the reader with the colonizer's values but, rather, helps them understand and respond to their own historical situation (in this case, the brutal war being waged against them by the Guatemalan regime of García Lucas). Menchú rejects the belief that the Bible, or the tale of Judith and Holofernes, themselves effect change: "It's more that each one of us learns to understand his reality and wants to devote himself to others. More than anything else, it was a form of learning for us."[5] Through this statement, she articulates a process of reading practiced by many of the world's Native peoples – a process that actively selects and invents, rather than passively accepts, from the literate materials exported to them by the dominant Euro-Spanish culture. For Menchú, this transculturation of meaning emerges from the act of biblical reading in the contact zone.

In her book *Imperial Eyes: Travel Writing and Transculturation*, Mary Louise Pratt defines a contact zone as the space of colonial encounters where people who are divided both geographically and historically come into contact with each other and establish ongoing relations, usually involving conditions of severe inequality and intractable conflict.[6] She coins this term, instead of borrowing the more Eurocentric "colonial frontier," because she wants "to foreground the interactive, improvisational dimensions of colonial encounters so easily ignored or suppressed by diffusionist accounts of conquest and domination."[7] For Pratt, a "contact" perspective treats the bonds among colonizers and colonized (for example, Quiché and *Ladinos*) as implying co-presence, mutual influence and interlocking understandings that emerge from deep asymmetries of power. In this essay I will read the biblical book of Ruth through just such a contact perspective forged by the interaction of biblical narrative, the realities of Anglo-European imperialism and the traditions

of Cherokee women. This rereading is marked not only by the colonial history of Indian–white relations but also by the persistence of American Indian traditions; not only by Anglo-European genocide but also by Native "survivance";[8] not only by subjugation but also by resistance.

Scholars have traditionally regarded the book of Ruth as one of the Hebrew Bible's literary jewels: "a brief moment of serenity in the stormy world."[9] According to Herman Gunkel, for example, Ruth represents one of those "glorious *poetical narratives*" that exhibits "a widow's love lasting beyond death and the grave."[10] Feminist biblical critics have persuasively challenged this view by exposing its masculinist and heterosexist bias. For these interpreters, Ruth's love embodies the love of a woman-identified woman who is forced into the patriarchal institution of levirate marriage in order to survive. It is here – with this struggle over the meaning of women in the text – that I wish to begin my own articulation of the difficult and often dangerous terrain charted by the contact zone. Like Menchú, I hope that my reading of Ruth will function as a form of learning that will enable Native people both to understand more thoroughly how biblical interpretation has impacted us, and to assert our own perspectives more strongly. It seems fitting, then, that this journey begin with a crisis: the journey of Naomi and her husband Elimelech into Moab, the scandalous country of Lot's daughters.

The Daughters of Lot

> Thus both daughters of Lot became pregnant by their father. The firstborn bore a son, and named him Moab; he is the ancestor of the Moabites to this day (Gen. 19.36–7, NRSV).

> While Israel was staying at Shittim, the people began to have sexual relations with the women of Moab. These invited the people to the sacrifices of their gods, and the people ate and bowed down to their gods. Thus Israel yoked itself to the Baal of Peor, and the Lord's anger was kindled against Israel (Num. 25.1–3, NRSV).

There was a famine in the house of bread – the literal meaning of the name "Bethlehem" – and only the threat of starvation motivated Elimelech, a god-fearing Israelite, to forsake his home for the country harboring the sexually promiscuous and scandalous Moabites. Even worse, once he and his family arrive there, their two sons defy the Hebrew proscription against foreign marriage by taking the Moabite women Orpah and Ruth as wives. Indeed, for centuries the Israelites had reviled this people as degenerate and, particularly, regarded Moabite women as the agents of impurity and evil. Even the name "Moab" exhibits this contempt, since it allegedly originates in the incestuous liaison between Lot and his daughters. According to the biblical narrative in Genesis 19, Lot's daughters devise a plan to get him drunk on succeeding nights so that they can seduce him. Both women become pregnant through this relationship and both have sons. Lot's eldest daughter openly declares her son's origins when she calls him Moab, or "from my father." We glimpse the result of their actions in Deuteronomy which declares that, even to the tenth generation, "no Ammonite or Moabite shall be admitted to the assembly of the Lord" (Deut. 23.3).

As Randall Bailey notes in his fascinating essay on sex and sexuality in Hebrew canon narratives,

> the effect of both the narrative in Genesis 19 and the laws in Deuteronomy 23 . . . is to label within the consciousness of the reader the view of these nations as nothing more than "incestuous bastards". Through the use of repetition in the narrative in Genesis 19 . . . the narrator grinds home the notion of *mamzērîm* [bastards].[11]

Further, according to Bailey, this dehumanization through graphic sexual innuendo enables one to read other parts of the Deuteronomic history – David's mass slaughter of the Moabites in 2 Sam. 8.2 or the ritual humiliation of the Ammonites in 2 Sam. 12.26–31 – as warranted and even meritorious.[12]

The belief in Moabite women as a hypersexualized threat to Israelite men prophetically augurs the Christian attitude toward the indigenous women of the Americas. Indeed, as early as 1511, an anonymous Dutch pamphleteer vouched that "these folke lyven lyke bestes without any reasonablenes . . . And the wymen be very hoote and dysposed to lecherdnes."[13] Significantly (and, I would add, symptomatically), no less a personage than Thomas Jefferson, the second President of the United States and a framer of its Constitution, forges an important link between the Israelite attitude toward the Moabites and the Christian attitude toward American Indians in his own discourse on the book of Ruth. After finishing his *Notes on the State of Virginia* (1787)[14] – one of the most important influences upon Euramerican attitudes toward Native peoples – Jefferson submitted the manuscript for comments to Charles Thomson, then Secretary of Congress. Thomson's remarks were included in the published version because, as Jefferson enthused, "the following observations . . . have too much merit not to be communicated." In his response to the section that describes the nation's "Aborigines," Thomson observes that an alleged lack of "ardor" in Indian men most probably originated in the forwardness of their women:

> Instances similar to that of Ruth and Boaz are not uncommon among them. For though the women are modest and diffident, and so bashful that they seldom lift up their eyes, and scarce ever look a man full in the face, yet being brought up on great subjection, custom and manners reconcile them to modes of acting, which, judged of by Europeans, would be deemed inconsistent with the rules of female decorum and propriety.[15]

Jefferson endorses Thomson's remarks by locating the relevant biblical passage: "When Boaz had eaten and drank, and his heart was merry, he went to lie down at the end of the heap of corn: and Ruth came softly, and uncovered his feet, and laid her down. Ruth 3.7."[16] Although cloaked in the rhetoric of Enlightenment gentility, the statements by Thomson and Jefferson nevertheless disseminate a cautionary tale that is quite similar to the one concerning the Moabites: both American Indian and Moabite women exist as agents not only of evil and impurity but also of men's sexual frigidity. Given such negative representations, we need to investigate why the biblical author of Ruth chooses to foreground precisely this ideological nexus by consistently identifying the protagonist as "Ruth of Moab."

Ruth 2.6 provides an insightful glimpse into this process. After Elimelech and his two sons die, Naomi and Ruth return to Bethlehem. Naomi subsequently, and

recklessly according to some critics, sends her daughter-in-law into the fields of Boaz, a relative of her late husband, who notices the young widow and asks his servant to whom she belongs. "The servant who was in charge of the reapers answered, 'she is the Moabite who came back with Naomi from the country of Moab.' " The redundant doubling of ethnic markers in this passage – the Moabite from the country of Moab – emphasizes the text's construction of Ruth not only as a *gērāh*, or resident alien, but also as an alien who comes from a despised and barbaric country. However, the significance of this particular repetition has been construed in widely variant ways.

For example, the rabbis who wrote *Ruth R.* believe that it reinforces Ruth's role as a paradigmatic convert to Judaism who "turned her back upon wicked Moab and its worthless idols to become a God-fearing Jewess – loyal daughter-in-law, modest bride, renowned ancestress of Israel's great King David."[17] The *Iggereth Shmuel* expands this view and suggests that the quality of Ruth's faith even surpasses that of Abraham since, unlike Ruth, he only left home after God commanded him to do so.[18] For more contemporary critics the message of Ruth's identity is not one of conversion, but rather of "interethnic bonding" that parallels the gender bond established when Naomi's daughter-in-law "clings" to her husband's mother instead of returning home.[19] William Phipps articulates this position when he argues that the repetition of "Ruth the Moabite" connotes "vital religion and ethics in a time of bigotry and mayhem,"[20] and acts as an antidote to the xenophobia of the postexilic Jewish community. Rather than rejection of the Moabites and acceptance of the Israelites, then, Ruth's story conjures a vision of ethnic and cultural harmony through the house of David, which claims her as a direct ancestress.

While the presentation of Ruth as a character manifesting the virtues of tolerance and multiculturalism is appealing, Robert Maldonado's attempt to develop a *malinchista* hermeneutics[21] complicates this view by exposing its political and historical ambiguities. For Maldonado, a theologian of Mexican and Hungarian descent, the biblical figure of Ruth foreshadows the existence of *La Malinche*, or Doña Marina, the Aztec woman who became a consort of, and collaborator with, the conquistador Hernán Cortés. *La Malinche*'s legacy endures not only in historical Mexican consciousness but also in its linguistic vernacular: "*Malinchista* is a common term for a person who adopts foreign values, assimilates to foreign cultures, or serves foreign interests . . . The usage ties the meaning of betrayal in Mexican Spanish to the history of colonialism and Indian White relations . . . '[22] Yet *La Malinche* harbors deeper and even more personal levels of betrayal, since she was sold as a young girl to some Mayan traders – an experience that generated the bilingualism so crucial to her equivocal status. After she had been acquired by Cortés she was "given" to one of his officers and subsequently married to another conquistador. We begin to glimpse at least some of the complex and disturbing elements underpinning *La Malinche*'s collaboration with her colonizers. The similarities between the story of Doña Marina and the actions of Ruth lead Maldonado provocatively to ask: "Could Ruth be a Moabite Malinche?"[23] Maldonado answers his own question with a strong "maybe" – precisely because of the redundant identification of Ruth described above, as well as his own investment in *mestizaje*, or the resistant discourse of racial and cultural mixing.

American Indians have a much more suspicious attitude toward the privileging of mixedness, be it *mestizaje, métissage* or life in the borderlands. After all, "mixing" is precisely what Thomas Jefferson proposed as the final solution to the seemingly irresolvable "Indian problem." To a visiting delegation of Wyandots, Chippewas and Shawnees he confidently predicted that "in time, you will be as we are; you will become one people with us. Your blood will mix with ours; and will spread, with ours, over this great island."[24] And what better way to accomplish this commingling than with the paradigm of intermarriage that we glimpse in the book of Ruth? Indeed, one could argue that this "moment of serenity in the stormy world of the Hebrew Bible" exists as the prototype for both the vision of Thomas Jefferson and all those who facilitated conquest of indigenous peoples through the promotion of assimilation.

This social absorption prophetically evokes the fate of many American Indian women and children. In the historically matrilineal Cherokee culture, for example, Jefferson's vision of "mingling" and the realities of intermarriage wreaked havoc upon tribal organization and development. Wives now went to live with their white husbands – a practice that was contrary to the ancient custom of husbands residing in their wives' domicile. Further, according to Wilma Mankiller (the former Principal Chief of the Cherokee Nation), the children of these relationships assumed their fathers' surnames and became heirs to their father's, rather than their mother's, houses and possessions.[25] Intermarriage between whites and Indians severely disrupted the traditions of Cherokee women, since a genealogy that had for time immemorial passed from mother to son or daughter now shifted to the father and drastically curtailed women's power. In contrast to Maldonado, I would argue that the book of Ruth similarly foregrounds the use of intermarriage as an assimilationist strategy.

Soon after Ruth marries Boaz, the text states that she conceives and bears a son.

> Then Naomi took the child and laid him in her bosom, and became his nurse. The women of the neighborhood gave him a name saying, "A son has been born to Naomi". They named him Obed; he became the father of Jesse, the father of David (4.13–17).

As Danna Nolan Fewell and David Gunn note, through this announcement Ruth effectively disappears into the household of Boaz, and the legacy of the future king David closes the door upon her story.[26] In other words – although Fewell and Gunn do not use these terms – Ruth's assimilation becomes complete through Obed's transfer to Naomi, the proper Jewish woman, and to Boaz, the Israelite husband. The issue then becomes, what motivates this effacement and what ideological ends does it fulfill?

Even to begin answering this question, however, we must first understand how Ruth is linked to two seemingly disparate female icons – one from the Hebrew Bible and the other from the annals of American Indian history: Rahab and Pocahontas. Both of these women have played important roles in the construction of national narratives and both, like *La Malinche*, have been mythologized as facilitating conquest through their relationships with colonizing men.

The Anti-Pocahontas Perplex

> You made a decision. My place is with you. I go where you go.
> (Stands With A First to John Dunbar in *Dances with Wolves*)

Rahab, of course, is Ruth's other mother-in-law and the Canaanite prostitute who gave birth to Boaz (see Mt. 1.5). The events leading to this remarkable transformation of status are memorialized in the book of Joshua, ch. 2, and can be briefly summarized as follows. Joshua, who was leading the Israelite invasion of Canaan, sends two spies to reconnoiter the city of Jericho. These two men "entered the house of a prostitute whose name was Rahab and spent the night there" (2.1). When the king of Jericho hears of the spies' presence, he orders Rahab to surrender them. She refuses and hides them under stalks of flax that she had laid out on the roof. After nightfall she visits the men and requests that, since she has dealt kindly with them, they might in turn spare her and her family "and deliver our lives from death." Jericho does indeed fall: "But Rahab the prostitute, with her family and all who belonged to her, Joshua spared. Her family has lived in Israel ever since" (Josh. 6.25). Further, she is extolled in the Greek Bible as a paragon of faith and granted a high status as the ancestress of David and Jesus. Like her daughter-in-law Ruth, Rahab embodies a foreign woman, a Canaanite Other who crosses over from paganism to monotheism and is rewarded for this act by absorption into the genealogy of her husband and son – in this case, into the house of Salmon and, ultimately, of David. And, like Ruth, she represents the position of the indigene in the text, or of those people who occupied the promised land before the invasion of the Israelites.

However, the narrative figures of Rahab and Ruth conjure not only the position of the indigene in the biblical text but also the specific cultural and historical predicament of American Indian women. Cherokee scholar Rayna Green has identified this predicament as "the Pocahontas Perplex" – one of Euramerica's most important master narratives about Native women. It is named for the daughter of Powhatan and the mythology that has arisen around one of the most culturally significant encounters between Indians and whites. In this version of the story Powhatan Indians capture Captain John Smith and his men while they are exploring the territory around what is now called Jamestown, Virginia. After marching Smith to their town, the Indians lay his head on a large stone and prepare to kill him with their clubs. Precisely at that moment, Pocahontas – the favorite daughter of Powhatan – uses her body as a human shield and prevents Smith from being executed. She then further intercedes on behalf of the English colonists, who were starving after a long winter, and consequently saves not only the colonists but also the future of English colonization.[27]

As a master narrative with an ideological function, the Pocahontas Perplex construes the nobility of Pocahontas and other Indian women as "princess" who

> "must save or give aid to white men". As Green notes, "the only good Indian – male or female, Squanto, Pocahontas, Sacagawea, Cochise, the Little Mohee or the Indian Doctor – rescues and helps white men". But the Indian woman is even more burdened by this narrow definition of a "good Indian", for it is she, not the males, whom white men desire sexually.[28]

A consequence of this desire is that the "good" feminine image also implies the "bad" one. She is the Squaw whose degraded sexuality is vividly summarized in the frontier song "Little Red Wing": She "lays on her back in a cowboy shack, and lets cowboys poke her in the crack."[29] The specter of the Squaw – also known as a daughter of Lot – retroactively taints Rahab and Ruth; after all, the former earns her living as a prostitute and, according to Thomas Jefferson and company, the latter's behavior in the biblical counterpart of the cowboy shack was shockingly immoral. Such a debased starting point enables the scriptural stories to proclaim even more stridently the metamorphosis of Rahab and Ruth into the Israelite version of the Pocahontas Perplex. In this scenario, Salmon and Boaz stand in for John Smith. The result, however, remains the same. An indigenous woman forsakes her people and aligns herself with the men whom Yahweh had directed to "break down their altars, smash their pillars, burn their Asherah poles with fires, and hew down the idols of their gods, and thus blot out their name from their places" (Deut. 12.3).

From an American-Indian perspective, then, the midrashic interpretation of Ruth as the paradigmatic convert who "turned her back upon wicked Moab and its worthless idols to become a God-fearing Jewess"[30] seems a much more accurate description of the text's actual function than Robert Maldonado's appeal to some undecidable state of *mestizaje*. Indeed, even Ruth's name affirms the hermeneutic acumen of the rabbis, since it derives from the Hebrew root *rwh*, meaning "watering to saturation".[31] However, whereas the success of this ideological irrigation inspires rejoicing on behalf of the Israelites, it is an instance of mourning for American Indian women. Yet another relative has succumbed to – been filled up by and 'saturated' by – a hegemonic culture.

Is there no hope in the book of Ruth? Is it nothing but a tale of conversion/assimilation and the inevitable vanishing of the indigene in the literary and social text? In fact, there does exist a counter-narrative – a kind of anti-Pocahontas – whose presence offers some small hope to the Native reader: the sign of Orpah, sister-in-law of Ruth and the woman who returned to her mother's house.

"They broke once more into loud weeping. But while Orpah kissed her mother-in-law goodbye, Ruth clung to her" (Ruth 1.14, translation by Sasson). The figure of Orpah is only mentioned twice in the book of Ruth – 1.4, which names her as one of the "Moabite wives", and 1.14, which describes her decision to part ways with Naomi and Ruth. Unfortunately, however, most contemporary scholars mimic the biblical text by leaving her to return home unattended, both literally and critically. Traditionally, Orpah generated much more scrutiny, although much of it was negative. According to midrashic literature, for example, her name allegorically connotes the opposite of Ruth's, since it originates in the root '*orep*, that is, the nape of the neck, and describes how she turns the back of her neck to Naomi when she decides to return to Moab. "That the sages name Orpah for this moment in her history indicates that they also consider it the most important part of her story"[32] – and it explicitly charges her with the narrative role of abandoner.[33] Some writers even suggest that she later becomes the mother of Goliath, the famous enemy of Israel, and that Goliath himself was "the son of a hundred fathers".[34] But what else could one expect from a "daughter of Lot?"

William Phipps expresses a more current and enlightened view of Ruth's sister-in-law:

> Orpah displays wrenching ambivalence, deciding first one way and then another. She finally takes Naomi's common-sense advice and, after an affectionate goodbye, returns "to her people and to her gods". Her life is difficult enough without taking responsibility for an older widow in a land presumed to be governed by a deity different from the ones she worships (the Moabite Stone refers to Chemosh and to goddess Ashtar, or Ishtar)...She does the prudent thing and heads for her family home to await an arranged remarriage.[35]

While I do not disagree with Phipps's summary, I also believe that he fails to recognize what is perhaps the most important element of Orpah's decision. She does not just take the path of least resistance – the path of prudence, freedom from responsibility and passivity. Rather, Orpah returns to *bêt 'immāh*, "her mother's house."[36] Carol Meyers observes that the use of *bêt 'immāh* is quite rare in the Hebrew Bible and indicates a family setting identified with the mother rather than the father.[37] In fact, she notes, each biblical passage using this phrase shares a similarity with all the others: a woman's story is being told; women act as agents in their own destiny; the agency of women affects other characters in the narrative; the setting is domestic; and finally, a marriage is involved.[38] Meyers further concludes that all biblical references to "the mother's house" offer female perspectives on issues that elsewhere in the Bible are viewed through a predominately androcentric lens. I would argue that the female perspective offered by 'the mother's house' in Ruth is a profoundly important one for Native women, since it signifies that Orpah – the one whose sign is the back of her neck – exists as the story's central character.

To Cherokee women, for example, Orpah connotes hope rather than perversity, because she is the one who does not reject her traditions or her sacred ancestors. Like Cherokee women have done for hundreds if not thousands of years, Orpah chooses the house of her clan and spiritual mother over the desire for another culture. In fact, Cherokee women not only chose the mother's house, they also owned it (along with the property upon which it stood as well as the gardens surrounding it). Read through these eyes, the book of Ruth tells a very different story indeed.

Ojibway poet Kimberly Blaeser illuminates this transformative process of reading through a concept she describes as "response-ability". In her essay, "Pagans Rewriting the Bible", Blaeser defines response-ability as the need of American Indian people to "reconsider, reevaluate, reimagine what [religious] terms might mean or have meant to Indian people as well as what they might come to mean to all people."[39] This is precisely what Rigoberta Menchú accomplishes in her choosing of Judith over Moses and in her insistence that the meaning of any biblical text reflect her people's reality. It is also what I have tried to effect in my own rereading of Ruth through a Native perspective and, more particularly, through the perspective of Cherokee women. I have reconsidered the dominant exegesis of Ruth as either a paradigm of conversion or a woman-identified woman. I have reimagined this literary jewel of the Hebrew Bible as the narrative equivalent of a last arrow pageant.

During the implementation of the Dawes Act,[40] the "last-arrow pageant" was a public ritual that marked the translation of American Indian identity into its more "civilized" white counterpart. Etymologically, the word "translation" means

"carried from one place to another", or transported across the borders between one language and another, one country and another, one culture and another.[41] In the context of last-arrow pageants, participants performed and acknowledged their own translation into the idiom of Euramerican culture:

> This conversion of Indians into individual landowners was ceremonialized at "last-arrow" pageants. On these occasions, the Indians were ordered by the governments to attend a large assembly on the reservation. Dressed in traditional costume and carrying a bow and arrow, each Indian was individually summoned from a tepee and told to shoot an arrow. He then retreated to the tepee and re-emerged wearing "civilized" clothing, symbolizing a crossing from the primitive to the modern world. Standing before a plow, the Indian was told: "Take the handle of this plow, this act means that you have chosen to live the life of the white man – and the white man lives by work." At the close of the ceremony, each allottee was given an American flag and a purse with the instructions: "This purse will always say to you that the money you gain from your labor must be wisely kept."[42]

For "Ruth the Moabite," the translation from savagery to civilization (or from Asherah to Yahweh) similarly involves the relinquishing of her ethnic and cultural identity. For Orpah, it necessitates a courageous act of self and communal affirmation: the choosing of the indigenous mother's house over that of the alien Israelite Father.

In this interpretation, my responseability as a person of Cherokee descent and as an informed biblical reader transforms Ruth's positive value into a negative and Orpah's negative value into a positive. Such is the epistemological vertigo inspired by reading in the contact zone. Indeed, paraphrasing Blaeser, recognizes that life – or meaning in the book of Ruth – cannot be produced for easy consumption. Chinese feminist theologian Kwok Pui Lan echoes a similar sentiment in her statement that "these attempts at indigenization [of the Bible] show clearly that biblical truth cannot be pre-packaged, that it must be found in the actual interaction between text and context in the concrete historical situation".[43] I can only hope that my indigenization of Ruth has located new meaning in the interaction between biblical text and American Indian context – a meaning that resists imperial exegesis and contributes to the empowerment of aboriginal peoples everywhere.

NOTES

1 In Wendy Rose, *Going to War with All my Relations: New and Selected Poems* (Flagstaff, AZ: Entrada Books, 1993).
2 "Deracination" comes from the Latin word meaning "to uproot or to alienate."
3 Rigoberta Menchú, *I, Rigoberta Menchú: An Indian Woman in Guatemala*, ed. E. Burgos-Debray; trans. A. Wright (London: Verso, 1984), 80.
4 Menchú, *I, Rigoberta Menchú*, 131.
5 Menchú, *I, Rigoberta Menchú*, 135.
6 Mary Louise Pratt, *Imperial Eyes: Travel Writing and Transculturation* (London: Routledge, 1992), 6.
7 Pratt, *Imperial Eyes*, 7.

8 The term "survivance" is used by Gerald Vizenor (Chippewa) to describe the complicated gestures of Native survival in the contact zone of contemporary American culture.
9 Danna Nolan Fewell and David M. Gunn, *Compromising Redemption: Relating Characters in the Book of Ruth* (Louisville, KY: Westminster/John Knox Press, 1990), 11.
10 H. Gunkel, *What Remains of the Old Testament, and Other Essays*, trans. A. K. Dallas (New York: Macmillan, 1928), 21.
11 Randall Bailey, "They're Nothing but Incestuous Bastards: The Polemical Use of Sex and Sexuality in Hebrew Canon Narratives," in Fernando F. Segovia and Mary Ann Tolbert (eds), *Reading from This Place. I. Social Location and Biblical Interpretation in the United States* (Philadelphia: Fortress Press, 1995), 121–38 (131).
12 Bailey, "They're Nothing," p. 132.
13 As cited in Robert F. Berkhofer, Jr, *The White Man's Indian: Images of the American Indian from Columbus to the Present* (New York: Random House, 1978), 10.
14 T. Jefferson, *Notes on the State of Virginia,* ed. William Peden (New York: W. W. Norton, 1982).
15 Jefferson, *Notes*, 201.
16 Jefferson, *Notes*, 297. Since in Hebrew "feet" is often used as a euphemism for a man's genitals, Ruth is clearly initiating some sort of sexual encounter with Boaz.
17 Kathryn Pfisterer Darr, *Far More Precious than Jewels: Perspectives on Biblical Women* (Louisville, KY: Westminster/John Knox Press, 1991), 72.
18 Darr, *Far More Precious*, 72.
19 The verb "to cling" is particularly revealing here, since its customary usage involves the relationships of husbands to wives and of humans to Yahweh. Both womanist and feminist critics have used this linguistic turn to argue for Ruth's status as a woman-identified woman. Or, a woman who embodied the capacity "to care passionately about the quality of another woman's life, to respect each other's choices, and to allow for each other's differences" (Renita Weems, *Just a Sister Away: A Womanist Vision of Women's Relationships in the Bible* (San Diego: Lura Media, 1988), 34).
20 William E. Phipps, *Assertive Biblical Women*, Contributions in Women's Studies, 128 (Westport, CT: Greenwood Press, 1992), 67.
21 R. Maldonado, "Reading Malinche Reading Ruth: Toward a Hermeneutics of Betrayal," *Semeia*, 72 (1995): pp. 91–109.
22 Mary Louise Pratt, " 'Yo soy la malinche': Chicana Writers and the Poetics of Ethnonationalism," *Callaloo*, 16 (1993): 859–73 (860); as cited in Maldonado, "Reading Malinche," 99.
23 Maldonado, "Reading Malinche," 101.
24 T. Jefferson, *The Writings of Thomas Jefferson*, ed. A. E. Bergh (Washington, DC: Thomas Jefferson Memorial Association of the United States, 1907), 464.
25 Wilma Mankiller with Michael Wallis, *Mankiller: A Chief and her People* (New York: St Martin's Press, 1984), 26.
26 Fewell and Gunn, *Compromising Redemption*, 105.
27 While most Americans still believe in the myth that Pocahontas loved John Smith, a growing body of scholarship has significantly revised this tale of their encounter. Rayna Green and Kathleen Brown are among those who have persuasively argued that Smith's own account of his captivity, near-execution and rescue by Pocahontas eloquently testifies to yet another example of misrecognized and misinterpreted cultural difference. Brown, for example, contends that Smith's recording of Pocahontas covering his body with her own was most probably part of an adoption ritual in which Powhatan defined his relationship to him as one of patriarchal dominance ("The Anglo-Algonquian Gender Frontier", in Nancy Shoemaker (ed.), *Negotiators of Change: Historical Perspectives on American Indian Women* (London: Routledge, 1995), 26–48 (39)). Unfortunately,

"Smith understood neither the ritual adoption taking place nor the significance of Powhatan's promise to make him a werowance and to 'for ever esteeme him as [he did] his son Nantaquoud' " (40). Green (in "The Pocahontas Perplex: The Image of Indian Women in American Culture," *Massachusetts Review* (autumn, 1975): 698–714) provides a further gloss. She notes that, as the daughter of the tribe's leader and a woman of considerable status, Pocahontas served as Smith's "mother," for he had to be reborn, after a symbolic death, as one of the tribe. Thus, Pocahontas was not delaying Smith's execution and thwarting her own people when she threw her body over his. She was in fact acting on behalf of her people (35).

28 Green, "The Pocahontas Perplex," 703.

29 Green, "The Pocahontas Perplex," 711.

30 Darr, *Far More Precious*, 72.

31 In *The Feminine Unconventional: Four Subversive figures in Israel's Tradition* (Minneapolis: Fortress Press, 1990), Andre LaCocque observes that most biblical exegetes "stubbornly propose" the Syriac translation of "Ruth" as an abbreviation of *Re'uth*, or female companion. Like other scholars who have carefully studied the book of Ruth, LaCocque persuasively argues that, philologically, the name "Ruth" has nothing to do with *r'h* (to be a companion), but rather is a cognate of *rwh* (to water to saturation). See his discussion, 115–16.

32 Leila Leah Bronner, "A Thematic Approach to Ruth in Rabbinic Literature", in A. Brenner (ed.), *A Feminist Companion to Ruth*, Feminist Companion to the Bible, 3 (Sheffield: Sheffield Academic Press, 1993), 146–69 (155).

33 M. Bal, *Lethal Love: Feminist Literary Readings of Biblical Love Stories* (Bloomington: Indiana University Press, 1987), 74.

34 Bronner, "Thematic Approach," 155.

35 Phipps, *Assertive Biblical Women*, 53.

36 "But Naomi said to her two daughters-in-law, 'Go back each of you to your mother's house' " (Ruth 1.8).

37 Carol Meyers, "Returning Home: Ruth 1.8 and the Gendering of the Book of Ruth," in Brenner (ed.), *A Feminist Companion to Ruth* (Feminist Companion to the Bible, 3; Sheffield: Sheffield Academic Press, 1993), 85–114 (91).

38 Meyers, "Returning Home," 109–10.

39 Kimberly M. Blaeser, "Pagans Rewriting the Bible: Heterodoxy and the Representation of Spirituality in Native American Literature," *Review of International English Literature*, 25.1 (1994): 12–31 (13).

40 Passed in 1887 and named for its sponsor, Massachusetts senator Henry L. Dawes, the Dawes Act attempted to detribalize American Indians by privatizing communally held Indian lands and partitioning reservations into 160- and 80-acre lots subject to sale or lease by the government. Between 1887 and its end in 1934, the Dawes Act reduced the total land base of American Indian peoples by two-thirds.

41 J. Hillis Miller, *Topographies: Crossing Aesthetics* (Stanford, CA: Stanford University Press, 1995), 316.

42 Ronald Takaki, *A Different Mirror: A History of Multicultural America* (Boston: Little, Brown & Co., 1993), 235–6.

43 Kwok Pui-lan, *Discovering the Bible in the Non-Biblical World: The Bible and Liberation* (Maryknoll, NY: Orbis Books, 1995), 11.

11

On Naming the Subject:

Postcolonial Reading of Daniel 1[1]

Philip Chia

> We live in an age that cannot name itself. For some, we are still in the age of modernity and the triumph of the bourgeois subject. For others, we are in a time of leveling of all traditions and await the return of the repressed traditional and communal subject. For yet others, we are in a postmodern moment where the death of the subject is now upon us as the last receding wave of the death of God.
>
> *On Naming the Present*, David Tracy

Introduction

Postcolonial criticism, a newcomer,[2] came to be recognized as a distinct category in new literary criticism only in the 1990s. From the publication of Frantz Fanon's *The Wretched of the Earth* (1961) and *Black Skin, White Masks* (1952, English, 1968), who identified a devastating pathology at the heart of Western culture, a denial of difference, to the recent title of Gail Low's *White Skins Black Masks: Representation and Colonialism* (1996), who examined the representational dynamics of colonizer versus colonized in the African and Indian writings of Haggard and Kipling, much of colonial discourse has emerged and elapsed.[3] Some viewed it as a replacement or substitute for Third World Theology or Postmodernism, but I take it differently because of the difference in their agenda and interest. My interest in postcolonial discourse and biblical studies, however, evolved not because it is in fashion as a new toy of literary approach for some critics, nor is it because of the need for a replacement for the term "Third World Theology" or "Asian Theology." Rather, it is a matter of life experience as a biblical interpreter in contexts that warrant such an interest. By life experience, I refer, firstly, to my birth and in a postcolonial country[4] and secondly, reading the Bible from a place which is about to enter into a post-colonial era.[5] It is with this self-interest and life experience that I proceed to provide a postcolonial reading of Daniel 1.

First published in 36 from *Jian Dao*, 7 (1997): 17–36.

Dan 1:1–2 Who is More Powerful, The Colonizer or the Colonized?

> Dan 1:1 In the third year of the reign of Jehoiakim king of Judah, Nebuchadnezzar king of Babylon came (בָּא) to Jerusalem and besieged (צָּר) it. 2 And Adonai (my Lord) gave (וַיִּתֵּן אֲדֹנָי) Jehoiakim king of Judah into his hand, with some of the vessels of the house of God; and he brought (בָּא) them to the land of Shinar, to the house of his god, and placed (בָּא) the vessels in the treasury of his god.

At the beginning of Daniel 1,[6] the narrator introduces the presence of four different powers – two human and two divine – king of Judah, king of Babylon, God of Jerusalem, and god of the land of Shinar. According to Nebuchadnezzar's point of view, human conflict reflects a divine conflict, the king of Babylon's victory over the king of Judah reflects a victory of the god of Babylon over the god of Judah, as suggested by the action of Nebuchadnezzar to transfer temple vessels from Jerusalem to the treasure-house of his god in Shinar.[7] Though this may be a common understanding in the ancient world, it does not seem to be the issue at hand according to the narrator's point of view. As pointed out by Fewell,[8] "the issue is not between Nebuchadnezzar and his god, on the one hand, and Jehoiakim and his god, on the other. Two of these four parties, namely Jehoiakim and Nebuchadnezzar's god, quickly fade into the background and, essentially, die to the story. Nebuchadnezzar and the narrator's God emerge as the only two characters to survive the exposition. Their relationship is curiously conflicted." Fewell is right in recognizing the fade-in and fade-out of characters, but she missed the irony by over-emphasizing the conflicting elements of the story.[9] In fact, it was the irony at play here, rather than the birth of a conflicting relationship between Nebuchadnezzar and the narrator's god. The irony is twofold and not difficult to recognize. Firstly, although according to Nebuchadnezzar, he and Adonai were enemies, they are in fact allies; both sought after the defeat of Jerusalem, except that Nebuchadnezzar did not know it. According to the narrator, it was Adonai who gave Jehoiakim king of Judah into Nebuchadnezzar's hand (v.2a). Secondly, just as Nebuchadnezzar thought that he had defeated the god of Jerusalem by transferring the temple vessels to the land of Shinar (v.2b), the narrator is not slow to point out that it was Adonai who gave Jehoiakim, king of Judah, to him "along with some of the vessels of the house of God" (v.2a).

What is the purpose of the narrator in presenting such irony in the story? According to Fewell, the purpose of the narrator is fourfold. First, it is to offer a theological explanation for the defeat of Jerusalem and the destruction of the temple. Second, it is to present a world in which Adonai is the sovereign Lord who is able to manipulate foreign rulers, even unbelievers, and is in control of events. Third, it is to reflect the anger of Adonai upon the people who have gone against Adonai's will. Fourth, by participating in the destruction of Jerusalem, Adonai brings an end to the "older story," which "foreshadows" a "new story" about to be unfolded with the possibility of hope.[10] Though the scheme is attractive, I would argue, on the contrary, that the presence of the irony reflects a kind of postcolonial ideology within the narrator's literary articulation. This introductory story serves to represent the narrator's reclaiming of the "true" past. It sets the stage with an overtone of postcolonial sentiment by which the narrator develops the

characters in the story that is to follow. I shall also demonstrate in the following, through the character of Daniel who mirrors the narrator's postcolonial ideology, the narrator is able to articulate a sentiment of resistance to the dominating power of the colonizer (Nebuchadnezzar), which is not uncommon in the exilic period.

In the first irony, Nebuchadnezzar was depicted by the narrator as an arrogant fool, who thought that it was by his own military might that the victory was won, without realizing that it was Adonai, the God of the narrator, who gave the enemy into his hand, as told from the narrator's point of view. The narrator, the colonized, as a subjugated subject under the imperial force of the Babylonian army, though he cannot help but to accept the fact that they were defeated, nonetheless, resists to admit the history as told from Nebuchadnezzar's point of view. Rather, the colonized narrator preferred to offer another story with regards to the happenings in the past; "it was 'my Lord' who gave the king of Judah into your hand."

Frantz Fanon in *The Wretched of the Earth* argued that in order for the colonized people to find a voice and identity, they must, first, reclaim their own past. Secondly, they must begin to erode the colonizer's ideology by which their past had been devalued. In order to reclaim their "true" past, the narrator of Daniel 1 resolves to offer a "history" that devalued the colonizer (Nebuchadnezzar as an arrogant fool), rather than being devalued. By pronouncing the passiveness of Nebuchadnezzar in his imperial act, the narrator is able to demote the colonizer from a taker to a receiver. As the table is being turned around, identity of the colonized is being up-graded, from the passive manipulated to the active manipulator, and from the powerless loser to the powerful giver.

To erode the ideology of the colonizer, the narrator presents a different picture by contrasting Adonai's action with Nebuchadnezzar's activity. Adonai actively gives (וַיִּתֵּן אֲדֹנָי) so that Nebuchadnezzar could come (בָּא), take (בָּא) and place (בָּא) vessels from the temple of Jerusalem in the land of Shinar. Words are carefully chosen to express the disapproval of the colonizer's view of history. The action of Nebuchadnezzar was characterized by the use of בָּא three times. Though the word may be one of the most frequently used verb in the Old Testament,[11] one of its frequent usages is to refer to a temple worshiper who comes to the sanctuary together with the community of faith to pray and bring sacrifices (Deut. 12:5; 31:11; 2Sam. 7:18; 1Kg.8:41; Isa. 30:29; Jer. 7:2,1; Ps.5:7[H8]; 42:2[H3]). The coming of Nebuchadnezzar to Jerusalem is an event actively anticipated and realized by the will of Adonai, just as it is Adonai's will that people should come and worship in the temple. Upon Nebuchadnezzar's coming בָּא Adonai gives נתַן from the Jerusalem temple. The colonizer (Nebuchadnezzar) plays right into the hand of the colonized (the narrator) who is mirrored in Adonai's action and represented by the character of Adonai in the narrative. Such literary articulation is one of the common characteristics of postcolonial criticism.

In the second irony, just as Nebuchadnezzar thought that he had defeated the god of Jerusalem by transferring the temple vessels to the land of Shinar (v.2b), the narrator immediately points out that it was Adonai who gave Jehoiakim, king of Judah, to him "along with some of the vessels of the house of God" (v.2a). It is a common phenomenon for the colonizer to feature the god of the colonized as weak, heathen, and incapable of defending its worshipers' interests. Postcolonial criticism calls to the awareness of false representation of the deity, religion and culture of the

subaltern, marginalized and colonized.[12] Through the play of irony, not only is the narrator able to represent the colonizer as the weak and dependent receiver, rather than the strong and independent taker, s/he is also able to elevate his/her identity by mirroring Adonai as a representation of the colonized. Although it is not at all wrong to argue as Fewell did, that the purpose of the narrator is to offer a theological explanation for the conquest of Jerusalem and the destruction of the temple, it might have downplayed the political, cultural, and religious sentiment of the dissidents in exile.[13]

Fewell discussed this introductory story under the heading of "Two Sovereigns," with a view of presenting the conflicting relationships between the sovereignty of Nebuchadnezzar and that of the narrator's God. The story as presented to me, however, is more towards a struggle for power and superiority between the colonizer and the colonized. Nebuchadnezzar, the colonizer, comes, besieges, takes and places, moves in and out of the promise land of the narrator as if it was no one's land. Such freedom of access to land, people, and vessels,[14] on the part of Nebuchadnezzar, which is understood as a kind of imperial force and colonizing power, is being represented as an event that is being authorized at a higher level than that of the colonizer, namely the God of the narrator; a divine power that is higher than that of Nebuchadnezzar's human power. By appealing to the divine power, the colonized is able to transcend, for the moment, the mere historical fact of being defeated and colonized, elevating oneself as superior to the imperial colonizer.

Thus, the stage is set, ready for the characters to play their roles. Voices of the colonized shall be heard, and the identity of the colonized as a superior subject, rather than a subjugated subject will be articulated in the following development of the Daniel story.[15]

Dan 1:3–7 The Process of Colonization and Neocolonization

> 3 Then the king commanded Ashpenaz, his chief eunuch, to bring some of the people of Israel, both of the royal family and of the nobility, 4 youths without blemish, handsome and skillful in all wisdom, endowed with knowledge, understanding learning, and competent to serve in the king's palace, and to teach them the letters and language of the Chaldeans. 5 The king assigned them a daily portion of the rich food which the king ate, and of the wine which he drank. They were to be educated for three years, and at the end of that time they were to stand before the king. 6 Among these were Daniel, Hananiah, Misha-el, and Azariah of the tribe of Judah. 7 And the chief of the eunuchs gave them names: Daniel he called Belteshazzar, Hananiah he called Shadrach, Misha-el he called Meshach, and Azariah he called Abednego.[16]

The story continues with a picture of the royal palace where Nebuchadnezzar administers his colonial affairs. The narrator presents a picture that unveils the colonizing strategy of the colonizer (Nebuchadnezzar) on the colonized (Israelites). Nebuchadnezzar commands his chief eunuch Ashpenaz to bring some of the people of Israel with the following qualifications: (a) of royal family and of nobility, (b) youth without any blemish מוּם, (c) handsome in appearance, (d) showing aptitude for all kinds of learning, (e) well informed and quick to understand.

These prerequisites would reflect their knowledge of Jewish language, tradition and culture. The purpose is clearly for "maximizing the efficiency of Babylonian rule," as suggested by Smith-Christopher.[17] The selection brings before Nebuchadnezzar the best minds of the Israelites, the elite. By such act, Nebuchadnezzar segregated the best of the best from the rest of the Israelites, so he can rule them in a "downward filtration" manner.

There are at least four different elements that are of interest to postcolonial criticism, according to Nebuchadnezzar's colonial policy: (1) Segregation (vv.1–4a), (2) Language (v.4b), (3) Education (v.5b), (4) Naming (vv.6–7).

Segregation is a common practice of the colonizer's political strategy, to divide and rule. Even before the Babylonians, Assyrian imperial policy practiced the dispersal of captives and dissemination of colonial knowledge for the purpose of control and domination. The selection of the best of the best Israelites, even including the "royal seed," is in fact a form of neocolonialism, in that colonized elite are being transformed or re-educated in order to serve the purpose of the colonizer. Fewell recognized the danger in such an act of selecting the "royal seeds," but Nebuchadnezzar, a well-seasoned colonizer, has strategy to turn the potential danger around for his own advantages, to rule his subjugates with the colonized elite. Neocolonialism has proven to be an effective strategy in many of the Commonwealth countries.

This group of selected colonial elite will need to go through a series of educational processes. They are to "learn the letters and language of the Chaldeans" (v.4b). As remarked by Ashcroft, "[L]anguage is a fundamental site of struggle for postcolonial discourse because the colonial process itself begins in language."[18] The learning of the language of the Chaldean also implies the instruction in Chaldean culture. As observed by Fewell, the term Chaldean could either designate "a class of professional sages (cf. 2:2–10; 3:8–12; 4:7; 5:7)," which therefore refers to a field of professional knowledge, or used as an ethnic label (cf. 5:30; 9:1). The "choice of the term 'Chaldean' rather than 'sage' or 'magician' suggests that the training involves national (and thus political) as well as professional indoctrination."[19] Some have suggested that "three years of study is mentioned in Persian sources as the time required for training in knowledge of religious matters."[20] Nebuchadnezzar's strategy to re-educate the elite of Israelites is to indoctrinate and infiltrate the colonized minds, a form of neocolonialism. Philip G. Altbach observes well, "Colonial educational policies were generally elitist. In India, British educational elitism assumed the title of 'downward filtration' – a system by which a small group of Indians with a British style education supposedly spread enlightenment to the masses . . . 'French assimilationist' policies also worked in this direction. Indigenous cultures, in many cases highly developed, were virtually ignored by colonial educational policy."[21] Braj B. Kachru painfully recalls that "[T]he English language is a tool of power, domination and elitist identity, and of communication across continents."[22] Ashcroft also observes that the process of colonization necessarily involves "the suppression of a vast wealth of indigenous cultures beneath the weight of imperial control." Nebuchadnezzar practices colonialism in his military operation to besiege Jerusalem (1:1–2), and promotes neocolonialism on the captives in Babylon (1:3–4). Such are the tactics of the colonizer in order to colonize their subjugate, with a view of consolidating and expanding their imperial kingdom.

Through re-education, the culture, religion, and knowledge of the colonized are transformed in order to serve the purpose of the colonizer. Colonialism takes place in Jerusalem and neocolonialism takes place in the Babylonian kingdom.

The next logical move for Nebuchadnezzar, the colonizer, is to name their subjugates. The Jewish names of the four Judean youths were carefully noted before changing them to Chaldean names, as articulated by the narrator. Daniel is renamed as Belteshazzar, Hananiah renamed as Shadrach, Misha-el as Meshach, and Azariah as Abednego. Although scholars do not agree on the precise meaning of their names, most would think that their new Chaldean names have to do with Babylonian religions and the names of Babylonian deities. The significance of the names, however, lies not so much in their meaning; rather, it lies in the fact that as subjugator/colonizer;, they are being named by their subjugator/colonizer; "it is done by a power that assumes the authority to make such a change," as Smith-Christopher remarks.

The naming of the subject, as in the creation story, carries with it a notion of domination and lordship over the subject. The naming or re-naming in biblical literature is also a sign of inferior, subordinate and dependent status; Eliakim was renamed by Pharaoh Neco as Jehoiakim (2 Kg. 23:34), and Mattaniah was changed to Zedekiah by Nebuchadnezzar (2 Kg. 24:17). Ashcroft, in *The Post-colonial Studies Reader*,[23] has captured the essence of naming the subject in the act of colonization.

> One of the most subtle demonstrations of the power of language is the means by which it provides, through the function of naming, a technique for knowing a colonised place or people. To name the world is to 'understand' it, to know it and to have control over it... To name reality is therefore to exert power over it, simply because the dominant language becomes the way in which it is known. In colonial experience this power is by no means vague or abstract. A systematic education and indoctrination installed the language and thus the reality on which it was predicated as preeminent.

The naming of Daniel and his friends in Chaldean language also means the change of their Jewish identity to one of a hybridity. The emphasis on identity as doubled, or hybrid, or unstable is one characteristic of the postcolonial approach to reading literature.[24] By the change of names, they have been transformed into Chaldeans with Jewish blood. Yet, they are supposedly to take it as an honor to serve the Babylonian empire with all honesty and loyalty, as any Babylonian would do. From this moment onward, Daniel and friends will have to live with a hybrid identity, mentally, socially, and physically. Though this might be some kind of a torture, and not much can be done with regards to the change of their names by their colonizer, yet the narrator continues to use their Jewish name in the narrative and throughout the book as a means of resistance to colonial rule. Such resistance can appear in different forms and in other areas of their lives, as the narrator develops the story, increasing the reader's anticipation.

On the naming of Daniel's Chaldean name, Fewell suggests that they might be engineered by their colonizer to go through a classic model of *a rite of passage*, "a ritual designed to facilitate a person's passing from one phase of life into another."[25] With the three stages in the classic model of ritual process,[26] Fewell concludes that

> [T]his match between Nebuchadnezzar's plan and a rite of passage strengthens our understanding of the training as not simply professional education. The young men are to learn the Babylonian profession, and confess Babylonian allegiance. Such a transformation benefits the king; the captives must be made to see that such a transformation benefits them as well. The narrator, however, leaves the reader two options for judging what is happening to the young Judeans. In one sense their rite of passage is a promotion from prisoners to professional. But in another sense, the passage is a demotion from "royal seed" to servanthood.

There is a difference, however, in the cultural anthropological model of Victor Turner and that of Nebuchadnezzar's strategy in Daniel 1. Though there may be some resemblance in the two situations, there is a spirit of resistance, politically and religiously, in Daniel's case, on the one hand, and they were forced to accept the transformation and brainwashing as prisoners of war, on the other. The model of a rite of passage is, after all, an observed phenomenon in primitive society in transition.

Identity and name are very personal belongings – being and existence are rooted in them. The change of one's name without one's consent or by force, not only is an insult to one's integrity and dignity, but also a denial of the right to ancestry. As pointed out by Samuel Huntington, "[P]eople define themselves in terms of ancestry, religion, language, history, values, customs and institutions."[27] For hundreds of years, the naming of Chinese people by the westerner has been a painful experience. For instance, the two names, Mao Ze-dong or Deng Xiao-ping, are never required by western media to reverse the order in introducing their names, while it is a common practice to reverse the order of the names for all other Chinese names (almost one-fourth of the entire world population). If one insisted on writing one's Chinese name according to the order of the Chinese characters, then it will almost certainly be mistaken by a westerner who will take the last character as the last name or surname. One's ancestrial tradition is defined by one's surname. There is a saying in Chinese, "Standing, I don't change my surname, Sitting, I don't change my name," which means one will stand by one's own words once uttered. This shows the importance of one's name in Chinese culture, like many others. Under the British rule, English education has forced many colonized people to change their names and identities. Often, names that reflect the western religion, i.e., Christianity, are taken with little knowledge of it, like that of Daniel and friends' Chaldean names.

That the narrator carefully articulated this element of name changing into the narrative of Daniel under Nebuchadnezazar, the colonizer, is by no means an accident. It is a voice for human integrity and dignity. The voice of dissident is being transmitted in the form of character play, through the action of Daniel who resisted the temptation of status at the risk of his life, as the story develops in the next section. With a new socio-political status for Daniel and the youths, king Nebuchadnezzar can expect the best of their service for his kingdom. Although as Fewell observed, "[T]he reader might even be tempted to consider Nebuchadnezzar a generous, tolerant monarch with worthy aesthetic and intellectual values," the narrator seems to have another thought in mind – to carry on his/her scheme of resistance to colonial rule, as the story develops further into Daniel's resistance to the eating culture of the palace.

Dan 1:8–16 The Resistance and Resolution[28]

> 8 But Daniel resolved that he would not defile himself with the king's rich food, or with the wine which he drank; therefore he asked the chief of the eunuchs to allow him not to defile himself. 9 And God gave Daniel favor and compassion חֶסֶד in the sight of the chief of the eunuchs; 10 and the chief of the eunuchs said to Daniel, "I fear lest my lord the king, who appointed your food and your drink, should see that you were in poorer condition than the youths who are of your own age. So you would endanger my head with the king." 11 Then Daniel said to the steward whom the chief of the eunuchs had appointed over Daniel, Hananiah, Misha-el, and Azariah; 12 "Test your servants for ten days; let us be given vegetables to eat and water to drink. 13 Then let our appearance and the appearance of the youths who eat the king's rich food be observed by you, and according to what you see deal with your servants." 14 So he hearkened to them in this matter, and tested them for ten days. 15 At the end of ten days it was seen that they were better in appearance and fatter in flesh than all the youths who ate the king's rich food. 16 So the steward took away their rich food and the wine they were to drink, and gave them vegetables.

In this section, the narrator continues to mirror his/her resistance to colonial power through the character of God and the act of Daniel. The colonial power, however, is represented not by Nebuchadnezzar himself in the first person this time, but by his representative, the chief eunuch Ashpenaz. There are two implications to this change in character representations. First, it provides a look into how successful is the neocolonization scheme of Nebuchadnezzar, as reflected through the service of the eunuch, who probably is enlisted to serve in the palace in the way Daniel and others did. Second, it allows the voices of those who are colonized under imperial rule against their will to be heard, through the act of Ashpenaz and Daniel. Some scholars might incline to think that the sympathy of Ashpenaz towards the youths is a sign of kindness to foreigners in the Babylonian court. But this is contrary to the narrator's purpose of the characterization of the eunuch in the story. The act of the eunuch is clearly to convey a postcolonial ideology. Although he is entrusted with a high position in the court of Babylon and physically he is beyond redemption, yet in all human dignity and in the spirit of resistance, he is willing even to risk his career and life (v.10) for the sake of colonial resistance. Smith-Christopher is right in commenting that "[T]he friendship between Daniel and Ashpenaz, therefore, is the solidarity of the oppressed, both of whom serve the imperial will under threat of death; and this solidarity crosses ethnic lines, as Ashpenaz obviously admires Daniel's courage. This is hardly a sign of positive attitudes toward Babylonians!"[29] The high official position of the Ashpenaz in Nebuchadnezzar's administration might suggest that he has been transformed with colonial knowledge and wisdom, whereby he is put in charge of all other eunuchs. The courage of Daniel to resist, might once again awaken his soul and spirit. Ashpenaz decided to go along with Daniel's way even at the risk of his own life. The interactions between Ashpenaz and Daniel may well fit into another characteristic of postcolonial criticism, namely, the stress on "cross-cultural" interactions. The narrator, furthermore, supports the act of resistance by Daniel and Ashpenaz to colonial power, through the characterization of God, "And God gave Daniel favor and compassion in the sight of the chief of the

eunuchs" (v.9). With the חֶסֶד of God who delivers and protects with power, the narrator presents, once again, the powerlessness of the colonizer in face of the power of the God of חֶסֶד who has covenantal responsibility towards Daniel, the colonized (cf. 1:1–2).[30]

The resistance is carried out through a simple act on the part of the colonized, Daniel and friends, the rejection of food. Like any resistance to colonial rule, life is always at risk, and so is Daniel's life. The decision to put the weight of resistance on the simple daily survival matter of food and drink, is by no means a coincidence. Food and drink,[31] which are basic for survival, also reflect and represent one's culture and religion, especially in the Jewish tradition. By granting food to Daniel, it represents the permission to live; and the food from the royal table means special status and quality of life granted by the king. The refusal to receive food from the royal table by Daniel, not only is a struggle to make known his voice of resistance to colonial power, but is also a challenge to the colonizer's claim of life controlling power, let alone the promise of quality life by the colonizer. Fewell[32] and Philip Davies[33] have both observed that, "there are political dimensions to the king's food. The food and wine are, in other words, the symbols of political patronage; to consume them would be tantamount to declaring complete political allegiance." The consuming of the food, on the part of Daniel, not only would declare "complete political allegiance," but also proclaims a victory on the part of the king as the colonizer who has the power over life and death (as in western colonial history). If Daniel, the colonized, accepted the foods offered by the King, his acceptance would be an admission, on the part of the culture and religion he represents, of the colonizer's superiority. That itself is defiling for Daniel culturally and religiously.[34] Davies is right in observing the act of Daniel's resistance as "a denial of the king's implicit claim to be sole provider."[35] Goldingay[36] also perceptively comments that although meat and wine are foods of festivity as in Isa. 22:13, the attitude of the exiles ought to be mourning for the destruction of Jerusalem, as the psalmist of Ps. 137 painfully mourned. Thus, whether for cultural, religious, or nationalistic reasons, Daniel's resistance to the food from the king's table lends a strong support to a postcolonial reading of his act as a resistance to colonial power.

To recapitulate the scene, the narrator's plot is simple; the refusal of Daniel and three friends to partake of the food created the tension and crisis which require a resolution. The suspense that comes with it anticipated the resolution through the act of God who is carefully articulated as a character in the hands of the narrator. In the first story in Dan.1:1–2, the narrator has represented the story that it was Adonai who gave the victory into Nebuchadnezzar's hand. In this story, no longer is it Nebuchadnezzar; instead, it is his chief eunuch, who is also in the control of the narrator's God who not only protected the four youths, but also preserves the life of the eunuch. In fact, it was the preservation of the colonized youths whereby the eunuch's life was redeemed. The strategy and power of neocolonialism is once again eliminated and turned around, instead, to demonstrate the providence of the God of the colonized narrator. The challenge to colonial power's universal claim on the right to physical life and death is thus brought to a close, declaring victory to the colonized Daniel and God of the narrator. Daniel lives and looks far better than those who are well fed by the king's rich food after ten days (v.15). The narrator has made his/her point on the resistance to colonial power and victory to the colonized.

The next challenge, as plotted by the narrator, is a comparison of wisdom and knowledge of the colonizer and the colonized.

Dan 1:17–21 The Success of the Subjugated

> 17 As for these four youths, God gave them learning and skill in all letters and wisdom; and Daniel had understanding in all visions and dreams. 18 At the end of the time, when the king had commanded that they should be brought in, the chief of the eunuchs brought them in before Nebuchadnezzar. 19 And the king spoke with them, and among them all none was found like Daniel, Hananiah, Misha-el, and Azariah; therefore they stood before the king. 20 And in every matter of wisdom and understanding concerning which the king inquired of them, he found them ten times better than all the magicians and enchanters that were in all his kingdom. 21 And Daniel continued until the first year of King Cyrus.

The story continues with the narrator's articulation of the providence of God who protects and provides the colonized with wisdom and knowledge, whereby the Babylonian kingdom is sustained.[37] Although no specific dramatic act is included in this section, it serves as a conclusion to Daniel 1, whereby Daniel stands as a winner in front of the king as a contrast to a captive's position at the beginning of the chapter. It also sets the position for Daniel's colonial career as unfolded by those stories that is to follow in the rest of the book; as Daniel continues to serve from Nebuchadnezzar to "the first year of King Cyrus" (v.21).

The narrator is quick to present the result of the challenge, that the wisdom and knowledge of Daniel and three friends are found "ten times better than all the magicians and enchanters that were in the kingdom." It is not difficult to perceive the narrator's implicit reason for such comparison of knowledge and wisdom of Daniel and friends with the rest of the kingdom's – to demote the claims to superiority in knowledge by the colonizer. But the narrator is careful in articulating the postcolonial ethos. In v. 17, the pride in the superiority of the narrator is presented as the act of God who gives the youths "knowledge and skill in all learning and wisdom" (נזדט והשכבל-ספר וחאכנזה). But Daniel alone has another added value, he has "understanding in all visions and dreams" (הכיז ככל-חזווחלנזות), which makes him superior to all the others and he continues to serve till the time of Cyrus. The test is conducted by no other than king Nebuchadnezzar himself (v.19), lest one should question the integrity and thoroughness of the test. Nebuchadnezzar comes into the scene again, at this last section of the chapter, and forms the conclusion to the contest that sets forth from the beginning of the chapter on who is more powerful. The narrator carefully manipulated the contest in such a way that it was through the mouth of the king that the confirmation of superiority of the colonized over those of the Babylonian kingdom's intellectuals is pronounced. The confession of the superiority of Daniel by the words of Nebuchadnezzar is in sharp contrast to the conqueror image that the narrator presented at the beginning of the story. The long-standing service of Daniel, according to the last verse of the chapter, testifies and satisfies the postcolonial mindset of the narrator, that Israelites are far more superior and powerful than the Babylonians.

It is clear, by now, that throughout the chapter, the characterizations of Daniel, friends, and God enabled the narrator to mirror a postcolonial ethos, and to claim a victory over the colonial power of Nebuchadnezzar. It is by the God of the narrator, through Daniel and friends, that the Babylonian kingdom stands and is being sustained.

Conclusion

This reader of Daniel 1, as one who has been colonized, identified with the narrator, Daniel, and the God of the colonized. The search for identity of the subject in a postmodern world is a common experience and many can testify to its agonizing rite of passage. This is also true of a postcolonial experience. One of the agonizing features in the search for identity of the colonized is the naming of oneself as the subject/object of/by the colonizer. The experience of Daniel is too much of a common experience of the colonized, say for those who experienced the British colonial rule, and subsequent neocolonial rule. This essay draws on the narrator's literary articulation of the colonial power versus the colonizer's God as a voice for those who have lived under the colonial rule.

The identity of the colonized is often in a hybrid situation. On the one hand, there is the identity by birth or native origin identity, and on the other, there is the identity imposed, at different layers, by the colonial reality. Although Daniel does not have any means of power or position that allows him to resist the colonizer's invitation to a new identity by naming him with a name in the colonizer's language, his courage to resist with his own stomach sets an unprecedented example for the many who struggled to live under colonial and neocolonial power, often without human dignity. The narrator's silent protest is reflected in the continuous use of the name Daniel throughout the story. Like any other resistance to domination, life is always at risk. Daniel jeopardized not only his own fate, but also the lives of the eunuch and his fellow countrymen by refusing to follow the food custom of his colonizer.

Eating habits and food custom are the most basic of all cultural differences. By changing one's food custom or eating habits, cultural identity is often being called into question. A visit to any food court will prove the case in point. Daniel's resistance thus immediately hauls the story into suspense, a confrontation between the colonizer and the colonized: a cultural confrontation or a conflict of culture?[38] What lies behind is also the religious factors embedded within the different cultures. Without any military means of offending the colonizer, the narrator resorted to religious power in the narrative; as a matter of faith, he confronts the situation and emerges with a victory. As it has always been, from the beginning of the story to the end, the tension has been that of a conflict and confrontation between two religious powers. Such a religious confrontation is not uncommon in most, if not all, of the racial and cultural disputations in human history. Recently, it is even being argued by Samuel Huntington to be a new order of confrontation that threatens the existence of humankind in the next century, "clashes of civilizations are the greatest threat to world peace, and an international order based on civilizations is the surest safeguard against world war."[39]

"Peoples and nations are attempting to answer the most basic question humans can face: Who are we?" So writes Huntington, and concludes that, "We know who we are only when we know who we are not and often only when we know whom we are against."[40]

NOTES

1 This essay is dedicated, in memory of Hong Kong, named as a British Subject for more than a hundred years, and shall be renamed as a "special administration region" when it returns to China's sovereignty; and to those Chinese nationals who hold BNO passports, a subject with hybrid identity. [Hong Kong reverted to Chinese rule on July 1, 1997.]

2 Not even mentioned in Jeremy Hawthorn, *A Concise Glossary of Contemporary Literary Theory* (2nd edn, 1994), nor David Lodge (ed.), *Modern Criticism and Theory: A Reader* (1988, 8th impression 1993), but found in Peter Barry, *Beginning Theory: An Introduction to Literary and Cultural Theory* (Manchester: Manchester University Press, 1995), and Keith Green and Jill Lebihan, *Critical Theory & Practice: A Coursebook* (London: Routledge, 1996). It was also in the 1996 AAR/SBL Annual Meeting's program, e.g., the theme on "Postcolonialism and Biblical Studies" was discussed in the Ideological Criticism Group.

3 Some of the representative literatures are Edward Said, *Orientalism* (New York: Pantheon, 1978) and *Culture and Imperialism* (New York: Vintage Books, 1993); Homi Bhabha, *Nation and Narration* (London: Routledge, 1990) and *The Location of Culture* (London: Routledge, 1994); *The Empire Writes Back: Theory and Practice in Post-colonial Literature* (London: Routledge, 1989), ed. Ashcroft and *et al.*, and Gayatri Chakravorty Spival, *The Post-colonial Critic*, ed. Sarah Harasym (London: Routledge, 1990). Over to this side of the Pacific, publications in Chinese include those of Liao Ping-hui, *Modernity in Re-vision: Reading Postmodern/Postcolonial Theories* (廖炳惠：《回顧現代：後現代與後殖民論文集》) (Taipei: Rye Field Publishing Company, 1994); Zhang Jingyuan (ed.), *Postcolonial Criticism and Cultural Identity* (張京媛編：《後殖民 理論與文化認同》) (Taipei: Rye Field Publishing Company, 1995), and Zhu Yau-wei, *Post-orientalism: A Strategy for Chinese and Western Cultural Critical Discourse* (朱耀偉：《後東 方主義》) (Taipei: Camel, 1994).

4 I was born in the year my country gained independence from the Great British Empire. My entire primary and secondary education was done at a time when the country was going through a process of national decolonization and assuming a postcolonial era, only to be haunted by neocolonialism.

5 Hong Kong Island was offered to become the British Crown of Colony according to the "Treaty of Nanjing" signed in 1842. Kowloon peninsula (South of Boundary Street including Stone Cutter Island) was offered to the United Kingdom according to the "Treaty of Beijing" in 1860. In 1898, the "Extension of Hong Kong Boundary" agreement was signed, which concluded the leasing of the land from south of Shenzhen River to the north of Boundary Street including Lantau Island and some other 235 outlying islands to the Great British Empire in terms of 99 years, due on June 30, 1997. The Chinese Government, however, declared the treaties were unfair and would not be accepted. Hence, the "Sino-British Joint Declaration" was announced after negotiations from both sides in 1984, and declared that Hong Kong will become a Special Administration Region upon the handover of the sovereignty back to China. Thus, Hong Kong, an island community of six and a half million people will be ushered, by fate, into a postcolonial era, precisely on July 1st, 1997, at 00hr.

6 Similar experience may be drawn from Daniel 1:1–2 for the people of Hong Kong, in the sense of a meta-narrative. HK 1:1 In the Twenty-second year of the reign of Hsün-tsung, the Emperor of China, Queen Victoria of the British Empire sent an army to China and besieged it. 2 The Emperor of China was invited to sign the Treaties, and Hong Kong was graciously offered as a sign of peace and gift to her Majesty for a ninety-nine years lease, and along with the offer were some of the vessels of the house of the Emperor, which were brought back to the land of Britain and placed in the British Museum.

7 On the issue of placing foreign vessels in the house of the treasure in Shinar, Daniel L. Smith-Christopher, "Daniel," in *The New Interpreter's Bible, Volume VII* (Nashville: Abingdon, 1996), 38–9, comments that "the Babylonians were highly aware of the propaganda value of placing captured religious symbols "under" the Babylonian gods in the Babylonian imperial shrines, thus symbolizing the captivity of conquered gods as well as people. Since the Jews did not have an image of their God, the Babylonian used their temple vessels instead. Note that these materials were not merely melted down, but kept intact so as to serve as symbols of the Jews' subordinate position in relation to Babylonian imperial and religious power."

8 Danna Nolan Fewell, *Circle of Sovereignty: Plotting Politics in the Book of Daniel* (Nashville: Abingdon, 1991), 13–15.

9 Focusing on their potential conflicting relationship, Fewell argued that "On the one hand, Adonai and Nebuchadnezzar are allies. They have both sought the same thing – the defeat of Jerusalem. On the other hand, Nebuchadnezzar does not recognize Adonai as the source of his victory. He does not know this god and he offers this god no credit. Thus the potential conflict is born," 14–15. I think it is absurd that if Nebuchadnezzar who is conscious of the king of Judah as his enemy should ever want to recognize Adonai as his source of victory or offer this god any credit for his victory.

10 She argued that "[B]y pairing Adonai's will with Nebuchadnezzar's activity, the narrator braces the story with a certain theological worldview." 15.

11 D. J. A. Clines counted 2,565 occurrences in *The Dictionary of Classical Hebrew, Volume II*, ו-ב (Sheffield: Sheffield Academic Press, 1995); while Elmer Martens counted 2,570 times in *Theological Workbook of the Old Testament*.

12 As pointed out by Peter Barry, "the first characteristic of postcolonial criticism is – an awareness of representations of the non-European as exotic or immoral "Other"." *Beginning Theory*, 192–3.

13 Daniel L. Smith-Christopher rightly observes that "Most literary analysis of these stories, however, has tended to overlook their potent sociopolitical power as stories of resistance to cultural and spiritual assimilation of a minority by a dominant foreign power," *The New Interpreter's Bible, Volume VII*, 20.

14 Such event can find resemblance in the modern history of China and Southeast Asia, which provided testimonies to western imperialism and colonizing power that left with them marks of brutality and cruelty, along with others, on the land and people of Asia.

15 D. W. Lee Humphreys, on the other hand, in "A Life-Style for Diaspora: A Study of the Tales of Esther and Daniel," *JBL* 92:2 (1973): 211–23, argues that "Daniel are tales of a particular type, which along with their considerable entertainment value, develop a particular theological emphasis addressed to the emerging Jewish communities of the Persian and hellenistic diaspora. They suggest and illustrate a certain style of life for the Jew in his foreign environment."

16 HK1:3 Then the Queen commanded her governors, The Right Honourables Sir Henry Pottingger (1843–4), Sir John Francis Davis (1844–8), Sir Samuel George Bonham (1848–54), Sir John Bowring (1854–9), Lord Rosmead (1859–65), Sir Richard Graves MacDonnell (1866–72), Sir Authur Edward Kennedy (1872–7), Sir John Pope Hennessy (1877–82), Sir George Ferguson Bowen (1883–5), Sir George William Des

Voeux (1887–91), Sir William Robinson (1891–8), and Sir Henry Arthur Blake (1898–1903), to enlist the people of Hong Kong, both of the rich family and nobility, 4 youths without blemish, handsome and skillful in all wisdom, endowed with knowledge, understanding learning, and competent to serve the Queen of the British Empire, and to teach them the letters and language of the Anglo-Saxons. 5 The Queen constituted them to learn the eating and drinking habits, as well as dinning manners of the high society and of royal and noble life style. They were to be educated for three years and at the end of that time they were to serve the Royal Service for her Majesty, the Queen of the Great British Empire. 6 Among these were Cheung Ah-san, Kwang Ah-see, Chong Ah-hwa, and Sia Phng-yng of the southern province of China. 7 And the headmaster gave them new names because they are difficult to pronounce, Cheung Ah-san he called James Cheung, Kwang Ah-see he called Andrew Kwang, Chong Ah-Hwa he called Thomas Chong, and Sia Phng-yng he called Philip Sia. Leaving all their Chinese given names in void and position their names in reverse order.

17 *The New Interpreter's Bible, Volume VII*, 39.

18 Ashcroft, et al. (eds), *The Postcolonial Studies Reader*, 283.

19 *Circle of Sovereignty*, 16.

20 *The New Interpreter's Bible, Volume VII*, 39.

21 "Education and Neocolonialism," in Ashcroft, et al., (eds), *The Postcolonial Studies Reader*, 452.

22 "The Alchemy of English," in Ashcroft, et al., (eds), *The Postcolonial Studies Reader*, 291.

23 Ashcroft, et al., (eds), *The Postcolonial Studies Reader*, 1.

24 As pointed out by Peter Barry, *Beginning Theory*, 195.

25 *Circle of Sovereignty*, 17.

26 The three stages are: first, they are separated from their community and put in seclusion (so Nebuchadnezzar's first command in v.3). Once secluded from normal society, they endure a temporary "betwixt and between" or "liminal" existence in which they are taught special knowledge that will enable them to function in their new roles... These included experiences in the liminal stage are designed to bring about a change of being, a change of identity. Third, the process is reintegration into society. *Circle of Sovereignty*, 17.

27 Samuel Huntington, *The Clash of Civilizations and the Remaking of World Order* (New York: Simon and Schuster, 1996), 21. He also points out that "For peoples seeking identity and reinventing ethnicity, enemies are essential, and the potentially most dangerous enmities occur across the fault lines between the world's major civilizations," 20.

28 HK1:8 But Cheung Ah-san resolved that he would not defile his ancestors with the Queen's new name; therefore he asked the Headmaster to allow him not to defile his ancestors by retaining his Chinese name.

29 *The New Interpreter's Bible, Volume VII*, 42.

30 Katherine Doob Sakenfeld, *The Meaning of* Hesed *in the Hebrew Bible* (Missoula, Mont.: Scholars Press, 1978).

31 Smith-Christopher has an interesting analysis of " 'Food and Power' in the Hebrew Bible," 40–2.

32 *Circle of Sovereignty*, 19.

33 *Daniel*, Old Testament Guides (Sheffield: Sheffield Academic Press, 1985), 90–1.

34 Scholars generally agreed that the issue of defilement here is not on eating foods that have been offered to idols, because "Daniel does accept 'vegetables' from the royal supply, so the likelihood that he wanted to avoid any Babylonian food that had been dedicated to pagan deities seems not to be the issue here," as argued by Smith-Christopher, 40.

35 *Daniel*, 91.

36 *Daniel*, Word Biblical Commentary (Dallas: Word Books, 1989), 18–19.

37 It is not surprising to find resemblance in modern history of western colonization that the culture and economy of the colonizer is sustained by exploitation on the colonies' wealth of resources, human and natural.

38 Samuel Huntington has a very convincing presentation on the coming conflict of civilizations, as a conflict of cultures, with an up-to-date analysis of international happenings in the last few years, in *The Clash of Civilizations and the Remaking of World Order* (New York: Simon and Schuster, 1996).

39 Ibid., 125.

40 Ibid., 21.

12

DECOLONIZING YAHWEH: A Postcolonial Reading of 2 Kings 24–25[1]

Kari Latvus

1 Destruction and Deportation

Two chapters, containing 50 verses, at the end of Kings (2 Kings 24–5) describe how the political and social independence of the southern state of Judah was lost. A major theme in the biblical story before this moment is: how to get the land and live in it. After this point the question is reloaded: how to survive without the land or how to get it back. The destruction of Jerusalem and its temple, as well as the deportation of part of the population are *the* core crisis in the Hebrew Bible. The political element of the momentum is focused on the collapse of the Davidic dynasty as the sovereign ruler of Judah. As a social result Judah was split, dispersed, and brought into the deepest possible interaction with the multicultural Orient. Both the political and social dimensions caused the condition of uncertainty and a threat to ethnic identity. The origin of process lay in external reasons, namely the politics of Babylon, which followed the pattern created by the Assyrian superpower: to conquer surrounding nations which were colonized so as to be provinces or vassal-nations of the empire. Colonialism in different forms has left permanent marks on the history of nations.

All these issues naturally strongly affected the Israelite's way of practicing their religion and expressing their faith in God. This meant that the relationship between Yahweh and Israel was reformulated to fit better with the individual and collective experiences and reality shared by the Israelites. In other words: the colonial politics of Babylon had a connection with the forms and contents of theology.

The aim of the present study is twofold. Firstly, it is intended to clarify the message of the end of the story, especially the so-called rehabilitation of Jehoiachin. Secondly, this paper tries to articulate how colonialism affected theology.

Unpublished paper.

2 The Postcolonial View

Before going into the analysis of the text a few remarks are needed about the terms *colonialism* and *postcolonialism*. As historical phenomena imperialism and colonialism are expressions of the politics which grow from the soil of political, financial, and cultural attempts to achieve hegemony in a certain geographical area or on the ideological level. The forms of colonialism vary and its aims are plural but somehow it is possible see the basic structure of it: it is always related to the power. Power to rule, power to trade, or to promote culture and ideology – just to give few examples. Colonialism is an ancient phenomenon and it is currently present as well.[2]

The analysis of colonialism in its varying forms has developed into a fruitful approach and gained the title postcolonial, which has been further applied into the biblical text with the title *postcolonial criticism*. Among the pioneers who have explored the new experiments and methodological guidelines especially R. S. Sugirtharajah and Fernando F. Segovia should be highlighted.[3]

> Postcolonialism's critical undertaking is a fusion of a variety of methods ranging from the now unfashionable historical-criticism to contemporary literary methods. . . . It thrives on inclusiveness and is attracted to all kinds of tools and disciplinary fields, as long as they probe injustices, produce new knowledge which problematizes well-entrenched positions, and enhances the lives of the marginalized. (Sugirtharajah, *Postcolonial*, 99–100)

In the research of ancient texts a fruitful approach is offered by analysis of power relations and their consequences. Thus there is need to notice:

> on the one hand, a political, economic, and cultural centre – more often than not symbolized by a city; on the other hand, any number of margins politically, economically, and culturally subordinated to the center. (Segovia, *Decolonizing*, 125–6)

Postcolonial criticism does not imitate liberation hermeneutics but obviously owes a lot to this tradition. Both approaches share a commitment to "the other" (not in power, ignored, marginalized) and also both emphasize empowerment of the oppressed.[4] Liberation theology/hermeneutics was, however, a child of modernity and a battering ram against the fortified castles of traditionalism. As such it represented the ideological approaches and atmosphere of the 1970s–80s.

3 Analysis of the Text: Power, Center, Margins

Deuteronomistic history (DH) ends with the colonial manifestation of the power of imperial Babylon. The story focuses on the detailed description of Babylon's military force and the action against Judah and its capital Jerusalem. In the plot of the story, four separate campaigns (24:1; 24:2; 24:10; 25:1) focus on the symbols of national identity: the members of the royal dynasty, Jerusalem and its walls, the royal palace and the temple of Yahweh. Imperial power is articulated through the destruction of city (25:9–10), through the partial slaughter of royal family and officers (25:7, 21) and also through the deportation of various groups (24:12, 14, 15–16; 25:7, 11).

In the list of deported or killed people several specific groups are mentioned: the royal family, court circles, leaders of the army, artisans, smiths, priests of varying status, and scribes (24:14–16; 25:18–21). The writer's interest is focused on those who are somehow connected to the royal court or have wealth or status in society based on certain professional skills. Besides these mentioned groups a large part of the nation which is left in Judah is labelled just "poor people of the land" (24:14).[5] One minor observation is that the list of deported people has a parallel version in the following passage (24:12a–14//15–17). The central difference in the latter text is the non-existence of margins: poor are not even mentioned.

After the first deportation there is a remaining population, the so-called "poor." The plot of the story requires, however, that non-deported people were able to establish a new society, have a new royal court, recruit a new army – and even were able to rebel against the colonial power in less than ten years. Finally an unsuccessful rebellion caused a new destruction of capital, including the temple, palace, houses of Jerusalem, and its walls (25:1–10). The rest of the *city population*, the rest of the skilled people, and even pro-Babylon allies (25:11) were deported. The poor people were left to work in vineyards and in fields. In the story only seven words are enough to describe the conditions of this anonymous majority of the nation, but nearly 70 words are needed to articulate the slaughter of priests, officers, and scribes in high rank, some mentioned even by name (25:12, 18–21).

Once more the plot of the story requires that the poor were able to run the society. From among "the remaining poor" grows a more or less established society including political groups, representatives of royal family, and officers of forces. "Remaining poor" seems to be a very flexible expression as a synonym for all those who are not worth mentioning. It seems that even when the rest of the city (25:11) or the whole of Judah is exiled (25:21) "you always have the poor with you" (John 12:8). The poor do not have names or quantity: no homes, burnt or saved; no children to be mentioned. They are just an unnumbered, unnamed, and non-located group somewhere. They are "the other" at a crucial moment of the nation's life. The poor represent the deepest margin compared to the political center of Babylon, because they are not even important enough to be named, killed, or deported. It seems obvious that the writer/s of the story do not identify themselves with the poor or even with the people that remained in Judah, but rather with those who are linked with the deported part of the society: those who work with the royal house and temple and those who work with the high-ranking officers and priests.

Another dimension of the colonization process is linked with the deeds of Babylon. Cruelty and killings committed by Babylon are articulated on several occasions in the story but always in connection with a reminder that Israelite rebellion is an original cause of the act. Jehoiakim rebelled against Babylon (24:1) and *Yahweh* sent nations to attack Judah. Jehoiachin "did what was evil in the sight of the Lord" (24:9) and Nebuchadnezzar attacked and colonized Judah. Zedekiah did evil and rebelled (24:19; 25:1) which caused major destruction in Jerusalem. On every occasion where the Babylonian empire uses violence or destroys the royal palace or temple, on every occasion when Babylon carries away the treasures or valuable things, there is always a preparatory section in the plot of the story where responsibility or the actual cause is pushed into Israelite hands. Their rebellious activities

effected the punishment given by Babylon. Actually Babylon does not look so bad at all, but is only a loyal servant in the mechanism of the inevitable larger historical logic.

4 End is Not Despair or Hope but Colonization

Let us now turn to the last verses in 2 Kings 25:22–30, which offer an illuminating sample of the writer's subordinated attitude. That means a positive understanding of the colonial power. In the words of Gedaliah (25:24) Babylon is hailed as a new master which they should "not be afraid of." Instead Babylon should be "served" and the colonial power would let good things happen: "it shall be well with you." The last phrase is very common in Deuteronomy to express good things given by Yahweh: Deut 4:40; 5:16, 26; 6:3, 18; 12:25, 28; 22:7. Also fear before the divine and before God is often expressed with "Do not fear" (Deut 1:21; 20:3; Josh 10:25, etc.). In deuteronomistic theology the basic verb to describe Israel's relation to Yahweh or other gods is "to serve." Contrary to the main line of deuteronomistic history, in this passage it is the foreign nation, not Yahweh, which should be served. The key words of this passage are also central deuteronomistic expressions but their focus in this setting has been changed. It seems as if the deuteronomistic Yahweh-talk had been transferred into a new context to create loyalty towards the colonial power, as if it would be the divine. Imperial power is seen and described by divine notions in order to underline how good it actually is.

The last paragraph of 2 Kings has presented a classical dilemma. Shall we read it as a sign of nationalistic hopes (Wolff)[6] or is it merely a pessimistic ending of a sad story (Noth)?[7] Until now there has not been a clear solution, but a cautious leaning towards the optimistic reading.[8] Postcolonial criticism offers a possibility, on this occasion, to find a new solution.

Therefore we should take into consideration the interpretation that the last episode reflects colonialism more than anything else. This means that the final verses continue the "subordination" line of the previous passage and show the good but controlled relations Jehoiachin had with Babylon. Babylon is described as a good and understanding power, showing how merciful a king Evil-Merodach is. The king has released and rehabilitated Jehoiachin's vassal status,[9] given him a high rank in the imperial court, and provided Jehoiachin's daily needs. All this happens, however, under the strict control of the imperial power. Jehoiachin is eating from the hand of the colonial power and his position is valued among other dominated rulers in Babylon. The end of 2 Kings is not merely a pessimistic conclusion of the book, nor is it an expression of nationalistic hopes, but it is a sign of the inner colonization of the writer. The main message of the writer focuses on the good relations between empire and subordinate. Rebellion or nationalistic hopes to have one's own king are far beyond these lines.[10]

Let me find an example about this attitude from the recent history of my own nation, Finland. Finland was known some decades ago as an example of politics in which the political and ideological activities were harnessed to good relations with the former Soviet Union. The policy of concessions was, even in the worldwide discussion, named as a process of *Finlandization*. Thus the minor partner has to

know its geopolitical realities and make the right and logical conclusions. Politics becomes geopolitics based on *Realpolitik*. It means that you are forced to have good relations with a nearby existing superpower.

For some this was a negative example of losing the absolute independence to articulate one's own national needs and opinions; for others this very same attitude saved the national structures while some important areas of life were self-censored. Whatever the evaluation is of those past decades, all agree that *Finlandization* as a phenomenon was real in some sense and influenced Finnish politics, decision-making, culture, and historiography. Through this example I do not mean to say that Finland and Judah can be understood to be similar at a social, political, or national level. What I do hope to show is the meaning and influence of colonialism on mental processes.

With the help of the colonial optic it is possible to read the last paragraph of Kings in a new light. The writer obviously is aware of political realities and within these limits describes the changed status of the deported Judean king. Jehoiachin is partly rehabilitated, but only within the frameworks allowed by superior forces.

5 Colonialism's Impact on Yahweh

Finally, there is a need to clarify what the role of Yahweh is at the end of 2 Kings. Earlier in this study it was noticed that poor people were mentioned on just a few occasions and in a minor role. As a parallel to this we can recognize that Yahweh is also mentioned very seldom. On the other hand, the role of Yahweh is prominent in the plot of the story. Three different things are said about Yahweh: kings of Judah did the evil in Yahweh's sight (24:9, 19), colonial military acts happened according to Yahweh's will (24:2, 3, 13), and the whole episode was motivated by the anger of God (24:20; cf. 24:3).

What is the relation between Yahweh and "the other," the poor? According to the classical liberation theological view, God is the liberator of poor and oppressed people, as in the Exodus story. On this occasion we can notice the opposite: Yahweh belongs to the coalition of Babylon, together with rulers like Jehoiachin and Gedaljah. The people on the margin do not have any specific preferential status or option in God's view in this story. However, in the story, Yahweh is a divine actor who motivates and pulls the strings behind the curtains and thus also becomes an ally of colonial powers. The more Yahweh is seen as the ruler of the historical events – as in DH – the more Yahweh is also responsible for the imperialistic policy of Babylon. Because Yahweh's acts are motivated by his anger, the whole God-talk changes. In the pre-deuteronomistic tradition Yahweh was seen as a source of blessing and life, guidance, and protection. In short: in earlier traditions Yahweh was seen as a creator of life (J-story; early form of Deut 11–16). Compared to this DH represents a different view. The major reasons for this change are the events described at the end of Kings. Actually the main reason for the changed theological thinking was the colonial policy and acts of Babylon. Reality created by political powers was thus transposed in theology.

Passages dealing with the anger of God are not limited to the last chapters of Kings but are important in the whole of DH. For example in Deuteronomy the anger of

God occurs four times more often than the love of God – which usually is understood to be among the main themes of Deuteronomy.[11] According to this study the relevant hypothesis is to presume that the whole deuteronomistic talk about the anger of God is strongly influenced by Babylonian colonialism.

6 Is it Possible to Decolonize Yahweh?

This study has underlined the strong influence of Babylonian colonialism on the attitude and thinking of the writer(s) of 2 Kings 24–5. When these chapters are interpreted in the current situation, it is worth considering if there is also a need to reconsider the possibilities of *decolonizing* the image of Yahweh. The first step in this process is to have a renewed analysis of DH using the tools of postcolonial criticism. Results of this study ought to be tested through the whole of DH. The second step is to see the larger theological context inside the Hebrew Bible balance the theological map.[12] The third step in the decolonization process is to compare the theology of exilic/post-exilic times with the current understanding about God, about life, and especially about "the other," available in the present world. This means there is a need for critical analyses of colonial power in the biblical writings and in their present readings. If the image of God was once colonized there is still perhaps a chance to decolonize these images, in order to find adequate concepts for current God-talk.

NOTES

1 This text was kindly revised and commented by Anthony Addy.
2 About the terms imperialism, colonialism and neo-colonialism see Sugirtharajah, *Postcolonial Critisicm and Biblical Interpretation*, 24–5. A classical work is E. Said, *Orientalism*.
3 To mention some writings: R. S. Sugirtharajah, *Asian Biblical Hermeneutics and Postcolonialism. Contesting the Interpretations*. BiSe 64 (Sheffield Academic Press, 1999); *The Bible and the Third World: Precolonial, Colonial and Postcolonial Encounters* (Cambridge University Press, 2001); *Postcolonial Critisicm and Biblical Interpretation*. Oxford University Press, 2002; Fernando F. Segovia, *Decolonizing Biblical Studies. A View from the Margins* (Orbis Books, 2000) – Warm thanks to both mentioned persons, who have also greatly encouraged me personally to do this analysis.
4 Sugirtharajah, *Postcolonial*, 103. For comparison between liberation hermeneutics and postcolonial interpretation see also pages 103–23. See also Segovia, *Decolonizing*, 121–6.
5 Hobbs, *2 Kings*, 344, 353, translates "the less important of the population." According to him "the term often, though not exclusively, indicates the lower strata of society."
6 Wolff, "Das Kerygma des deuteronomistischen Geschichtswerkes," 310–11.
7 Noth, *Überlieferungsgeschichtliche Studien*, 108. Following this view Würthwein, *Die Bücher der Könige 1. Kön. 17–2. Kön. 25*, 481–4: a national anecdote without any special theological intention.
8 Among the representatives of optimistic interpretation are Gerhard von Rad, *Theologie des Alten Testaments I*, 355–6; Erich Zenger, "Die deuteronomistischen Interpretation der Rehabilitierung Jojachins," *BZ*, 12 (1968): 16–30; Jones, *Commentary on 1 and 2 Kings*, 647–9.
9 Zenger, "Die deuteronomistischen," 23–5.

10 This view is supported by Begg, "The Significance of Jehoiakin's Release: A New Proposal," 53–5 and Long, *2 Kings*, 289.
11 More detailed in Latvus, "God, Anger and Ideology," *JSOTS*, 279: 74–7.
12 Important counter theme to the power of God is the weakness of God. See Gerstenberger, *Theologies in the Old Testament*, 224–34; Latvus, "God," 89–94.

REFERENCES

Begg, Christopher T. (1986). "The Significance of Jehoiakin's Release: A New Proposal." *JSOT*, 36: 49–56.

Gerstenberger, Erhard S. (2002). *Theologies in the Old Testament*. Minneapolis: Fortress Press.

Hobbs, T. R. (1985). *2 Kings*. Word Biblical Commentary, vol. 13. Waco: Word Books.

Horsley, Richard A. (2001). *Hearing the Whole Story. The Politics of Plot in Marks's Gospel*. Louisville, KY.: Westminster John Knox Press.

Jones, G. H. (1984). *Commentary on 1 and 2 Kings*. Grand Rapids: Wm. B. Eerdmans Publishing Company.

Latvus, Kari (1998). "God, Anger and Ideology. The Anger of God in Joshua and Judges in Relation to Deuteronomy and the Priestly Writings." *JSOTS*, 279. Sheffield: Sheffield Academic Press.

Long, Burke O. (1991). *2 Kings. The Forms of the Old Testament Literature*, vol. X. Wm. B. Eerdmans Publishing Company.

Noth, Martin (1967). *Überlieferungsgeschichtliche Studien. Die sammelnden und bearbeitenden Geschichswerke im Alten Testament*. Tübingen: Max Niemeyer Verlag.

von Rad, Gerhard (1962). *Theologie des Alten Testaments I. Die Theologie der geschichtlichen Überlieferungen Israels*. Munich: Chr. Kaiser Verlag.

Said, E. (2003). *Orientalism*. [1978] 25th anniversary edn. New York: Vintage Books.

Segovia, Fernando F. (2000). *Decolonizing Biblical Studies. A View from the Margins*. Maryknoll, NY: Orbis Books.

Sugirtharajah, R. S. (1999). *Asian Biblical Hermeneutics and Postcolonialism. Contesting the Interpretations*. BiSe 64. Sheffield: Sheffield Academic Press.

—— (2001). *The Bible and the Third World: Precolonial, Colonial and Postcolonial Encounters*. Cambridge: Cambridge University Press.

—— (2002). *Postcolonial Criticism and Biblical Interpretation*. Oxford: Oxford University Press.

Wolff, Hans Walter (1964). "Das Kerygma des deuteronomistischen Geschichtswerkes." in *Gesammelte Studien zum Alten Testament*. Munich: Chr. Kaiser Verlag.

Würthwein, Ernst (1984). *Die Bücher der Könige 1. Kön. 17–2. Kön. 25*. ATD 11,2. Göttingen: Vandenhoeck & Ruprecht.

Zenger, Erich (1968). "Die deuteronomistischen Interpretation der Rehabilitierung Jojachins." *BZ* 12: 16–30.

13

Mark and Empire: "Zealot" and "Postcolonial" Readings

Stephen D. Moore

Nation

> They came to the other side of the sea, to the country of the Gerasenes. And when he had stepped out of the boat, immediately a man out of the tombs with an unclean spirit met him. He lived among the tombs; and no one could restrain him any more, even with a chain; for he had often been restrained with shackles and chains, but the chains he wrenched apart, and the shackles he broke in pieces; and no one had the strength to subdue him. Night and day among the tombs and on the mountains he was always howling and bruising himself with stones. When he saw Jesus from a distance, he ran and bowed down before him; and he shouted at the top of his voice, "What have you to do with me, Jesus, Son of the Most High God? I adjure you by God, do not torment me!" For he had said to him, "Come out of the man, you unclean spirit!" Then Jesus asked him, "What is your name?" He replied, "My name is Legion; for we are many." (Mk. 5:1–9)

What's in a name, not least a name that gestures simultaneously to demonic possession and colonial occupation – if, indeed, it does? "Since the text explicitly associates Legion with numerousness," one leading Markan scholar has recently protested, "we have no reason to think of a covert reference to the occupation of Palestine by Roman legions."[1] No reason whatsoever, perhaps, unless our desire is for a Mark for whom the occupation of Palestine by Roman legions *is* a concern – or for *which* that occupation is a concern, "Mark" now naming the text rather than the author; for even what cannot plausibly be ascribed to an author's intentions can always be ascribed to the text that invariably exceeds them. That, apparently, is the dual lesson of "precritical" biblical exegesis and poststructuralist literary theory. Yet we need not break free of the current of mainstream biblical criticism in order to encounter readings of Mark's Gerasene episode attuned to colonial issues. Even the improbably prolonged moment in Markan scholarship of which Gundry's

First published in Catherine Keller et al., *Postcolonial Theologies: Divinity and Empire*. St Louis: Chalice Press, 2004, 134–48.

monumental commentary is a consummate product – the "historical-critical" moment, with its single-minded preoccupation with the gospel's "original" context, coupled with the evangelist's putative intentionality, and the corollary exclusion (necessarily incomplete) of contemporary contexts from the task of exegesis – yields a small but significant trickle of assertions that Roman military occupation, no less than demonic possession, was indeed in view in this pericope. And in recent years, with the multiplication of "political" readings of Mark, and of early Christian texts and traditions more generally, that assertion has become almost commonplace.[2] With the emergence of a newly sharpened focus on "empire" within New Testament studies, moreover – a focus enabled, on occasion at least, by the conceptual tools and critical vocabulary of extra-biblical postcolonial studies – we do have, pace Gundry, compelling reasons for hearing in Mark 5:9 a dual reference to demonic possession *and* colonial occupation.

The fraught tale of the Gerasene demoniac, then, seems to be a logical enough place from which to launch a "postcolonial" reading of the gospel of Mark, centered on the perennial and intractable issues of land, invasion, occupation, and liberation. If the demons are, by their own admission, to be identified analogically with the Roman "army of occupation,"[3] then the demoniac may be identified in turn as the land and people under occupation – which, it may be argued, is why the demons earnestly entreat the exorcist "not to send them out of the country [*exô tês chôras*]" (5:10). And if the act of exorcism is to be accorded anticolonial significance in *this* pericope, why should it not be accorded similar significance in every other exorcistic episode in Mark, that most exorcistic of gospels (see 1:23–7, 32–4; 6:7, 13; 7:24–30; 9:14–29; cf. 3:11–12, 14–15, 22–30; 9:38)? Jesus' earlier boast that his plundering of the property of the "strong man" portends the end of Satan's empire (3:23–7) could then be read as equally portending the end of Rome's empire, the latter being implicitly construed as but an instrumental extension of the former. To begin to read Mark in this way is tantamount to using 5:9 ("My name is Legion...") as a "hermeneutical key" with which to unlock the gospel as a whole. Such keys generally break off in the lock, as the history of biblical scholarship never tires of telling us, and so I do not intend to overuse this one.[4] But it may at least open up a reading that will lead to an as yet unforeseeable destination.

To set foot, however tentatively, on this interpretive path is to begin to read the narrative of the Gerasene "demoniac," and much else in the larger narrative in which it is embedded, as *allegory*, to read as the Markan Jesus himself has taught us to read (4:13–20) – a strategy that accrues added interest from recent (heated) debates concerning the extent to which so-called national allegories, in which literary representations of individual colonial subjects stand in allegorically for the histories and destinies of entire colonized peoples, may be seen as a defining characteristic of contemporary postcolonial literatures. Allegory, in any case, once unleashed, cannot easily be contained—not unlike the Gerasene demoniac himself whom no shackle or chain can restrain (5:4), and who thereby becomes an allegory of allegory itself. It would not be unduly difficult to track allegory's inexorable verse-by-verse rampage through this entire pericope, should strategy demand it. In the event, a few sample steps will suffice to relay a sense of the dance.

They came to... the country of the Gerasenes (5:1). The Hebrew root *gr* – means "banish," "drive out," "cast out," as more than one commentator has observed, and

so, by extension, commonly signifies exorcism. The exorcist has landed, but on what shore? Hardly "the land of the exorcists"; "the land in need of exorcism" better suits the context. The very name of the country in which he has just set foot "hails" Jesus, then, and "interpellates" him, as the Marxist critic Louis Althusser might have said – and by which he might have meant that the name, simultaneously a summons, reaches out subtly yet imperiously to mold and manipulate the one thus called.[5] Jesus has arrived among a people whose very appellation constitutes a preexisting appeal to (and hence a covert construction of) his (now) manifest destiny to drive out the powers that possess them.

[A] man out of the tombs with an unclean spirit [en pneumati akathartô] met him (5:2). The peculiar *en* should be allowed its full, engulfing force here. It signifies that the possessed subject's identity has been utterly submerged in that which possesses him – as is indeed evident from that fact that, in the dialogue that ensues, *it* speaks in him, through him, and for him. One would be hard-pressed to find a more apt image – or allegory – of the colonial subject's self-alienation when compelled to internalize the discourse of the colonizer.

[N]o one could restrain him any more, even with a chain; for he had often been restrained with shackles and chains, but the chains he wrenched apart, and the shackles he broke in pieces; and no one had the strength to subdue him. Night and day... he was always howling and bruising himself with stones (5:3–5). Possession is *maddening*, eliciting spectacular acts of masochistic resistance. Here, the national allegory projects onto the parallel screen the disastrous and increasingly desperate armed rebellion that culminated with the Roman decimation of Jerusalem and its temple. When the occupying power is too overwhelming, armed resistance can only effect self-annihilation – which, however, is also self-immolation; and from the ashes of martyrs rebellion is reborn.

And the unclean spirits came out and entered the swine; and the herd... rushed down the steep bank into the sea... (5:13). The reason for the pigs's lemming-like rush into the sea is unstated. The simplest explanation would seem to be that the exorcist has compelled them to do so, thereby cleansing the land of their polluting presence. Not to put too delicate a point on it, the Romans are here shown up for the filthy swine that they are, and triumphantly driven back into the sea from whence they came – the dream of every Jewish peasant resister, as one of our own sages has observed.[6] Cleansing the (com)promised land of unclean occupants so that God's people can possess it more completely is a theme thoroughly rooted in the Israelite myth of origins. (The companion theme of prior liberation from bondage is also discernible in the pericope, the phantasmic destruction of the Romans in the sea serving to evoke the mythic destruction of the Egyptians in the sea.) But whereas in the Israelite conquest narratives the invaders are charged with sweeping the land clean, now it is the invaders themselves who must be swept into the sea. Genocide and nationalism share a certain fastidious tidiness, it would seem – which, no doubt, is why the former has at times sprung fully formed from the head of the latter.

And it is not just the invaders who must be swept away, but the comprador class who have made the invaders' continuing control of the land and its people possible. The first step in ridding the land of the polluting Roman presence, it emerges (once we begin to survey larger stretches of the narrative, employing Gerasa as our vantage point), is to rid it of the collaborating local elites. In due course, Mark's Messiah will

embark on his single-minded march to Jerusalem (cf. 10:32–4). But to what end? Primarily, so that he may enact the symbolic destruction of the Jerusalem temple, essential seat of power of the indigenous elite: "Then they came to Jerusalem. And he entered the temple and began to drive out [*ekballein*] those who were selling and those who were buying in the temple..." (11:15). Again, we are faced with an exorcism of sorts: The spectacle is one of expulsion, cleansing, dispossession, and repossession. Thematically, at least, this pericope is intimately imbricated with that of the Gerasene demoniac. The "cleansing" of God's house ("My house [*ho oikos mou*] shall be called a house of prayer..." – 11:17) performed with such passion by Mark's Messiah, and seen as so threatening by the Jerusalem elites ("And when the chief priests and the scribes heard it, they kept looking for a way to kill him..." – 11:18), is a symbolic prelude to the "cleansing" of the entire land that properly belongs to the owner of the house (cf. 12:1ff), a cleansing that the exorcism at Gerasa anticipated.

The Messiah's symbolic destruction of the temple precipitates his own destruction, however, his public annihilation on the colonial cross. But in engineering Jesus' own obliteration in retribution for the symbolic destruction of their temple (11:18; cf. 14:58; 15:29–30), the local elite unwittingly and catastrophically engineers the *actual* destruction of the temple, according to Mark, and as such their own inevitable eradication. Consider the positioning of the "temple-cleansing" incident. It interrupts the two-part anecdote of Jesus' cursing and thereby blasting an unproductive fig tree (11:12–14, 20–2). The "temple-cleansing" material thus forms the filling in a narrative sandwich. It is, indeed, one of the more notable examples of Mark's celebrated "sandwich technique" (the menu also includes 3:20–1 [22–30] 31–5; 5:21–4 [25–34] 35–43; 6:7–13 [14–29] 30–2; 14:53–65 [66–72] 15:1–5), and is generally regarded as one of the less enigmatic examples of the device, the material in the two outer layers of the sandwich imposing a relatively transparent meaning on the material in the middle layer: The destruction of the unproductive fig tree portends the destruction of the "unproductive" temple.[7] Mark thereby obliquely signals his conviction that the Roman annihilation of the temple and city that brought the Jewish rebellion of 66 CE to a catastrophic close was an act of divine retribution. The sandwich is followed almost immediately by the parable of the vineyard and the tenants (12:1–12), which deftly reinforces the message: "What then will the owner of the vineyard do? He will come and destroy the tenants... [T]hey [the chief priests, the scribes, and the elders] realized that he had told this parable against them..." (12:9, 12).

Of course, the Jerusalem temple's destruction is itself but the eschatological prelude to Jesus' parousia, as the ensuing apocalyptic discourse (13:1–37) makes plain. And what the parousia will signify, among other things, is the unceremonious cessation of the Roman empire, as of every other human *basileia* ("empire"). Jesus will bump Caesar off the throne. Is this the telos, then, toward which everything in the Markan narrative is tending? Yes and no, it seems to me. Yes, because a reading of Mark along these lines – a "zealot" reading, if you will – is not only possible; in certain contexts – straitened contexts, especially, occasioned by overt state-sponsored oppression, akin to that experienced, or anticipated, by the Markan community itself – a reading of Mark as anti-imperial resistance literature, pure and simple, may be absolutely necessary. And no, because such a reading, in order to

run smoothly, must aqua-glide over the intense ambivalence that, on an alternative reading, can be shown (and will be shown below) to characterize and complicate Mark's representations of empire. Practices of reading acutely attuned to such complexities are a signal feature of contemporary postcolonial theory, and not the least of its benefits for the biblical critic. Outside of biblical studies, postcolonial studies has tended to be infused and enabled by a generic poststructuralism, itself intimately attuned to the inherent instabilities of discourse and representation. Postcolonial biblical criticism has, to date, been less shaped by poststructuralism, tending instead, in some of its more notable manifestations, to operate under the aegis of a hermeneutic of suspicion and in the mode of ideology critique.[8] Like its extra-biblical counterpart, however, it brings complexly unstable texts into view. A defining feature of "postcolonial" biblical exegesis, indeed, as distinct from (although by no means in opposition to) "liberationist" biblical exegesis, is a willingness to press a biblical text at precisely those points at which its ideology falls prey to ambivalence, incoherence, and self-subversion – not least where its message of emancipation subtly mutates into oppression. We have seen, in miniature at least, one way in which an unreserved reading of Mark as anti-imperial resistance literature might proceed. It remains to inquire how else a reading of Mark attuned to issues of empire might unfold.

Empire

Let us begin again, then, this time by noting that Mark altogether lacks the snarling, fang-baring hostility toward the Roman state that possesses Mark's near-contemporary, and yet more apocalyptic, cousin, the book of Revelation, a text that shares with Mark an intense preoccupation with the prospect of persecution and likewise proffers an apocalyptic solution to that problem: "The one who endures to the end will be saved," is Mark's summation of the solution (13:13), but it could just as easily be John's. The face of Rome comes into explicit focus in Mark only in 15:1–39, Jesus' trial before the Roman prefect of Judea and his public execution at the hands of the Roman military. But the expression on that face is curiously difficult to decipher. How is the figure of Pontius Pilate in Mark to be construed? As a basically benign but morally feeble official who would release the accused if he could but is unable to out-maneuver, or is merely unwilling to override, the Sadduceean elite and the vociferous mob whose strings they control? Or rather as himself a consummate manipulator, who unblinkingly dispatches the peasant troublemaker while skillfully contriving to make it seem as though he is simply acceding to the impassioned demands of the peasant's own countrymen? The only other Roman official who makes an explicit appearance in Mark, albeit a cameo one, is, if anything, still more ambiguously delineated. What does the Roman centurion's celebrated pronouncement in 15:39 actually amount to? In declaring the bloody corpse dangling before him to have "truly... [been] God's Son" (*Alêthôs houtos ho anthrôpos huios theou ên*) is he, in good crypto-Christian fashion, succeeding spectacularly where Jesus' own disciples have so singularly failed, effortlessly coupling the concepts of divine sonship and dishonorable death where they could not, and thereby giving climactic and definitive expression to Mark's *theologia crucis*? Or is he merely engaging in

grim gallows humor ("Some Son of God!"), unwittingly giving expression thereby to a "truth" that is not his but belongs to the evangelist/ventriloquist instead? Unaware that he is a dummy, is the centurion simply parroting the derision of everybody else in the vicinity of the cross (15:29–32), not least the local elites with whom his commander is in cahoots: "Those who passed by derided him . . . In the same way, the chief priest, along with the scribes, were also mocking him among themselves and saying, . . . 'Let the Messiah, the King of Israel, come down from the cross now . . .' Those who were crucified with him also taunted him" (15:29–32)? Jesus' sole explicit pronouncement on Rome in Mark – "Give to [Caesar] the things that are [Caesar's], and to God the things that are God's" (12:17) – is itself no less enveloped in ambiguity, as its history of reception amply attests. It can be, and has been, read to mean that because, in accordance with Israelite tradition and theology, everything belongs to God, nothing is due to Caesar;[9] far more frequently, however, it has been read unabashedly as an affirmation of the imperial status quo. In consequence of these assorted uncertainties, it seems to me, Mark's stance vis-à-vis Rome cannot plausibly be construed as one of unambiguous opposition. Turning now to less explicit or immediate representations of Rome in Mark, my working assumption instead is that Mark's attitude toward Rome is imbued with that simultaneous attraction and repulsion – in a word, ambivalence – to which Homi Bhabha, in particular, has taught us to be attuned when analyzing colonial or anticolonial discourses.[10]

The clamor of Roman legionaries breaching the walls of Jerusalem and putting its inhabitants to the sword can dimly be heard in Mark 13:14–20, according to the dominant critical reading. Earlier in the apocalyptic discourse, Jesus' disciples are forewarned that they must stand before Roman governors or client kings, just as Jesus himself did, and possibly be executed for their testimony, just as he himself was (13:9–13). When the Son of Man returns in the clouds "with great power and glory" (13:26), however, as he is soon destined to do, his behavior and demeanor will be markedly different from his Messianic counterpart in Revelation, who, on his own return through an "opened heaven," will be riding at the head of the "armies of heaven," "to judge and make war," armed with the "sharp sword" of his mouth "with which to strike down the nations," which will result in a nightmarish mountain of rotting human flesh upon which "all the birds that fly in midheaven" will be invited to gorge (Rev. 19:11–21, author's trans.). What of the parousia of the Markan Messiah? What preordained plan of action will he execute when he makes his own appearance on the clouds? We are told only that "he will send out the angels, and gather his elect from the four winds, from the ends of earth to the ends of heaven" (Mk. 13:27). The Markan parousia is, in essence, a search-and-rescue mission, not a punitive strike, as in Revelation. Nowhere in Mark are Roman officials who have persecuted Christians, nor even Judean collaborators with Rome who have conspired to murder their Messiah, threatened explicitly with a post-parousia reckoning. Whereas in Revelation, Rome's imminent destruction, and its eschatological consignment, in the guise of the Beast, to "the lake of fire and sulfur" (Rev. 20:10) is an immense and intense preoccupation, in Mark the only characters threatened with the Son of Man's displeasure at his return and with the everlasting torments of hell are Jesus' own disciples (8:38; 9:42–9). In marked contrast to the Apocalypse of John, Mark's "Little Apocalypse" (chapter 13) predicts

not the destruction *of* Rome, but rather an act of destruction *by* Rome (the demolition of city and temple, that is, and the concomitant decimation of the Judean populace) – a particularly arresting symptom of the profound ambivalence that attends Mark's representation of the empire.

Mark's anti-imperial invective really only extends to the local elites. Indeed, far from predicting divine punishment of Rome for the destruction of Jerusalem and its temple and the attendant massacre of its people, Mark appears to interpret this destruction and slaughter as divine punishment of the Judean elites for their exploitation of the common people (7:9–13; 11:12–21; 12:38–44), as we have already seen, coupled with their rejection of the Galilean Messiah (12:7–12). So whereas Rome in Revelation embodies and epitomizes intractable opposition to and alienation from the God of Israel and his salvific interventions in human history, Rome in Mark is merely God's instrument, his scourge, which he employs to punish the indigenous Judean elites. (Rome therefore occupies roughly the same role in Mark's deuteronomistic theodicy as in that of his contemporary Josephus, as the latter's *Jewish War* 5.395 in particular suggests: "Indeed, what can it be that hath stirred up an army of the Romans against our nation? Is it not the impiety of the inhabitants?") Mark thereby falls prey spectacularly to the divide-and-rule strategy entailed in the Roman policy of ceding administrative authority to indigenous elites in the provinces. As has been remarked with regard to the advantages to modern European empires of indirect rule in colonial Africa, "popular resentments and hatreds could be deflected on to the local officials while the ultimate authority could remain remote, unseen and 'above the battle' "[11]– at least until, as in the case of the Jewish revolt and its suppression many centuries earlier, the ultimate authority finds it necessary temporarily to relinquish its godlike remoteness and relative invisibility in order to intervene decisively and irresistibly in the corrupt affairs of its creatures in an attempt to contain the chaos that its own administrative policies has created.

And yet even if Mark lacks the explicitly hostile attitude toward Roman rule evident in Revelation, he also lacks the explicitly "quietist" attitude toward Roman rule evident in at least two other first-century Christian texts, namely, the letter to the Romans (cf. 13:1–7: "Let every person be subject to the governing authorities; for there is no authority except from God, and those authorities that exist have been instituted by God. Therefore whoever resists authority resists what God has appointed, and those who resist will incur judgment") and 1 Peter (cf. 2:13–17: "For the Lord's sake accept the authority of every human institution, whether of the emperor as supreme, or of governors, as sent by him to punish those who do wrong and to praise those who do right"). Generally speaking (and putting it rather too mildly), Mark does not enjoin its audience to respect human authorities. Every human authority in Mark, indeed, whether "religious" or "political" (a distinction largely meaningless, however, in the context), is a persecutor, or potential persecutor, of John, Jesus, or the disciples of Jesus, aside from three incidental, but rule-proving, exceptions: the synagogue leader, Jairus (5:22ff.); the scribe commended by Jesus for not being "far from the [empire] of God (12:28–34); and the Sanhedrin member, Joseph of Arimathea (15:42–6). In addition, Jesus is repeatedly represented in Mark as urging his followers not to aspire to authority, glory, power, or wealth (9:33–7; 10:17–31, 35–44; cf. 12:41–4), but to adopt for emulation instead such liminal role models as the child (*paidion*) and the servant (*diakonos*) or slave (*doulos*) (9:35–7;

10:13–16, 42–5; cf. 13:34). Mark's relentless narrative undermining of Jesus' own elite corps of disciples (4:13, 40; 6:52; 7:18; 8:21, 32–3; 9:5–6, 33–4, 38–9; 10:35–45; 14:10–11, 32–46, 50, 66–72), themselves the repositories of significant authority by the time the gospel was written, may be regarded as a further component of this elaborate anti-authoritarian theme.

There *is*, however, one major human authority figure in Mark whose authority is not the object of repeated narrative erosion but rather of constant reassertion and reification, that figure being, of course, Jesus himself. The question then arises: In attributing absolute, unassailable authority to Jesus, is Mark merely mirroring Roman imperial ideology, deftly switching Jesus for Caesar (to replay the ending of the "zealot" reading performed earlier), but thereby undercutting the Gospel's anti-authoritarian thematics and inaugurating an empire of God that inevitably evinces many of the oppressive traits of the Roman empire it displaces?[12] This question is best addressed within the framework afforded by another, more encompassing question: What does the empire of God in Mark actually amount to?

Arguably, Mark's deployment of the term *basileia* ("empire") may be deemed an instance of what postcolonial theorist Gayatri Spivak has dubbed *catachresis*, originally a Greek rhetorical figure denoting "misuse" or "misapplication." As employed by Spivak, the term designates the process by which the colonized strategically appropriate and redeploy specific elements of colonial or imperial culture or ideology; as such, it is a practice of resistance through an act of usurpation.[13] In any Roman province, the primary referent of *basileia* would have been the *imperium Romanum*. Mark's practice of catachresis, as it pertains to *basileia*, can therefore be said to border on the parodic. "The time is fulfilled, and the [empire] of God has come near," Mark's ragtag peasant protagonist proclaims (1:15), marching through the remote rural reaches of southern Galilee and drawing assorted other peasant nonentities in his wake, fellow builders-to-be of this latest and greatest of empires. The intrinsic, indeed surreal, unlikelihood of this Empire of empires begs elucidation, and as such is virtually the sole topic of Jesus' first extended public address in Mark (one of only two), namely, his parables discourse (4:1–33). (His other extended "sermon," the apocalyptic discourse [chap. 13], also has the advent of God's empire as its topic, although it is delivered from the other side of the eschatological curtain.) The parables of the seed growing in secret (4:26–9) and of the mustard seed (4:30–2) contrast the present concealment (cf. 4:11–12) and seeming inconsequentiality of the empire of God with its impending and impressive public manifestation, as does the parable of the sower (4:1–9, 14–20), albeit to a lesser degree. Mark's next explicit mention of the empire of God glosses its imminent public disclosure as the moment when the seemingly vanquished Son of Man will reappear in unequivocal majesty (8:38–9:1). But the next several occurrences of the term play again on the paradoxically inglorious character of the present as opposed to future empire of God. Physical deformity will pose no obstacle to membership in the imperial ranks ("better for you to enter the [empire] of God with one eye" [9:47]), nor will childlikeness (which, on the contrary, will be a necessary qualification: "whoever does not receive the [empire] of God as a little child" [10:15]). Social status, however, epitomized by wealth, *will* pose a near-insurmountable stumbling block to membership ("How hard it will be for those who have wealth to enter the [empire] of God!" [10:23]), which is to say that those who have benefited most

egregiously from participation in Caesar's empire will be least eligible for admittance to God's empire. The latter pronouncement occurs in the immediate context of others that, as we have already noted, proffer servanthood and slavery as the supreme models for Christian existence, in marked contrast to the practice of the "Gentiles" (read: Romans) – a cluster of countercultural sayings and anecdotes (9:30–10:45, passim) that, in the absence of anything else approximating a Markan "Sermon on the Mount," gives much-needed (if still insufficient) substance to its singularly unimperial concept of divine empire, as it translates into Christian practice.

The present empire of God, then, dimly conjured up in Mark, seethes with countercultural valence. But is it effectively domesticated and defused by the coming empire of God? Is the Markan Jesus' self-proclaimed ethic of self-giving and self-emptying ("the Son of Man came not to be served but to serve"), culminating in his voluntary submission to torture and execution ("and to give his life [as] a ransom for many" [10:45]), in the end but the means to an end, that end being (not to put too subtle a point on it) incomparable personal power and authority ("Then they will see 'the Son of Man coming in clouds' with great power and glory" [13:26])? And what of Jesus' disciples? Neither Matthew nor Luke hesitate to extend the eschatological "no pain, no gain" formula to disciples: "You are those who have stood by me in my trials, and I confer on you, just as my Father has conferred on me, [an empire]...and you will sit on thrones judging the twelve tribes of Israel" (Lk. 22:28–30; cf. Matt. 19:28).[14] Mark, however, in intriguing contrast, seems reticent about unequivocally promising eschatological power and glory to disciples who successfully imitate Jesus' practice of embracing a self-abnegating way of life fraught with the risk of violent death: Jesus readily promises the suffering ("The cup that I drink you will drink"), but is noticeably evasive on the matter of the reward ("but to sit at my right hand or at my left is not mine to grant" [10:39–40]). Mark's curious caution in this regard, whatever its motivation might have been, arguably lends its ethics a "contemporary feel" that Matthew's and Luke's lack. To deal in broad generalizations for a moment, from within the enabling assumptions and convictions that have characterized many modern experiments in community (not least, socialist experiments), a teleology of otherwordly reward has tended to be seen as serving only to devalue a community ethic built on egalitarianism and mutual service. The tendency instead has been to regard the community thereby constructed as sufficient "reward," in and of itself, for the sacrifices that subtend it. Mark comes closer than most early Christian writings to approximating this perspective. Mark 10:29–30 is particularly notable in this regard: "Truly I tell you, there is no one who has left house or brothers or sisters or mother or father or children or fields, for my sake and for the sake of the good news, who will not receive a hundredfold now in this age – houses, brothers and sisters, mothers and children, and fields with persecutions" (cf. 3:31–5). The concluding clause – "and in the age to come eternal life" – is interestingly akin to an afterthought: In contrast to the painstakingly itemized rewards of the present age, it is devoid of detail or substantive content. All of this, too, contrasts starkly, yet again, with Revelation, whose only real ethic is an ethic of endurance, and which so scrupulously itemizes the spectacular benefits due to those who, through their endurance, have earned admittance to the heavenly city (21:1–22:5).

Apocalypse

To the extent that Mark can be said to locate the primary rewards for the radical community experiment that it advocates in the liminal communities themselves that will come into being in consequence, must its christology be said to stand in tension with its ethics? By insisting on returning "with great power and glory" (13:26), does Mark's Jesus betray Mark's own latent desire for a top-heavy, authoritarian, universal Christian empire, an über-Roman empire, so to speak – the kind that will arrive all too soon, anyway, unbeknown to Mark, long before Jesus himself does? By insisting on returning in imperial splendor (however muted, relative to Revelation and even the other synoptic gospels), does Mark's Jesus relativize and undercut the radical social values that he has died to exemplify and implement? Can radical apocalypticism, in other words, only ever stand in tension or outright contradiction with radical ethics? Or to put it yet another way, can radical apocalypticism only mirror imperial or colonial ideologies (and reflect them in a convex mirror, what is more, so that what was oppressively oversized to begin with now towers above the heavens: "And then they will see 'the Son of Man coming in clouds' "), or can it instead be consonant with a counter-imperial or counter-colonial ethic?

Yes and no, it would seem to me (yet again); it all depends on how apocalypticism is to be construed. A radical ethic that shatters every previously imaginable social structure (not that Mark's ethic goes quite that far) is, in its own way, also radically apocalyptic, portending the end of the world as we know it. Mark's apocalyptic discourse (13:1–37) does not, however, portend the end of the Roman imperial order, but rather its apotheosis. To discover a counter-imperial apocalypse in Mark, we must look elsewhere. Conveniently, however, we will find what we need on the very threshold of Mark 13. The Markan anecdote traditionally labeled "The Widow's Mites" (12:41–4) may be read as encapsulating, or at least adumbrating, a counter-imperial apocalyptic ethic.

Traditionally, the widow's donation "out of her poverty" (*ek tês hysterêseôs autês*) of "everything she had, all she had to live on" (12:44) has been construed as an exemplary action enthusiastically lauded by Jesus, the woman's absolute self-giving dramatically prefiguring his own self-emptying in death. In recent years, however, a sharp reaction to this hallowed typological interpretation has set in, not least because the interpretation, at its least palatable, has traditionally been presented to the poor as an enticement to donate beyond their means to the church. In the revisionary recasting of the anecdote, the woman is read as epitomizing instead the oppressed peasantry mercilessly bled dry by the indigenous, Rome-allied elites.[15] The latter reading, unlike the former, enables interpreters to posit a high degree of narrative continuity between the anecdote about the widow and the apocalyptic discourse that succeeds it: It is because of what has been done to the weakest of the weak in its name that the Jerusalem temple has been marked by God for demolition, as Jesus immediately goes on to imply: "Do you see these great buildings? Not one stone will be left here upon another; all will be thrown down" (13:2). The congeniality of this line of interpretation to an emancipatory reading of Mark is, however, severely undercut, it seems to me, by Mark's neo-deuteronomistic theodicy, which, when pressed, promptly implodes in horrific absurdity: Impoverished denizens of

Jerusalem, such as this widow, would have been among the first to fall victim, if not by slaughter then by starvation, to the Rome-administered divine retribution against the city and temple – a retribution that the Roman-Judean administration, through its exploitation of the common people, had (in accordance with the theodicy imputed to Mark) provoked in the first place. The divine response to the unjust suffering of the poor, on this reading, is to escalate that suffering beyond measure: "For in those days there will be such tribulation [*thlipsis*] as has not been from the beginning of the creation which God created until now, and never will be" (Mark 13:19, author's trans.).

A third reading of the widow anecdote is, however, possible. This one piggybacks on the traditional ecclesiastical reading, the first one summarized above, and similarly styles the woman as an exemplary figure – not because she anticipates and dimly adumbrates Jesus' self-emptying, however, but rather because she exceeds it. The woman's voluntary self-divestment of "everything she had, all she had to live on" – at once an absolute and a thankless gesture – may be read as an act of epiphanic extravagance whose immeasurable immoderation thrusts it outside every conventional circle of economic exchange. As Jacques Derrida has remarked, apropos of his own liminal concept of a gift beyond reciprocity,

> the gift is precisely, and this it what is has in common with justice, something that cannot be reappropriated. A gift is something which never appears as such and is never equal to gratitude, to commerce, to compensation, to reward. When a gift is given, first of all, no gratitude can be proportionate to it. A gift is something you cannot be thankful for. As soon as I say "thank you" for a gift, I start canceling the gift, I start destroying the gift, by proposing an equivalence, that is, a circle which encircles the gift in a movement of reappropriation.[16]

Read from this angle, the widow's self-divestment, as expenditure without reserve and absolute gift, would represent (with only a minimum of hyperbolic torquing) the breaking through, or breaking out, of "something inconceivable, hardly possible, *the* impossible" even.[17] In common with other radically countercultural currents in Mark that we have pondered – only more so – this gift beyond reciprocity would hint at liminal experiments in community that apocalyptically deconstruct the world as we know it. The anecdote of "The Widow's Mites," then (mighty mites, indeed!), would be the real site of apocalypse in Mark, not the so-called apocalyptic discourse that follows, rather lamely, on its heels, and for which it ostensibly prepares. Having already surpassed that for which it prepares, the anecdote renders the apocalyptic metanarrative superfluous and hence expendable. And the non-imperial apocalypse preemptively unveiled in the anecdote, far from undercutting the radical ethic that informs much of the preceding narrative, instead epitomizes it. What the widow's action prefigures, if anything, is not so much Jesus' self-divesting investment – the Markan cross, in the end, is merely a bold entrepreneurial wager that yields an eschatological empire – but rather the expenditure without reserve exemplified by yet another anonymous woman in the narrative, the one who "wastes" on Jesus (*eis ti hê apôleia hautê . . .*) the "alabaster jar of very costly ointment of nard" (14:3–4), and whose tale is told almost immediately *after* the (official) apocalyptic discourse. Sandwiched between two women of whom he is apparently in awe, Mark's Jesus nonetheless fails to learn the lesson wrapped up in

the absolute gift that he lauds, not once but twice, and cancels his planned parousia accordingly. In the end, then, Mark's gospel refuses to relinquish its dreams of empire, even while deftly deconstructing the models of economic exchange that enable empires, even eschatological ones, to function.

NOTES

1 Robert H. Gundry, *Mark: A Commentary on His Apology for the Cross* (Grand Rapids, Mich.: Eerdmans, 1993), 260.

2 See, for example, Ched Myers, *Binding the Strong Man: A Political Reading of Mark's Story of Jesus* (New York: Orbis Books, 1988), 190–4; Herman C. Waetjen, *A Reordering of Power: A Socio-Political Reading of Mark's Gospel* (Minneapolis, Minn.: Augsburg Fortress Press, 1989), 115–18; John Dominic Crossan, *Historical Jesus: The Life of a Mediterranean Jewish Peasant* (San Francisco: Harper San Francisco, 1991), 314–18; Richard A. Horsley, *Hearing the Whole Story: The Politics of Plot in Mark's Gospel* (Louisville, Ky.: Westminster John Knox Press, 2001), 140–1, 47; Richard A. Horsley, *Jesus and Empire: The Kingdom of God and the New World Disorder* (Minneapolis: Fortress Press, 2003), 100ff; R. S. Sugirtharajah, *Postcolonial Criticism and Biblical Interpretation* (New York: Oxford University Press, 2002), 91–4.

3 A token force, to be sure, stationed primarily at Caesarea – but able to call on the Syrian legate and his legions whenever the paucity of its numbers instills hope of effective armed resistance in the native populace.

4 A determination reinforced by reading a prepublished version of Laura E. Donaldson's "Gospel Hauntings: The Postcolonial Demons of Biblical Criticism," in Fernando F. Segovia. (ed.) *Postcolonial Biblical Criticism: Interdisciplinary Intersections*, The Bible and Postcolonialism (Sheffield, England: Sheffield Academic Press, forthcoming), which incisively underscores the hazards of imposing a unitary meaning on the gospel exorcisms. Not least among these hazards is a certain gender blindness. While the Gerasene wails at the top of his lungs, notes Donaldson, the demon-possessed daughter of Mark 7:24–30 (Matthew 15:21–8) is mute; while he engages in frenzied activity, she lays immobile on her mattress; and while he vividly inhabits the main narrative, she is absent from it. Such stereotyping, as she further observes, subverts any attempt to lump men and women together under the master term "the colonized."

5 Louis Althusser, "Ideology and Ideological State Apparatuses (Notes Towards an Investigation)," in Louis Althusser (ed) *Lenin and Philosophy and Other Essays* (London: New Left Books, 1971).

6 See Crossan, *Historical Jesus*, 314.

7 The standard study detailing and advancing this interpretation is that of William R. Telford, *The Barren Temple and the Withered Tree*, JSNT Sup 1 (Sheffield, England: JSOT Press, 1980).

8 One thinks immediately of Musa W. Dube, *Postcolonial Feminist Interpretation Interpretation of the Bible* (St. Louis, Mo.: Chalice Press, 2000); or Tat-siong Benny Liew, *Politics of Parousia: Reading Mark Inter(con)textually*, Biblical Interpretation (Leiden and Boston: Brill, 1999).

9 See, most recently, Horsley, *Hearing the Whole Story*, 36, 43, 112–13.

10 See Homi K. Bhabha, *The Location of Culture* (London and New York: Routledge, 1994), 85–92, 129–38.

11 Peter Worsley, *The Third World*, 2nd edn., Nature of Human Societies Series (Chicago: University of Chicago Press, 1970), 38.

12 As Tat-siong Benny Liew has, in effect, recently argued (Liew, *Politics of Parousia*, 93–108). Pivotal to his argument is a reading of the Markan parousia (13:24–7), in tandem with the Markan passage on Gehenna (9:43–8), as a show of ultimate force and authority that "will right all wrongs with the annihilation of the 'wicked' " (Liew, *Politics of Parousia*, 107). As my earlier remarks indicate, I find Mark's parousia to be a much milder and more muted affair.

13 See, for example, Gayatri Chakravorty Spivak, "Identity and Alterity: An Interview – Gayatri Chakravorty Spivak with Nikos Papastergiardis," *Arena: A Marxist Journal of Criticism and Discussion*, 97 (summer 1991): 70.

14 Compare, too, Mark 14:25 and Matthew 26:29. If, with the majority, we assume Markan priority, then we see that Matthew has changed the Markan Jesus' declaration, "Truly I tell you, I will never again drink of the fruit of the vine until that day when I drink it new in the kingdom of God," to "I tell you, I will never again drink of this fruit of the vine until that day when I drink it new *with you* [*meth' hymôn*] in my Father's kingdom."

15 See, for example, Liew, *Politics of Parousia*, 73; and Horsley, *Hearing the Whole Story*, 216–17.

16 Jacques Derrida, "The Villanova Roundtable," in John D. Caputo (ed.), *Deconstruction in a Nutshell: A Conversation with Jacques Derrida*, (New York: Fordham University Press, 1997), 18.

17 John D. Caputo, *The Prayers and Tears of Jacques Derrida: Religion without Religion* (Bloomington: Indiana University Press, 1997), 177, his emphasis. Here, I have been embroidering and expanding some passing, but illuminating, comments of Caputo on the widow's gift.

14

Tyranny, Boundary, and Might:

Colonial Mimicry in Mark's Gospel

Tat-siong Benny Liew

Most scholars who read Mark's Gospel in light of Roman colonization of Palestine in the first century CE have interpreted the Gospel as a document for liberation. Those who note Mark's polemic for liberation frequently describe the Gospel in purely positive terms. For Ched Myers (1992), Mark rejects imperialistic Roman oppression, repudiates the temple's exploitative economy, and advocates to build a just and egalitarian community of sharing and mutual service by the way of the cross (which Myers equates with Mahatma Gandhi's nonviolent resistance). Herman C. Waetjen (1989) understands Mark to be a condemnation of an old order, which is (1) represented by the temple and by the power of Jewish and Roman establishment, and (2) characterized by binary exclusion, hierarchical oppression, and economic dispossession. Instead, Jesus' new order, according to Waetjen's reading of Mark, is typified by egalitarian and familial relationships. Similarly, Robert G. Hamerton-Kelly (1994), applying René Girard's theory on ritual scapegoating to the Gospel of Mark, argues that Mark presents a gospel that challenges the "sacred" or the violent system that rules the world. While Jesus' death on the cross exposes the way the "sacred" – which includes both Jewish and Roman social formation – is dependent on violence, Jesus' resurrection signifies the possibility of a new community that is characterized by love and inclusiveness.

One may question, however, the one-sidedness of such liberational readings in light of current developments within colonial/postcolonial studies. In recent years, such studies have moved beyond the old politics of blame to scrutinize how nationalism often becomes an antonym of liberation, and decolonization a synonym of neocolonialism.[1] One may also trace the limits of such liberational readings to the oppressive role the Bible itself has played in the history of colonization.[2] Rather than taking the easy way out by saying that whatever problems the Bible may have been associated with are results of "misinterpretation," I agree with Rey Chow (1993: 21)

First published in *Journal for the Study of the New Testament*, 73 (1999).

that we need to learn from the way Michel Foucault handles the problem of the Gulag; that is, being willing to confront a predicament as an understandable evolution of its founding texts or theories rather than condemning it as an unacceptable error.[3] But more importantly, my dissatisfaction with the aforementioned readings of Mark is related to my personal history. Caught within the larger history of Hong Kong, my personal history is one that sensitizes me to colonial power relations, and predisposes me to "a diasporic consciousness" (Chow 1993: 22) that refuses to idealize anything.

Writing and Reading Diaspora

Two of my childhood memories may serve to illustrate this sensitivity and consciousness. For many children who grew up in colonial Hong Kong, our first encounter with British colonialism was nothing less than a literal educational experience. On the first day of class in a church-related school, we were told that we needed a "proper" name – meaning English and/or Christian – for school.[4] Being the fifth child of my family, I was fortunate to benefit from the experiences of my four older siblings. Since neither my father nor my mother knew English, it was my eldest sister who gave me my English name the night before my first day in school; and she did so by basically flipping through an English dictionary until she found a name that "sounded good but was not overused." I still remember, however, the anxiety and embarrassment felt by many of my classmates as they scrambled to come up with an English name for each other, or waited nervously to receive a new name from the teacher. Feeling the "need" for an English and/or Christian name but yet unwilling to be named by a stranger, many young people from Hong Kong end up with some rather "unconventional" English names like "Apollo" or "Cinderella."

My other childhood memory is really a cluster of memories that prompted me to distance myself from Chinese communists as well as from British colonials. Many years before Tiananmen Square (1989) and the current uproar surrounding Tibet (indirectly because of the release of two Hollywood movies), I have become aware of the oppressions within mainland China through relatives who live under that communist regime. I remember stories about two older cousins, who, at the time of Mao Ze-dong's Cultural Revolution, were removed from grade school and placed in different bakery training programs without consent; to this day, my cousins remain largely illiterate. I remember my uncle and aunt who, after swimming every single day for a year in different public swimming pools (to avoid the attention of suspicious Red Guards) to build up their stamina, risked their lives in shark-infested waters for three days in order to sneak into Hong Kong in search of a better life. I remember letters from relatives telling about their need for clothing and food. I remember when, as a little boy, I accompanied my mother to the train station for her trip into the mainland to help provide for these needy relatives; what I witnessed were like scenes taken directly from movies about the Japanese occupation of Hong Kong during the Second World War. The train station was filled with people, mostly middle-aged women who, like my mother, were carrying an unreasonable number of unreasonably big bags;[5] some, like my mother, dragged these bags along with bare hands, others had them strapped on both ends of a long bamboo pole, which they

carried across their shoulders. I knew what was in my mother's bags, and from the look of things, I knew similar things were filling other peoples': underwear, towels, shirts, pants, socks, and canned food.[6]

In hindsight, I now realize that what I saw that morning in the train station is a striking display of the parallel exploitation experienced by those who live in colonial Hong Kong and those who live in communist China. As these people pushed and ran to catch a train to provide help and relief for their relatives in mainland China, they did not only look like political refugees and fugitives themselves; more importantly, they demonstrated a loss of faith in "the system." Their pushing and shoving against each other was not a result of impatience, but because of a deep realization that having a ticket did not necessarily mean that the agreement that a ticketholder made with the train company would be honored. My mother has provided me with a lifetime of examples of this lack of faith in institutional promises. This mindset that I had always interpreted as impatience and irrational anxiety was a source of great frustration to me right up to the day it was announced that Hong Kong Chinese carrying British passports would not be allowed to settle in the United Kingdom to escape the 1997 transfer of Hong Kong back to Chinese rule.

My "diasporic consciousness" continues, of course, with my move to North America. Once again, Chow puts it so appropriately and beautifully; speaking of her own migration from Hong Kong to the United States, she becomes, in effect, "a kind of diasporic person in diaspora" (1993: 23). While I have spent the majority of the last seventeen years in the United States, my "diasporic consciousness" has been heightened, in no small measure, from two separate stints in Canada that amount to five and a half years. As Bart Moore-Gilbert points out (1997: 10–11), Canada is perhaps the best illustration of how complex and ironic colonial relations can be. Living under the shadow of both British colonialism of yesterday and United States imperialism of today, Canada itself has internally colonized at least two significant cultures that have been making a lot of noise in the last few years: the French-speaking Quebecois and the recent, financially well-off immigrants from Hong Kong. To complicate matters even further, these two internally colonized cultures have, in turn, taken on the colonizer role vis-à-vis the native Indian population and the "rest" of the Chinese Canadian community respectively. For example, in the words of a former parishioner of mine who moved from Hong Kong to Canada twenty years ago and has been working as a self-employed consultant, recent investor-immigrants from Hong Kong are the worst employers, because "they will not be satisfied until they suck the last drop of blood out of their employees."[7]

It is with this kind of "diasporic consciousness", this sensitivity to colonization and refusal of idealization, that I approach Mark's Gospel. Since reading diaspora "make[s] room for reciprocal critique and multiple commitments" (Cheung 1997: 10; see also Said: 1993: xxvi–xxvii), my reading of Mark involves a simultaneous claiming and disclaiming of Mark.[8] Without denying the elements of anti-colonial protests that Myers, Waetjen, and Hamerton-Kelly have suggested for Mark's Gospel, I want to examine if Mark duplicates any colonial ideology or contains any traces of – turning Bhabha's term (1994c) on its head – "colonial mimicry."[9] After all, Spivak has argued in "The Rani of Sirmur" (1985) that "colonial worlding" involves not only the construction of the colonizers, but also the potential internalization of that constructed world on the part of the colonized.[10] Looking at the way

Mark (1) attributes absolute authority to Jesus, (2) preserves the insider-outsider binarism, and (3) understands the nature of "legitimate" authority, I intend to argue that Mark has indeed internalized the imperialist ideology of his colonizers.

Jesus' Absolute Authority

Despite all of Mark's anti-authority rhetoric that others have suggested, one may question if Mark is concerned with breaking up the very makeup of authority, or merely wishes to replace one authority by another. The way he contrasts the teaching and the authority of Jesus and the Jewish leaders in the first healing miracle (1.21–8) and the first controversy story (2.1–12) of the Gospel, seems to suggest that the issue for Mark has more to do with the categories of authority – whether it is new and substantial, or traditional and hollow – than its constitution. Alan Sinfield, writing about King James's insistence to distinguish "a lawful good king" from "an usurping tyrant," calls such a distinction a "characteristic of the ideology of absolutism" (1992: 98–9). Does Mark's representation of Jesus' authority, then, duplicate an absolutist ideology?

The authority of Mark's Jesus is, first of all, closely related to the authority of the Hebrew scripture.[11] Time after time, Mark presents Jesus as one who can quote and expound scripture to justify his own teachings and actions, whether the issue at hand concerns the Sabbath (2.23–8), his practice of speaking in parables (4.10–12), ritual cleanliness (7.1–8), responsibility to parents (7.9–13), the acceptability of divorce (10.2–12), the assurance of eternal life (10.17–22), the operation of the temple (11.15–17), the credibility of resurrection (12.18–27), the first commandment (12.28–31), the relationship between David and the messiah (12.35–7), or the apocalypse (13.24–7).[12] As if Mark is afraid that his readers may not come into agreement with Jesus, Mark is careful to point out that the way Jesus uses and interprets scripture is recognized as valid by the crowd (11.18; 12.37b) as well as by the scribe who questions him about the "first commandment" (12.32–3). Effectively silencing all his critics (12.34c), this scribal recognition, in effect, shows that Jesus is a sort of master scribe. At the same time, however, Mark indicates that this Jesus is much more than a master scribe who understands scripture; he is, in fact, its very fulfillment. In addition to Jesus' own references to scripture as a prophecy of his upcoming suffering and ultimate glory (9.12–23; 12.10–11; 13.26; 14.21, 27, 48–9, 62; 15.33), Mark also has "many" (11.8) chanting the "hosanna chorus" at Jesus' entry into Jerusalem (11.9–10), thus identifying Jesus as the promised messiah. One must also not forget that at the broader narrative level (that of the implied author or narrator), this entire story about Jesus begins with a scriptural allusion to Isaiah (1.1–3).[13]

This understanding that Jesus is the very fulfillment of Jewish scripture is perhaps best underscored by two scenes. The first is the parable of the wicked tenants (12.1–11), which asserts that Jesus, who holds a special status as "beloved son" (12.6b) and "heir" (12.7), will conclude the succession of servant-prophets sent by God to re-establish God's claim of ownership of the "vineyard." The other, Jesus' transfiguration (9.2–8), though sequentially earlier, may actually be more forceful in making this point. The transfigured Jesus is, first of all, greeted by Moses and Elijah,

who personify the law and the prophets. After Peter rashly proposes to make "three tents" or "dwellings" (9.5d) for the conversation partners, three things happen: (1) a cloud overcomes them; (2) a heavenly voice is heard "repeating"[14] the announcement that Jesus is God's "beloved son" (9.7c), followed by the command, "listen to him" (9.7d); and (3) Moses and Elijah disappear from the scene altogether. While this command to "listen" has been rightfully linked to the disciples' inability to take seriously Jesus' passion predictions within this "on-the-way" section of the Gospel (8.22–10.52) or, a little more specifically, their obsession with the dazzling sights associated with Jesus' transfiguration (Tolbert 1989: 206–7), the disappearance of Moses and Elijah after this command to "listen" may also signify what is wrong with Peter's proposal: Peter should not have placed Moses, Elijah and Jesus as equals.[15] Granted that Moses and Elijah are respectively the great law-giver and the great prophet of the Hebrew scripture, the son's appearance fulfills and brings with him the authoritative interpretation of that tradition.[16]

The authority of Mark's Jesus, then, is ultimately dependent on his status as God's beloved son and heir. Burton Mack cites Philipp Vielhauer to argue that Mark has effectively positioned one story at the beginning of the Gospel (Jesus' baptism, 1.9–11), one at the middle (Jesus' transfiguration, 9.2–8), and one at the end (Jesus' crucifixion, 15.33–40) to declare Jesus as God's son, and thus "superimpose a script of divine approval and involvement for all of... [Jesus'] activities" (Mack 1988: 285); but I think Mark's consummate touch in making Jesus' status special and his authority absolute is found in one little word that he tucks away in the parable of the wicked tenants to qualify this "beloved son": "the owner still had *one* other person, a beloved son" (12.6; emphasis mine). In other words, there is no other heir other than Jesus; he is God's last authorized agent, God's one and only regent. This claim of singularity is, of course, an effective ideological weapon that leads to absolutism by allowing no comparison or competition.[17]

Some scholars are right in pointing out the distinction Mark makes between Jesus and God,[18] but the proximity between Jesus and God within the Gospel must also not be denied. This can be seen by the way Mark introduces his story as "the gospel of Jesus Christ" (1.1), but then has Jesus "proclaiming the gospel of God" (1.14) in the beginning of Jesus' ministry. The fluidity of Jesus as proclaimer and proclaimed is further demonstrated by how a Galilean leper, despite Jesus' command to be silent, goes around to "proclaim a lot" (1.45a) about how Jesus has healed him. Likewise, as Tolbert (1989: 228 n. 95) observes, the Gerasene demoniac, who is told by Jesus to report on what God has done for him, "departed... to proclaim in the Decapolis how much *Jesus* had done for him" (5.20a; emphasis mine) instead. In various places in the Gospel, we find Mark's Jesus associating himself with the gospel and God with statements such as "whoever is willing to lose his or her life *for my sake and for the sake of the gospel* will save it" (8.35b; emphasis mine), "whoever receives me receives not me but the one who sent me" (9.37c and d), and "there is no one who has left a house or brothers or sisters or a mother or a father or children or fields *for my sake and for the sake of the gospel*, who will not receive a hundredfold in this age, houses and brothers and sisters and mothers and children and fields along with persecutions, and in the coming age eternal life" (10.29c–30; emphasis mine).

This status allows Jesus, as Mack observes (1988: 199, 203), in Mark's many controversy stories, to "author" his own assumptions, arguments and pronounce-

ments that his opponents may not even share or accept. Rather than just being subjected to the authority of Hebrew scripture, Jesus becomes his own authority to give pronouncements that ask for decision without discussion.[19] For instance, in the controversy about fasting (2.18–22), Jesus simply declares "that from this time on, the meaning and purpose of fasting are defined, determined and dependant on the person of the Messiah-Bridegroom" (Trakatellis 1987: 17), which is Jesus himself. In fact, his authority is so absolute that he has the freedom and flexibility to override the instructions that he himself gives to others to follow. For example, while Jesus chides the scribes for exploiting the livelihood of poor widows (12.40–4), asks a rich man to sell all he owns so that he can give the money to the poor (10.17–22), and sends the Twelve out on a mission like minimalists both in terms of personal belongings taken and charity sought (6.7–13), he allows an undistinguished woman to anoint him at a leper's house with a jar of expensive nard that could have been sold for money to help the poor (14.3–9). He faults the Pharisees and the scribes for neglecting their parents with the excuse of the Corban offering (7.9–13); yet Jesus himself justifies his decision to ignore and shame his mother and siblings, whom he leaves standing outside calling for him, on the basis of a higher calling from God (3.31–5). Similarly, he forbids his disciples from excluding another exorcist because, he says, the exorcist is exorcizing in Jesus' name (9.38–40); at the same time, he reserves for himself the right to decide people's "proximity" to the kingdom (12.34), and to identify "false" prophets, even if they are also performing miracles in Jesus' name (13.21–2).

Jesus' status as God's *only* son and heir in Mark's Gospel seems to result in yet another hierarchical community structure. Despite the familial terms we have seen Mark use to describe the community of Jesus, Jesus' family, like most families on earth, is not devoid of its own pecking order. Alongside his language of brotherly and sisterly relations, we also find within Mark's Gospel the language of hierarchy that seems to undercut his egalitarian ideals. For instance, at the end of the "apocalyptic discourse" (13.34–7), Jesus describes his household in terms of a "lord" (Jesus himself) who "authorizes" his "servants" and "commands" his "doorkeeper" to various tasks before he goes on a trip. Since the parable begins and concludes with the warning that one should stay alert and awake (13.32, 35–7), the imagery is that of an institution where vertical structure and the threat of punishment are all accepted modes of operation.[20] Jesus is at the pinnacle of the hierarchy of his household, just as the Gentile or Roman rulers are at the pinnacle of their hierarchy of power, "lording over" (10.42b) and "exercising authority over" (10.42b) those who rank below them. Although Mark's Jesus forbids his disciples to treat each other in this manner and sets himself up as the model of a different way of relating (10.43–5), this is the kind of language that Mark uses to describe Jesus' interaction with his disciples. When Jesus sends the Twelve out on their mission, Jesus also "authorized" (6.7c), and "ordered" (6.8a) his disciples (see also 3.14–15); and as they get ready to move towards Jerusalem, Jesus also "commanded" (8.15a) the disciples to watch out for the "leaven" (8.15) or influence of the Jewish authorities. Jesus, as the "lord" of his household (13.35a) or the "shepherd" of his flock (6.34; 14.27), teaches and tells his disciples – or his servants, his sheep – what they should do and how they should live. Why? Because, after all, he is not just "another servant" (12.4a) sent by God, he is God's only "son" (12.6b) and "heir" (12.7),

whose sandals John the Baptizer is not even worthy to bend down to untie (1.7). No matter what imagery Mark uses, Mark is quite explicit that while there may not be any "next best" seats for James and John in the kingdom, there is a throne that belongs to Jesus and Jesus alone.[21]

With Jesus on the throne, his disciples are often reduced to, borrowing Patrick Brantlinger's phrase for colored characters in British literature, " 'sidekick' roles, as the loyal satellites – virtually personified colonies" (1988: 57) of the messiah. To keep a safe distance between himself and the "maddening crowd," Jesus tells the disciples to go and get a boat for him to teach in (3.9). As the disciples strain at the oars, Jesus is taking a nap at the stern (4.38). When there are miraculous feedings to be performed, the disciples are the ones who assume the ushering role of seating people, the table-waiting role of distributing food, and the janitorial role of picking up crumbs (6.39, 41, 43; 8.6–8; see also 8.19–20). In the latter part of the Gospel, they continue to act as Jesus' "gophers"; they are sent by Jesus to go for Bartimaeus (10.49), to go for the colt in the next village (11.1–7), and to go for the Passover preparation in the city (14.12–16). As Catherine Hall observes (1992: 243–4), "apprenticeship" (or Mark's "discipleship") is often just another name for "slavery" (or Mark's "servitude") in human history. While Mark faults the disciples for their hard heads and fearful hearts, and frowns at any possible inequality among them, he never questions the different and unequal status between Jesus and the disciples.

Current studies on colonial discourse have alerted us to the realization that even language of the family may encode oppressive and dominating relations (for example, Achebe 1988: 7–8; Hall 1992: 260–1). One may notice that the word "father" is conspicuously absent in Jesus' definition of the new family (3.33–5). When Jesus talks to his disciples about sacrifices involved in following him (10.28–30), he sort of reiterates this idea of a new family by promising to replace every sacrifice by a "hundredfold" (10.30a): "houses" (10.29c, 30a), "brothers" (10.29c, 30a), "sisters" (10.29c, 30a), "mothers" (10.29c, 30a), "children" (10.29c, 30a), and "fields" (10.29c, 30a). Every single sacrifice brings an over-abundant return except "father" (10.29c), which is explicitly stated as a possible loss but also noticeably left out in the list of promised rewards. Before we equate this curious absence and disappearance of "father" with the dismantling of authority or hierarchy, we must keep a couple of thoughts in mind. First, Mark's Jesus reintroduces an authoritative "father" figure for both himself and his disciples in the person of God, who has the last say on honor and shame (8.38), on forgiveness (11.25), on the time of the apocalypse (13.32), and on what happens and does not happen (14.36). Second, even if doing God's will makes one a mother or a sibling of Jesus, one must remember that within Mark's Gospel, God's will is arbitrated by and fulfilled in Jesus, the "beloved son" (1.11; 9.7; 12.6b) and "heir" (12.7) of God. Jesus' new definition of "family" does not automatically eliminate the interplay of power and subordination; quite the contrary, power always resides with the one who has the authority to define.

"Children" is another familial term that crops up in Mark's Gospel once in a while. According to Mark's Jesus, his followers should welcome and incorporate "children" (9.36–7) in their midst, and, at the same time, being "child-like" is "the disposition necessary for entry and continuing participation" (Horsley 1993: 421) in Jesus' community (10.13–16, particularly v. 15). In other places, we find Mark's

Jesus referring to his disciples as "the sons of the bridal party" (2.19b), and Jewish people as "children" (7.27b and c). Once, in the verses immediately preceding the discussion on sacrifice mentioned above, Jesus addresses his disciples directly as "children" (10.24). Even if one understands "children" as a symbol for something else (like those who occupy a marginal position in society), infantilization is still an insulting form of patronization at best, and an extreme form of victimization at worst.

Because of Jesus' unique and authoritative status, those who criticize him are "guilty of an eternal sin" (3.29b). Similarly, the disciples are instructed by Jesus that they are to demonstrate formally their rejection of those who reject them in their mission (6.10–11). When a disciple, Peter, rejects Jesus' first passion prediction, Peter instantly becomes "Satan" (8.33c), which is defined as one who has his or her mind on human rather than divine things (8.33d). Judging from the immediate literary context of Jesus and Peter's interaction (8.31–3), and from Mark's presentation of Jesus as God's son and heir, and thus the authoritative interpreter of God's will, it may be accurate to conclude that "Satan" becomes anyone who does not share the mind or obey the thoughts of Mark's Jesus.[22] Not only do these crude methods of polarization further fuel the absolute authority of Mark's Jesus,[23] they also lead to a duplication of the insider–outsider binarism.

The Binarism Remains

As the above episodes intimate, Mark's Gospel operates on a rather straightforward equation: those who respond favorably to Jesus, the authoritative interpreter and fulfillment of God's will, are "in," and those who do not are "out" (8.38). Granted that, as some have discussed (for example, Hamerton-Kelly 1994: 18; Kee 1983: 33–4, 95, 115; Kelber 1979: 30–42; Kingsbury 1989: 89–117), (1) this new criterion is opened to people of all heredity and ethnicity, and (2) the stories of the disciples and the "other exorcist" show that one's status as an "insider" may involve a few twists of surprise, understanding and following Jesus is still a prerequisite for inclusion.[24] The result, therefore, is not inclusiveness but the validation of a new criterion that is based on one's response to Jesus rather than other conventional measures. For example, what if that "other exorcist" is exorcizing in someone other than Jesus' name? Will there still be any question about his or her exclusion?

Mark's duplication of the insider-outsider binarism also involves violent destruction of those "outside" when the "ins" and "outs" become clear and absolute at Jesus' parousia. With Jesus reappearing in power and in judgment (8.38–9.1; 12.9–11; 12.36; 13.1–2, 26; 14.61–2), the parousia will bring about a realignment of socio-political power and the full establishment of God's reign, the "wicked" authorities will be destroyed, and the temple built by indiscriminating "builders" dismantled. In other words, the "outsiders" who "ousted" Jesus will, in turn, be completely "ousted." As the following statement from the Gospel shows, Mark actually has in mind something worse than a "tit-for-tat" policy: "What measure you measure with, it will be measured against you, *with added proportion*" (4.24c; emphasis mine).[25] The horror of this "interest-incurring" repayment of violence is reflected, for instance, in Jesus' comment regarding his betrayer that "it would have

been better for that person if he or she had not been born" (14.21c). Elsewhere, he talks about his eschatological judgment as an experience that is worse than drowning and mutilation, for it involves the torture of "never-dying" worms and "ever-burning" fire (10.42–8).

Presenting an all-authoritative Jesus who will eventually annihilate all opponents and all other authorities, Mark's utopian, or dystopian, vision, in effect, duplicates the colonial (non)choice of "serve-or-be-destroyed" (Said 1993: 168; see also p. 80). This (non)choice is, in turn, based on another colonial rationalization that Mark shares: namely that certain people have proven to be too barbaric, too evil or too underdeveloped to be given autonomy, or even the right to live.[26] Despite the Gospel's invocation of the Deity and its rhetoric that polarizes things divine and human (8.33; 11.30), it, like most human power systems, promotes "a hierarchical, punitive, and tyrannical concept of ruler and ruled, while claiming that it was all for the best" (Sinfield 1992: 167).[27]

Authority as Power

Mark's politics of parousia supports the use of power, then, at the same time as it is used to express dissatisfaction with the present political power. Actually, power is also a word that would nicely summarize how Mark understands and presents Jesus' authority (Mack 1988: 170, 205–6, 234–42; and Tolbert 1989: 135–6). Although the word "authority" is first used in association with Jesus' first public teaching (1.21–2), what we really find in that pericope is not the content of Jesus' teaching but the account of Jesus' first healing miracle (1.23–6). Immediately after Jesus has successfully exorcized the "unclean spirit" (1.23a) from the man, Mark has all the people in the synagogue who witness the miracle echo in amazement how Jesus' teaching is coupled with authority (1.27c and d). Yet again, the people's statement does not contain any recapitulation of what Jesus teaches; instead, there is a reiteration of the exorcism or healing miracle ("he commands even the unclean spirits, and they obey him," 1.27e).

Three observations can be made from the above pericope. First, Mark makes Jesus' teaching inseparable from Jesus' miracles; the (unknown) content of Jesus' teaching is known by his ability to heal, or his command over unclean spirits. Second, that power to perform miracles, or the ability to have his commands obeyed, is understood to be Jesus' authority. Third, concluding from the above, what Jesus has to teach is his power to do miracles. In other words, his message is his authority.

Mark restates these same points in another pericope that occupies a strategic location within the Gospel. The controversy story about Jesus healing a paralytic (2.1–12) is the last of a series of four healing stories that introduce Jesus' public ministry (1.21–2.12), and the first of a series of five controversy stories that feature Jesus' conflict with the Jewish authorities (2.1–3.6). Like the pericope concerning the healing of the man with the unclean spirit, Mark ties Jesus' healing of the paralytic together with Jesus' teaching, the content of which may be muddled at first glance. The unspoken questions of the scribes (2.6–7) and the ensuing response from Jesus make it clear that the controversy or the point that Jesus wants to teach

or get across is his authority – more specifically, his authority to forgive sins (2.5–8). To prove his authority, Jesus performs his miracle-working power. He gives the paralytic a 'three-point' command: the paralytic is to stand, pick up his mat and walk home. To the amazement of all, his command is obeyed point by point (2.9–12).[28]

This Markan understanding of authority as power can also be seen in other miracle and controversy stories, where, for example, Jesus overpowers death (5.35–43) and nature (4.35–41; 6.45–51) until people say "he has done all things well" (7.37b), or overwhelms his challengers until "no one dared to ask him any question any more" (12.34b). Although it works in opposite directions, this same understanding (authority as power) underlies both the Baptizer's deference to Jesus and the Nazarenes' rejection of him. The Baptizer's statement that he is not worthy to untie Jesus' sandals (1.7c) is sandwiched by two statements about Jesus' power: Jesus' superior strength (1.7b) and Jesus' baptism with the Holy Spirit (1.8). On the other hand, the Nazarenes are so convinced of Jesus' humble family background (6.2–3) that they conclude that Jesus' miracles must not be real, because the same assumption, put in negative terms, means that people without authority do not have real power.

Even though (1) not everybody responds, as Mark implies one should, in amazement, attention and silent obedience,[29] and (2) the faithlessness of the disciples and the hostility of the Jewish authorities leave Jesus dying alone on a Roman cross, Mark's understanding of Jesus and of authority remain the same. In fact, Mark's understanding of authority as power becomes obvious in the dramatic events associated with the parousia. According to Mark, the parousia is God's ultimate show of force (and authority) through Jesus. This event, which is often associated with the word "power" (9.1; 13.26; 14.61–2), will right all wrongs with the annihilation of the "wicked" (12.1–11; 13.24–5). I, for one, tend to think that Jesus' resurrection and return would be enough to undo his murder literally and establish his special place. But for Mark, such a scenario, which may solicit from some a somewhat contrite response similar to Herod's when he thinks John the Baptizer has come back to life in the person of Jesus (6.14), is not enough of a demonstration of authority. Authority is (over)power(ing); and it demands the submission of everybody, and thus also the annihilation of those who do not submit. In other words, vindication must become vindictive. The problem is that by defeating power with more power, Mark is, in the final analysis, no different from the "might-is-right" ideology that has led to colonialism, imperialism and various forms of suffering and oppression.[30] Mark's Jesus may have replaced the "wicked" Jewish-Roman power, but the tyrannical, exclusionary and coercive politics goes on.

Conclusion

While Mark's Gospel may contain critiques of the existing colonial (dis)order, it also contains traces of "colonial mimicry" that reinscribe colonial domination. Jesus, as God's son and heir, has absolute authority in interpreting and arbitrating God's will. One's response to this authorized revealer of God's will, then, becomes the new measure by which one's status within the old "insider–outsider" binarism is

determined. Mark's politics of parousia remains a politics of power, because Mark still understands authority as the ability to have one's commands obeyed and followed, or the power to wipe out those who do not. Despite Mark's declaration of an apocalypse, what we have in the Gospel are recurring themes of "empire" such as tyranny, boundary, and might.

NOTES

1 Barbara Harlow (1987), 154–97, for example, talks about how this has been the experience of Nigeria, Algeria, Kenya, Ghana, Egypt, and "third world" feminism. Several theorists are particularly associated with this emphasis within contemporary colonial/postcolonial studies, including, though not exhaustively, Homi Bhabha (for example, 1992, 1994c and 1994d,), from whom I borrow the term "colonial mimicry"; Gayatri Chakravorty Spivak (for example, 1990a, 381–2; 1990b, 44–5, 54, 135), who politicizes deconstruction by using it as a way to alert a critic to his or her own complicity in the very system which he or she critiques; Edward Said, whose later works have moved beyond the rigid "us-vs.-them" binarism of his *Orientalism* to accentuate the entangled relationships between 'friends' and "foes" (for example, 1993; 9, 12, 18–19, 54, 61, 168, 241–2, 273, 282), and talk about a postcolonial intellectual's role to attest to "an experience of colonialism that continues into the present" (1986), 54, and Trinh T. Minh-ha (for example, 1989, 80; 1991, 8, 88, 91–5, 100, 158–9; and 1992, 56), whose writings remind us that the idea that "domination is [often] propagated by the dominated" (Adorno, 1974, 121) has actually been theorized by an older generation of critics (like Lorde, 1983, 99; Lorde 1990, 287; and Soyinka, 1976, 127).

2 Mary Ann Tolbert (1994), for example, talks about the repressive role the Bible has played in dehumanizing and disenfranchising non-Christians (often meaning non-Europeans), blacks, Jews, women and homosexuals. Similarly, Vincent Wimbush (1995: 98–9) acknowledges the "cultural capital" the Bible represents in the United States. He sees the Bible as a cultural icon that helps justify this country's independence, its curelty against native Indians, its practice of slavery, as well as its imperialistic policies both within and without. Using a language that reminds one of Northrop Frye, both William Dean (1994), xvii–xx, 3–12, and Charles Mabee (1991), 108–9, cite previous studies to talk about a Puritan "myth" of American exceptionalism that was founded on the Bible. In addition, Werner Sollors (1986: 81–6) has related the New Testament to the "melting-pot" language of both J. Hector St. John de Crèvecoeur and Israel Zangwill – a language that has served to normalize the "west" and marginalize the "rest" within the United States (see Lim, 1992).

3 For Foucault, addressing the problem of Gulag means: "[not] question[ing] the Gulag on the basis of the texts of Marx or Lenin or to ask oneself how, through what error, deviation, misunderstanding or distortion of speculation or practice, their theory could have been betrayed to such a degree. On the contrary, it means questioning all these theoretical texts, however old, from the standpoint of the reality of the Gulag. Rather than of searching in those texts for a condemnation in advance of the Gulag, it is a matter of asking what in those texts could have made the Gulag possible, what might even now continue to justify it, and what makes it intolerable truth still acceptable today. The Gulag question must be posed not in terms of error (reduction of the problem to one of theory), but in terms of reality" (1980), 135.

4 Because of Hong Kong's colonial history, church-related schools continue to be viewed as the "best schools" available. Since a person does not necessarily begin his or her

educational pursuit in a church-related school, one may well experience what I am describing in the high school level as well as the grade school level. I should also clarify that this "(re)naming" procedure is not a standard practice in all church-related schools in Hong Kong; whether a student experiences it or not depends on the specific institutions and individual teachers one encounters.

5 Suitcases did not really become popular for most people in Hong Kong until the early or mid-1970s. In the late 1960s, most middle-aged women in Hong Kong traveled with huge bags made of nylon or canvas. Even in the late 1990s, many elderly Chinese still prefer these bags to suitcases.

6 Chow (1993), 20, relating similar childhood memories, talks about a woman who wore seven pairs of pants on her trip into mainland China. My discussion in this section is highly indebted to Chow, whose memories of Hong Kong in the late 1960s trigger in me many images and emotions that I thought I had forgotten.

7 My point here is not to compare oppression qualitatively or quantitatively. Rather than "authenticating" oppression, I am trying to emphasize the duplication of oppression.

8 It is with this same kind of sweet yet bitter feeling that I watched on TV the official return of Hong Kong to the People's Republic of China on July 1, 1997. My sense of pride and satisfaction as Hong Kong ended its status as a British colony was undercut by a sense of shame and sadness, because this Chinese government with which Hong Kong is re-uniting has been notorious for its oppression of its own people as well as its colonization of others (like the people of Tibet). It is even more sobering when one remembers how often this kind of colonial duplication actually happened in the history of the so-called "Judeo-Christian" tradition. Not long before Mark's Gospel, there were the Maccabeans, whose nationalist independence movement turned into tyrannical oppression (Bickermann, 1962); not too long after Mark's Gospel, Christianity was transformed from a marginal religion into the imperial (and imperialistic) religion of the Roman Empire (Olster 1994: 30–50).

9 For Bhabha, "colonial mimicry" is a strategy of the colonizers that backfires, because it requires, by definition, a "partial sameness". To use an accessible example from Renita Weems (1991), 60–6, slave-owners only presented the Bible to slaves in "partial" form for the purpose of "re-form-ation"; slaves were not allowed to read the entire Bible by themselves, but could only hear "expositions" of certain passages by white ministers. This "partial" encounter, or command to mimicry, however, gives slaves the room to maneuver without being chained to what is literally written in the Bible. Using both Jacques Lacan and Jacques Derrida, however, Bhabha pursues his argument in terms of the "ambivalence" or "hybridity" of a colonizer's psyche or a colonial text (for example, 1994b and 1994d). What is central to Bhabha's concern is, of course, the question of agency on the part of the colonized. Without denying agency, however, my "diasporic consciousness" also wants to push Bhabha's emphasis on "the mutualities and negotiations across the colonial divide" (Moore-Gilbert 1997, 116) to its logical conclusion; that is, to explore also the "ambivalence" or the "hybridity" of an anti-colonial text. While Bhabha tends to present "mimicry" as mainly a "menace" (1994c), 88, to the colonizer, I am using "mimicry" to refer to a reinscription or a duplication of colonial ideology by the colonized.

10 According to Moore-Gilbert (1997), 86–7, this emphasis on a "decentered" or "impure" subject also becomes a bridge for Spivak to deconstruct the exclusionary, and irresponsible understanding of biological or cultural determinism (for example, the view that "only women can talk about women," or "only Indians can understand Indians").

11 Given Mark's frequent allusions to Hebrew scripture, many of them stated with a formulaic introduction (for example, 1.2–3; 7.6–7; 11.17; 14.27), he seems to locate the source of truths and authorized actions outside of one's self, although ironically

many of his so-called "scriptural allusions" do not actually exist (for example, 1.2b; 14.21, 49).

12 Scriptual allusions may, of course, be implicit or explicit. For example, both Howard Clark Kee (1983), 111–12, and Joanna Dewey (1994), 480–1, 483, have suggested that Jesus' sea-crossing and feeding miracles in Mark (4.35–41; 6.30–52; 8.1–10) are implicit allusions to the Exodus event. For the purpose of demonstration, I have limited my list of examples here to Mark's explicit allusions only.

13 It should be noted that the first part of this so-called "allusion" (1.2b) cannot be found in Isaiah. Tolbert (1989), 239–48, has also argued for a minority position that this "allusion" refers specifically to Jesus rather than John the Baptizer. Since Mark's formulaic introduction to scriptural quotation ("as it is written", 1.2a) follows on from "the beginning of the gospel of Jesus Christ" (1.1), one does not have to take Tolbert's position to realize the overarching relationship between Jesus and the Hebrew scripture within Mark's Gospel.

14 Sequentially speaking, of course, this announcement repeats the one given at Jesus' baptism (1.11b) rather than the one stated in the parable of the wicked tenants (12.6).

15 This point is also clarified by the following verses that center on the Elijah figure (9.9–13). Tolbert (1989), 208, has argued convincingly that Mark does two things to identify the Baptizer with Elijah: (1) he describes the Baptizer with the same words that the Hebrew scripture uses to describe Elijah (1.6; see also 2 Kgs 1.8); (2) he emphasizes the same word "all" (1.5a; 9.12a) in describing the extent of both the Baptizer's and Elijah's work. What one still needs to remember, then, is how the Baptizer declares in the first chapter of the Gospel that he is not even worthy to bend down to unite Jesus' sandals (1.7).

16 In addition to what I have discussed regarding Jesus acting as the authoritative interpreter and adjudicator of cultic and other traditions of law, Mark's presentation of Jesus as a greater lawgiver can be seen in his claim to establish a "new" covenant with his blood (14.22–5). Let me also give a few examples of Jesus acting as a greater prophet whose words will remain even if heaven and earth do not (13.30–1). These examples will include his three passion predictions (8.31; 9.31; 10.32–4), the finding and the borrowing of a colt for Jesus to ride into Jerusalem (11.1–6), the preparation of the Passover meal (14.12–16), and the failure of the disciples at the time of Jesus' passion, including Peter's denials (14.17–21, 27–30, 50–1, 66–72). As Tolbert (1989), 259, points out, presenting Jesus as such a master prophet gives Jesus an air of "omniscience" and adds credibility to Jesus' predictions about the apocalypse or his parousia, which are not yet fulfilled within the Gospel (13.1–26; 14.28, 62; 16.7). While I see the transfiguration account as the episode that clearly establishes Jesus as the fulfillment of Hebrew scripture, Tolbert (1989), 249, following Kee (1975), 166, sees this establishment as being made in Mk 11, and understands, along with Norman Perrin and Dennis C. Duling (1982), 250, the transfiguration as "proleptic of the parousia" (Tolbert, 1989), 204 n. 49.

17 In addition to our previous discussion of how Mark's Jesus is being presented as a greater scribe, a greater lawgiver and a greater prophet, the brief controversy about the relationship between David and the Messiah (12.35–7) may be interpreted as an attempt to establish Jesus as also a greater king (see Trakatellis, 1987, 81).

18 According to many, Mark has a so-called "low" Christology because of its lack of a birth narrative. To adapt Regenia Gagnier's phrase about the working class, the absence of a birth narrative makes Jesus lack "differentiation from the undifferentiated masses" (1991), 141, until his baptism. For more specific examples, see Tolbert (1989), 268 n. 55, who sees 13.32 as an indication of the distance between Jesus and God; or Waetjen (1989), 168, who features 10.18 as the basis of his argument.

19 According to Jacob Neusner (1975), 115, this is shown in the controversy stories by the order as well as the number of arguments Mark gives to each side: the single argument

Mark gives to the Jewish leaders initially is often countered by two arguments made by Jesus. For more discussions on Mark's rhetorical constructions of these controversy stories, see Dean-Otting and Robbins (1995), and Parrott (1993).

20 Regarding this parable, Donald H. Juel makes the statement that "the use of institutional imagery is unmistakable" (1994), 87. Juel goes on, however, to use this parable to pursue his argument that the church was already a settled institution at the time of Mark's writing, and that Mark is concerned with the church's complacency rather than its persecution.

21 Of course, there are those commentators who are so excited by Mark's language of equality that they do not make any mention of this duplication of hierarchical ideology within Mark's Gospel; see, for example, Belo, (1981), 261–2. While Waetjen acknowledges that the messiah or Christ title is associated with a royal ideology that is "essentially elitist" and vertical in structure, he insists, in the same breath, that Mark's Jesus is establishing a community that has an "essentially egalitarian" structure (1989), 144–5; see also 97. Likewise, Hamerton-Kelly admits that Jesus, as "master," is set apart from the disciples, but he also follows that up by qualifying Jesus' authority over his disciples as only "informal" (1994), 73–4; see also 111. Perhaps because of his sensitivity to the menace of the British monarchy, it is the Canadian literary critic Frye (1982), 87–8, 91, 99–101 who actually devotes several pages to wrestling with the royal and loyal ideology that permeates the New Testament, although he, like the New Testament scholars cited above, ends up denying the potential danger of the New Testament writings.

22 This Markan emphasis on obedience and loyalty is also reflected in Jesus' remark that "if a house is divided against itself, that house will not be able to stand" (3.25). Mark's negative portrayal of the disciples, however, does not only disappoint Jesus within the Gospel narrative, it may also be disappointing to those who read the Gospel and, as a result, spur the readers on to greater obedience and faithfulness to the person and mission of Jesus (Tolbert, (1989), 224). In light of Mark's duplication of colonial ideology, its rhetorical and emotional power may be related to Susan Stewart's argument (1984), 70–103, that when an anti-hegemonic movement turns hegemonic, it often involves 'gigantic' emotions of obedience, loyalty and faithfulness. Or, as Brantlinger writes, "At the heart of all authoritarian politics lies the desire to abolish dialogue (particularly the language of others), to use words strictly in the imperative mode, to call forth acts of heroism and devotion. This desire seeks to subject 'every possible language, every future language, to the actual sovereignty of [a] unique Discourse which no one, perhaps, will be able to hear'" (Brantlinger, 1988, 57; see also Mikhail M. Bakhtin's consistent characterization of such monologic, authoritative and obedience-imposing language as "dead" language in Bakhtin, (1981), 259–422). I am also reminded of a comment by an anonymous Vietnamese worker: "A society that imposes on its people a single way of thinking, a single way of perceiving life, cannot be a human society" (cited in Trinh (1992), 51). May be that is why Mark's Jesus, in response to the Sadducees' question, likens resurrection life (or life after the parousia?) to being angels in heaven (12.25), whose existence, as far as we can tell from the Gospel, is limited to serving Jesus (1.13c) and being on call to do his bidding (13.26–7, 32).

23 One may say that Mark's Jesus, being surrounded by "erroneous disciples" and "evil opponents", appears much like Brantlinger's description of a prototypical colonial hero or missionary who encounters both "amusing" and "dangerous" obstacles: lesser natives who need to be taught and demonic savages who need to be overcome (1988), 181. Like these figures, the fact that Jesus ends up being killed does not diminish, but exaggerate his stature.

24 Notice that the insider-outsider binarism and the hierarchical subordination mentioned earlier often go hand in hand. Instead of demonstrating inclusiveness, the ironic change of the disciples from privileged insider to pitiful outsider, for example, may function to

create a sense of vulnerability that helps "insiders" stay inside. Various scholars have pointed out the repeated Markan emphasis on to "beware" and be "watchful" (8.15; 13.5, 9, 23, 33, 35, 37; 14.34, 37–8; for example, Kee (1983), 75, 159–60; and Mack (1988), 330). Whether it is through warnings of Satan, persecution, selfish desire for wealth and power (4.15–19), false prophets (13.5–6, 21–2), or the uncertainty of the final hour (13.32–7), I agree with Waetjen (1989), 201, that Mark's Gospel seems to foster an identity or subjectivity that is insecure and vulnerable.

25 For scholars who insist that Mark has moved beyond the repayment of violence with violence, see Hamerton-Kelly (1994), 27, 31–2, 40; Waetjen (1989), 78; and most recently, Beck (1996). In contrast, see Arthur P. Mendel (1992), 39–43, who argues that Mark, like Revelation, depicts an apocalyptic vision that is inherently violent. My interpretation also differs from Trakatellis's (1987), 21, which argues that Jesus' death on the cross is sufficient to prevent the Gospel from ending up in some kind of triumphalism.

26 This repetitive violence in Mark seems nothing more than a new cycle of neocolonial rule, and it becomes more stark in light of the recent formation of the controversial Truth and Reconciliation Commission in South Africa, which aims to chart a future that would include all, even those who have participated in the crimes and atrocities of apartheid.

27 Various critics such as Frantz Fanon (1991), 88, 93–5, and Julia Kristeva (1986), 479, have commented on and expressed regret over this violent kind of "colonial mimicry" by anti-colonial and counter-cultural communities. While Fanon explains this mimicry of vicious violence in terms of the "Manichaeism" of the colonial world, Kristeva does so by using Girard's theory on ritual scapegoating. Contrary to Hamerton-Kelly, who takes Jesus as the only scapegoat being sacrificed in the Gospel of Mark, I think there is evidence to suggest that Mark is guilty of duplicating the scapegoating mechanism in his promised expulsion of the "wicked tenants", which may, in turn, involve another level of "scapegoating" (charging Jewish authorities for the evil of Roman colonialists) within Mark's narrative. I am afraid the way Hamerton-Kelly presents the Christian gospel as a necessary corrective to the scapegoating violence that the Hebrew scripture "essentially disguises" (1994), 2–3, is also guilty of anti-Jewish implications.

28 One may further argue that similar points about Jesus' teaching, miracles and authority are made within the series of healing stories (1.21–2.12) and the series of controversy stories (2.1–3.6), both of which involves the healing of the paralytic (2.1–12). A brief summary account of Jesus preaching and exorcizing throughout Galilee (1.35–39) is inserted right in the middle of the series of four healing stories, with two healing stories before (the healing of the man with the unclean spirit, 1.21–28; and the healing of Simon's mother-in-law, 1.29–34) and two healing stories after it (the healing of the leper, 1.40–45; and the healing of the paralytic, 2.1–12). Somewhat similarly, the series of controversies is made up of a conflict story that involves a healing in the beginning (the healing of the paralytic, 2.1–12), three conflict stories that feature rhetorical arguments instead of miraculous cures (the question of eating with tax-collectors, 2.13–17; the question about fasting, 2.18–22; and the question of plucking and eating grain on the Sabbath, 2.23–27) and another conflict story that involves a healing at the end (the healing of the man with a withered hand, 3.1–6). Both series also start with a story in which the word "authority" is specifically mentioned (1.22b, 27d; 2.10).

29 These emphases are brought out by the repeated occurrence of words like "amaze" (1.27; 2.12; 6.2, 51; 9.15; 10.32; 12.17), "hear" (4.3, 9, 23–4; 8.18; 9.7), "obey" (1.27; 4.41), and "follow" (1.17–18; 2.14–15; 3.7; 6.1; 8.34; 10.21, 28, 32, 52; 14.51, 54; 15.41), as well as the Markan commands to silence (1.25, 34, 43–4; 2.12; 5.43; 7.36; 8.30; 9.9).

30 As Samuel Fleischacker seeks to wrestle with "the moral, even epistemological validity" of authority in contemporary sensibilities, he is quick to assert that authority is illegitimate if it is ultimately a matter of power (1994), 84.

REFERENCES

Achebe, Chinua (1988). "An Image of Africa: Racism in Conrad's *Heart of Darkness*," in *Hopes and Impediments, Selected Essays, 1965–1987*. Portsmouth: Heinemann, 1–13.
Adorno, Theodor W. (1974). *Minima Moralia: Reflections from a Damaged Life*, trans. E. F. N. Jephcot. London: New Left Books.
Bakhtin, Mikhail M. (1981). *The Dialogic Imagination: Four Essays*, ed. Michael Holquist; trans. Caryl Emerson and Michael Holquist. Austin: University of Texas Press.
Beck, Robert R. (1996). *Nonviolent Story: Narrative Conflict Resolution in the Gospel of Mark*. Maryknoll, NY: Orbis Books.
Belo, Fernando (1981). *A Materialist Reading of the Gospel of Mark*, trans. Matthew J. O'Connell. Maryknoll, NY: Orbis Books.
Bhabha, Homi (1992). "Postcolonial Authority and Postmodern Guilt," in Grossberg, Nelson and Treichler (1992), 56–68.
——(1994a). *The Location of Culture*. New York: Routledge.
——(1994b). "The Other Question: Stereotype, Discrimination and the Discourse of Colonialism," in Bhabha (1994a), 66–84.
——(1994c). "Of Mimicry and Man: The Ambivalence of Colonial Discourse," in Bhabha (1994a), 85–92.
——(1994d). "Signs Taken for Wonders: Questions of Ambivalence and Authority Under a Tree Outside Delhi, May 1817," in Bhabha (1994a), 102–22.
Bickermann, Elias (1962). *From Ezra to the Last of the Maccabees: Foundations of Post-Biblical Judaism*. New York: Schocken Books.
Brantlinger, Patrick (1988). *Rule of Darkness: British Literature and Imperialism, 1830–1914*. Ithaca, NY: Cornell University Press.
Cheung, King-kok (1997). "Re-viewing Asian American Literary Studies," in idem (ed.), *An Interethnic Companion to Asian American Literature*. New York: Cambridge University Press, 1–36.
Chow, Rey (1993). *Writing Diaspora: Tactics of Intervention in Contemporary Cultural Studies*. Bloomington: Indiana University Press.
Crèvecoeur, J. Hector St. John de (1957). *Letters from an American Farmer*. New York: Dutton [1782].
Dean, William (1994). *The Religious Critic in American Culture*. Albany: State University of New York Press.
Dean-Ottig, Miriam, and Vernon K. Robbins (1995). "Biblical Sources for Pronouncement Stories in the Gospels." *Semeia*, 64: 95–116.
Dewey, Joanna (1994). "The Gospel of Mark," in Elisabeth Schüssler Fiorenza (ed.) *Searching the Scriptures*. II. *A Feminist Commentary*. New York: Crossroad, 470–509.
Fanon, Frantz (1991). *The Wretched of the Earth*, trans. Constance Farrington. New York: Grove Weidenfeld.
Ferguson, Russell, Martha Gever, Trinh T. Minh-ha and Cornel West (eds) (1990). *Out There: Marginalization and Contemporary Cultures*. New York: The New Museum of Contemporary Art.
Fleischacker, Samuel (1994). *The Ethics of Culture*. Ithaca, NY: Cornell University Press.
Foucault, Michel (1980). *Power/Knowledge: Selected Interviews and Other Writings, 1972–1977*, ed. and trans. Colin Gordon. New York: Pantheon.
Frye, Northrop (1982). *The Great Code: The Bible and Literature*. Toronto: Academic Press.
Gagnier, Regenia (1991). *Subjectivities: A History of Self-Representation in Britain, 1832–1920*. New York: Oxford University Press.
Girard, René (1977). *Violence and the Sacred*, trans. Patrick Gregory. Baltimore: Johns Hopkins University Press.

Grossberg, Lawrence, Cary Nelson and Paula Treichler (eds) (1992). *Cultural Studies*. New York: Routledge.
Hall, Catherine (1992). "Missionary Stories: Gender and Ethnicity in England in the 1830s and 1840s," in Grossberg, Nelson and Treichler (1992), 240–76.
Hamerton-Kelly, Robert G. (1994). *The Gospel and the Sacred: Poetics of Violence in Mark*. Minneapolis: Fortress Press.
Harlow, Barbara (1987). *Resistance Literature*. New York: Methuen.
Horsley, Richard A. (1993). "The Kingdom of God and the Renewal of Israel," in Norman K. Gottwald and Richard A. Horsley (eds), *The Bible and Liberation: Political and Social Hermeneutics*. Maryknoll, NY: Orbis Books, rev. edn, 408–27.
Juel, Donald H. (1994). *A Master of Surprise: Mark Interpreted*. Minneapolis: Fortress Press.
Kee, Howard Clark (1975). "The Function of Scriptural Quotation and Allusions in Mark 11–16," in E. Earle Ellis and Erich Grässe (eds), *Jesus und Paulus: Festschrift für Werner Georg Kümmel*. Göttingen: Vandenhoeck & Ruprecht, 165–88.
——(1983). *Community of the New Age: Studies in Mark's Gospel*. Macon, GA: Mercer University Press.
Kelber, Werner H. (1979). *Mark's Story of Jesus*. Philadelphia: Fortress Press.
Kingsbury, Jack Dean (1989). *Conflict in Mark: Jesus, Authorities, Disciples*. Minneapolis: Fortress Press.
Kristeva, Julia (1986). "Women's Time," in Hazard Adams and Leroy Searle (eds), *Critical Theory Since 1965*. Tallahassee: University Press of Florida, 471–84.
Lim, Shirley Geok-lin (1992). "The Ambivalent American: Asian American Literature on the Cusp," in Shirley Geok-lin Lim and Amy Ling (eds), *Reading the Literatures of Asian America*. Philadelphia: Temple University Press, 13–32.
Lorde, André (1983). "The Master's Tools Will Never Dismantle the Master's House," in Cherrie Morraga and Gloria Anzaldúa (eds), *This Bridge Called My Back: Writings by Radical Women of Color*. Brooklyn: Kitchen Table, 98–101.
——(1990). "Age, Race, Class, and Sex: Women Redefining Difference," in Ferguson, Gever, Trinh and West (1990), 281–87.
Mabee, Charles (1991). *Reading Sacred Texts through American Eyes: Biblical Interpretation as Cultural Critique*. Macon, GA: Mercer University Press.
Mack, Burton (1988). *A Myth of Innocence: Mark and Christian Origins*. Philadelphia: Fortress Press.
Mendel, Arthur P. (1992). *Vision and Violence*. Ann Arbor: University of Michigan Press.
Moore-Gilbert, Bart (1997). *Postcolonial Theory: Contexts, Practices, Politics*. New York: Verso.
Myers, Ched (1992). *Binding the Strong Man: A Political Reading of Mark's Story of Jesus*. Maryknoll, NY: Orbis Books.
Neusner, Jacob (1975). *Early Rabbinic Judaism*. Leiden: E. J. Brill.
Olster, David M. (1994). *Roman Defeat, Christian Response, and the Literary Construction of the Jew*. Philadelphia: University of Pennsylvania Press.
Parrott, Rod (1993). "Conflict and Rhetoric in Mark 2:23–28." *Semeia*, 64: 117–37.
Perrin, Norman, and Dennis C. Duling (1982). *The New Testament: An Introduction*. New York: Harcourt Brace Jovanovich.
Said, Edward (1978). *Orientalism*. New York: Vintage.
——(1986). "Intellectuals in the Post-Colonial World." *Salmagundi*, 70–71: 44–64.
——(1993). *Culture and Imperialism*. New York: Alfred A. Knopf.
Sinfield, Alan (1992). *Faultlines: Cultural Materialism and the Politics of Dissident Reading*. Berkeley: University of California Press.
Sollors, Werner (1986). *Beyond Ethnicity: Consent and Descent in American Culture*. New York: Oxford University Press.

Soyinka, Wole (1976). *Myth, Literature and the African World.* New York: Cambridge University Press.
Spivak, Gayatri Chakravorty (1985). "The Rani of Sirmur," in Francis Barker, Peter Hume, Margaret Iverson and Diana Loxley (eds), *Europe and Its Others.* Colchester: University of Essex Press, I: 128–50.
——(1990a). "Explanation and Culture: Marginalia," in Ferguson, Gever, Trinh and West (1990), 377–94.
——(1990b). *The Post-Colonial Critic: Interviews, Strategies, Dialogues,* ed. Sarah Harasym. New York: Routledge.
Stewart, Susan (1984). *On Longing: Narratives of the Miniature, the Gigantic, the Souvenir, the Collection.* Baltimore: Johns Hopkins University Press.
Tolbert, Mary Ann (1989). *Sowing the Gospel: Mark's World in Literary-Historical Perspective.* Minneapolis: Fortress Press.
——(1994). "Reconstituting the World: Feminism, Power, and the Bible," 20th Antoinette Brown Lecture. Vanderbilt Divinity School, March 24.
Trakatellis, Demetrios (1987). *Authority and Passion: Christological Aspects of the Gospel According to Mark,* trans. George K. Duvall and Harry Vulopas. Brookline: Holy Cross Orthodox.
Trinh, T. Minh-ha (1989). *Woman, Native, Other: Writing Postcoloniality and Feminism.* Bloomington: Indiana University Press.
——(1991). *When the Moon Waxes Red: Representation, Gender and Cultural Politics.* New York: Routledge.
——(1992). *Framer Framed.* New York: Routledge.
Vielhauer, Philipp (1964). "Erwägungen zur Christologie des Markusevangeliums," in Erich Dinkler (ed.), *Zeit und Geschichte: Dankesgabe an Rudolf Bultmann zum 80.* Tübingen: J. C. B. Mohr, 155–69.
Waetjen, Herman C. (1989). *A Reordering of Power: A Socio-Political Reading of Mark's Gospel.* Minneapolis: Fortress Press.
Weems, Renita (1991). "Reading *Her* Way through the Struggle: African American Women and the Bible," in Cain Hope Felder (ed.), *Stony the Road We Trod: African American Biblical Interpretation.* Minneapolis: Fortress Press, 57–77.
Wimbush, Vincent (1995). "Reading Texts as Reading Ourselves: A Chapter in the History of African-American Biblical Interpretation," in Fernando F. Segovia and Mary Ann Tolbert (eds) *Reading from this Place.* I. *Social Location and Biblical Interpretation in the United States.* Minneapolis: Fortress Press, 95–108.
Zangwill, Israel (1910). *The Melting-Pot.* New York: Macmillan.

15

Maori "Jews" and a Resistant Reading of John 5.10–47

Mary Huie-Jolly

Johannine Christology makes a division between those who honor Jesus, the "Son," as the equal of God, and those who refuse to accept these claims. It associates "the Jews" with resistance to Jesus' claims to sonship: "Whoever does not honour the Son, just as the Father does not honour the Father" (5.23b).[1] Many scholars could argue that social location makes a difference in determining who makes these claims and who does not. When John 5 was first written, exalted claims concerning Jesus as Son of God figured in a feud between a marginal Johannine group and synagogue authorities.[2] Yet in a situation of colonization the Johannine sonship Christology resonates with claims of superiority and dominance.

Interestingly after the Anglo-Maori land wars of the 1860s and early 1870s, in New Zealand's Bay of Plenty region, some Maori referred to themselves as "Jews" rather than Christians.[3]

Chief Tiopira Te Hukiki, a former lay teacher of Anglicans, reasoned thusly with missionary Leonard Williams in 1878: "You have not visited us for years, and now that you have come to us again you find that we have given up the way of the Son and have adopted instead the way of the Father."[4] This phenomenon was not new. Four decades earlier Henry Williams of the Church Missionary Society (CMS) found "about half the people profess Christianity," the other half "call themselves Jews or unbelievers"; the missionary also found other groups of "Jews" in the district.[5]

Again, at the beginning of the twentieth century, certain Maori who had earlier been regarded as converts of the missionaries, now in response to colonial practices which undermined their tribal lands and way of life, called themselves "Jews" and began to leave the way of the Son.[6]

I am not the first to explore the complex historical reasons for this development.[7] My aim is simply to bring the act of "turning away from the way of the Son" into

First published in Musa Dube and Jeffrey and L. Staley, *John and Postcolonialism*. London: Continuum, 2002, 94–110.

conversation with a post-colonial reading of John 5, for John constructs a dominating Christology which has affinities with the universalizing claims of later colonialist Christianity. In the Maori act of "turning away" I do not see any clear historical connection between the particular text of John 5 and the colonization of New Zealand. However, the claims of John 5 that Jesus is the "Son," just like "God the Father" are consistent with later Christian creeds. The creeds persisted in the religion associated with British imperialism. This, in turn, supported the attitudes of religious and cultural superiority often associated with colonial expansion. Both John 5 and politically dominant Christianity present a universal absolute claim to the divine sonship of Jesus. I will suggest that the identification with the Jews by certain Maori was a decision to "leave the way of the Son" and to resist colonial domination.

Polarizing "the Jews" in constructing christological authority

The Johannine group's conflict over sonship claims is presented by the narrator as if it had come from the mouth of Jesus himself (5.17, 19–47). The narrator relates a healing of Jesus and accusations by "the Jews" concerning his Sabbath action (5.9–10, 16, 18). Jesus replies in the form of a legal defense, arguing that as Son he can do nothing but what the Father is doing (5.17, 19). The adversarial presentation of "the Jews" as those who persecute, and do not honor Jesus, appears to reflect the drama of the Johannine group in feud with a synagogue community as much or more than events during the time of the life of Jesus.[8] Thus, John 5 represents Jesus as "the Son" who calls God "my Father" and acts just like God. And calling God "my Father", is regarded as "making himself equal to God" (5.18). It is answered by an even more exalted claim; absolute authority over life, and absolute judgment are given to the Son by the Father (5.21–3).

The exalted Johannine confession of Jesus as Son would have been regarded as an offense within the profoundly monotheistic culture of the synagogue. But the claim of absolute authority over life and judgment given to the Son by the Father, provided legitimacy and a basis for the Johannine community's identity and authority. For the Johannine group that was no longer under the jurisdiction of synagogue observant Judaism, the Son became the authority, independent of the synagogue.

The Sonship claims do not simply argue that Jesus' Sabbath action was justified. Much more than that, they establish a functional unity between the Son and the Father: the Son acts just like the Father in creating life and in judging, thus establishing equality between Father and Son (5.20–2). The exalted claims for Jesus clearly represent the resurrection faith of the Johannine church: Jesus, exalted to the throne of God, is endowed with all the power of God.[9]

The Polarizing Structure of John 5.16–47

The Sonship claim intends to make a universal claim: "that all may honour the son" (5.23); but practically speaking it is unenforceable outside the group. It serves only to draw a boundary between those within and without, labeling the outsiders as under judgment, and pressuring those within to conform utterly or else be condemned. John 5.16–47 thus structures division between those who honor the Son as

God, and those who refuse to honor him and the division is made at the expense of people who the text calls "the Jews" (5.10, 16, 18). Furthermore, the claims concerning Jesus' Sonship are placed within a polarized, trial-like format in which they function as a defense of Jesus in John 5.16–47.[10]

In the supplementary section on authentic witnesses (John 5.31–47) the "Jews" are blamed for having never even heard the Father's voice, for lacking his word, not believing Jesus whom the Father sent, refusing to come to him, not having the love of God, giving glory only to one another, and not God, and, finally, are accused by Moses for not believing Jesus' words (Jn 5.37–47). By association they are those who, in the hour of judgment, will not hear his voice and having done evil they will face "judgment" (Jn 5.29).

In its original context, Jn 5.16–23 was presented in the literary form of a forensic defence in reply to accusations; but it was not originally enforceable as a law over those "outside" whom it called "the Jews." The forensic reply had teeth only for the marginal group that constructed it. This is in marked contrast with later colonialist situations, where Christianity, with its "Son equals the Father" Christology, was the dominant religion supported by economic and political powers of imperialism.

Is Jesus' identity with God a claim consistent with imperial domination?

John 5.21–3 is consistent with later creedal norms. The creed "the Son is one substance with the Father" is a derivative statement. It seems to be consistent with the Johannine statement of the son's identity with the action and judgment of God the Father.

> The Son can do . . . only what he sees the Father doing; for whatever the Father does the Son does likewise . . . For as the Father raises the dead and creates life so also the Son gives life to whom he will. The Father . . . has given all judgement to the Son that all may honour the Son even as they honour the Father. Whoever does not honour the Son does not honour the Father . . . (Jn 5.21–3).

> I believe in one God the Father Almighty . . . And in one Lord Jesus Christ, the only-begotten Son of God . . . God of God, Light of Light, Very God of Very God, Begotten not made, Being of one substance with the Father . . . (The Nicene Creed 325 CE).

> We all with one voice teach that it should be confessed that our Lord Jesus Christ is one and the same God . . . *homoousious* with the Father as to his Godhead, and the Same *homoousious* with us as to his manhood . . .[11]

These statements function as theological norms in the institutional church. Because they are similar to Jn 5.17–23, the original text and the derivative creeds reinforce each other and function as one unitary norm of Christian discourse. Statements of Jesus' identity with God, from a position of superior authority and power, were statements well suited to dominance. They presupposed the deity of Christ by relying on concepts of a Johannine logos Christology. This served the imperial councils and creeds as 'the highroad of developing Christian orthodoxy'.[12]

In John 5, the Jews who refuse to confess Jesus' sonship stand before the Son as their judge. The norm set out in Jn 5.21–3 clarifies the institutional status quo. As in

the creeds, the role of giving honor to Jesus "just as" God the Father is honored. In addition, it explicitly elaborates the role of dishonor which, though not stated in the creed, follows the same structure and is logically its converse: those who do not honor the Son do not honor the Father (5.23b).

In a church associated with imperial political authority this text wields great authority. Its negative characterization of "the Jews" reinforces contemporary trajectories of anti-Judaism. And its absolutism threatens indigenous cultures and alternative responses to Jesus.

The forensic trappings of John 5 serve to intensify and clarify an ideology of divine expectation for absolute honor for Jesus, and conversely, to blame all who refuse to grant him this honor. To fail to honor Jesus as God is to fail to honor God (5.23). And indirectly such failures are aligned with the "Jews who sought to kill him," and who refuse to believe his testimony (5.18, 43–7). From a position of political power, the Sonship claim dominates. It is consistent with the institutional creeds of politically dominant Christendom; and its Christology, based on the absolute superiority of divine power, resonates with colonial claims to superior power: "God gave all power to the Son that they may honour the Son just as they honour the Father, whoever does not honour the Son does not honour the Father..." (Jn 5.23).

The claim to Sonship draws on the common desire to honor God through obedience to him. According to John's logic, those who do not honor the Son, do not honor the Father, and are identified, within the larger narrative, with the Jews who resist by refusing to accept that the Son is just like God the Father. Likewise, following the loss of their ancestral lands, certain Maori, who were deeply literate in the Maori Bible (a legacy of Christian missionaries) chose to distinguish themselves from the Christianity of the missionaries over the issues of Jesus' Sonship.

Missionary and Maori

From their earliest contact with European missionaries to New Zealand, Maori identified with the biblical accounts of the children of Israel. Like the Israelites, Maori tribes were knit together by their ties of kinship, genealogy, and their lore of sacred journeys.[13] The sense of tribal affinity with the stories of the Hebrews impelled them with a powerful desire to read this sacred lore. Reading and writing also spread rapidly among Maori, in part, because communication by written marks was seen as an almost magical art. Biblical literacy was a factor in their conversion because the printed text was regarded as *tapu* (holy);[14] and the eventual translation of portions of the Bible into Maori in the 1830s sustained the powerful enthusiasm for literacy.[15]

People took learning back to villages, where the newly literate passed on knowledge to home tribes. By the 1850s Maori were more literate than Pakeha (the Maori name for New Zealanders of European descent). Literate Maori often became the teachers of others, so that the Scriptures were received and used by Maori for Maori in dynamic interaction with their traditional religion.[16] Biblical messages also spread orally, sometimes preceding the Pakeha missionaries. Occasionally, European missionaries found Maori villages where people could recite whole passages of scripture, and words of hymns from memory, to which they then composed own their

tunes.[17] Whole liturgies were memorized by Maori attending Christian services, and they assimilated aspects of their own culture as an indigenous response to Christianity.[18]

However, the enthusiastic reception of the Bible in Maori did not lead Maori to an uncritical acceptance of missionary Christianity. The early missionaries, following the explorers and whalers, were among the first Europeans to live among Maori. The missionaries themselves came from distinct groups representing diverse perspectives,[19] but in general their motivations centered around conversion of the Maori to Christianity. Yet the link between religion and empire was sometimes taken for granted. Samuel Marsden, of the Anglican Church Missionary society (CMS), gives an indication of this attitude in his 1816 account of "The First Sabbath-day observed in New Zealand":

> On Sunday morning, when I was on deck, I saw the English flag flying, which was a pleasing sight in New Zealand. I considered it as the signal and dawn of civilization, liberty and religion, in that dark benighted land . . . I flattered myself [the British colors] would never be removed, till the natives of that island enjoyed all the happiness of British subjects . . . [I preached from Luke] . . . "Behold! I bring you glad tidings of great joy . . ." The natives told Ruaterra[20] that they could not understand what I meant. He replied that they were not to mind that now, for they would understand bye and bye . . .[21]

The missionary's role became more complicated and new conflicts emerged when colonial settlement, beginning in the late 1830s, brought land hungry Europeans to New Zealand. Colonial rule hastened the alienation of land from Maori by legal and illegal means. The sale and confiscation of their lands took the substance of life from the original Maori inhabitants. Furthermore, since law and religion were part of the overall framework of Maori society, mission involvement in religious and moral teaching was easily understood, but the relationship between missionaries and government authorities was ambiguous. The growth of the settler population and the grab for more land conflicted with the missionaries' attempt to safeguard and protect the Maori interests.[22] The missionaries, particularly those from the Church Missionary Society, were caught up in this ambiguity; some of them became land holders in their own right and were accused of duplicity.[23] As a colonial society became established in New Zealand, the initial influence of the missions declined.

Often, missionaries tried to curb the worst excesses of colonial exploitation of Maori land. For example, they were instrumental in negotiating and promoting the Treaty of Waitangi in 1840. This Treaty between the British Crown and most Maori tribes enshrined protection of Maori forest, fisheries, and cultural treasures by law. It turned land purchasing from the Maori into a government monopoly. The Crown bought the land and then sold or leased it to settlers.[24] But the legacy of the treaty was ambiguous. The English version of the Treaty saw it in terms of Maori ceding their sovereignty to the Crown, and yet in the Maori version, it also ensured Maori sovereignty, *rangatiratanga*, over their own lands.[25]

The status of the missionaries with the Maori converts was also ambiguous in the colonial period. Colonial settlement was accompanied by pressure for more land, and land was often confiscated in war even from Maori who had not fought the

British. But confiscation as punishment was a clear breach of the Treaty. When missionaries acted as chaplains in the wars of the 1860s and accompanied army and government officials in battle, Maori assumed they were in solidarity with the Crown, and that their role would be to recite chants to ensure victory and defeat the "enemy." The missionaries, perhaps naively and mistakenly, assumed that they could act as army chaplains and at the same time act in good faith to protect Maori from colonial exploitation.

Revd J. W. Stack, speaking of such a battle in the Waikato said: "No wonder the majority of the Maoris lost their belief in the divine origin of the Christian religion which they strongly suspected was a political intervention to beguile the unwary, and to render them more easily subjugated."[26]

In traditional Maori society, religion and law were one. For as Elsmore observes,[27] the institution of *tapu* (the sacred and off-limits) formed the basis of civil order and its spiritual aspect was seen in ritual practices. This unity did not change with the coming of the Pakeha, since the "social laws of that society were laid out in the new scriptures."[28] Added to this was the fact that the missionaries and the early governors were often seen together. These features of Pakeha behavior reinforced Maori assumptions that for the Europeans as well, the religious and secular laws were not separate.[29]

Missionaries often were held accountable for other problems caused by colonization. They were seen as those who "induced the people to accept Christianity," then brought in "arms to oust the simpleton from his land."[30] One Maori speaker put it in these words: "The missionaries were sent to break in the Maoris as men break in a wild horse; to rub them quietly down the face to keep them quiet, while the land was being taken from them."[31]

Missionaries were instrumental in getting people to sign the Treaty, believing that it would protect Maori interests.[32] A Maori saying indicates a different interpretation: "They [the missionaries] made parsons and priests of several members of the Maori race, and they taught these persons to . . . look up and pray; and while they were looking up the Pakehas took away our land."[33]

An old song of the Nga-Puhi people about Samuel Marsden, the first missionary to New Zealand, carries a similar message:

> [Marsden's] message was this: God is in heaven, look therefore to the sky. But the Maori people turned and gazed below to the land, the soil of Aotearoa. They beheld it decayed away with the iron spade, the iron axe, the flaming red blanket and the iron Jew's harp. Thy goods O Governor! Alas the land has gone adrift on the great ocean of *Kiwa*.[34]

Maori saw the *mauri* (the life principle) of anything living or nonliving as the dwelling place of the protecting deities.[35] *Karakia* was a chant or prayer connecting humans to helpful or unhelpful *atua* (deities), by a process of loosing and binding.[36] If connection by *karakia* was polluted in any way, then the deity withdrew and its protection was therefore no longer present.[37] As Michael Shirres explains, the power to make *karakia* effective came from the *atua*. *Mana* (power and status) and the power to reap advantage from *karakia* came from the gods. But most importantly, the failure of *karakia* was linked to acceptance of Western Christianity, indicating that the effectiveness of the chants ceased when people accepted the new faith. The time before *te taenga mai o te Rongopai* (the coming of the good news) was seen as a time

when people were *tapu* (sacred) and *karakia* had power. Formerly *karakia* had power and so had people. But from the time the Gospel arrived here sickness commenced. It was because of people being made *noa* (ordinary, no longer sacred) that sickness commenced. From the time the gospel arrived the people were made *noa*.[38]

> This was the spiritual state of the Maori after some decades of continuing contact with the alternative system of the Pakeha ... When a cure was sought, a *tohunga* [holy person] might be called in, but the power of these figures was most often inadequate to affect any cure against Pakeha diseases. The *Atua* Pakeha was therefore acknowledged to be stronger than the *atua* Maori, and Pakeha medicine the only remedy against *mate* (diseases, curses and death) of the Pakeha.[39]

Bronwyn Elsmore decries the missionaries' use of this crisis to encourage belief in the superiority of the Pakeha God.[40] When Maori were defeated in battles against Pakeha and Christian Maori who had sided with the government, God was seen to be on the side of the Pakeha.[41]

Europeans often regarded the sacred traditions of the Maori as absurdities in contrast to the biblical epics. All this led to loss of status for the Maori. In a conversation between James Stack, an early Wesleyan missionary to New Zealand, and the son-in-law of Chief Te Puhi from Waitangi, Stack writes:

> The chief's son-in-law requested conversation on the creation, before I commenced he wished to know if after I had done I would listen to his traditions. I endeavoured to speak to him on the Mosaic Creation, Fall of Man etc as far as the Flood. But soon perceived that he had a far greater desire to talk than to listen. Finding his patience beginning to exhaust I finished when he commenced telling me a long round of absurdities but with all the spirit imaginable.[42]

In response to the confiscation of land and loss of *mana*, due to Pakeha colonial domination, some Maori turned away from the religion of the missionaries. Instead, they identified with the political situation of the ancient Israelites. They, too, were captive in their own land, subject to imperial domination by a foreign race.[43] According to Irvine Roxburgh, "The unconcealed wish of many colonists and even politicians for a war of extermination of the Maori race, went to give a strong colour to the native belief that the white man's desire for land was the controlling factor [in the unjust labelling of Maori as rebels for their defence of their homeland]."[44]

However, Allan Davidson cautions against stereotyping the "colonial and indigenous worlds" of New Zealand. He notes that the missionaries were in fact influenced by humanitarianism and paternalism. Whereas the colonial world was based on self-interest and aggrandisement, the influence of Social Darwinism from the 1870s brought a "different attitude towards Maori as a dying race and was used to justify assimilationist thinking and actions," says Davidson; there was no one voice in colonialist Christianity, for nineteenth-century colonialism was influenced by a "growing pluralism, sectarianism and secularism."[45]

As I have argued, complex social forces led certain Maori in the late nineteenth and early twentieth centuries to identify themselves as "Jews" as distinct from Christian subjects of the religion of empire. First, the Scriptures had become their

own, and they were free to select and adapt them to their particular social, and religious concerns. Secondly, they felt empathy with the stories of the Hebrew tribes, affinity between with the religion of ancient Israel and traditional Maori practices. And thirdly, during and after the wars of the 1860s there was a degree of "aggressive defiance" in identifying themselves with "Jews." This became the Maori way of saying they were "the chosen people."[46]

Te Kooti Rikirangi, a member of the Rongowhakaata sub-tribe of Ngati Porou, was a man of no traditional chiefly rank, who was deeply learned in Scripture, having gained literacy in the mission schools. When he was unjustly exiled without trial, he escaped with a gathering of followers around him. By claiming the authority of Jehovah, he led a religious movement called *ringatu* (the word means the upraised hand, recalling Moses's hands upraised as the harbinger of "the Jews"). Ringatu forays into the "promised land," which Te Kooti resolved to take back from "Canaan," as he called the places occupied by the colonial settlers, brought sporadic fighting with the colonists.

After a visit to Te Kooti and his followers around 1877, Missionary Thomas Grace noted that their order of service was based on the prayerbook and their faith was not so different from his own – "except that it did not look to the Christian Saviour in its prayers. Rather it looked directly to God".[47] Reflecting on his visit, Grace wrote in his annual letter to the Christian Missionary Society in 1877:

> In early years they received Christianity (and I may say Colonization) at our hands, without doubting and to a great extent on credit. Colonization, war, Confiscation... have followed each other in quick succession; while the expectations anticipated from representations made when they signed the Treaty of Waitangi have not been realized. And now they turn and question their first advisers and look at the whole of our connection with them as a scheme to get their lands from them... These things, together with the course some of our brethren took in the [Anglo-Maori] war, has completely changed our position with these people. Nor is the change less than has come over their own minds as regards the management of their religious affairs. Formerly they consulted us in all matters connected with their teaching and worship... Now they assume the entire management of their own spiritual affairs and seem to consider they have a perfect [right] to do so... they have clearly never intended to renounce Christianity and go back to heathenism – on the contrary. Whatever individual exceptions they now make – they have lost confidence in us as a body and look upon us with distrust and suspicion, and have determined to manage their own religious affairs.[48]

Other religious movements associated with prophetic figures like Te Kooti emerged from this period as well.[49] Judith Binney, Te Kooti's biographer, sees the faith of his people as

> Essentially concerned with the problems of the colonised. It gave them the framework for analysing their own situation; it also offered them a unique relationship with God... resting on the covenanted relationship between them and God, or the politics of the Exodus whereby the destiny of the people is urged as being in their own hands.[50]

In conclusion, biblical stories of land and tribal identity connected Maori with Israelite lore and this identity with Israel fueled the resolve of Te Kooti and others to

battle as Israelites for land against the Canaanite (the European settlers) during the time when the settlers' greed led to war and further confiscation of land.

John's Jews and Maori resistance

From their first contact with Christianity, Maori were encouraged by the missionaries to believe that their tribes were descendants of the people of Israel.[51] But it was, I suggest, their alienation from colonialism and, by association, Christianity as the colonial religion, which fueled their identification with the Jews in the negative Johannine sense of associating "the Jews" with unbelief. Maori identification with the New Testament role of the Jew as enemy of the Christians (or in Johannine terms with "unbelief"), was an act of resistance to colonial Christianity.

Elsmore would seem to support my hypothesis.

> When seen in light of the scriptures, the religious significance between the Maori and Pakeha cultures was major. In the New Testament it was shown that the Christian and the Jews were opposed, and in fact references to the Jews in the later scriptures were to the effect that they were set apart from the Christians for their unbelief. Those termed "Jews" were those who had rejected both Jesus and his teachings, and had even persecuted and killed him. To give to the Maori the idea that they were descended from this race, and in addition to give him the proof of this in the word of God, was therefore almost the equivalent to instructing him that it was his duty to reject the message of Christianity and become rather, as that people of old.[52]

John 5 initially presents the Jews as the accusers of Jesus who "seek to kill him" (5.18). But Jesus quickly moves from the role of the accused to the role of all-powerful judge (5.19–23). The claim that Jesus is the Son just like God the Father, turns the tables, and the Jews change roles. By questioning and refusing to accept the claim that Jesus the Son is just like God, they refuse to honor the all-powerful judge. Jesus' speech reiterates the dominion of the Son as equal to God. It requires hearers to accept or reject him on these same terms. By implication, to respond appropriately to God's demands, to be just and right, requires one to honor God by also giving honor to the Son in those absolute terms.

The negative role in which John's Gospel casts "the Jews" is not unlike anti-Jewish attitudes reflected in the correspondence of Henry Williams, an early CMS missionary to New Zealand. Williams recorded in 1839 that he once met a man named Mr Merning who told Williams of his first arrival in Taranaki, New Zealand. Merning and his companion were greeted by men carrying muskets, so to protect themselves they had called out that they were missionaries, at which point they were heartily welcomed. Williams commented that Merning was "an infidel and his companion a Jew, both enemies to our cause, but in this instance it was convenient for them to hail for Missionaries."[53]

The religion of "the Son just as God," the same substance as the Father, is enshrined in the creeds of Western Christendom where it continued to be normative within the religion of the British Empire during the colonization of New Zealand. Indirectly, then, to refuse to submit to the Son who is vested with the absolute power of God, is, in the ideology of empire, to associate oneself with those placed outside

the realm. It is to identify, as certain Maori did, with the Jews, who are outside the religious ideology of Christendom's loyal subjects. But as Davidson notes: "it was Maori who identified themselves in this way, they demanded this status for themselves, rather than having it imposed by Pakeha."[54]

The Jews are marginalized in John's gospel within the legal motif of a trial. Foiled as the unbelievers who accuse and do not believe the testimony of Jesus, they are judged by God for their refusal to accept the equality of the Son with God (5.23). In the symbolic order of later developments in institutional Christianity, their refusal to believe in the Son as one with the Father, places them outside the fold.

Rudolf Bultmann comments on this Johannine line of reasoning as part of what he characterizes as a "cosmic trial." The "trial" is characterized by the witness, accusation, and reply format repeated throughout John.

> Just as in the rest of the Gospel, the Jews in John 5 appear as the opponents of Jesus, and as the opponents of his witness. This, then, is the prelude to the struggle which runs through the whole of the life of Jesus: it is a struggle between Christian faith and the world as represented by Judaism. It is a struggle that is continually represented as a trial, where the "Jews" are under the illusion that they are the judges, whereas in fact they are the accused before the forum of God.[55]

The "cosmic trial" is a forensic theme in John's Gospel, one which scholars have identified as a device designed to present the reader's decision for or against Jesus in universal terms. The outcome of the cosmic "trial" is consistent with the plot structure of John 5. A division develops between the approved behavior of honoring Jesus as God and the reproach and dishonor attending those who refuse to conform to this behavior as the norm of faith.

John 5.17–23 gives testimony that Jesus is equal to God by arguing in absolute and universal terms for the divine superiority of the Son. In situations of politically dominant Christianity, such texts legitimate an imperial Christology that wields enormous social power when associated with institutions and communities gathered around the traditions of the authority of Jesus.

When, after the missionary period in New Zealand, some Maori who had become Anglicans changed their minds and willingly identified themselves as "Jews," their identity was tied up with the Israelites in a political sense. On one hand, they identified with the stories of the Israelites whom Scripture presents affirmatively with a divine mandate to drive out the Canaanites (who for them represented the European settlers). But, on the other hand, they were willing to self-identify as "Jews" in a negative sense as "unbelievers." They did this in order to empower themselves.[56] In an age of colonial Christianity. I suggest that their self-identification as "Jews" who had turned away from the way of the Son, was a defiant act of resistance to the dominant claims of empire.

The Nicene creed is ideologically consistent with Jn 5.17–23 in that both seek to regulate the status of the Son as equal to the status of the Father; thus text and creed function as one unitary norm, as statements ordering discourse.[57] I am not aware of any quotations from John 5 or creeds derivative of it in the historical documents of colonial New Zealand. Yet both John 5 and New Zealand colonial documents reflect attitudes of imperial religious ideology: "The Father raises the

dead and creates life so also does the Son . . . and the Father does not judge anyone but he has given all judgment to his Son that all may honour the Son just as they honour the Father, whoever does not honour the Son does not honour the Father" (Jn 5.21–23).

On the one hand, the way of the Son equates Christ with the absolute power of God the Father who raises the dead and creates life (5.21). On the other hand, it argues that honoring the power of God as it is given to the Son is the criteria for inclusion as a loyal subject of the Father: whoever does not honor the Son does not honor the Father (5.23).

John's "high Christology" was not formulated as a challenge to Roman political power. It was formulated in order to counter criticism for linking Jesus with God. It did this by solidifying expressions of Jesus' divine authority in superior, absolute terms. Later, in a Christian imperial context, its exalted image of Jesus as the unique Son, God from above from the beginning, resonated with the culture of subsequent imperial rule, and later Western colonial subjugation.

Davidson affirms that colonial nineteenth-century Christianity was in a "self-assured expansionist mode" in New Zealand.[58]

> In taking colonialist forms of ministry, its ways of organising the Church, its modes of worship, old world values and ideals dominated Maori Christian behaviour. That is not to say there was not a process of adaptation in the new environment; there was and that is in itself significant. In their expansionist mode, colonial Christians could very easily ride roughshod over the values of indigenous peoples. They were happy to assimilate Maori Christians into their own Church structures on their own terms. But, whenever the question of Maori having some control over their own spiritual destiny was raised, this was largely squelched. It is therefore not surprising that some Maori expressed their Christianity and religious beliefs outside the structures of both missionary and colonialist Christianity.[59]

Former Anglican chief Tiopira Te Hukiki's comment "You have not visited us for years and now that you have come to us again you find that we have given up the way of the Son and have adopted instead the way of the Father"[60] indicates a change of affiliation. If the "way of the Son" was perceived as ideologically connected with the claims of superiority presumed and imposed by colonial rule of New Zealand, it may have represented, for some Maori, the way of Pakeha domination; to leave the "way of the Son" was to refuse to bow to colonialism's claim of absolute power and instead to identify with the Jews as an act of defiance. To do so is to resist absolute imperial claims, just as in John's gospel the Jews refuse to conform to the Johannine ideology that Jesus the Son is equal with God the Father. Some Maori resisted allegiance to the divine Son of God because of the colonial connection. The absolute religious claims and the dominance imposed by the religion of Empire meant that to "leave the way of the Son" was to challenge the universal and "superior" claims of colonialist Christianity. Maori who defiantly identifed with "the Jews" shook the dust of empire from their feet. They challenged the core of colonialist Christian confession, as reflective of the very structure of nineteenth-century British colonial thought. It was a form of resistance to elude the imperial net of social control.

NOTES

1 See also Jn 1.11–12; 8.37–59; 10.31–9.
2 John Ashton describes it as a "family quarrel"; see his summary of Johannine scholarship on the conflict with "the Jews" in *Understanding the Fourth Gospel* (Oxford: Clarendon Press, 1991), 131–59.
J. Louis Martyn, *History and Theology in the Fourth Gospel* (Nashville: Abingdon Press, 2nd edn, 1979), 29–37, 70; Wayne A. Meeks, "Equal to God," in Robert T. Fortna and Beverly R. Gaventa (eds), *The Conversation Continues: Studies in Paul and John in Honor of J. Louis Martyn* (Nashville: Abingdon Press, 1990), 309–21; Jerome H. Neyrey, *An Ideology of Revolt: John's Christology in Social-Science Perspective* (Philadelphia: Fortress Neyrey, 1988); and Bruce J. Malina, *The Gospel of John in Sociolinguistic Perspective* (Protocol of the Forty-Eighth Colloquy; Berkeley, CA: Center for Hermeneutical Studies in Hellenistic and Modern Culture; Graduate Theological Union and the University of California, 1985), see the conflict depicted in the text as reflective of the conflict that defined the Johannine community.
3 Bronwyn Elsmore, *The Religion of Matenga Tamati* (Auckland: Reed, 1997), 23. In the subsequent discussion of this type of response, I focus on certain actions which are not necessarily representative of all or even most Maori. For a fuller account which gives attention to local variations, see the historical studies by Keith Sinclair, *Kinds of Peace: Maori People after the Wars, 1870–85* (Auckland, NZ: Auckland University Press, 1991); Bronwyn Elsmore, *Like Them that Dream: The Maori and the Old Testament* (Tauranga: Tauranga Moana, 1985); and Anne Salmond, *Two Worlds: First Meetings Between Maori and Europeans 1642–1772* (Auckland: Viking, 1991).
4 Judith Binney, *Redemption Songs: A Life of Te Kooti Arikirangi Te Turuki* (Auckland: Auckland University Press, 1995), 296.
5 Elsmore, *The Religion of Matenga Tamati*, 22.
6 The Maori prophet Rua Kanana is a notable example; on his life, see Judith Binney, G. Chaplin and C. Wallace (eds), *Mihaia: The Prophet Rua Kanana and his Community at Maungapohatu* (Auckland: Auckland University Press, 1996); and Peter Webster, *Rua and the Maori Millennium* (Wellington, NZ: Price Milburn for Victoria University Press, 1979).
7 For historical accounts beyond the scope of this paper, see Sinclair, *Kinds of Peace*; Binney, *Redemption Songs*; Elsmore, *Like Them that Dream*. The historical novel, *Season of the Jew*, by Maurice Shadbolt (Auckland, NZ: Hodder & Stoughton, 1986), also provides a helpful introduction to this period.
8 Jn 7.13, 9.22, 12.42 and 16.2 similarly refer to conflict over the confession of Christ in connection with fear of expulsion from the synagogue.
9 See Mary R. Huie-Jolly, "Threats Answered by Enthronement: John 5.17–27 with Reference to the Divine Warrior Myth in Psalm 2 and Daniel 7", in Craig A. Evans and James A. Sanders (eds), *Early Christian Interpretations of the Scriptures of Israel: Investigations and Proposals* (JSNTSup, 148; SSEJC, 5; Sheffield: Sheffield Academic Press, 1997), 196–200.
10 Mary R. Huie-Jolly, "The Son Enthroned in Conflict: A Socio-rhetorical Interpretation of John 5.17–23" (unpublished PhD dissertation, University of Otago, Dunedin, New Zealand, 1994), 235–7.
11 The Definition of Chalcedon 451 CE, cited by Justo L. González, *A History of Christian Thought: From the Beginnings to the Council of Chalcedon* (Nashville: Abingdon, rev. edn, 1987), 379.
12 James D.G. Dunn, *Christology in the Making: An Inquiry into the Origins of the Doctrine of the Incarnation* (London: SCM, 2nd edn, 1989), xxx–xxxi.

13 Elsmore, *Like Them that Dream*, 62–76.
14 Allan K. Davidson, *Aotearoa New Zealand: Defining Moments in the Gospel–Culture Encounter* (Geneva: WCC, 1996), 6–7.
15 Elsmore describes the hunger for literacy (Elsmore, *Like Them that Dream*, 23–5): Portions of the Scriptures, printed in Maori as early as 1827, fed an amazing eagerness to learn to read: "Books books . . . We are ill for want of books" (Elsmore, *Like Them that Dream*, 24). Reading and writing were not prized initially for their link to Pakeha religion but because writing itself was seen to be magical. If writing could make one understand another *Atua* [god], then the Pakeha *Atua* must be more powerful than *Atua* Maori. Learning the art of conveying messages through cryptic markings had immense appeal. Missionaries allowed translation of the Scriptures only in Maori to ensure that the literate Maori were kept from non-Christian influences. The books were seen as possessing great power and were in demand for their protective qualities. People from the tribes flocked to mission stations for lessons. In Poverty Bay, for example, after 1840, for example, the Church Missionary Society's Revd Henry Williams taught outdoors with cut out letters.
16 Allan K. Davidson and Peter J. Lineham, *Transplanted Christianity: Documents Illustrating Aspects of New Zealand Church History* (Palmerston North, NZ: Massey University Printery, 3rd edn, 1995), 37.
17 Elsmore, *Like Them that Dream*, 25.
18 Davidson, *Aotearoa New Zealand*, 7–8.
19 Allan Davidson, "The Interaction of Missionary and Colonial Christianity in Nineteenth Century New Zealand", in *Studies in World Christianity*, vol. 2, part 2 (Edinburgh: Edinburgh University Press, 1996), 145–66, explores distinctions and confluence between diverse missionaries and their context in relation to the colonial world.
20 A Maori chief, and nephew of Te Pahi and Hongi Hika, Ruaterra taught the Maori language to Marsden and offered him hospitality and protection (Davidson and Lineham, *Transplanted Christianity*, 22).
21 Davidson and Lineham, *Transplanted Christianity*, 27–8, citing the *Missionary Register*, November 1816, 470–1.
22 Davidson, *Aotearoa New Zealand*, 10.
23 Davidson, unpublished personal correspondence to the author, 26 April, 2000, 1.
24 Sinclair, *Kinds of Peace*, 15.
25 Sinclair, *Kinds of Peace*, 16.
26 Elsmore, *Like Them that Dream*, 48, cites J. W. Stack, *More Maoriland Adventures* (Wellington, 1936), 183.
27 Elsmore, *Like Them that Dream*, 47
28 Elsmore, *Like Them that Dream*, 47.
29 Elsmore, *Like Them that Dream*, 47.
30 Elsmore, *Like Them that Dream*, 32.
31 Elsmore, *Like Them that Dream*. Elsmore, 33, cites Revd T. G. Hammond, *In the Beginning* (Auckland, 1940), 72.
32 Settler greed for more land brought more and more breaches in the Treaty and was a major factor leading to sporadic armed conflict and war. Although until the 1980s the Treaty had been regarded with pride as something setting New Zealand apart in its dealings with indigenous peoples. But it carries the painful legacy of promises disregarded and broken.
33 Elsmore, *Like Them that Dream*, 32, cites *The New Zealand Parliamentary Debates* (1903), vol. 142, 1141.
34 Elsmore, *Like Them that Dream*, 32, cites Apirana T. Ngata and I. L. G Sutherland, "Religious Influences," in Sutherland (ed.), *The Maori People Today: A General Survey* (Wellington, 1940), 346–7.

35 Elsmore, *Like Them that Dream*, 43.
36 Michael P. Shirres, *Te Tangata: The Human Person* (Auckland: Snedden & Cervin, 1997), 78, 82.
37 Elsmore, *Like Them that Dream*, 43.
38 Shirres, *Te Tangata*, 86.
39 Elsmore, *Like Them that Dream*, 43.
40 Elsmore, *Like Them that Dream*, 43.
41 Elsmore, *Like Them that Dream*, 47.
42 Davidson and Lineham, *Transplanted Christianity*, 35, citing W. M. S. NZ Correspondence, J. W. Stack to W. M. S secretaries, 29 March, 1826 (Journal No. 1), 2.
43 Elsmore, *Like Them that Dream*, 71–2.
44 Irvine Roxburgh, *The Ringatu Movement: A Phenomenological Essay on Culture Shock in New Zealand/Aotearoa* (Christchurch, NZ: Cadsonbury, 1998), 39, cites James Cowan, *The New Zealand Wars and the Pioneering Period* (Wellington, 1923), 9.
45 Davidson, unpublished personal correspondence to the author, 26 April, 2000, 2.
46 Davidson, unpublished personal correspondence to the author, 26 April, 2000, 1.
47 Binney, *Redemption Songs*, 297.
48 T. Grace is cited in Binney, *Redemption Songs*, 296.
49 The various Maori prophets and their particular historical contexts are quite distinct. For a fuller historical introduction, see Elsmore, *Like Them that Dream*, and Sinclair, *Kinds of Peace*.
50 Binney, *Redemption Songs*, 298.
51 Early nineteenth-century Christian interpretation of Genesis was that all people came from Adam and Eve the first parents. This encouraged missionaries to suggest that Maori might be a lost tribe of Israel. The view was widely accepted by Maori who, from the period of first contact with Europeans, "firmly believed that his origins were in the same people of which he read in the new scriptures". Elsmore, *Like Them that Dream*, 71.
52 Elsmore, *Like Them that Dream*, 88.
53 Elsmore, *Like Them that Dream*, 18–19, cites Henry Williams, Journal, 11 November, 1839, found in Lawrence M. Rogers (ed.), *The Early Journals of Henry Williams 1826–40* (Christchurch: Pegasus, 1961), 450.
54 Davidson, unpublished personal correspondence to the author, 26 April, 2000, 1.
55 Rudolf Bultmann, *The Gospel of John: A Commentary* (trans. G.R. Beasley-Murray; Oxford: Basil Blackwell, 1971), 50, 84–97, 145, 172, 237–84
56 Davidson, unpublished personal correspondence to the author, 26 April, 2000, 2.
57 My discussion is dependent upon Michel Foucault's view of the relationship between social practice and the statements that provide normative shape to their institutions. See Michel Foucault, *The Archaeology of Knowledge*, trans. A.M. Sheriden-Smith (London: Tavistock, 1972).
58 Davidson, "Interaction," 162.
59 Davidson, "Interaction," 162.
60 Binney, *Redemption Songs*, 296, cites the *East Coast Historical Records*, 80. Cleric James Stack understood this to be a statement of Maori autonomy from their former teachers, and a powerful belief in their unique relationship with God. The Maori thought that this familial relationship with God their Father "had been intentionally concealed from them by their English teachers for political reasons."

16

God at the Crossroads: A Postcolonial Reading of Sophia

Mayra Rivera

At the crossroads
Where her spirit shocks
She comes sweeping
Through the night,
Spirits and hounds
Baying behind her.
Her wings keep me warm.[1]
Does not [Sophia] call,
And does not understanding raise her voice?
On the heights, beside the way,
At the crossroads she takes her stand . . .[2]

At the crossroads Sophia takes her stand . . .[3] But why there? Is the crossroads not a confusing, dangerous place to take a stance? Who would turn to such a space of diverging paths, conflicting choices, contingency, and crisis – in order to find Wisdom? Who would look for God at a crossroads? In our postmodern world, crossroads, borderlands, *fronteras* traverse the lives of an increasing number of people. These are the ones who experience firsthand the risks and tragedies of crossing paths. But they also encounter the paradoxes, ironies, and creative potential of the crossroads. Thus, for Chicana feminist poet Gloria Anzaldúa, images of crossroads evoke the complexities of life at the Southwest/Mexican border and of the *mestiza* identities that it brings forth.[4] The crossroads also lead Anzaldúa to meditate more generally on the psychological, sexual, and spiritual borderlands found wherever different persons or groups come in contact with one another. At these multiple crossroads, one encounters *los atravesados* ("the crossed"): "squint-eyed, the perverse, the queer, the troublesome, the mongrel, the mulatto, the half-breed, the half-dead."[5] *Los atravesados*; those who do not fit the dominant categories; those whose presence shocks. Not from here; not from there.

First published in Catherine Keller et al., *Postcolonial Theologies: Divinity and Empire*. St Louis: Chalice Press, 2004, 186–203.

Crossroads also converge on my postcolonial feminist perspective – a perspective that is more (or perhaps less) than a theoretical choice. Raised in what has been called "the oldest colony in the world,"[6] I can hardly ignore the complexities, perplexities, and subtleties to which postcolonial theory attends. "Puerto Rico," like the rest of "Latin America," endured – indeed, emerged from – the early conquests of Spanish and/or Portuguese empires. Unlike the rest of Latin America, however, Puerto Rico got trapped in the conflict between the old Spanish empire and the then-emerging US empire, which left it, to this date, subject to the US. Politically, I am a US citizen by right of birth in a country with no right to participate in the US electoral process. "Racially" as much African and Taína as Spanish, linguistically nurtured by a Spanish too anglicized for Spain and an English too foreign for the US, I share a Protestantism brought with the US invasion but transformed by the Catholic and African heritages of our culture. As a woman moving always on crisscrossing paths, living and loving all the while between two starkly different patriarchies – how could I not feel strangely attuned to *los atravesados*? Is this a symptom of my secret taste for the *in-between*? Perhaps. It certainly signals my alertness to the strategies and limits of systems of domination through classification. It betrays my familiarity with the desires and frustrations of this power, its endless demands to the other to yield her secrets, to perform a given role, to inform – and with its resulting puzzlement, fascination, fear, and denial.

Perhaps it is not so surprising, then, that a divine figure who takes her stand at the crossroads, a female whose origin remains uncertain – she who seems to escape fixed theological categories – has caught my attention. And so do the reactions that she elicits: puzzlement, disavowal, abject horror as she reappears – and also, though rarely, intense appreciation. Among theologians, Sophia has been recognized in the multidimensionality of the Trinity as Spirit-Sophia, Jesus-Sophia, and Mother-Sophia,[7] or, contrastingly, as "a principle 'other' than [God's] hypostases," as the "living and loving substance" of God.[8] Most theologians see Sophia as a mere primitive precursor of the Logos and thus quickly turn to the Logos to continue the conversation. Although some suspect that "Western theology constantly hovers on the brink of sophiological problems,"[9] Sophia's presence goes often simply unnoticed.

A scrutiny of ancient testimonies of Sophia's presence begins to bring into focus the complexities of Sophia's identity. But it does not dispel its uncertainties. Biblical scholars' debates around the "origin" of Sophia tend to place her somewhere – else. Somewhere *other*. She must be, they argue, the daughter of somebody else's goddess, be it the "Canaanite love goddess, Astarte, the Mesopotamian goddess Ishtar, the Egyptian goddess Maat, the Semitic mother goddess . . . the Hellenized form of Egyptian goddess Isis."[10] A female divinity cannot be *native* to Israel – can she? Biblical scholars also debate whether she bears any resemblances to real women in Israel. Was her portrayal inspired by Israelite women? Or was Sophia created by male scribes trying to set a standard for appropriate female behavior? And what about her relation to the Creator? "The LORD created me," she announces in Proverbs 8, "at the beginning of his work, the first of his acts of long ago . . . When he established the heavens, I was there."[11] But she also describes herself as a source of life. God or not-God? Creator or creature? Native woman or foreign goddess? Here also, Sophia stands at the crossroads: not from here; not from there.

The questions that biblical and theological scholars raise about Sophia's origin and identity are crucial to my engagement with her, for it seems to me that the figure of Sophia raises those questions, that she has precisely that effect. How then should one approach Sophia? Postcolonial thought, I suggest, will help us engage this elusive character. Postcolonial theory's analysis of the complexities of identity, the perplexities of power, and the subtle strategies of subversion within situations of oppression seems well suited for reading Sophia. For it is in the indefiniteness of her identity that I approach Sophia – as a living hybrid. I intend to test how the postcolonial concept of hybridity may offer us liberating possibilities even within a textual terrain marked by structures of domination, indeed within that very space in which Sophia has – remarkably – managed to survive. What postcolonial theorist Homi Bhabha writes of the hybrid can be applied to Sophia: Even if she is "an effect of colonial power," her "irremediably estranging"[12] presence may disrupt the categories that authorize the very exercise of power: patriarchal, social, national, or cosmological. She "reverses the effects of colonial representation, so that other 'denied' knowledges enter upon the dominant discourse and estrange the basis of its authority, its *rules of recognition*."[13] Might a postcolonial theology, then, give voice to a Sophia who "disturbs, intervenes, unsettles, interrogates, ironizes, denaturalizes and transgresses by refusing to 'fit' into established categories"?[14]

Encountering Sophia

The first full biblical personification of Sophia appears in the book of Proverbs.[15] There, Sophia introduces herself as a proclaimer of truth: "Hear, for I will speak noble things. And from my lips will come what is right; for my mouth will utter truth . . . " (Prov. 8:6–7a). "My fruit is better than gold" (8:19). Sophia claims to have been an active participant in the creation of the world as well as its source of love, strength, justice, and life: "Whosoever finds me finds life" (8:35). Proverbs' readers are thus advised to love Sophia: to take her instruction instead of silver, to wait for her, and to keep her ways in order to see their days multiplied and years added to their life (9:11). But Proverbs seems at least as interested in the shadowy figure who serves as Sophia's foil, the one the text names the Strange (or Foreign) Woman, against whom it advises: "Do not let your hearts turn aside to her ways; do not stray into her paths, for many are those she has laid low, and numerous are her victims. Her house is the way to Sheol . . . " (Prov. 7:25–7). In this Strange Woman, the Foreign Woman, we see Proverbs' personification of the Other. In other (later) books in the Hebrew Scripture – Sirach, Baruch, and Wisdom of Solomon – Sophia is also represented in roles associated with the Divine.[16] Their ambiguous responses to her suggest their bewildering reactions to the complex identity of Sophia, the hybrid.

Already in her first appearance in the book of Proverbs, her gender alone makes Sophia stand out as a rarity in the Bible. So no wonder she raises numerous questions for her feminist readers. What was the writers' intention in creating this female image? Was Sophia imagined as a reflection of real or idealized women's roles in Proverbs' community? Was she meant as an exaltation of women? Or was she intended as a controlling symbol defining acceptable behavior for women? Most

feminist biblical scholars argue that only the social roles of real women, or an idealization of them, can explain Proverbs' disposition to imagine Sophia as female. Carole Fontaine holds that both Sophia and the Strange Woman "embody the social roles, positive and negative, which women filled within the society at large and the wisdom movement in particular."[17] Similarly, Silvia Schroer considers the roles of personified Sophia to reflect the counseling functions that women did perform in the community.[18] It is further believed that the decentralization of authority resulting from the lack of formal public structures during the postexilic period brought about an increase in the importance of the family, thus heightening women's authority.[19] But the strong presence of the Strange Woman in the text and her striking similarities with Sophia do not allow a simple reading of Proverbs' "intentions." Rather, they invite us to ponder the complexities and ambiguities of its agenda.

Despite difficulties determining the dates of compilation of the book of Proverbs, most biblical scholars locate it in the post-exilic period. This period was characterized by the conflicts between the "Israelites" who returned to Judah after the Babylonian exile and those who had stayed in the land. Both groups were claiming political power, religious authority, and territorial rights. Hence, the returning group faced the challenge of finding a way to legitimize its own claims over and against those of the people who had been inhabiting the land for fifty years. Ironically, at the end of their oppression under Babylonian rule, some of the formerly colonized struggled to assert their role as ruling power through the exclusion of others. The returning elites attempted to define an Other against whom a communal self could be asserted, thus performing – perhaps mimicking – a typical colonial scene. Homi Bhabha describes this sort of self-legitimating process as that in which the "narratorial voice" of authority articulates the narcissistic demand "that the Other should authorize the self, recognize its priority, fulfill its outlines."[20] Naturally, that self-legitimating process produced narratives that combined and confused social practices with an ideological rhetoric of identity. Writing on Proverbs, Claudia Camp points out that such processes of identity-formation involve internal as much as external battles; they entail the definition of those inside and outside the internal spheres of power, as well as those inside and outside the community.[21]

These processes, however, come fraught with contradiction. Do we perhaps see in Proverbs the marks of the incongruities produced by its own attempt to define a pure identity? It is the very attempt to construct a stable self-definition that prompted the construction of a "myth of historical origination,"[22] a myth based on (real or fictitious) genealogies.[23] The identity of the "others" was constructed on equally fictitious, even anachronistic, genealogies.[24] The deep ambiguity and ironic outcomes of these projects are exemplified by the fact that "those called 'foreign' were often residents of the land; those called 'strange' were often former members of a priestly lineage."[25] Also integral to the agenda of creating the community's identity was an increased emphasis on separation from "others," typically expressed as admonitions against intermarriage. Rather than protecting the borders against the possible intrusion of the other, these admonitions typically function, according to postcolonial theory, as rhetorical masks to cover the absence of a pure identity. In other words, discourses against mixing with the other most often attempt to hide the fact that the other is already among us, indeed, integral to us.

In addition to the words *foreign* and *strange*, which are prominent in the book of Proverbs, *Woman* was also a crucial element in constructions of identity, and it was strongly associated with both *foreign* and *strange*. Camp notes that the Hebrew Bible frequently collapsed language of "illicit sex, illicit worship and intermarriage with foreigners, especially foreign women."[26] Thus, these discourses about the *outsiders* relied on associations between *foreign, strange*, and *woman*. As a consequence of these close associations, it was not unusual to find references to "women's blood standing for all pollution, foreign wives standing for all things foreign, adulterous women standing for idolatrous Israel." As a result, *woman* could readily function as a signifier of strangeness.[27] In Camp's words, "*Proverbs* makes the metaphorical connection between woman and the strange, thus identifying woman as that which is not proper to 'Israel.' National/ethnic distinction has been assimilated to and named by gender distinction."[28] The figure of a woman is, then, suggestive of threats to national identity, religious faithfulness, ritual purity – that is, threats to the social order and, as a consequence, to the cosmological order as well.

In the textual homeland of Sophia, femaleness is anything but a neutral sign reflecting social realities. It is a problematic sign – and a sign of the problematic – in regard not only to gender roles but also to a conglomerate of categories, all highly contested in the political, social, and religious arenas. Camp's conclusion does not exclude the possibility that women did perform roles analogous to those in which Sophia is portrayed. It does alert us, nonetheless, to the strong tensions and instabilities that lie behind deceptively simple categories: woman, foreigner, strange. "In the Borderlands/You are the battleground/Where enemies are kin to each other; /You are at home, a stranger..."[29]

This gendering of otherness is epitomized in the Strange Woman, Proverbs' representation of oppositional otherness.[30] And it might be the Strange Woman who best captures the text's intentions. Be that as it may, my main interest is in that which escapes those intentions. For all its harsh admonitions against the Other, the divine image that one encounters in Proverbs conforms neither to the text's insiders (the young men who receive Proverbs' advise) nor of its characterization of the antithetical Other. Proverbs' divine figure is actually a female, a female who resembles the "Other." We look at her. We are puzzled, disturbed. In a community in which identity is defined in reference to its male members, doesn't the fact that Sophia is a female make her an odd image of authority? Moreover, if her gender is like that of the "Other," if *woman* stands for *strangeness*, are we not forced to ask if the "we" (the *insiders* of Proverbs' community), of which Sophia is an authorized image of identity, is already strange to itself?

Socially, religiously, and even cosmologically, Sophia occupies the space of the hybrid. In her manifold *in-betweenness* she "intervenes in the exercise of authority not merely to indicate the impossibility of its identity but to represent the unpredictability of its presence."[31] "Out in the street... in the squares... [a]t the busiest corner..." (Prov. 1:20, 21) – literally and symbolically, Sophia stands at the crossroads. "On the heights, beside the way, at the crossroads she takes her stand; beside the gates in front on the town, at the entrance of the portals she cries out" (Prov. 8:2–3). The contrast with Proverbs' "capable wife," undoubtedly a "proper Israelite woman," is telling. In the case of the "capable wife," it is her husband who

is "known in the city gates" (Prov. 31:23). Sophia instead stands there herself. She is where the text locates honorable men and "loose women" (Prov. 7:12) – thus resisting any simple opposition to the Strange Woman. She is at the crossroads of "proper" gender roles.

Depicted as mother, lover, and wife, Sophia is not a stable sign of any of those categories. Consider the role of wife. Like the "capable wife," Sophia is beloved (Prov. 4:6–9; 7:4). Like the "capable wife," Sophia brings "favor of the Lord" to those who find her (Prov. 18:22, 8:35). But Sophia violates Proverbs' admonitions to restrain her speech and to guard her mouth (Prov. 9:13); instead, she follows other Proverbs instructions: to cry out, raise the voice, seek, and search. These instructions, however, were not addressed to women but to young men: "Cry out for insight, and raise your voice for understanding" (Prov. 2:3). Sophia is "almost the same, but not quite,"[32] for she doesn't cry out to receive wisdom but to offer it. The "capable wife" brings happiness; Sophia brings life. Almost the same, but not quite.

Sophia's speech also betrays her hybridity. Is the language of Israel her "first language"? On the one hand, there is no doubt that Sophia is closely related to Israel and that she is well versed in its traditions. Her words are recognized as the language of Israel, and her "call . . . is the voice of the Lord."[33] Wisdom of Solomon even identifies Sophia as the fountain of wisdom for Israel's great king Solomon. But her speeches also betray her relation to Babylonian Ishtar, Canaanite Astarte, and especially to the Egyptian goddess Maat. As Maat, she is "an amulet worn for protection and life."[34] Also like Maat, Sophia declares her existence before creation and her authority over kings.[35] She even resembles the already hybrid Isis. Sophia's use of the formula "I am" (Prov. 22:17ff) resembles that of the Egyptian *Wisdom of Ameneope*.[36] "Like Isis, she is concerned with justice; like Isis, who taught writing and the arts of civilization and humanity, Sophia continues to instruct the wise in the arts, particularly scripture; like Isis, Sophia is concerned with the protection of kings and rulers."[37] All these traits, however, are intrinsic to the character of Sophia herself, who Proverbs exalted as the ideal native and who confidently walks Israel's streets, speaks JHWH's words, and demands to be heard and followed (Prov. 8:32). Yet the fact that she can be compared to – perhaps even confused with, but not identified as – a "foreign woman" threatens the very basis of the "rules of recognition." In her, the boundaries between the native and the foreign blur. She is "*neither One . . . nor the Other . . . but something besides*, which contests the terms and territories of both."[38] Biblical scholars have had to admit (not without disappointment) that she has "clearly borrowed" "the style of a specific Egyptian divine proclamation . . . ideas which had roots *elsewhere*."[39] In other words: *Sophia speaks with an accent*. "'Denied' knowledges" have entered the privileged discourse and "estrange[d] the basis of its authority."[40] Moreover, not only does Sophia evidence the presence, always already within Israel, of traditions from the *outside*; but her proclamation also carries the wisdom of the *inside* to the *outside* of Israel, to "whosoever" finds her (Prov. 8:35), whosoever loves her (Prov. 8:17–20).

And if Sophia's social context places her in an interstitial position between the normative subject and the multitudinous *other*, her cosmological position is also at the crossroads. She moves between the divine and the created realms. Just what type of being is Sophia? On the one hand, she unmistakably resembles God.[41] Who but

God can claim, as Sophia does: "Whosoever finds me, finds life" (Prov. 8:35)? Expanding Proverbs' portrayal, the authors of Wisdom of Solomon assert that Sophia is all-pervasive, all-powerful, and enlivening (Wis. 7:22, 27; 8:1), that she gives immortality (Wis. 10:17), that she has been the protecting and delivering power in Israel's history (Wis. 10), and that she is omniscient (Wis. 9:11). But the text will not allow for an easy substitution of Sophia for God, or an equation of Sophia with God, either. Sophia stands in and as the difference, the interval, between God and creation. Her very origin at once asserts her unity with God and makes a difference, although admittedly a very fluid one. In her presence God founded the earth; she is an intimate in the knowledge of God.[42] In the beginning was Sophia; Sophia was with God, and Sophia was God.

This ontological undecidability creates, when noticed, theological discomfort. To explain the indeterminacy of Sophia's ontological identity, Roland Murphy describes her as a feminine apparition of God – of a male God, that is. "Wisdom is truly the *form* in which JHWH makes *himself* present and in which *he* wished to be sought by man."[43] She is "He" – *present*? "He" wishes to be sought as a female? He wants to be seen as what "He" is not – a female? It seems that God is slipping through the forms, moving between the names.

In fact, the neat distinction between the male God's presence and the female "form" in the proposal just cited cannot withstand intrusion by Sophia herself. Her own self-descriptive oration destabilizes this implicit dualism from within, from inside the womb, and "from the beginning." The many difficulties with the interpretation of Proverbs 8:22–31 are noted and strongly debated among biblical scholars. But then again, it is precisely from the reverberations of the effects of Sophia that the present postcolonial reading draws its energy.

> The Lord *begot me*[44] at [as] the beginning of his work,
> the first of his acts of long ago.
> Ages ago I was *poured out* [as from the waters of the womb],[45]
> at the first, before the beginning of the earth.
> When there were no depths I was *brought forth*,[46]
> when there were no springs abounding with water.
> Before the mountains had been shaped,
> before the hills, I was *brought forth*.[47]
>
> vv.22–5

In this account of the beginning, God is not only expecting to be *sought* in the form of a woman; God is *delivering*. If God gives birth, pours out from God's womb, and brings forth, how can we discriminate God from Goddess? Where can we draw the line? Is *She* God? Is *He* Goddess? As Sophia emerges from the depths of God's womb, from God's own maternal waters, she reveals fluid communion – rather than absolute opposition – as the difference between God and creation. In this scene of God's maternal fecundity, divinity comes forth from God, revealing a Creator that defies characterization as merely over and against creation.

In Proverbs' account, creation generates intervals between the Creator and Sophia and between Sophia and creation, not as empty gaps, but as openings for the flux of divine delight:

and I was daily his delight,
    rejoicing before him always,
rejoicing in his inhabited world
    and delighting in the human race.
        vv. 30b–31

This clear parallelism between God's delight in Sophia and Sophia's delight in the created world links God and creation in a relational joy.

If Proverbs' writers were anxious about a Strange Woman who could incite the desire of the young men of Israel, imagine how disturbing would have been a hybrid Sophia, who could excite not only Israel's men but also Israel's God! The erotic undertones of these passages provoke disturbed scholarly looks: "in vv. 30f. the Egyptian idea of a deity caressing personified truth (ma-at) has *somehow*... found its way into our didactic poem."[48] In this desire of God for Sophia, it is the deity who seems out of God's "proper" place.

Proverbs' Readers

Readers of Proverbs, ancient and contemporary, Jewish and Christian, have felt the lure of Sophia. "All that you may desire cannot compare with her" (Prov. 8:11). Their reactions have been diverse. Solomon, for instance, shamelessly hymned his erotic desire "to take [Sophia] for... bride and become enamored of her beauty" (Wis. 8:2). For the rabbis, Solomon's desire for Sophia spoke to *their* yearning for the Torah, the reservoir of God's Wisdom. "Learn where is wisdom," Baruch exhorted his readers, "so that you may at the same time discern where there is length of days, and life" (Bar. 3:14). "She is the book of the commandments of God, the law that endures forever. All who hold her fast will live" (Bar. 4:1). It was thus to the Torah that some dedicated their passion. "Let him kiss me with the kisses of his mouth!" (Song 1:2) inspired a rabbi to imagine the encounter with God's speech in startling terms: "The *dibbur* [i.e., commandment or utterance] itself went in turn to each of the Israelites and said to him, 'Do you undertake to keep me?'... He would reply, 'Yes, yes,' and straightway the commandment kissed him on the mouth and taught him the Torah."[49] A lovingly incarnate word indeed. But patriarchy recognizes the dangers of desire and the risks of the "Yes, Yes." Such unconditional openness to the other may undermine the supposed autonomy of the patriarchal subjects. A felt desire may elicit fear. Patriarchy responds by asserting its control over her. For instance, instead of boasting, like Solomon did, about his yearning for Sophia, Sirach imagines himself "pursuing her like a hunter and lying in wait on her paths" (Sir. 14:22). The contrast between a hunter-like pursuit – seeking to grasp and possess a desired/feared other – and Proverbs' image of God's delight – rejoicing in Sophia's joy in creation – is striking. Already desire morphs into domination.

Nationalism is also haunted by the ghosts of its desires repressed at the boundaries between its "we" and the others. Quite frequently these ghosts have the shape of a woman. Indeed, nationalism often blames its own vulnerability on *her*: on her who lures men of the nation to transgress its borders or on her who falls prey to – or says "yes" to – an invading other, on her who conceives a hybrid.[50] Strange Women of

ancient or modern worlds. But as the hybrids populate the *in-between* spaces – the regions of forbidden and forgotten encounters between the national "we" and its others – they stand as disturbing reminders of the vitality of these denied spaces. These hybrids, *mestizos*, literally born from colonizer and colonized, are joined by other hybrids – by choice or chance – *atravesados*, who also resist dominant classifications. They do not suit nationalist projects. It is not the fact that they are different from the dominant subject that makes them strange, but that their difference cannot be classified. When not dismissed as aberrant, their hybridity is simply disavowed by forcing the hybrid into recognizable categories of "outsiders" or "insiders."[51] That seems to have been the reaction of many of Sophia's readers: They repeatedly attempted to fix her within established boundaries. Sirach was emphatic in securing Sophia's location *within* Israel's borders, calling the Creator "himself" to utter the decree: "Make your dwelling in Jacob, and in Israel receive your inheritance" (Sir. 24:8) – as if to reassert the stability of the boundaries between the inside/outside, national/foreign. For others, the important boundary was that between heaven and earth. First Enoch had Sophia "settled permanently among the angels" (Enoch 42:1–2). Even Philo anxiously tried to confine Sophia to a heavenly house.[52] But soon many claimed to have heard her voice, crying out loud again, walking the streets again, from Galilee to Jerusalem and beyond.

Just as the rabbis encountered Sophia in divine commandments and thus in the Torah, early followers of Jesus felt they were in Sophia's presence. New Testament texts show traces of early christological interpretations inspired by the traditions of Sophia. In these christologies, Jesus is depicted either as Sophia's prophet or as Sophia herself. Luke's saying "Sophia is justified by all her children" (Lk. 7:35), the portrayal of the Spirit descending upon Jesus in the form of a dove (a symbol related to the Near Eastern love goddess), and the "I am" orations are all viewed as remnants of Sophia christologies. Like Sophia, Jesus himself has been recognized as a border crosser,[53] a *Mestizo*,[54] "the hybrid being par excellence in John's Gospel"[55] – as one who transgresses the accepted boundaries of class, gender, religious purity, and, above all, the human-divine divide.

When we come to an explicit description of Christ in cosmological terms in the Fourth Gospel, however, it is not Sophia we find, but Logos. We see *He*, the Logos, not She, standing in the beginning with God and as God. What has happened? After reading Sophia declare, "The LORD begot me as the beginning of his work, the first of his acts long ago,"[56] the prologue's proclamation of a *male* figure *as the beginning* triggers feminist concerns. Not only does the feminine get excluded from this influential beginning, but this male figure has apparently mirrored and mimicked the role of Sophia. "John transfers the powers and attributes of Sophia to the Logos and then identifies Christ as incarnate Logos."[57] Thus, "the male Logos absorbed the female Sophia (for clearly patriarchal reasons) and so brought about her disappearance."[58]

Patriarchy turns gender into a trap. But should we concede Sophia's disappearance? Might Sophia be mocking the gender rules of recognition? For Daniel Boyarin, the presence of the Logos in John's prologue represents not the patriarchal erasure of Sophia, but her dynamic presence in Jewish thought. I noted that strands of the Jewish tradition associated Sophia with the Torah. Aramaic Targums also witness a tacit association between Wisdom and the Word of God, *Memra* (another feminine

term). The usage of the term *Memra* in Palestinian Aramaic translations of the Bible parallels the functions of Logos in Logos theologies; *Memra* was used of God as creating, speaking to humans, self-revealing, punishing the wicked, saving, and redeeming.[59] As evidence of the connection between the targumic *Memra* and the Logos of John, Boyarin refers to the midrash of the "four nights," thought to be part of a paschal liturgy. It begins with the night of creation and culminates in the night of the Messiah. This midrash reads Genesis 1:3 as "Through his Memra there was light." This interpretation of Genesis 1 through the hypostasized Memra is consonant with John's account of the beginning through the hypostasized Logos. Boyarin concludes that the prologue of John was a midrash on the opening verses of Genesis, implicitly invoking Proverbs 8 as its hermeneutical intertext. "The primacy of Genesis as exegeted text explains why we have here 'Logos' and not 'Sophia,' without necessitating the assumption of a 'Word' tradition of Genesis in alleged conflict with a 'Wisdom' tradition . . . The preacher of the Prologue of John had to speak of Logos here, because his homiletical effort is directed at the opening verses of Genesis, with their majestic: 'And God said: Let there be light, and there was light.' "[60] Therefore, he argues that the prologue should be read as "a recognizable and coherent instance of traditional midrash on Genesis 1 interpreted via *Proverbs* in such a way as to produce a hypostasized Memra/Logos."[61] Thus, the gender shift is explained as a by-product of the hermeneutical process.

Uncovering this apparent accident of translation – from a feminine Sophia/Memra to a masculine Logos – can hardly, however, erase the history of appropriation of a male Logos as the bestower of patriarchal power.[62] We had best pay heed to Derrida's warning: "Never treat as an accident *the force of the name* in what happens, occurs or is said in the name of religion."[63] But the boundary between Sophia and Logos may nonetheless prove fruitful for feminist postcolonial re/namings.

Ancient readers of Logos did not construe the gender difference between Sophia and Logos as an insurmountable boundary. No friend of female images, Philo nonetheless admitted the fluidity of Sophia's identity. Moses, he observed, "has disclosed that the lofty and heavenly Sophia is many-named; for he calls it 'beginning' and 'image' and 'vision of God'."[64] Likewise, Justin, for whom Christ was the Logos who personified the Torah,[65] acknowledged that she/he whom "God has begotten as a Beginning . . . is called by the Holy Spirit the Glory of the Lord, sometimes Son, and sometimes Sophia, and sometimes Angel, and sometimes God, and sometimes Lord and Word."[66] Sometimes Sophia, sometimes Logos, and sometimes God – this is a "begetting" that differentiates without cutting off.

The boundary between a feminine Sophia and a masculine Logos was not an obstacle for Origen either. In Origen's systematic treatise *De Principis*, Sophialogy is clearly assumed as the foundation for christology. "We have first to ascertain what the only-begotten Son of God is, seeing He is called by many different names, according to the circumstances and views of individuals. *For he is termed Sophia*, according to the expression of Solomon: 'The Lord begot me – the beginning of His ways and among His works, before He made any other thing . . . In the beginning . . . He brought me forth . . . ' " (1.2.1). Thus Origen opens his section "On Christ." For this third-century father, the gospels witnessed to Sophia as Son, the first-born who "is not by nature a different person from Sophia, but one and the

same" (1.2.1). Begotten as beginning, Origen explains, Sophia is generated eternally "as the brilliancy which is produced from the sun" (1.2.2). Indeed, the Father never existed "even for a single moment, without begetting his Sophia" (1.2.2). Because Sophia contains "the beginnings and causes and species of the whole creation" (1.2.2). God is always already differing from and in relation to creation, desiring to create (4.1.35), and rejoicing in the creation (1.4.4). "That Sophia in whom God delighted when the world was finished" reveals "that God ever rejoices" (1.4.4). It is indeed Sophia's desire to reveal God. This revelation, however, is not external to her, for "she *outlines first in herself* the things which she wishes to reveal to others" (1.2.8). Sometimes Sophia, sometimes Logos, sometimes God.

The image outlined in John's prologue, however, is seldom encountered as she who is called by many names, whose identity resists dominant categories, whose presence shocks. Instead, Logos became the alibi for our disavowal of Sophia – as much Jewish as Christian. Whereas Christians moved to name Logos as a purely Platonic concept, Rabbinic Judaism, in an "attempt to separate itself from its own history of now 'Christian' Logos theology," "suppressed all talk of the Memra or Logos."[67] Another attempt to secure her within established boundaries: "Make your dwelling . . . " – this time among Christians? Not only have we denied the "other" gender its divinity in the reification of Logos' maleness, we have also contained the challenges of her/his ontological undecidability in neat demarcations between human and divine. As historian of early Christianity Rebecca Lyman observes, after Nicaea the Logos was absorbed into a separate divine realm, and it "could no longer belong to both sides of the divide and provide a link between Creator and Creature."[68] Is this another command to Sophia to "settle permanently among the angels"? Has Sophia's power to disrupt, her capacity to call into question, to open new spaces, become neutralized by endless attempts to locate and fix her?

Concluding Remarks

God begot Sophia as the beginning . . . Ages ago, Sophia was poured out at first, before the beginning of the earth. As the beginning, Sophia emerges as the site of God's self-differentiation from creation. Beginning, interval, difference, and at the same time the opening of a space for relation. Not severance, but eternal begetting and continuous divine delight, and thus also the opening of a possibility for human delight. As God rejoices in Sophia and Sophia takes pleasure in the human race, would humans not partake in their joy, mirroring their passion, delighting in her who cries out at the crossroads, but who is also met in the intimacy of a kiss? This invitation to participate in God's joy is also a challenge: to open ourselves to the other. Can we find joy in her who is simultaneously as close as a caress and irreducibly different? For despite persistent attempts to locate, to define, to fix, and to grasp Sophia's identity, her location at the crossroads, her puzzling foreign accent, her undecidable ontological position,[69] will not be resolved. Her identity remains indefinable and, for that matter, open.[70] Her presence is perplexing; her spirit shocks. Indeed, Sophia's distinctive mark is to remain inappropriable in predetermined categories, but existing between them as their constant challenge.

What Bhabha says of the hybrid is also true of Sophia: Her hybridity is "not a third term that resolves the tension between two cultures [or two religions or two ontological poles] ... [It] creates a crisis" for "authority based on a system of recognition."[71] *Wisdom* overflows knowledge. Do we glimpse in this resistance to closure what Christian tradition has called divine *transcendence*?

God's transcendence, God's unassimilable otherness, is sensed in the excess that haunts all theological assertions, in the instability of the names, in the "impossibility of identity ... the unpredictability of presence."[72] Unlike traditional models that imagine God's transcendence as over and against creation, the transcendence that Sophia represents is neither absent nor untouchable, but a challenging closeness that is always beyond grasp: "Divinity drawing near and passing by."[73] She transcends our "world" not by being detached from it, but by opening the world to what it has not received, to what has been pushed outside – by crossing its borders. While exceeding theological constructions, her unforeseeable presence haunts theological certainties; it lurks as a "strange guardian in the margin,"[74] as though to keep us from idolatry. Constantly calling into question the certainty of the system, transcendence, as Kathryn Tanner argues, "becomes the model for the resistance to the Same, which all those who resist the status quo might follow in a solidarity that involves no ordinary identification according to general categories."[75]

A postcolonial optic helps us recognize just such modes of resistance and the solidarities of unexpected identifications; this reading of Sophia finds these modes of resistance intrinsically linked with divine transcendence. We have seen Proverbs' community struggling to assert its identity by repressing its complex and messy relationships with others, only to be haunted by their return in the face of none other than divinity itself. Sophia embodies the very complexities that authoritative discourse could not control. In the midst of a text marked by projections of otherness designed to consolidate the authority of a group, Sophia takes her stand at the crossroads. It is from there – from the forbidden or forgotten spaces between the self-asserting "we" and the repulsed Other – that Sophia cries out.

Sophia outlines in herself what she wishes to reveal: She traces herself as a hybrid. Almost a foreign woman, but not quite. It is perhaps not strange to have found ancient and contemporary reactions to Sophia that resemble our own reactions to *los atravesados*: endless demands that they yield their secrets, that they perform recognizable roles, that they identify unambiguously with the insiders or just accept to belonging *elsewhere*. Some have even pursued them like hunters and laid wait in their paths. Spirits and hounds are baying behind them. Puzzlement, fascination, fear, denial, and even violence. Crying out from the crossroads, *los atravesados* may also be strange guardians at the margins. Facing their undefinable specificity may save us from idolatries of national identity, of established categories of sexual difference, of the assumed inevitability of our economic system. Sophia in her transcendence thus serves as a figure of the multiple others that haunt not only theological systems, but social ones as well.[76] In that challenge there is also an opportunity, an opening of a new space of relations. Perhaps even of new beginnings.

NOTES

1 Gloria Anzaldúa, "Canción de la diosa de la noche," in *Borderlands/La Frontera: The New Mestiza* (San Francisco: Aunt Lute Books, 1999), 218.
2 Proverbs 8: 1–2. NRSV uses the word *wisdom* rather than *Sophia.*
3 Prov. 8:2. "Sophia" is used in the Septuagint to translate *Hokmâ*, the Hebrew word for "wisdom." Because Proverbs gives wisdom personal attributes, I will use Sophia as a personal name.
4 During Spanish/Portuguese colonial control over Latin America, the word *mestiza/o* was used to refer to the offspring of a Spaniard and an Amerindian. Currently, Latin Americans tend to use the word *mestizaje* more generally to refer to the complex intermixture – biological or cultural – that comprises the Latin American heritage. That is, the meaning of *mestizaje* has been expanded to include Spanish, Amerindian, African, and, in many cases, U.S. cultural influences. It is related to the term *hybridity*, but it alludes specifically to the Latino context.
5 Anzaldúa, *Borderlands*, 25.
6 José Trís Monge, *Puerto Rico: The Trials of the Oldest Colony in the World* (New Haven, Conn., & London: Yale University Press, 1997).
7 Elizabeth A. Johnson, *She Who Is: The Mystery of God in Feminist Theological Discourse* (New York: Crossroads, 1992).
8 Sergei Bulgakov, *Sophia: The Wisdom of God*, trans. Xenia Braikevitc, Library of Russian Philosophy (Hudson, N.Y.: Lindisfarne, 1993), 55, 35.
9 Ibid., 5.
10 Johnson, *She Who Is*, 92.
11 Prov. 8:22, 27.
12 Homi K. Bhabha, *The Location of Culture* (London and New York: Routledge, 1994), 114.
13 Ibid. (italics added).
14 Susan Stanford Friedman, *Mappings: Feminism and the Cultural Geographies of Encounter* (Princeton, NJ: Princeton University Press, 1998), 89.
15 See Prov. 1:20–33; 8; 9:4–6.
16 See Sir. 24; Bar. 3:9–4:4; Wis. 7–9.
17 Carole R. Fontaine, "The Social Role of Women in the World of Wisdom," in *A Feminist Companion to Wisdom Literature*, ed. Athalya Brenner (Sheffield, England: Sheffield Academic Press, 1995), 46.
18 Silvia Schroer, "Wise and Counseling Women in Ancient Israel: Literary and Historical Ideas of the Personified Hokmâ," in *Feminist Companion*.
19 Gail Paterson Corrington, *Her Image of Salvation, Female Saviors and Formative Christianity* (Louisville, Ky.: Westminster/John Knox Press, 1992), 117.
20 Bhabha, *Location of Culture*, 98.
21 Claudia V. Camp, *Wise, Strange and Holy: The Strange Woman and the Making of the Bible* (Sheffield, England: Sheffield Academic Press, 2000), 31.
22 Bhabha, *Location of Culture*, 74.
23 Camp, *Wise, Strange and Holy*, 32.
24 Ibid.
25 Ibid., 15.
26 Ibid., 17.
27 "Female ethnic foreignness," according to Camp, "is intimately linked, via several different modes, to other significant conceptual fields; it is linked, by ideological framing, to worship of foreign gods; by metaphor, to sexual strangeness (adultery, prostitution and, in general, women's control of their own sexuality); by extension of the sexual

metaphor, to deceitful language; by metonymy to correct ritual practice; by moral logic to evil; by onto-logic to death; and by patri-logic, to loss of inheritance and lineage." Ibid., 29.

28 Ibid., 59.
29 Anzaldúa, *Borderlands*, 216.
30 See Prov. 2:16–19; 5:11; 6:24–35; 7:14–20; 9:16–17.
31 Bhabha, *Location of Culture*, 114.
32 Ibid., 86.
33 Roland E. Murphy, *The Tree of Life, An Exploration of Biblical Wisdom Literature* (Grand Rapids, Mich.: Eerdmans, 1996), 138.
34 Claudia V. Camp, *Wisdom and the Feminine in the Book of Proverbs* (Decatur, Ga.: JSOT Press, 1985), 29.
35 Ibid.
36 Murphy, *Tree of Life*, 161.
37 Corrington, *Her Image of Salvation*, 107.
38 Bhabha, *Location of Culture*, 25 (italics original).
39 Gerhard von Rad, quoted in Murphy, *Tree of Life*, 138 (italics added).
40 Bhabha, *Location of Culture*, 114.
41 She is all-pervasive, enlivening, and all-powerful (Wis. 7:22, 27; 8:1).
42 She is an "associate in his works" (Wis. 8:4). "She is a breath of the power of God and a pure emanation of the Almighty" (Wis. 7:25).
43 Gerhard von Rad, quoted in Murphy, *Tree of Life*, 138. (italics added).
44 The translation "begot me" is well supported among biblical scholars. See, for example, Carole R. Fontaine, "The Social Role of Women in the World of Wisdom," in *Women's Bible Commentary*, ed. Carol A. Newsom and Sharon H. Ringe (Louisville, Ky.: Westminster John Knox Press, 1998); Murphy, *Tree of Life*, 136; William McKane, *Proverbs: A New Approach* (Philadelphia: Westminster Press, 1970); and Leo G. Perdue, *Proverbs* (Louisville, Ky.: Westminster John Knox Press, 2000). NRSV translation: "The Lord created me at the beginning of his works."
45 As translated by Perdue, *Proverbs*, 144. Another possible translation is "I was hidden in the womb in antiquity," McKane, *Proverbs*, 352.
46 "Literally, 'was given birth,'" Perdue, *Proverbs*, 143. See also McKane, *Proverbs*, 352.
47 See note 46.
48 Gerhard von Rad, quoted in Murphy, *Tree of Life*, 138, italics added. Camp points out that the word used in this passage for "delight" is "used to describe Samson's play before the Philistines, as well as Isaac's intimate activity with Rebekah (Gen 26.8)" Camp, *Wise, Strange and Holy*, 109.
49 David Winston, *Logos and Mystical Theology in Philo of Alexandria* (Cincinnati, Ohio: Hebrew Union College Press, 1985), 16.
50 Her own vulnerability is overlooked – even when miscegenation, a colonial strategy for the assimilation of the "native" other into the colonizer's "race," involves the possession of the native woman, her rape. Colonialism and patriarchy intermix.
51 An example of this strategy can be seen in the nationalist discourse of Mexico, where *mestizaje* is the authorized image for the "we" of the nation, leading to the exclusion of the native population from that "we." For a discussion of these dynamics and its challenges for postcolonial thinkers, see Josefina Saldaña-Portillo, "Who's the Indian in Aztlán? Re-Writing Mestizaje, Indianism, and Chicanismo from the Lacandón," in *The Latin American Subaltern Studies Reader*, ed. Ileana Rodríguez (Durham, N.C., and London: Duke University Press, 2001).
52 Elisabeth Schüssler Fiorenza, *Jesus: Miriam's Child, Sophia's Prophet, Critical Issues in Feminist Christology* (New York: Continuum, 1994), 138.

53 Leticia A. Guardiola-Sáenz, "Border-Crossing and Its Redemptive Power in John 7.53–8.11: A Cultural Reading of Jesus and the *Accussed*," in Jeffrey L. Staley (ed.), *John and Postcolonialism*, The Bible and Postcolonialism, vol. 7 (London and New York: Sheffield Academic Press, 2002).
54 Virgilio Elizondo, *Galilean Journey: The Mexican-American Promise* (Maryknoll, NY: Orbis Books, 1993).
55 Guardiola-Sáenz, "Border-Crossing," 151.
56 Prov. 8:22.
57 Joan Chamberlain Engelsman, *The Feminine Dimension of the Divine* (Philadelphia: Westminster Press, 1979), 114.
58 Silvia Schroer, *Wisdom Has Built Her House: Studies on the Figure of Sophia and the Bible* (Collegeville, Minn.: Liturgical Press, 2000), 120.
59 Daniel Boyarin, "The Gospel of the Memra: Jewish Binitarianism and the Prologue to John," *Harvard Theological Review*, 94. 3 (July 2001): 257.
60 Ibid., 14.
61 Ibid., 7.
62 The maleness of the Logos becomes especially pernicious when, in later two-natured christology, Logos becomes Son and doubles the maleness of the historical Jesus. Virginia Burrus, "Radical Sex and the Hybrid Christ: Unorthodox Reflections on Patristic Theology," unpublished manuscript.
63 Jacques Derrida, "Faith and Knowledge: The Two Sources of 'Religion' at the Limits of Reason Alone," in Gianni Vattimo (ed.), *Religion*, Cultural Memory in the Present (Stanford, Calif.: Stanford University Press, 1998), 6 (italics added).
64 David Winston, *Philo of Alexandria: The Contemplative Life, The Giants, and Selections* (New York: Paulist Press, 1981), 92.
65 M.J. Edwards, "Justin's Logos and the Word of God," *Journal of Early Christian Studies*, 3.3 (1995).
66 Justine Dialogue 61.1, quoted by Boyarin, "Gospel of Memra," 282.
67 Ibid., 246, 254.
68 J. Rebecca Lyman, *Christology and Cosmology: Models of Divine Activity in Origen, Eusebius, and Athanasius* (Oxford, England: Clarendon Press, 1993), 179. See also Virginia Burrus, "Creatio Ex-Libidine: Reading Ancient Logos Differently," Yvonne Sherwood and Kevin Hart (eds) in *Derrida and Religion: Other Testaments*, (New York: Routledge, 2004)
69 T. Minh-Ha Trinh, *Woman Native Other* (Bloomington and Indianapolis: Indiana University Press, 1989), 104.
70 Both Schroer and Murphy insist on the irreducible undecidability of the text's ontological claim. Schroer, *Wisdom Has Built Her House*, 28; Murphy, *Tree of Life*, 136.
71 Bhabha, *Location of Culture*, 114.
72 Ibid.
73 Johnson, *She Who Is*, 124.
74 Gayatri Chakravorty Spivak, *A Critique of Postcolonial Reason, Toward a History of the Vanishing Present* (Cambridge, Mass.: Harvard University Press, 1999), 176.
75 Kathryn Tanner, "Creation as a Mixed Metaphor" (paper presented at "Interstitial Initiations: Counterdiscourses of Creation," First Transdisciplinary Theological Colloquium, Drew University, September 30–October 1, 2001), 2.
76 Denouncing the idolatry of the Western economic system by calling attention to its others (not an Other defined by the system but those others disavowed by it) has been a distinctive element of liberation theology. Latin American liberation philosopher Enrique Dussel explains: "The 'other' ('the widow, the orphan, the foreigner,' in the prophets' formulation, or under the universal name of 'the poor person') confronting the system is

the metaphysical reality beyond the ontological being of the system. As a result he or she is 'exteriority,' what is most alien to the system as a totality, 'internal transcendence' . . . he or she is the 'locus' of God's epiphany in those who are non-system . . . " Enrique Dussel, "An Ethics of Liberation: Fundamental Hypotheses," in Eduardo Mendieta (ed.), *Beyond Philosophy: Ethics, History, Marxism, and Liberation Theology*, (Lanham, Md.: Rowan & Littlefield, 2003), 139.

PART IV
Postcolonial Concerns

INTRODUCTION:
Postcolonial Concerns

R. S. Sugirtharajah

The essays in this section contain major postcolonial interventions. One of the ways in which the colonizer controlled the native was through translation. The first two essays here deal with this issue. Dora R. Mbuwayesango's "How Local Divine Powers were Suppressed: A Case of Mwari of the Shona" begins by asserting that Mwari, the Supreme Being of the Shona, had no specific gender and could speak through both men and women. Using examples from colonial versions of the Bible, she shows persuasively how colonial missionaries chose Mwari as the equivalent of Yahweh but how, more damagingly, Mwari was transformed into a male God, thus rejecting all the traditions, institutions, and myths that accompanied this Supreme Being. In short, Mwari had been colonized and the Shona people had been robbed of their tradition. Her essay ends with two proposals. One is that the translation of the Bible should be independent of the evangelizing project to which it has been inextricably tethered. The other is to move away from the practice of translating the Bible through European languages and work directly from Hebrew-Shona and Greek-Shona lexicons. Her plea is that the Shona should be permitted to discern biblical truths through Shona and their direct encounter with biblical languages, rather than through the medium of English.

Hephzibah Israel's essay examines the response of the Protestant Tamil community to the Bible and its religious vocabulary. It looks at the nineteenth-century conflict between missionaries and the Protestant Tamils over the revision of the Tamil Bible and the alternative strategies offered by Tamils employing Tamil poetic genres. One of those who opposed the missionary translations was Vedanayaka Sastri. The central contention of Sastri and those who opposed the missionary translations was based not on doctrinal or denominational differences, but on the use of the Tamil language and the failure of missionaries to follow the rules of Tamil grammar and literary traditions. This approach of the Tamil Protestants, in Israel's view, was motivated by a need to redefine their identity to meet the changing political and social circumstances of the Tamil community.

One of the concerns of postcolonialism is the misperception and misrepresentation of the "Other." In her essay, Karen King seeks to recover the figure of Mary

Magdalene, who had been simultaneously canonized and castigated. Her essay is a postcolonial project to erase that past defamation. She retells the story of how a very powerful, exemplary, and devoted leader was turned into a repentant sinner by the patriarchal exegesis, not only to fit in with its view of women but also to discredit and undermine Mary Magdalene's significance as a model for leadership in the Church. Using the Gospel of Mary, discarded by the canonizers, King presents a picture of Mary not only as a person of spiritual maturity and strength of character but also as a figure of authority and leadership within early Christianity. King's essay revisits the question of the canon and the importance of subjecting both canonical and non-canonical books to a feminist hermeneutics of suspicion.

The volume ends with an essay by the Filipino American, Eleazar Fernandez, which deals with one of the tragedies of colonialism – the dislocation of people who settle in strange countries and alien locations, often as minorities. Fernandez's interpretation of the Exodus deviates from the traditional reading and does not extract the themes which normally accompany the story – "liberation", "conquest", "release," and "election." Unlike the canonical narrative which begins with and moves out of Egypt, in Fernandez's Exodus the narrative starts with Canaan/Philippines and ends up with Egypt/USA. In this revised framework, the story does not dwell on the heroics of Moses in Egypt, but on Jacob and his descendants, especially on Joseph and the events which originally led him to Egypt. Fernandez's "Moses," therefore, does not lead people out of Egypt but into Egypt. Unlike the biblical Israelites, Filipino-Americans have no intention of leaving Egypt/USA, but have decided to throw in their lot with the new land of their dreams, with some dreams unfinished, and some nightmarish. For Fernandez, the narrative is about immigration and settlement. Such an experience for Fernandez is not a one-time event led by Moses, but an ongoing struggle for freedom.

17

How Local Divine Powers were Suppressed:

A Case of Mwari of the Shona

Dora R. Mbuwayesango

Before the colonization of Zimbabwe by the British in 1890, the country comprised many different political entities that were united religiously by the belief in a Supreme Being. This Supreme Being was commonly known by the personal name "Mwari." The different political entities paid allegiance to Mwari in different ways. Zimbabwe can be divided into two major superficial regions, that is, Mashonaland and Matabeleland. In Mashonaland, the language is mainly Shona, although with different dialects. The language in Matabeleland is predominantly Ndebele. The Ndebele, to a limited extent, respected the Mwari cult that was centered in Matopo Hills in Matebeleland.[1] The Shona understand Mwari to be a genderless spirit, neither male nor female. The attributes of Mwari all have to do with Mwari's transcendence and creative activities.[2] Thus, these attributes include *Nyadenga* (of the sky), *Mutangakugara* (the first to exist), *Muumbi* (the one who forms), and *Musikavanhu* (the creator of humanity). Also, Mwari does not discriminate and can speak through women and even through objects, as well as through men.

Colonialism and Christianity came to Zimbabwe simultaneously. In fact, the two aided each other in "christianizing" and dominating the indigenous peoples. The partnership of colonialism and Christianity is well expressed in one of David Livingstone's letters, discussed by John Kirk:

> That you may have a clear idea of my objects, I may state that they have more in them than meets the eye. They are not merely exploratory, for I go with the intention of benefiting both the African and my own countrymen. I take a practical mining geologist to tell of the mineral resources of the country, an economic botanist to give full report of the vegetable productions, an artist to give the scenery, a naval officer to tell of the capacity of river communications, a moral agent to lay a Christian foundation for

First published in Musa W. Dube, *Other Ways of Reading: African Women and the Bible*. Atlanta: Society of Biblical Literature, 2001, 63–77.

> anything that may follow. All this machinery has for its ostensible object the development of African trade and promotion of civilisation; but what I can tell none but such as you, in whom I have confidence, is this. *I hope it may result in an English colony in the healthy high lands of Central Africa.*[3]

Robert Moffat, one of the great missionary pioneers, also expresses the connection between missionary and colonial ventures in Africa:

> It is where the political organization is most perfect, and the social system still in its aboriginal vigour, that the missionary has the least success in making an impression. Where things have undergone a change and the feudal usages have lost their power, where there is a measure of disorganization, the new ideas which the gospel brings with it do not come into collision with any powerful political prejudice. The habits and modes of thinking have been broken up, and there is a preparation for the seed of the word.[4]

The European settler group that succeeded was the British South Africa Company (BSA Company) under Cecil Rhodes, after whom the country was later named Rhodesia. There were several European missionary organizations involved in Zimbabwe, although the initial missionary ventures had little success. The first missionary to operate in the country was Gançalo da Silveira, a Portuguese Jesuit, who was killed. The second phase of missionary activities in the country took place in the seventeenth century, when the Dominicans set up missions in the eastern part; by the end of that century, they had abandoned the missions. The next to attempt the evangelization of the Shona peoples were the Congregationalists, who worked among the eastern Shona in the 1870s. The Dutch Reformed Church, the Berlin missionary society, and Anglicans also made tentative efforts in Mashonaland in the 1880s, but these missionary ventures were unsuccessful. It was only after Cecil John Rhodes had occupied Mashonaland that the missionaries started to experience success. Rhodes personally encouraged missionary work by allocating generous tracts of land to thirteen different societies during the 1890s. Later the Methodists and other missionary groups entered the country.

The missionaries found no need to explain the concept of God to the Shona people. In fact, they discovered that the Shona were a very spiritual and monotheistic people who believed in the Supreme Being by the name of Mwari, whose cult flourished in the Matopo Hills near Bulawayo. This cult seems to have been one of the strongest elements that united the different groups comprising the Shona.

> So many different clans are presented among the staff at each shrine as to make it likely that the location of the cult in the Matopos is to be regarded as an ancient structural feature. We find that priests, dancers, consecrated women and messengers are drawn from such diverse groups as the Karanga, Kalanga, Mbire, the Hera, Rozvi, and the Venda.[5]

The widespread belief in Mwari in the Matopo Hills is demonstrated by Daneel, who records finding a system of messengers and tribute in operation among Matonjeni and the districts of Chilimanzi, Gutu, Victoria, Melsetter, Bikita, Ndanga, Chibi, Chipinga, Belingwe, Gwanda, Plumtree, Nyamadlovu, and centers in Vendaland both north and south of the Limpopo.[6]

The Quest for a Shona Word for the Biblical Deity

One of the challenging tasks for the missionaries was to make the biblical deity relevant and acceptable to the Shona. While the missionaries eventually adopted the name Mwari to designate the biblical god (*Elohim* or *Yhwh* in the Old Testament, and God the Father in the New Testament), the history leading to that conclusion is reflected in the translations of the Bible, liturgical texts, and the catechisms of the different missionary organizations operating in Mashonaland.

Before the standardization of Shona language, the missionary groups had different preferences for Shona terms for the biblical deity. The first was *Modzimo* or *Mudzimu*, which was used in writings between 1899 and 1912 by the Lutheran and Dutch Reformed churches operating among the Karangas.[7] The second Shona term to refer to the biblical deity was *Wedenga*, "of the sky." This was found in writings of the Dutch Reformed Church and the Church of Sweden in 1909 and 1927, respectively.[8] The term *Wedenga* was also combined with *Mudzimu* as *Mudzimu Wedenga*, "the Ancestral Spirit of the Sky."[9]

In Shona, the term *Mudzimu* refers only to the ancestral spirit. Its early use among the Karanga seemed to have been influenced by the corresponding Sotho term *Molimo*, due to the missionary misunderstanding of that term. As Smith points out, the Tswana (the people of Botswana) were responding to a specific question posed by the missionaries: What is "the cause of all appearances in nature and the origin of all good and evil that happens to them without any act of their own?"[10] Attempts to correct this misunderstanding, as demonstrated by Louw's qualification with *Wedenga*, did not catch on.[11]

Other missionary organizations used the term *Mwari* exclusively from the beginning, especially the Anglicans, Methodists, and, later, groups such as the Salvation Army, who operated among the Eastern Shona and the Zezuru.[12]

The Roman Catholic Church was characterized by initial diversity in the terms used for the biblical deity before the general acceptance of *Mwari*. Some Catholics – in particular the Dominicans and the Catholic translations at Waddilove – used *Mwari* from the outset.[13] Jesuit Catholic publications, however, used *Yave* from 1898.[14] The first edition of the Catholic Shona-English dictionary gives the following entries as translations of the English word *God: Yave* (a foreign word); *Mwea mukuru* (the great spirit); *Mwari* (the great spirit, according to native understanding); *Murenga* (the god of war, a word introduced from the Matabeleland in the last rebellion: the cry was, *Murenga wamuka* [the God of war has risen]).[15]

Although *Mwari* finally became the accepted Shona term for the biblical deity, the discussion that ensued between 1921 and 1924 in Catholic circles reveals the underlying distinctions between the Shona deity and the biblical deity. For example, Father Richartz argued that, although the Shona gods might be honored as gods or have godlike traits, their names were sullied by unworthy associations, and, if used, they would confuse the simple. The term *Mwari*, he said, would be unsuitable because it did not connote the notion of judge – an essential ingredient of the Christian belief – nor the notion of creation in the strict sense. He also considered the views of those who went to the Mwari shrines as concerned only for material matters. Thus the use of the term would be bound to bring in many false notions.[16]

Also, Father Luobiere objected to the term *Mwari* for the Christian God on the grounds that it lacked moral connotations, in that both the good and the wicked are equally Mwari's offspring, and after death all would be treated alike.[17] Even non-Catholics such as Bullock weighed in on the debate, to express their reservation about the equation of Mwari and the Christian God: "I should be the last to advocate the translation of our word God by the Chishona word *Mwari*."[18] By the early 1960s, however, the Jesuits had joined the other Christian societies in using *Mwari* to refer to the Christian God. For example, one of the most influential persons in the standardization of the Shona language, Father Michael Hannan, used *Mwari* in his New Testament translation of 1966 and listed *Mwari* as one of the Shona terms for God, the Supreme Being, in his Shona dictionary.[19]

The missionary translation of the Bible was aimed at replacing the Shona Mwari with the biblical God in everything else but the name. If the missionaries had come to introduce a new God to the Shonas, they might have met much resistance, as happened in the earlier mission ventures. The adoption of the Shona name Mwari for the biblical God was in reality the religious usurpation of the Shona. The missionaries took the Shona captive by colonizing the Shona Supreme Being. The results of this religious colonization can be demonstrated by analyzing texts that were now taken to speak of Mwari, the Shona God.

The Effects of the Adoption of the Shona Term Mwari

Due to the similarities between the Shona culture and the culture depicted in the Old Testament, the effects of the missionary adoption of the term *Mwari* will be considered mainly from the Old Testament context. There are several ways to refer to the deity in the Old Testament. One of the ways is by personal names, such as Elohim as in Gen. 1:1, or Yhwh in Exod. 3:4, or a combination of the two, Yhwh Elohim, in Gen. 2:4. Another way is by a construct chain made up of Elohim with a proper name, such as Elohe-Abraham, Elohe-Isaac, and Elohe-Jacob (Exod. 3:6). In other passages the name El may be juxtaposed to a place name, as in El Shadday or El Bethel.

The direct equation was made between Elohim and Mwari in Shona Bibles. Thus, for example, the first verse in Genesis reads *Pakutanga Mwari vakasika denga nenyika*... (In the beginning Mwari created the heavens and the earth...). The earlier Bible translation had *Tenzi* in place of *Yhwh*, based on the English use of LORD to signify that divine name.[20] *Tenzi* means a variety of things depending on the context. It can mean "master," or "owner," or even "employer." The earliest and most recent translations use *Jehova*, based on a German transliteration and misunderstanding of the concept behind the vowel pointing.[21]

As a written record the Bible became the authentic voice on Mwari and Mwari's ways. The Shona believe that Mwari is the creator and the ultimate controller of the universe, the Supreme Being. However, the authentic way to describe Mwari's creative activity has come to be understood as that found in the Bible. The equation thus overruled the way the Shona spoke about and dealt with their deity. The missionaries designated the Shona as primitive and uncivilized in their understanding of God. While the Shona believed that Mwari had created everything, the missionaries granted no validity to the myths that describe the details of these

creative activities. The equation of Mwari and Elohim resulted in the suppression of the Shona stories about Mwari's activities as creator. The Shona were basically an oral people, with no written documents. The Shona myths and folktales were not given the same status as the written material that the missionaries introduced to the Shona.

The biblical story of creation appears to be in line with the belief of the Shona that Mwari is the creator of the universe and of humanity. The details in the story, however, distort the details in Shona belief. The most evident distortion is found in Gen. 1:26–8, which depicts the creation of humanity. While to feminists this account provides positive testimony for the equality of male and female before the biblical deity,[22] the depiction of the deity distorts the basic belief about the form of the Shona deity. In the Shona Bible translation, Mwari is given a human form. In the Shona religious traditions, however, Mwari was truly holy, set apart from creation.[23] Mwari had no form or image. Mwari was truly a spirit without sexuality or gender,[24] but, in the Bible, Mwari is given human form (Gen. 1:26–7). Although the story seems to portray Mwari as having both male and female attributes, by the time of the ancestral stories later in Genesis, Mwari has acquired male gender. In Genesis 18, when the deity by the name of Yhwh appears to Abraham, there are three men with whom Abraham carries on a conversation and has a meal. Two of the men, identified as "messengers," leave Abraham and continue to Sodom. The implication is that the third "man" is actually the deity (Gen. 18:22).

In the Old Testament, the deity is presented as male in subtle ways. In languages that have grammatical gender, masculine forms are generally used. In the Prophets in general, and particularly in Hosea and Ezekiel, the metaphor that represents the relationship between the deity and Israel is that of husband and wife. In this metaphor, the deity is the husband and the wife is Israel. The clearest reference to the deity as male in the Old Testament is in Isa. 63:16, in which the term *father* is used to address the deity.

The biblical stories of creation are products of Jews in the exilic period whose basic aim was to preserve their beliefs in the face of the religious and cultural threat represented by the Babylonian environment. It is significant that these "priestly" writers did not replace Elohim with Babylonian gods such as Marduk. *Elohim* is not a generic term for the deity but a specific name, just as *Mwari* is for the Shona. To take over the name Mwari is to rob the Shona of their traditions and to colonize Mwari. The Shona were a people whose traditions were passed orally from generation to generation. With no written records to concretize those traditions, the missionaries replaced the unwritten records of the Shona with the Bible. As a result, the Bible now talks about Mwari, but *whose* Mwari?

In the stories of the Old Testament, Mwari becomes the god of the Hebrews who had dealings with the Hebrews and not with the Shona peoples, and in the New Testament the only way to Mwari is through *his* son Jesus Christ. This pattern is made clear when *Mwari* functions as the term for God in the story of the rise of Israel as a nation. The call of Moses in Exodus 3 needs special attention, because it demonstrates clearly how the biblical god is tied to the nationhood of Israel. That crucial account, however, must be set in its narrative context.

The book of Genesis begins by considering the world in broad spectrum and gradually narrows to focus on a specific family, the family of Abraham, who is

promised a land and nationhood (Genesis 12). The story moves through the descendants of Abraham – Isaac and Jacob. The book of Genesis, however, closes with Abraham's descendants in Egypt, where they end up because of famine in the promised land (Genesis 50).

The book of Exodus opens with the *bene yisrael* (children of Israel), at the death of Joseph, as a population of only seventy (1:1–5). When Joseph and his brothers died, the *bene yisrael* experienced a population surge – "they multiplied and grew exceedingly strong, so that the land was filled with them" (1:7). The Pharaoh, who did not know Joseph, saw the *bene yisrael* as a threat and devised measures to keep their population growth and strength in check (1:8–22). The story of the birth and survival of Moses, the founder of Israelite religion, relates to Pharaoh's attempts to suppress the growth of the Israelites. Moses is rescued by Pharaoh's daughter and subsequently grows up in the Egyptian environment (2:1–10). But Moses identified with the Hebrews. One day he saw an Egyptian mistreating a Hebrew man, and he killed the Egyptian and hid his body in the sand. When Pharaoh learned what Moses had done, he sought to kill him, and so Moses fled to Midian (2:11–22).

After a while, the Pharaoh who sought to kill Moses died, but the Hebrews continued to suffer in Egypt and groaned and cried; their cry for deliverance rose to Elohim. "Elohim heard their groaning, and Elohim remembered his covenant with Abraham, Isaac, and Jacob. Elohim looked upon the Israelites, and Elohim took notice of them" (2:24–5). The name Elohim is repeated five times in 2:23–5. More significant, however, is the connection between Elohim and the ancestors of the Israelites. When, in Shona Bibles, Elohim is replaced by the name Mwari, it becomes Mwari who remembers the covenant that Mwari made with the ancestors of Israel, not with the ancestors of the Shona. Thus, the Shona deity becomes the special God of the Hebrews. For the Shona to relate to their deity, they have to adopt the traditions in the Bible. These traditions have no room for the ways in which various groups of the Shona deal with Mwari, such as through the epics or myths about how Mwari, through the leadership of a *mhondoro* (a spirit of the founding ancestors), led each group to its current location.

Exodus 2 concludes by noting what was taking place in Egypt. Chapter 3, however, goes back to the scene in Midian, in which Moses is in exile. While in Midian, herding his father-in-law's flock, Moses has an encounter with the deity. The encounter takes place at a location identified as Horeb, the mountain of Elohim. The story is characterized by interchangeable use of the biblical deity's two names, Elohim (*Mwari*) and Yhwh (*Tenzi* or *Jehova*).[25] A messenger of Yhwh appears to Moses in a flame, in a bush that is ablaze but not consumed. Moses investigates this unusual phenomenon, and when Yhwh sees that Moses has turned aside to look, Elohim (Mwari) calls and Moses responds. The voice that calls identifies itself with the construct form of Elohim (*elohe*), juxtaposed with the names of Moses' ancestors, Abraham, Isaac, and Jacob (3:6). Once again the deity is identified in relationship to the ancestors of Israel – Abraham, Isaac, and Jacob. In Shona Bibles, the text reads, "Mwari vaAbraham, Mwari vaIsaka, naMwari vaJakobo." Thus Mwari is identified exclusively with the Israelites, and the connection between Mwari and the Shona is disregarded. The Shona traditions about how different mediators, such as Chaminuka, Nehanda, and Kaguvi, serve as spokespersons of Mwari are discredited and superseded by the biblical traditions. For example, the Mazezuru, a branch of

the Shona, have a tradition about how Chaminuka became the link between Mwari and the people. Prior to Chaminuka's time, at a place called Maringari, was a special tree, *muti usinazita* (a tree without a name). According to Shona tradition, the tree fell and became a log from which shoots continued to sprout. The people would hear a voice, giving instructions and providing them with food. The voice was first identified as Mwari's voice and later replaced by Chaminuka, such that Mwari now speaks through Chaminuka and the people speak to Mwari through Chaminuka.[26]

The biblical account of the encounter between Moses and the Israelite God continues with the deity's identification with a people: "I have observed the misery of my people who are in Egypt" (Exod. 3:7). The Hebrew people belong to a specific deity, Elohim, who has come to deliver them from their sufferings at the hands of their oppressors. The connection between the people and this deity is made even clearer. This deity has come down to bring them "out of the land of Egypt to a good and broad land, a land flowing with milk and honey, to a country of the Canaanites, the Hittites, . . . and the Jebusites" (3:8). This deity has a grand scheme for the Israelites – a scheme that involves replacing other peoples in the land. For Africans, this picture of the divine purpose is ironic in the face of the Shona peoples' displacement by the European settlers.

Moses' response to this grand scheme relates to his specific role. He is to go to Pharaoh and demand that Pharaoh give the Israelites freedom. Moses initially wants to know what qualifies him for this role: "Who am I that I should go to Pharaoh, and bring the Israelites out of Egypt?" (3:11). The deity's response is that Moses' qualifications are inconsequential to the grand scheme of deliverance. What is significant is that the deity will be with him.

Moses then wonders how to communicate the identity of the deity. The deity had identified itself as the God of the Israelite ancestors. Moses now says, "If I come to the Israelites and say to them, 'The God of your ancestors has sent me to you,' and they ask me, 'What is his name?' what will I say to them?" (3:13). There are three parts to the deity's response. The first part seems to be the deity's refusal to respond and give its name: *Ehyeh asher ehyeh* ("I am who I am").[27] But this is the not the final response. The second part tells Moses how to respond to the Israelites' question: "Thus you shall say to the Israelites, '*Ehyeh* . . . has sent me to you' " (3:14b). The deity gives its name as *ehyeh*, which means "I am" in English and translates as *ndiri* in Shona. But that is not the final answer either. Moses is again told what to say to the Israelites: "Yhwh, the God of your ancestors, the God of Abraham, the God of Isaac, and the God of Jacob, has sent me to you" (3:15a). The God that Moses brings to the Israelites is none other than the God of their ancestors, who thus will fulfill the promise made to the ancestors. Thus, in Shona Bibles, Mwari becomes the name that stands for the new name revealed to Moses, and Mwari becomes the God of Abraham, of Isaac, and of Jacob, the God of the Hebrews.

This is a direct usurpation of the Shona deity by the biblical deity. Sanneh argues that the translation of Scriptures into vernacular languages assisted the Africans in preserving their names for the deity.[28] In fact, the translation of the Scriptures, at least as far as the Shona are concerned, resulted in the colonization of the Shona God. Mwari ceased to be the God of the Shona peoples and became the God of the Hebrews. Shona ways of relating to their deity are replaced by the new ways of

relating to Mwari as Yhwh. The missionaries, and the Bible as the missionaries interpreted it, thus had the final word on what is acceptable and not acceptable for Mwari's new identity; the ways of the Shona were deemed obsolete. The Mwari shrines became an abomination, the connection between the Mwari and the ancestors invalid. The list of activities abhorrent to Mwari, according to Deut. 18:9–13, include most of the ways the Shona people communicated with their God. The equation of *vadzimu* (the ancestors) with the "ghosts and spirits," with whom connection is prohibited in Deut. 18:11, demonizes the Shona ancestors.

Unshackling Mwari from Colonial Chains

The Bible played a large role in the colonization of Zimbabwe. The religious colonization of the Shona began with the colonization of the Shona deity Mwari. This colonization, as detailed above, occurred by equating the name of the Shona deity with the biblical god and by the consequent transformation of the Shona deity. For the Shona to relate to this god, they had to abandon their Shona identity and become Western. Their own religious traditions suddenly were deemed incompatible with Mwari.

There is no doubt that Christianity is now one of the major religions of Africa. Mainstream Christianity, however, is plagued by having remained a foreign religion. It continues to make Shona Christians feel inadequate for being Shona, because Shona understandings of Mwari are suppressed. There are several ways to deal with this problem. The Bible entered Zimbabwe as a propaganda tool. The writing of African languages was developed in order to translate the Scriptures, since the missionaries wanted Shona words to make their message less foreign and thus acceptable to the Shona; that is the basis on which the Shona name of deity was appropriated and transferred to the biblical god. The Bible was also used as a text in schools, so that the adaptation of the deity was imprinted on those learning how to read and write. The power of the written word is demonstrated clearly by how the Bible suppressed oral traditions and led the biblical word to be seen as more authentic than the oral traditions it superseded. Shona values and beliefs had been transferred from generation to generation through folktales, but this process gradually ended and was replaced with the written word. Shona folktales were not accorded the same validity as the Bible, because they were said to be "myths," or unreal stories.

While the past cannot be undone, it is crucial now that the translation of the Shona Bibles be done independent of the evangelization of the Shona. In such a project, as Bird points out,

> The aim of the Bible translator... should be to enable a modern audience to *overhear* an ancient conversation, rather than to hear itself addressed directly.... It is not the translator's duty to make her audience *accept* the author's message, or even [to] identify themselves with the ancient audience.[29]

This also calls for a move from translating the Bible through European languages such as English, and instead to working directly from the Hebrew and Greek texts.

There should be a Hebrew-Shona dictionary and Greek-Shona dictionary to allow the Shona to meet the Bible, not on English terms, but on the terms of Shona and of the original languages.

The inadequacy of the Bible to the Shona people's experience is expressed well by Canaan Banana, a Zimbabwean theologian, who argues not only for a translation from the original languages, but even for a rewriting of the Bible.

> This would include revision and editing to what is already there, but would also involve adding that which is not included. . . . I see that a re-written Bible, one that is more universal, embracing the rich plurality of the human experience in response to God, would be a more authentic and relevant document in today's world.[30]

The assumption behind Banana's proposal is that the Christian deity and the Shona deity are one and the same. This assumption still falls into the trap of making Mwari compatible with Christian concepts. In my judgment, the two should be kept separate and distinct. There should be separate documents containing the Shona stories and traditions about their deity. The Shona traditions should have authenticity apart from the Bible.

In the project I propose, the Hebrew names of God would be maintained in order to maintain the differences between Mwari and Yhwh Elohim. The pen should rescue the Shona deity. Writing merged Mwari with the biblical god, and it is through writing that the identification of Mwari with the genderless Shona deity will be reclaimed.

NOTES

1 The limited allegiance of the Ndebele to Mwari can be demonstrated by the function of the Mwari cult during the first Ndebele-Shona uprising against the British settlers in 1896.

2 The claim that Mwari was divided into three – Father, Mother, and Son – is an attempt to make African religions compatible with the Christian concept of trinity.

3 John Kirk, *Zambezi Journals and Letters*, ed. Reginald Foskett, vol. 1 (Edinburgh: Oliver & Boyd, 1965), 309. Italics are mine.

4 Cited in J. P. Wallis (ed.), *The Matabele Mission* (London: Chatto and Windus, 1945), 70–1.

5 G. Fortune, "Who Was *Mwari?*" *Rhodesian History: Journal of the Central African Historical Association*, 4 (1973): 5. Also, J. M. Schoffeleers and R. Mwanza, "An Organizational Model of the Mwari Shrines," in J. M. Schoffelers (ed.), *Guardians of the Land: Essays on Central African Territorial Cults* (Gwelo, Rhodesia: Mambo Press, 1978), 308.

6 M. L. Daneel, *The God of the Matopo Hills* (London and The Hague: Mouton, 1970), 56–7.

7 *Buke eo ko Ravisa Tshekaranga* (The book for learning Karanga language) (Middleburg, South Africa: 1899); Rev. Wedepohl, *Mashoko e Buke eo Modzimo* (Compiled Bible stories) (Berlin: Evangelical Missionge-sellschaft, 1902); J. T. Helm and A. A. Louw, *Evangeli ea Mattheus* (Translation of Matthew's Gospel) (London: British Foreign Bible Society, 1904); *Nziyo dzechiKaranga dze "De Ned. Ger. Kereke pa Mashonaland"* (Karanga hymns for the Mashonaland Church) (Cape Town: Citadel Press, 1910); *Vunzo dzeshoko ro Mudzimu* (Questions on the Word of God) (Fort Victoria, Rhodesia: Morgenster Mission, 1912).

8 *Vunzo dzeshoko roWedenga* (Questions about the Word of God) (Fort Victoria, Rhodesia: Morgenster Mission, 1909); *Mashoko e Bibele* (The Bible stories) (Belingwe, Rhodesia: Southern Rhodesia Church of Sweden Mission, 1927).
9 C. S. Louw, *Manual of the Chikaranga Language* (Bulawayo, Rhodesia: Philpott & Collins, 1915), 203.
10 E. W. Smith, *African Ideas of God* (London: Edinburgh House, 1950), 116–17.
11 Louw, *Manual of the Chikaranga Language*, 203.
12 For example, for Anglicans: *Minamato neZwiyimbo Yamana we-Sangano* (London: SPCK, 1900); Methodists: H. E. Springer, *A Handbook of Chikaranga* (Cincinnati: Jennings & Graham, 1905); Salvation Army: *Chizezuru and Ckinyanja Songs* (Cape Town: Salvation Army, 1920).
13 *Testamente Itswa ya She Wedu Jesu Kristu no Rurimi rwe Chishona* (The New Testament of our Lord Jesus Christ in Shona) (London: British & Foreign Bible Society, 1907); F. Mayr, *Katekisima re Makristo e Sangano re Katolike* (Pinetown, South Africa: Miriannhill, 1910).
14 A. M. Hartmann, *Rugwaro rgwo Kunamata* (Chishawasha, Rhodesia: Jesuit Mission, 1898); E. Biehler, *Zwinamato Zwineitikwa* (Roermond, Holland: J. J. Romen, 1906).
15 *English-Chiswina Dictionary with an Outline Chiswina Grammar* (Chishawasha: Jesuit Mission, 1906).
16 Fortune, "Who Was *Mwari?*" 8.
17 Ibid., 9.
18 Charles Bullock, *The Mashona* (Cape Town: Juta, 1928), 124; idem, *The Mashona and the Matabele* (Cape Town: Juta, 1950), 147.
19 M. Hannan, *Chitendero Chitsva* (Gwelo, Rhodesia: Mambo Press, 1966); *Standard Shona Dictionary* (Salisbury, Rhodesia: Rhodesia Literature Bureau, 1959 [1st edn], 1974 [2nd edn]).
20 *Bhaibheri rine Apokirifa* (Harare: Bible Society of Zimbabwe, 1979).
21 *Bhaibheri Magwaro Matsvene Amwari Testamente Yekare Testamente Itsva* (London: British and Foreign Bible Society, 1949); *Bhaibheri Magwaro Matsvene Amwari Namanyorero Anhasi* (Harare: Bible Society of Zimbabwe, 1995).
22 For example, Phyllis Trible, *God and the Rhetoric of Sexuality* (Philadelphia: Fortress Press, 1978), 18.
23 This is contrary to Mbiti's assertion that the Ndebele and Shona have a pantheon of God the Father, God the Mother, and God the Son. This conclusion is actually a distortion that comes from the influence of Christianity. The Shona have never conceived of God in such human terms, which to their traditions would appear to limit the deity.
24 Shona languages lack the complication of grammatical gender.
25 This is sometimes taken as evidence that the story results from the J and E sources, or traditions.
26 Michael Gelfand, *Shona Ritual with Special Reference to the Chaminuka Cult* (Cape Town, Wynberg, and Johannesburg: Juta, 1959), 13–14.
27 Or "I am what I am" or "I will be what I will be."
28 Lamin Sanneh, *Translating the Message: The Missionary Impact on Culture* (Maryknoll, NY: Orbis Books, 1989), 181.
29 Phyllis A. Bird, *Missing Persons and Mistaken Identities: Women and Gender in Ancient Israel* (Minneapolis: Fortress Press, 1997), 243.
30 Canaan S. Banana, "The Case for a New Bible," in R. S. Surgirtharajah (ed.), *Voices from the Margin: Interpreting the Bible in the Third World* (rev. edn; Maryknoll, NY: Orbis Books, 1995), 81.

18

Cutchery Tamil versus Pure Tamil:

Contesting Language Use in the Translated Bible in the Early Nineteenth-Century Protestant Tamil Community

Hephzibah Israel

Although one of the concerns of postcolonial theory is the politics of language use in both colonial and postcolonial societies and some postcolonial critics (Thiong'o 1986; Niranjana 1992; Dharwadker 1999; Devy 1999) have engaged with the political implications of the way language and translations function in colonial situations, (opening a new area in translation studies) very few have examined the role Bible translation has played in the formation of Christian communities and religious identity outside Europe. Scholars engaged in studying translations in the colonial period tend to see the practice of translation as participating mainly in other hegemonic colonial interventions within colonized societies. However, my examination of the Bible in Tamil translation revealed that it effected many different meanings in the culture it entered, interacted with factors already present in Tamil culture, and elicited heterogeneous responses, both complicit or resisting. I argue that translation projects undertaken by missionaries in the colonial context question neat polarities, such as colonizing/colonized languages, domesticating/foreignizing translations, and complicit/resistant audiences that continue to have currency in the present theoretical discourse on translation. In particular, I focus on the extent to which Protestant Tamils, as an interpretative community of faith, have been responsible in shaping a Protestant Tamil vocabulary and in defining themselves; and how different groups within the community have strategically claimed to represent Protestant Tamil identity at different points in time by using notions of "tradition," "purity," and the "sacred" in language.

The two primary objectives of the Protestant missionaries in nineteenth-century India were, one, to assimilate the Bible through translation into the language

Unpublished paper.

cultures of India; and, two, to create a Protestant identity for their converts. Since language is one of the markers of identity one of the primary tasks of the missionary translators was also to build a suitable Christian vocabulary in each language, so that the new Protestant Indians would be able to express their religious beliefs and identity in a vocabulary that was distinct from their previous religious affiliations. Regardless of the historical and cultural specificity of each individual's past, the convert was encouraged to fit into the universalized category of a "Protestant." The emphasis on standard translations and terminology was part of a larger interest in creating a homogeneous Protestant readership. As Sue Zemka has argued: "The Bible Society based and justified its existence on the belief that the exposure to Holy Scriptures created an abstract Christian subject with similar attributes of behaviour and belief regardless of cultural conditions, material environment, or pre-existing religious beliefs" (Zemka, 1991: 104). The aim was to replace certain local cultural practices, deemed as particularly "heathen," with Protestant ethics and values. The Protestant register of the languages used in the translated Bibles was meant to provide the convert with a distinct vocabulary to express this move towards the Protestant faith.

Terms from Tamil religious vocabulary were available as much to Protestant Tamils as to Protestant missionaries. The writings of both, which resulted in a substantial body of Tamil Protestant literature, reveal that choice of terminology has played a significant part in what has been accepted as Protestant at different points in the history of Protestant Christianity in Tamilnadu. Unfortunately, there is little surviving evidence from the eighteenth century of Protestant Tamil opinion on language use, choice of vocabulary, or the style of a new version of the Tamil Bible. However, within a hundred years of a Protestant Tamil vocabulary becoming visible as belonging to a distinct Protestant discourse, there were references to it as "missionary Tamil." As early as 1825, a letter written by a Protestant Tamil priest, Vicuvaca Nadan, solicits the support of "his fellow Native Priests and Superiors" for the revision of the existing Tamil Bible in order to remove the "missionary Tamil" used in it.[1] This label continues to be used, somewhat disparagingly, along with others, such as "padre" or "Christian Tamil," among Protestant Tamils even today to identify the terms peculiar to Protestant Tamil use.

Language choice has determined how Protestant Christianity was translated as one of the religious faiths available to Tamil society and how it interacted with the other belief systems. In the early decades of the nineteenth century, Evangelical Lutherans of Madras and Tanjore wrote several letters and petitions protesting against revisions of existing translations. Large sections of the Evangelical Lutherans belonged to the high-caste *Vellala* group who showed their self-consciousness as a religious community in their engagement with the question of Bible translation. They combined the issue of Bible translation with other differences that the congregations had with the missionaries: the observance of caste distinctions, the observation of Protestant and Tamil feast days, the use of Tamil musical instruments, and the writing of Protestant poetry according to Tamil poetic and religious traditions. All of these were referred to as "cruelties" imposed by the missionaries on the Protestant Tamil congregations. They protested against the proposed revision of the (eighteenth-century) Tamil Bible on the grounds that the highly Sanskritized version used a "pure" Tamil that best represented the Protestant Tamils as a com-

munity and themselves as belonging to a caste that enjoyed a high social standing in Tamil society.

In the long history of religious rivalry in Tamil society, religious language and poetry had functioned as a powerful instrument with which to express religious identity. Assailing the literary quality of Tamil had figured largely in earlier conflicts between Tamil Saiva, Buddhist, and Jaina sects. Inability to speak or sing good Tamil had been used to "expose" the perceived foreignness of Buddhist and Jaina poets in medieval Tamil society, an issue that was brought up again at the entry of Protestant Christianity into Tamil society in the eighteenth century. Religious rivalry between these religious systems had been expressed in claims about the use of "pure," "literary," or "correct" Tamil where the ability to use pure Tamil was viewed as an indication of knowing the true God. In this context, they were conscious that the peculiar form of Tamil, derogatorily termed "missionary" or "Protestant" Tamil, was one from which they wanted to disassociate themselves. Protestant Tamil congregations dominated by the Vellala caste at the beginning of the nineteenth century were keen to maintain a particular version of the Tamil Bible as representing appropriate language use, and thus, their own religious identity.

Protestant Tamil Objections to Rhenius's Revision of the Tamil Bible

Controversy began as a result of the appointment of Rhenius (1790–1837) by the British and Foreign Bible Society (hereafter BFBS) in 1814 to revise the German Lutheran missionary, Fabricius's (1711–91) revision of the New (1772) and translations of the Old Testaments (1776). Letters and petitions of protest from the Tanjore Evangelical congregations have survived. Conflict was at a height around 1825 when Rhenius's revision committee printed parts of the revised New Testament and circulated them for opinion. In spite of opposition, his New Testament was published in 1833 and the entire revised Bible in 1840 by the BFBS. There is no surviving evidence of Rhenius's revision committee considering or recording criticism from any Protestant Tamil groups. As Sastri, one of those responding to Rhenius's Bible revisions, claimed:

> I the general Poet of all the congregations examined and found in one page 10 or 20 and many more mistakes and with great sorrow wrote the first book Wedaviantchiapatram against their corrections [of the Tamil Bible] and sent it to the Revd Mr Haubroe . . . I earnestly begged him to consider that this deed was not good and that it was a great obstacle and infinite injury to Christianity [.?] he did not regard it, but rejected my advice.[2]

Protestant Tamil dissent has survived through unpublished manuscript versions of pamphlets and petitions written by Vedanayaka Sastri, some composed by him on behalf of the Tanjore Evangelical Church. In *Sādipēdaga sambāveney* (hereafter *SS*) or "Dialogue on the Distinction of Caste," written in both Tamil and in English in 1828, Sastri named his other texts in which "the unnatural language and confusions" of Bible revision were dealt with: "They have been shewn in our books viz. *Vēdaviatchiapatram, Kuttravilackam, Puduthiruthalin Kūkural* and *Pudutiruthalin*

Chōdeney." Except *kuttravilakam*, these have survived as manuscript copies. He stated in both *SS* and *Pututtiruttalin cōtanai* that *Vētaviātcia patram* was the first he wrote, followed by the others when the missionaries ignored it. The English preface to *Vētaviātcia patram* (hereafter *VP*) reveals that it was written in 1820 along with its companion piece *Kuttravilakam* to "expose an unjust correction and to protect the holy religion." *Pututtiruttalin Kūkural* (English title, "Noise of New Corrections," hereafter *PK*) was written jointly by the congregation of the Tanjore Evangelical Church in 1825 in response to a letter written to them by Vicuvaca Nadan, "a Native Priest at Combaconum" dated September 3, 1823. Written in Tamil (with an English Preface), in eight chapters, *PK* is a detailed refutation of every accusation or claim made by Vicuvaca Nadan in support of Rhenius's revisions and ends with a detailed textual analysis of the differences in translation of the Lord's Prayer in the two versions (i.e., Fabricius and Rhenius). After *PK*, Sastri wrote *Pututtiruttalin cōtanai* ("tribulation of the new corrections," hereafter *PC*). The pamphlet written in Tamil, may have had a preface and been dated originally, but is now missing. The main body of the pamphlet is a close textual analysis of the first chapters of the book of Genesis and the Gospel of Matthew in the two existing Bible versions, by which he attempted to prove that Fabricius's translation was superior to Rhenius's revision. To this, Sastri appended letters of petition written by the congregations of Madras and Tanjore to the "new missionaries who have created the new revision" (dated, 1819 and 1827) and a letter addressed to Sastri from a John Devasahayam (dated 1833).

Interestingly, Sastri combined the issue of Bible translation with other differences that he and his fellow Evangelical congregations had with the missionaries regarding observing caste distinctions in the church. In *SS* and *Sāditeratoo* ("Explaining Caste"), the English Preface to a collection of documents entitled *Jāti-tiruttalin payittiyam* ("The Foolishness of Amending Caste"), Sastri focused on controversial issues of caste between the congregations and missionaries of the Tanjore Evangelical Church. But while doing so, he connected the caste dispute with the controversy over Bible revision. In his mind, at least, the two were linked as "cruelties" imposed by the missionaries on the Protestant Tamil congregations.

Sastri and the Tanjore Evangelicals launched a critique of the Bible revision carried out by those they dubbed the "junior" or "new missionaries." Their targets were mainly Rhenius and other missionaries assisting him. They contrasted these to the "previous missionaries," which mainly referred to Bartholomäus Ziegenbalg (1682–1719) and Fabricius. Their arguments, in brief, were that Fabricius's translation was excellent; that the present efforts at revision only corrupted the previous translation; and that the revision was an imposition by the missionaries on Protestant Tamils who had not demanded a revision of the Tamil Bible they used. Significantly, their quarrel was not with theological or denominational differences or conflicting doctrinal interpretations of the biblical text. The focal point of their argument was the use of Tamil language, that is, whether the appropriate register of Tamil was being used for Bible translation. This concern of Sastri and his fellow protesters with the use of the Tamil language indicates their self-consciousness regarding the status of the Protestant Tamil community within Tamil society.

Three main arguments were offered in support of Fabricius: first, that Fabricius's knowledge of Tamil was superior to that of Rhenius; second, that Fabricius had help

from the "right" Tamil scholars; and third, that Fabricius used literary Tamil, whereas Rhenius did not. First, in order to prove that Fabricius's translation needed no revision, Sastri attempted to prove that Fabricius's knowledge of Tamil was superior to that of Rhenius. In *SS*, he claimed that Fabricius's knowledge of Hebrew, Greek, and Tamil philology had resulted in a Scriptures that "could be plainly understood by the learned and unlearned and put . . . in a most agreeable Tamil, expressing them by most delightful and sweet words rejoicing and edifying the mind like the joys of the garden of Eden and the gladness of the city of God the new Jerusalem" (*SS*, 1828). Likewise, in both *PK* and *PC*, he repeatedly emphasized that Fabricius and others before him translated according to rules of Tamil grammar and literary tradition, and followed principles of word conjunctions. Sastri's answer to aspersions on Fabricius's knowledge of Tamil was that he learnt Tamil from *tampirans* or learned scholars and by studying various Hindu scriptures. As further proof he claimed that the "previous missionaries" were able to write Tamil dictionaries and grammars only because they had studied the *Nanūl*[3] (*PK*, 1825).

In Sastri's opinion, Rhenius's accomplishments fell far short of the standards set by Fabricius. Rhenius,

> before he could learn accurately the Tamil for at least ten years fondly persuaded himself that he was a perfect scholar in Tamil, . . . and changed quite another way the 1st Book of Moses, the Gospels, Epistles, the Common prayer and hymn Book. These he altered so materially that they are now neither Eleckanam [grammatical] nor common Tamil both dialects being mixed and spoiled. (*SS*, 1828)

The new revision was completed in a hurry, using a Tamil that Sastri thought was neither grammatically correct, nor commonly used everywhere (*PK*, 1825). He referred to the revisers as those who under the guise of friendship, had pretended to revise the Bible as an act of goodwill but instead had only spoilt and destroyed their entire Bible and prayers (*PK*, 1825). By referring to the revision project as Rhenius's "meddling" with Fabricius's "golden" version of the Tamil Bible, Sastri implied the linguistic superiority of the latter over any attempts at revision. Further, Sastri's attempt to prove the superiority of Fabricius's skill as a translator by focusing specifically on his knowledge of Tamil indicates the premium placed on the use of Tamil in the religious context.

The second claim that Sastri made was that while the "previous missionaries" took the help of the right Tamil scholars to translate the Bible, the "junior missionaries" were assisted by wrong scholars, that is, "heathen munshis" who were against the Bible. The critics of Fabricius alleged exactly the opposite: Vicuvaca Nadan accused the missionaries who translated previously of not having used appropriate teachers (sastris) but of having sought the help of those who had no knowledge of the Tamil castras. In answer, Sastri in *PK* quoted passages from Ziegenbalg's Preface to the Tamil Bible of 1717[4] to prove that the missionaries had made considerable efforts to learn Tamil and from the right sources: that they had learnt Tamil from Tamil books and palmleaf manuscripts and after they had studied the books and manners of the people of the country, had decided to translate the Bible into Tamil. Later in the pamphlet, however, he acknowledged that the early Tamil books printed by Protestant missionaries might not have been entirely accurate but that Fabricius's

Tamil was faultless. Sastri explained this by claiming that Ziegenbalg did not have adequate help but that as Christianity spread in Tranquebar and Madras "learning and wisdom" increased and many Tamil scholars arose (*PK*, 1825). What he seems to be implying is that by the time Fabricius began translating the Bible, the spread of Christianity and mission schools had produced Tamil scholars who were also Protestants and could therefore help in the process of Bible translation better than Hindu Tamil scholars. In *SS*, Sastri accused Rhenius of paying considerable sums to "the heathen moonshees who blasphemed Christ, and thus frustrated the endeavours of the ancient Missionaries through the heathen Moonshees" (*SS*, 1828). The present revisers rendered the work of the previous missionaries,

> detestable and inelegant, believing even the heathen Moonshees words, who jested with and imposed on them on account of their ignorance in Tamil, and filled them with words not only ungrammatical, unmeaning and unsystematical, but also irreligious, perverting the Word of God, and blasphemous, and made those books to be laughed at by all who hear them uttering them and mixing in them all the Cutchery [mixed] Tamil and Gentoo [Telugu] words. (*SS*, 1828)

Sastri further claimed that these heathen *munshis* deceived the Europeans with their eloquence and art; however, their skills had been used to write books that were "entirely corrupting," which made them unsuitable for the translation of the Bible (*SS*, 1828). Again in *PC*, he asserted that the present missionaries had placed the holy scriptures in the hands of "heathen" *munshis* who knew neither *parāparaṉ* (that is, the Protestant God) nor the missionaries. In the Tamil preface to *VP*, Sastri condemned the new missionaries for seeking assistance not from "God's people" that is, Protestant Tamils but from those who "worship images." In his English preface to *VP*, Sastri continued his attack of the Hindu Tamil scholars involved in Bible translation:

> The Heathen Poets, . . . ridiculing thro' their ignorance the most respectable translation of the late Rev. Mr. Fabricius, thought that they could write more elegantly, and mixed their worldly ideas with the Divine truth. And thus they have entirely corrupted the Holy Scriptures, put them in Cutchery and Telunga [=Telugu] Tamul and filled them with many words which are against religious language and the very principles of Grammar. (*VP*, 1820)

Sastri's criticism gained substance by the fact that there were Protestant Tamils who could have adequately fulfilled the role of Tamil scholar to aid the missionary translators. Sastri himself would have been quite suitable for the task and so would the Protestant Tamil poet H. A. Krishna Pillai (1827–1900). Both missionaries and Protestant Tamils acknowledged that Sastri and Krishna Pillai had excellent command of the Tamil language, including its high literary style, along with a good grasp of the basic tenets of Protestant Christianity. However, it is significant that Sastri was not invited to help in any of the Bible translation projects either at a formal or informal level. Although Krishna Pillai was appointed Tamil *munshi* to assist in revising the Tamil translation of the Bible in 1858 (which led to the *Union Version* of 1871), this appointment lasted only for three weeks and he noted later that not a

day's work was done during this time.[5] In 1861, however, Krishna Pillai's brother Muttaiya Pillai, competed for the position of "Tamil Referee" for the Bible translation committee and was acknowledged in the committee's report as a "native referee" who had thorough knowledge of Tamil and practical experience in the work of translation (*Revision*, 1869: 13).[6]

The difference in positions between Sastri and Vicuvaca Nadan was that Sastri emphasized the importance of assistance from Protestant Tamil scholars whereas Vicuvaca Nadan stressed Tamil scholarship above the religious persuasion of the assisting scholars. Sastri's bias in favor of Protestant scholars of Tamil can be explained by his assumption that the primary target readership of the Tamil Bible was Protestant Tamils. For him, only Protestants could interpret and translate the Bible accurately for other Protestants. It is clear from Sastri's accusations that he viewed non-Protestant Tamil scholars as opponents to Protestant Tamils, who would take advantage of the missionaries' lack of Tamil scholarship to corrupt language use in the Tamil Bible. However, it was not only Hindu scholars he saw as adversaries since he often bracketed the Catholics (usually referred to as "Papists" by Sastri) with the "heathen moonshees": in a long diatribe against the barbarous use of Tamil in the revisions he referred to "the help of heathen moonshees and Papists who are enemies to the Christian religion and quite ignorant of its Mysteries and thus frustrated the intention and labours of the Honorable Societies" (*SS*, 1828). Nonetheless, Sastri thought that the Catholic missionaries' attitude to language and translation was better than the present project. It is significant that although he thought the eloquent use of literary Tamil important in Bible translation, he distrusted the eloquence of Hindu and Catholic scholars as one that corrupted or distorted the Protestant Bible.

The third important opposition that Sastri set up was the use of "pure" Tamil versus what he called "cutchery" Tamil, a term he used to indicate a mixture of Telugu and Tamil, replete with colloquialisms, region specific words and the Tamil spoken by lower castes. For want of "mature knowledge of the Tamil language," Sastri maintained, the new missionaries "changed the translations of our invaluable Bible etc into Cutchery Tamil, Telingu Tamil and a comical and barbarous language" (*SS*, 1828). In *PK*, he contended that the mixing of high and low, old and new words did not make a work dear to the learned. He rhetorically questioned whether they (he presumed to speak for the entire Protestant Tamil community) could reject their "golden" version by Fabricius in favor of a version using a mixture of Tamil, Telugu and Cutchery Tamil, which was "hateful to their souls" (*PK*, 1825).

When Sastri analyzed the merits of one word over another, he opposed "*ilakkana col*," that is, grammatically correct words to "*valaka col*," that is, colloquial, "customary" or regional Tamil words. In *PK*, for instance, he picked out 46 words from the first chapter of Fabricius's Gospel of Matthew to point out that they were all literary words used according to grammatical rules. He pointed out that all the 46 were found in dictionaries and *nikantukal*,[7] and were neither colloquial, nor words of an "ugly, improper" nature, spoken by lower castes or hunting tribes of the forest and mountainous regions. Nor were they the blabbering of foreigners who could not speak the language. The new revisions, according to Sastri, used colloquial Tamil, and destroyed the meaning, sweetness, and grammar of the original texts found in the previous translations. Likewise, in *PC*, Sastri claimed that the new revisions had

made the earlier translations defective (*palutu*, the Tamil word used also means rotten, ruin, a lie) and had completely spoilt them. It is important to mention at this point that Sastri compared the use of terms in the Tamil Bible with Catholic, Hindu and Muslim usage. For instance, he objected to the change from *nāmam* (name) to *tiru nāmam* (holy name) in the Lord's Prayer because the latter was used to refer to the mark worn by Vaiśnavites on their foreheads. It is significant that in his criticism of the older translations, Vicuvaca Nadan had made the same accusation against previous translators: they had used ungrammatical Tamil according to him, which was being corrected by the present revisers.

However, the one point both Sastri and Vicuvaca Nadan seem agreed upon was that a recognizably different kind of language use had developed among Protestant Tamils as a result of missionary translations and writings: the "missionary Tamil." In his letter, Vicuvaca Nadan claimed that the present missionaries were revising the earlier translations in order to correct the peculiarities of "missionary Tamil." Sastri, while acknowledging that the term had been used to refer to the Tamil used in the existing translations of the Bible, attributed it to the jealous attempts by "heathens," Catholics, and "other" people to defile the Protestant scriptures. He pointed out that because the "white man" had brought their religion to them, they were despised as those who followed the "white man's religion" or the "padre's (missionary) religion." It is significant that Sastri only expressed disdain at such name-calling but did not claim that such a difference in language use did not exist. He categorically stated in *PK* that Protestant Tamils would not forsake the true Veda (that is, the Bible) only because they were unable to bear the ridicule of its being termed the white man's Veda. He was thereby claiming status for Protestant Christianity in spite of admitting irregularities in the use of the Tamil language.

Sastri's conclusions as to which translation was acceptable were a result of using the method of comparison, by judging a translation's effect on its readers, and by making claims on behalf of custom and tradition. First, his method of comparing translations was in keeping with the usual standards his contemporary western scholars used. Like them, he analyzed which of the translations "slipped" from the meaning intended in the original. He pointed out that Fabricius had translated keeping the "sense" of the original in mind rather than translating literally. In his opinion, the revisers were unable to achieve the same. Sastri arrived at this conclusion by using the analytic tool of comparing several translated versions since none of the Protestant Tamils knew the original languages to study the difference between the original and the Tamil translation. He compared versions at two levels: first, he juxtaposed several Tamil translations to check whether the "sense" in all of them remained the same; and second, he compared the Tamil translations with the English version to see if there were any discrepancies between the two. For instance, in *PK* he pointed out that though the Tamil Gospels of Tranquebar (1758), Colombo (1754) and Madras (1771)[8] were translated by different missionaries at different times and places, there were differences only in the use of words but not in the sense they conveyed. This proof, according to him, made Protestant Tamils witness to the fact that the previous missionaries had translated without deviating from the sense of the original. While providing close textual analysis to support his points, he often highlighted discrepancies between the English and the Tamil revision. Analyzing the differences in the "Lord's Prayer" in the old and new Tamil versions in the second

half of *PK*, he compared the latest revision with not only previous Tamil Protestant and Catholic versions from Tamilnadu and Ceylon, but also pointed out that the Prayer as translated in the English, German, Portuguese, and Dutch versions matched the older Tamil translations but not the new. Significantly, he brought up the question of the validity of the English "Authorized Version" by suggesting that the revisers were actually jeopardizing its authority by not translating the Tamil version according to it. Further, by asking whether the English (he included the government, the Bible Society and other persons of importance) would have been happy to accept such tampering with *their* "Lord's Prayer," Sastri put himself and Protestant Tamils on a par with the English in making choices over the language and translation of religion for their community. Ironically, the missionaries who increasingly gave the English version an almost equivalent status to the original biblical texts found themselves judged by the same standards.

Another route by which he approached the problem of evaluation was by referring to a target readership. Unlike the missionaries who rather futilely attempted to balance the needs of both Christian and non-Christian audiences through a single translation, Sastri concentrated on the needs of the various sections of the Protestant Tamil community alone. In fact, he dismissed the judgment of "heathen" readers who would not know the difference between previous and present translations or good and bad texts, thus rendering their opinion of no account for evaluation. On the other hand, those brought up within a Protestant tradition, according to Sastri, would be able to recognize the superiority of one text over the other (*PK*, 1825). He seems to argue for a Protestant Bible exclusively for Protestant Tamils. While taking Protestant Tamil readership into account he covered several angles: the social position of the reader within Tamil caste hierarchy; the extent of literacy or lack of it; and dominant patterns of custom and tradition within the Protestant Tamil community.

Although Sastri did not name the high castes to which some Protestant Tamils belonged, it is clear that he positioned himself and his fellow-petitioners with them. He named some of the low-caste groups (*pallar, pariar, shānār, cakkiliyar*) as well as some hunting tribes who were part of the Protestant Tamil community. Sastri's understanding of the role and importance of the caste position of the Protestant Tamil readers was ambiguous and at times even contradictory. On the one hand, he thought that the Bible had to be translated into a Tamil equally accessible to Protestant Tamils of all castes. He claimed that this was what Fabricius had achieved (but was lacking in the recent revisions). Fabricius had, according to Sastri, used a level of Tamil that satisfied the literate high castes as well as the semi-literate low castes. It is difficult, however, to see how a version that used the high Tamil (generally unfamiliar to the lower castes) could possibly be accessible to them. His conviction that the non-literary, lower forms of Tamil spoken by lower castes should be kept out of the Tamil Bible stemmed from a desire to check censure from rival religious groups. At the same time, at several points in his pamphlets, he asserted that those belonging to the lower castes were illiterate and therefore unable to understand or judge the merits of Tamil texts for themselves. Sastri dismissed Vicuvaca Nadan's claims that the revisions had been given not only to those with sense (that is, the literate) but those without sense (the illiterate), and thus spread Christianity further.

Sastri's attack on a translation because it was inaccessible to lower castes does not stand since he thought them incapable of critical analysis in any case. What Sastri and his fellow-protestors resented most was that the missionaries were forcing a revision on them. Worse still, the missionaries were using the mission schools to propagate the unwelcome revisions among their youth:

> And when they found that these their unjust translations were not like by any one, they not only introduced them into all the Schools and forcibly made it a rule that these books alone should be learned, but also have thus brought it about, that none of the true and well translated religious books are to be had among the poor Tamil Christians. (*SS*, 1828)

As mentioned earlier, the third important element in Sastri's discussion of the reader's expectation was the part played by custom and tradition. In his textual analyses of passages in both *PK* and *PC*, Sastri pointed out that various terms introduced by the revisers were not customarily in use in all Tamil regions. Or, he pointed out that the customary understanding of a certain term could be in conflict with its dictionary meaning: he claimed that *kerpavati* used by Fabricius was the customary term used to refer to a pregnant woman; *karpavati*, used in the revision instead was a colloquial reference to *ganja* (Indian hemp) and in some places used to refer to women who had become sexually familiar with ascetics. Thus, when applied to the Virgin Mary's conception through the Holy Spirit it became a term of insult rather than respect. It is questionable, however, whether Fabricius was aware of this colloquial usage and deliberately favored one spelling over the other.

Sastri also used the argument of "custom" for translations that Protestant Tamils were accustomed to. The earlier translations had become accepted and customary versions for the present generation of Protestant Tamils. In *SS*, Sastri defended the earlier translations: "These books were accepted by all the congregations and its Missionaries with the greatest esteem and are read and used by us, our fathers and our children" (*SS*, 1828). Further, Sastri saw the revision of Fabricius's version, which had been used in all the churches for approximately 80 years, as an act of dishonoring the previous translators (*PK*, 1825). Fabricius's had been a single, uniform version accepted by all the Tamil churches for several years. In his opinion, the revisers were

> like a man who destroyed a stone house and built a Cottage [,] they hurted [sic] and destroyed all their [the previous translator's] works, which are so highly esteemed by all the Congregations . . . under the pretence that they would revise the Bible . . . which had been perfectly done and translated by the former Missionaries. (*SS*, 1828)

Sastri feared that the substandard Tamil used by the revisers would spread among Protestant Tamils through the mission schools. Significantly, he connected the erasure of Fabricius's Tamil with the erasure of the missionaries from the collective memory of the community:

> by introducing them, forcibly in the Congregations and Schools making the children from their infancy to practise this new Tamil, they trusted their intention would be accomplished within 20 years, and took away therefore, the precious translations of the

> ancient Missionaries from the use of all schools, and made them not only to forget them entirely, but endeavoured to eradicate the remembrance of the former Missionaries from our minds and that of our children. (*SS*, 1828)

Thus, one of Sastri's concerns was that a tradition established for more than a hundred years was being threatened. Though his emphasis here was on the loss of a textual tradition, elsewhere he connected this with the loss of other church traditions and rituals, which had been established by the Lutheran missionaries and which were now being changed by Anglican missionaries. This connection is apparent when in *SS* he claimed:

> I venture to say that as in the time of old when the wickedness increased amongst the people, and they began to build the tower of Babel, God did confound their languages, so when the Christians were ungrateful for the kindness and benefactions of their late Missionaries, God did send the Junior Missionaries as a whip for us to upset all our religious books, divine songs, the gladness of the holy festivals of the Lord, and the reasonable pleasure, suitable to enjoy at Marriages, Baptisms and other joyful days of the Congregation and abolish the urbanity of the Country which is the rank of Caste. (*SS*, 1828)

The repeated opposition of past and present, previous and recent in the arguments of the pamphlets under discussion highlight how the experiments and at times tentative strategies employed by previous missionaries were now being conferred a quasi-sacred status, as part of a received tradition, by some dominant groups amongst Protestant Tamils.

By the same token, any competing translation that threatened the special place a previous biblical version had in the community also threatened the social standing of the entire community. Sastri's many references to how other religious groups, both Christian and non-Christian, would react to the revised versions of the Tamil Bible reveal an anxiety about the status of the Protestant Tamil community. For instance, he feared that because Rhenius had distributed his revisions, "every where, these two kind of books being put in use for the Congregation and schools gives room to the Unitarians and Papists to laugh, and to alledge [sic] that our Religion [. . .] differs one from another, and caused an inexpressible confusion in religion among [. . .] the people" (*SS*, 1828). This meant that the prestige of the Protestant Tamil community was brought into question. In *PK* he warned that Protestant Tamils should be aware that "Papist scholars could hardly refrain from ridiculing them when they see books translated in several different ways" (*PK*, 1825). When he objected to the use of terms that he thought questioned the human incarnation of Christ in *PC*, he showed concern about Catholic accusations that the Protestants were denying the divine nature of Christ. Thus, on the one hand, Hindu scholars could not be trusted to provide accurate translations for biblical passages, perhaps even deliberately mis-translating in order to undermine the authority of the Bible. On the other hand, he was conscious of the rival gaze of the Catholics waiting to denounce Protestant methods as crude and ineffective. Revising a well-established and satisfactory Tamil translation provided the perfect occasion in Sastri's eyes for either rival religious party to attack or humiliate Protestant Tamils.

The rationale behind the protest launched by Sastri and other Lutheran Evangelical Tamils against the revision of Fabricius's version is clearer when placed within the political and cultural context of late-eighteenth and early -nineteenth-century Tanjore. Tanjore was ruled in succession by non-Tamil linguistic and cultural dynasties, that is, the Telugu Nayaks, the Marathas, and then the British and, thus, was in a period of transition. The influences brought in by them, however, were interacting with the Tamil religious and literary discourses that went back to an earlier period. Sastri and his contemporaries were highly conscious of the kind of Tamil in use in the Bible at a time when there were linguistic influences from Telugu and Marathi (besides Sanskrit) on Tamil. Sastri made a claim for Fabricius's use of a "pure" Tamil by pointing out that it was the reviser, Rhenius, who was using a Tamil mixed with gentoo (i.e. Telugu) and Marathi words. According to him, Rhenius's improper use of Tamil corrupted both the Protestant religion and the Tamil language. In this context, he could posit the more Sanskrit-based "missionary Tamil" of Fabricius as "pure" Tamil against the "cutchery" Tamil of Rhenius. For Sastri, "pure" Tamil was one that included Sanskrit terms but not words from other regional languages (this definition of "pure" Tamil was to change in the twentieth century where the presence of Sanskrit terminology made Tamil "impure"). Sastri, by arguing that Fabricius's version used a pure Tamil and was thus a "golden Version," could overcome criticism from rival religious detractors such as Catholics and Hindus. Most importantly, Sastri and his fellow Lutheran Evangelicals' insistence on the importance of using "pure" Tamil for their scriptures was an avenue by which they could lay claims to a better status for their religious community.

Whose Tamil and Whose Traditions?

Missionary sources on the subject of Tamil Bible translation, until the end of the nineteenth century, conveyed an impression largely of a missionary coalition of translators producing a finished piece of translation, handed over to a passive but grateful Protestant Tamil readership. However, sources outside Bible Society and missionary records[9] suggest that Protestant Tamils responded to the translated Bible in various ways, both implicit and explicit. These responses were not, however, in any way homogeneous or unified either in support of or against a particular translation; neither were the responses always a coherent and deliberate resistance to the authority and culture of the missionary agency. An important point of conflict has been Protestant Tamil terminology and the use of the appropriate register of Tamil language. This paper analyzed how religious and social conflicts as well as denominational rivalry between the different mission societies in the Tamil area, defined Protestant Tamil response to the question of terminology: that is, Protestant Tamils have participated as much in the south-Indian context of inter-religious antagonism expressed through disagreements over language use as responded to the Protestant missionary agenda for setting up differences between Protestant Christianity and other belief systems. The skill revealed by Protestant Tamils to assimilate Protestant Christianity on their own terms is a counter-assimilative move to that of Protestant missionaries.

In contrast, in the second half of the nineteenth century, other caste groups in the Protestant Tamil community colluded with the missionary project and accepted the

revised Tamil Bible because it was in their interest to do so. Upwardly mobile low-caste groups, such as the *Nadars*, who had converted in large numbers to the Protestant faith in the second half of the nineteenth century, found that the missionary program enabled them to ascend the social ladder through literacy, education, and government jobs. In contrast to the Protestants belonging to the higher-caste *Vellalas* who were reluctant to give up cultural practices that signaled their high status in Tamil society, these low-caste groups assimilated Protestant missionary interpretations of language and cultural practices. The missionary project to translate Protestant Christianity and the Bible into Tamil "high" culture while simultaneously providing a distinct religious and social identity offered lower-caste groups the opportunity to create an alternative social identity under the banner of a Protestant Tamil identity. These groups enthusiastically accepted the new translation of the mid-nineteenth century and went on to locate their Protestant identity in the highly Sanskritized "Protestant Tamil" of the *Union Version*. For these castes, the *Union Version* has acquired besides the religious, a symbolic power, and functions in the present to mark boundaries of identity and otherness. The technical terminology of the *Union Version*, which helped to shape the sacred areas of Protestant Tamil lives, had gradually come to be understood as the correct way to speak about the church and its doctrines. "Protestant Tamil" had become the only appropriate language for Protestant worship and expression of devotion.

The contradictory responses from two sections of the nineteenth-century Protestant Tamil community point to the extra-linguistic factors, socio-political and cultural, in South India that affected the formation of Protestant Tamil identity. Where one group of Protestant Tamils in the early nineteenth century resisted the Protestant mission's attempted to direct Protestant identity in a particular direction through institutional efforts at translating the Bible, another section of Protestant Tamils colluded with the missionary agenda. In both instances, the caste identity of each group played an important part in Protestant Tamil response. However, the important point is that these socio-political conflicts become visible most in the context of Bible translation that raises questions of appropriate and representative language use.

Further, the relatively short history of the Protestant Tamil community (as compared to the other religious traditions in Tamil society) has resulted in a need to establish a "past" for the community. Located in a culture of long and well-established religious traditions, one of the projects of Protestant Tamils has been to establish an unbroken thread of tradition and continuity from the early eighteenth century. The Tamil Bible could function as one such link with the past if there was only one standard version. Further, it confirmed their status as a religious community if they were seen not to have internal squabbles over their central sacred text: they often showed awareness of the derisive gaze of rival religious groups (especially Hindu and Catholic Tamil communities), none of whom had the similar problem of possessing multiple translations that were meant to indicate one sacred text. While Protestant missionaries also labored to arrive at one translation that could be established as a standard version to represent the Protestant Tamil community, their motive was different. For Protestant missionaries, one version of the Tamil Bible signified a unified Protestant Tamil community separated on a horizontal plane from the other religious communities in Tamil society but united vertically to the universal church. Protestant Tamils, however, supported the establishment of one

version because it provided them a vertical link with their past, so that it was possible to speak of a Protestant Tamil tradition. However, the politics of who decides which tradition is to be followed has also depended on caste movement within the Protestant Tamil community.

If the history of Protestant translations in Tamil society is viewed from the top down, from missionary records and the official missionary position, then the assimilation of Protestant Christianity into Tamil culture appears to participate in other hegemonic strategies of colonial power that sought to impose a rigid definition of how religious communities ought to relate with each other. However, the history of Protestant Bibles in Tamil translations, when viewed from the standpoint of the various sections of Protestant Tamils, indicates that the Protestant Tamils have adopted the translated Bible and its language on their own terms. Thus, in the colonial context, the hegemonic agenda of a translation project may be fulfilled not because of passive, complicit, consenting audiences, but because the audience saw the radical possibilities offered by the project to fight other hegemonic institutions and practices within their own social structures.

NOTES

1 This letter is quoted verbatim in Tamil in the unpublished pamphlet "Noise of the New Correction" (Tamil title, "pudutirutalin kūkural"), written by Vedanayaka Sastri and members of the Tanjore Evangelical Church in 1825. It is catalogued as VPC-VNS 27 in the United Theological College Archives, Bangalore.
2 Vedanayaka Sastri, *Sādipedaga Sambaveney*, unpublished manuscript in the United Theological College Archives, Bangalore, catalogued as VPC-VNS 42 (1828).
3 An ancient Tamil grammar.
4 The MSS wrongly gives the date 1817 as the year when Ziegenbalg's translation of the Bible was printed.
5 Hudson concludes that the position was nothing more than a title and a salary, and a way for some CMS and SPG missionaries to fulfill a responsibility they had assumed on behalf of a new convert (Hudson 1970: 269, 271).
6 *Revision of the Tamil Bible: Report of the Proceedings of the Delegates Appointed for the Revision of the Tamil Bible* (Madras, April 27, 1869).
7 Tamil term for metrical glossaries or thesauruses in verse.
8 These are dates provided by Sastri and are not necessarily the date of first publication of each translation.
9 For instance, the unpublished manuscripts of Vedanayaka Sastri on the revision of the Tamil Bible now located in the archives of the United Theological College, Bangalore.

REFERENCES

Unpublished sources (United Theological College, Bangalore)

Vedanayaka Sastri (1796). *Njānakumme*. Paper manuscript [VPC-VNS 48].
——(1810). *Sebamawley*. (Garland of prayers) Tanjore. [VPC-VNS 33].
——(1820). *Vētaviyātciyāpattiram*. [VPC-VNS 44].

——(1825). *Pututtiruttaln kūkural.* (Noise of the New Correction). [VPC-VNS 27].
——(1828). *Sādipēdaga sambāveney* (Dialogue on the Distinction of Caste). [VPC-VNS 42].
——(1829). *Pandegey Perasdābam* (Response to the Revised Order of the Lord's Supper). Madras: CMS (1825). [VPC-VNS 63].
——(N.d.). Dedication and Preface. *Case of the Caste Argument: Complaint of the Tamil Christians.* By Sastri. [VPC-VNS 34].
——(N.d.). *Pututtiruttalin cōtanai.* (The Tribulation of the Revision). [VPC-VNS 36].
——(N.d.). *Jāti-tiruttalin payittiyam* (The Foolishness of Amending Caste). Department of Oriental Printed Books and Manuscripts, catalogued as OR.11,742. London: British Library.

Printed sources

Bower, H. (1879–84). "Fifty-ninth Annual Report." *Annual Report of the Madras Auxiliary Bible Society.*
Devy, Ganesh (1999). "Translation and literary history – an Indian view," in Susan Bassnett and Harish Trivedi (eds), *Post-colonial Translation: Theory and Practice.* London: Routledge.
Dharwadker, Vinay (1999). "A.K. Ramanujan's theory and practice of translation," in Susan Bassnett and Harish Trivedi (eds), *Post-colonial Translation: Theory and Practice.* London: Routledge.
Niranjana, Tejaswani (1992). *Sitting Translation: History, Post-structuralism and the Colonial Context.* Berkeley: University of California Press.
Report (1811). *Reports of the British and Foreign Bible Society with Extracts of Correspondence.* London: British and Foreign Bible Society.
Report (1863). *Report of the Proceedings of the Delegates for the Revision of the Tamil New Testament at their Final Meeting, held on the Pulney Hills*, June–August.
Revision (1869). *Revision of the Tamil Bible: Report of the Proceedings of the Delegates Appointed for the Revision of the Tamil Bible.* Madras, April 27.
Rhenius, J. (1841). *Memoir of the Rev. C. T. E. Rhenius: comprising extracts from his journal and correspondence, with details of missionary proceedings in south India/by his son [i.e. Johann Rhenius].* London: James Nisbet & Co.
Thiong'o, Ng-ug-i wa (1986). *Decolonising the Mind: the Politics of Language in African Literature.* London: James Currey.
Zemka, Sue (1991). "The Holy Book of Empire: Translations of the British and Foreign Bible Society," in Jonathan Arac and Harriet Ritvo (eds), *Macropolitics of Nineteenth Century Literature: Nationalism, Exoticism, Imperialism.* Philedelphia: University of Pennsylvania Press.

19

Canonization and Marginalization: Mary of Magdala

Karen L. King

Mary of Magdala is best known in popular Western imagery and tradition as a repentant prostitute,[1] as the adulteress rescued by Jesus from men trying to stone her,[2] and as the woman sinner whose tears of repentance washed Jesus' feet in preparation for his burial.[3] Yet none of this is historically accurate. Nothing in the New Testament or early Christian literature provides a shred of evidence to support this portrait.

Historically Mary was a Jewish woman who followed Jesus of Nazareth. She came from the town of Magdala, located on the west shore of the Sea of Galilee, just north of the city of Tiberias. Apparently of independent means, she accompanied him during his ministry and supported him out of her own resources.[4] The New Testament Gospels[5] and other early Christian literature consistently portray Mary as a prominent disciple of Jesus.[6]

In the Gospel stories, she is said to have been present at the crucifixion[7] and to have been a witness to the resurrection.[8] Indeed, she is portrayed as the first or among the first privileged to see and speak with the risen Lord.[9] In the Gospel of John, the risen Jesus gives her special teaching and commissions her as an apostle to the apostles to bring them the good news.[10] The Gospel of Mary, an early second-century text discovered at the end of the nineteenth century in Egypt, also affirms that Mary received special teaching from Jesus and functioned as a leader among the disciples after the resurrection. The combined evidence strongly suggests that Mary was a visionary and leader in the Christian movement after Jesus' death.

How are we to understand and account for these different portraits, for the simultaneous *canonization* of Mary as a prominent disciple and her *marginalization* as a repentant prostitute?

The simplest answer is that the problem arose due to misguided exegesis. Starting in the fourth century, Christian theologians in the Latin West began confusing Mary

First published in *Concilium*, 3 (1998): 28–36.

of Magdala with Mary of Bethany.[11] They conflated the account of John 12.1–8, in which Mary of Bethany anoints Jesus in preparation for his burial, with the account of the unnamed sinner woman in Luke 7.36–50 who washed Jesus' feet with her tears and anointed them. From there it was an easy step to identify Mary of Magdala with the unnamed adulteress in John 8.1–11. Mary the disciple had become Mary the whore. We can perhaps see this confusion as simply an error – there are after all a lot of Marys to keep straight: Mary of Magdala, Mary of Bethany, Mary the mother of Jesus, Mary the wife of Clopas (Jesus' aunt), Mary the mother of James the younger and Joses (or Joseph), and of course the "other" Mary. But the simplicity of this answer is deceptive. The Eastern Orthodox churches after all never made this mistake. Even in the West, the connections were not made until relatively late. The church fathers of the early centuries knew nothing of Mary as a prostitute; they mentioned her primarily as an important witness to the resurrection. They are concerned, of course, to counter any hint that Jesus' command to Mary not to touch him (John 20.17) might imply that the resurrection was not physical, but no criticism is directed at Mary. Indeed Tertullian praised Mary because she approached Jesus to touch him "out of love, not from curiosity, nor with Thomas' incredulity".[12] The reason for the prohibition was simply that it was too early for touching; the resurrection had to be completed by Jesus' ascent.[13]

By the sixth century, however, another interpretation had become prevalent, exemplified in a sermon by Pope Gregory the Great in which he not only identified Mary of Magdala with the sinner women of Luke and John, but also drew the moral conclusion that would dominate the imagination of the West:

> She whom Luke calls the sinful woman, whom John calls Mary, we believe to be the Mary from whom seven devils were ejected according to Mark. And what did these seven devils signify, if not all the vices? . . . It is clear, brothers, that the woman previously used the unguent to perfume her flesh in forbidden acts. What she therefore displayed more scandalously, she was now offering to God in a more praiseworthy manner. She had coveted with earthly eyes, but now through penitence these are consumed with tears. She displayed her hair to set off her face, but now her hair dries her tears. She had spoken proud things with her mouth, but in kissing the Lord's feet, she now planted her mouth on the Redeemer's feet. For every delight, therefore, she had had in herself, she now immolated herself. She turned the mass of her crimes to virtues, in order to serve God entirely in penance, for as much as she had wrongly held God in contempt.[14]

Mary lost all semblance of the devoted disciple and visionary. She became a model for women to immolate themselves for their crimes of sexuality, vanity, and bold speech. Simple error is not sufficient to account for this unsavoury and totally fantastic portrait.

Certainly this invention is part and parcel of typical Western patriarchal constructions of gender roles, which all too often define women almost solely according to heterosexual roles in relation to men. As the Christian model of female sexuality redeemed, Mary took her place with two other prominent figures: the temptress Eve and the virgin mother Mary. Among them, they modeled the roles possible for women in the patriarchal script. But why choose Mary for the role of the repentant sinner? The serious effort necessary to contrive and sustain these strained exegetical

connections certainly show that it was not a casual exercise. Did they go to all this trouble simply because they wanted to fill the role with a well-known actor?

Let me suggest another possibility. Patriarchal exegetes invented this role for Mary of Magdala because they wanted to discredit the theology associated with her name and to undermine her significance as a model for the legitimacy of women's leadership. In short, the portrait of the repentant sinner was invented to counter an earlier and very powerful portrait of Mary as a visionary prophet, exemplary disciple, and apostolic leader.

That such a portrait of Mary existed as early as the second century is shown in a variety of works, most of which were discovered in Egypt within the last century.[15] Though it would be improper to construct a composite portrait of Mary from such varied materials,[16] these sources do agree in giving Mary a role, often a prominent role, among the disciples.[17] For example, in the Dialogue of the Savior, a second-century dialogue between the Lord and his disciples, Mary responds with particular insight to certain issues. The Lord himself exclaims at her response to a question: "You make clear the abundance of the revealer!"[18] At another point, the narrator breaks in to explain: "She uttered this as a woman who had understood completely."[19] Mary is clearly to be numbered among the disciples who fully comprehended the Lord's teaching.[20] In the canonical Gospel tradition, it is not entirely clear whether women are included among those who are commissioned to go forth and preach the gospel, though the account in Acts clearly indicates that women received the Spirit at Pentecost.[21] In contrast, the Sophia of Jesus Christ, a second-century revelation discourse given by Jesus to his disciples, clearly states that Jesus commissioned women as well as men to preach the gospel. Mary is included by name[22] among those special disciples to whom Jesus entrusted his most elevated teaching, and she takes a role in preaching the gospel.[23] The Gospel of Philip, a second-century Valentinian compilation, mentions Mary as one of the three Marys "who always walked with the Lord," and she is called his "companion."[24] What this designation means becomes clear later in the text when it is stated that the Lord loved her more than all the disciples and he used to kiss her often.[25] Kissing symbolizes the reception of spiritual teaching, as Jesus points out: "[And had] the word gone out from that place it would be nourished from the mouth and it would become perfect. For it is by a kiss that the perfect conceive and give birth. For this reason we also kiss one another. We receive conception from the grace which is in one another."[26] When the other disciples object to the apparent favoritism Jesus shows Mary, Jesus tells them that they should seek instead to be loved as she is, that is, they should seek the spiritual perfection she has achieved.

The theme of Jesus' special regard for Mary appears with special emphasis in the Gospel of Mary.[27] Here after the Savior's departure, Mary steps into his place, comforting the grieving disciples and encouraging them and turning their hearts towards a discussion of the Savior's words. The work also tells of a special revelation which the Savior had given to Mary in a vision containing advanced teaching about the nature of visionary experience and the journey of the soul after death. At Peter's request, she passes on this teaching to the other disciples. The Gospel of Mary exemplifies Mary's role as apostle to the apostles by portraying her as a prophet, teacher, and support for the other disciples.

The Gospel of Mary illustrates Mary's leadership by contrasting her strength of character and spiritual maturity with the fear, ignorance, and jealousy of other disciples. She alone had maintained her composure at the Savior's departure while the other disciples were weeping and fearing for their lives should they follow the Savior's command and go out and preach the gospel. In her vision, the Savior praises her for "not wavering" at the sight of him. While the other disciples exhibit jealousy and contention over the fact that the Savior loved her more than them, Mary only demonstrates care toward them, taking up her role of teacher and leader only in response to their need. The Gospel of Mary illustrates the characteristics of spiritual virtue in Mary's calm, in her unwavering faith, her care for the other disciples, her fearlessness in the face of possible persecution, and her advanced spiritual comprehension of Jesus' teachings. In this way, the Gospel of Mary holds up Mary as a model for Christian leadership based on spiritual maturity and prophetic insight. It is because she has achieved spiritual maturity that she is able to teach and care for the others.

Moreover, the Gospel of Mary addresses the topic of women's leadership directly by narrating a story about a controversy among the disciples over Mary's exercise of leadership. In the story, when she finishes teaching the other disciples about her revelation, Andrew and Peter challenge her. Andrew suggests that her teachings are "strange," but Peter goes further and questions whether the Savior could really have preferred a woman to them. Their complaints show that they have not really comprehended the Savior's teaching. Peter's remark is soundly condemned by Levi, who assures Peter that indeed the Savior did love her more than them, and for good reason. Peter's position is shown up for what it is: an ignorant jealousy which makes it impossible for Peter to see past the distinctions of the flesh to the spiritual insight of Mary's teaching. He is so focused on his loss of prestige at being instructed by a woman that he fails to learn from her teaching. The Gospel of Mary thus presents the clearest argument for the legitimacy of women's authority and leadership in early Christianity. By insisting that authority should be based on spiritual maturity rather than on sex/gender distinctions,[28] the Gospel of Mary opens up the possibility of an ungendered space in which both women and men could exercise legitimate leadership aimed at teaching, preaching, and exercising care for others. It also carefully ties spiritual development to a sharp critique of unjust domination, suggesting an integral connection between the politics of liberation and spirituality.

Controversy between Mary and other male disciples, especially Peter, appears in a number of other works as well,[29] illustrating that Mary was a figure around whom debates were waged over a number of issues, including the importance of visionary experience, the legitimacy of women's leadership, and the meaning of Jesus' teaching. The fact that a Gospel was written in her name and that she appears so prominently in these early writings shows that, like Peter and Paul, she was a figure to whom apostolic appeal was made. Mary of Magdala was therefore a much more important figure in the early church than the canonical portrait of the New Testament allows.

This information should lead us to approach the canonical texts afresh with a hermeneutics of suspicion.[30] For example, in the face of these powerful traditions about Mary, her absence from the Acts of the Apostles[31] takes on a different appearance. Rather than reading the silence in Acts as evidence that Mary was not

important to the early church, it is possible to ask if mention of her was omitted on purpose, and to what purpose. It is especially ironic that Mary is not named in the scene where Peter calls for a replacement for Judas to be chosen as "a witness to the resurrection." Although the writer of Acts surely understands women to have been present in the group of 120 persons Peter addresses,[32] Peter's speech makes it clear that only men will be considered.[33] Mary's explicit absence from the text is not oversight but strategic to the exclusion of women from positions of apostolic leadership. Because early Christian theology supporting women's leadership was linked with the name of Mary of Magdala, excluding Mary also operated to oppose the theologies[34] circulating in her name.

The Gospel of Mary[35] gives us a good idea of what at least one of those theologies may have looked like.[36] It constructed Christian identity apart from social gender roles, sex, and childbearing. It argued that direct access to God was possible for all through the Spirit. Leadership was exercised by those who are more spiritually advanced by giving freely to all without claim to a fixed hierarchical ordering of power. Jesus was understood as a teacher and mediator of wisdom, not as a judge or ruler, and theological reflection centered on the risen Christ, not on suffering as atonement for sin. Excluding the Gospel of Mary and marginalizing the figure of Mary of Magdala worked to erase an important source for reconstructing early Christian women's theologizing and for advocating the legitimacy of women's leadership.

The "revision" of Mary's history from apostle and prophet to repentant prostitute functioned on several fronts: it put Mary "safely" into the confines of patriarchal definitions of women, it undermined appeals to her to support women's leadership, and it undermined the theology associated with her name. So while the canonization of Mary gave her a positive role as a disciple of Jesus and witness to the resurrection, it was a role in line with the needs and requirements of patriarchal theology and one which stopped far short of portraying her as an important leader in formative Christianity. The later conflation of her with the sinner woman in Luke and the adulteress in John fashioned a character even more pliable to patriarchal purposes, and further countered the powerful tradition of her as a visionary prophet and apostle. Yet at the same time, even the limited portrait of Mary in the New Testament has been a resource for women in their attempts to legitimate their practices of leadership.

Reconstructing a more accurate historical portrait of Mary of Magdala is not merely a matter of correcting the errors of Western canonical exegesis; it requires including all the extant source materials about her for consideration. All the sources, canonical and non-canonical, need to be read through the lenses of a feminist hermeneutics of suspicion which recognizes the politics of historicizing narratives or appeals to apostolic authority.

It should now be clear, too, that doing justice to the historical Mary of Magdala will require problematizing the canon as a starting point for both historical reconstruction and theological reflection. The portrait of Mary in the New Testament as a prominent disciple of Jesus and an important witness to the resurrection, although a positive portrait, is nonetheless a selective one. Mary of Magdala and women in general were not marginal actors in the formation of Christianity; their marginality was produced in part by the process of canonization as part and parcel of the

theological development of "orthodoxy" which condemned every early Christian theology that was supportive of women's leadership as heresy. Canon and "orthodoxy" were devised in part to exclude women from positions of leadership and authority. They were not of course entirely successful. The invention of Mary as a prostitute has not kept women from appealing to her to legitimate their public preaching and teaching throughout the centuries. But insofar as it was successful, the cost has been high. A fuller and more accurate historical portrait of Mary of Magdala is one contribution toward rectifying that loss by providing an important resource for critical theological reflection and praxis.

NOTES

1 See the study of traditions about Mary of Magdala by Susan Haskins, *Mary Magdalen: Myth and Metaphor* (New York, 1993).
2 See John 8.1–11.
3 See Luke 7.36–50 conflated with John 12.1–8.
4 See Luke 8.1–3.
5 For a recent study of Mary of Magdala in the New Testament literature, see Carla Ricci, *Mary Magdalene and Many Others. Women who Followed Jesus* (Minneapolis, 1994).
6 See Mark 15.40–1; Matt. 27.55–6; Luke 8.1–3; John 19.25; Gospel of Philip 59.6–9(?).
7 Mark 15.40–1; John 19.25; Mark 15.47 and Matt. 27.61 also place her at the entombment.
8 Mark 16.1–8; Matt. 28.1–7; Luke 24.1–10; John 20.1, 11–13; Gospel of Peter 12–13.
9 Matt. 28.9–10; John 20.14–18; Mark 16.9; *Epistula Apostolorum*.
10 John 20.17; cf. Mark 16.17 and Matt. 28.7.
11 For a fuller treatment of this process, see Haskins, *Mary Magdalen* (n. 1), 90–7.
12 *Against Praxeas*.
13 See for example, Origen, *Commentary on John* 6.37; 10.21.
14 Gregory, *Homily* 33. Quoted from Haskins, *Mary Magdalen* (n. 1), 96.
15 For an excellent extended treatment of these materials, see Anni Marjanen, *The Woman Jesus Loved. Mary Magdalene in the Nag Hammadi Library and Related Documents* (Nag Hammadi and Manichaean Studies XL, Leiden, 1996).
16 One of the strengths of Marjanen's analysis is the clear distinctions he makes among the various portraits of Mary. She is not always shown to be superior to the male disciples; nor do texts which give her a prominent role necessarily treat women or female symbolization in a positive light (see especially his conclusions, *The Woman Jesus Loved* [n. 15], 216–25).
17 See the discussion by Elisabeth Schüssler Fiorenza, *In Memory of Her. A Feminist Theological Reconstruction of Christian Origins* (New York and London, 1983), esp. 139, 304–7, 332–3.
18 *Dial. Sav.* 140.17–19. Text and translation in Stephen Emmel, *Nag Hammadi Codex III.5 The Dialogue of the Savior* (Nag Hammadi Studies XXVI, Leiden, 1984), 80–1.
19 *Dial. Sav.* 139.11–13. Text and translation in Emmel, 78–9.
20 See *Dial. Sav.* 142.11–13, Emmel, 84–5.
21 See Matt. 28.16–20, Mark 16.14–20, where Jesus commissions "the eleven"; the audience of Acts 1.8 is more ambiguous, saying only "the apostles he had chosen" (1.2), but the Spirit clearly descends on a large group that includes both men and women (2.14). John is the least clear, saying only "the disciples" (20.19–23).

22 See *Soph. Jes. Christ* III 98.10 (BG 90.1) and III 114.9 (BG 117.13). Text in *Nag Hammadi Codices III. 3–4 and VI.1 with Papyrus Berolinensis 8502, 3 and Oxyrhynchus Papyrus 1081. Eugnostos and The Sophia of Jesus Christ* (Nag Hammadi Studies XXVII, Leiden, 1991), 69, 169.

23 In *Soph. Jes. Christ* III 119.1–16 (BG 126.5–127.5), the Savior gives them authority as "Children of the Light" over all things, and the "disciples" go out to preach. My translation, text, ibid., 177–8. Parrot's translation "Sons of Light" is incorrect given the explicit presence of five women disciples (III 90, 17–18).

24 *Gos. Phil.* 59.6–11. Text and translation in Bentley Layton (ed.), *Nag Hammadi Codex 11.2–7* (Nag Hammadi Studies XX, Leiden, 1989), 158–9.

25 See *Gos. Phil.* 63.34–6.

26 *Gos. Phil.* 58.34–59.6. Text and translation in ibid., 156–7.

27 For a more detailed discussion of this work, see Karen L. King, "The Gospel of Mary Magdalene", in Elisabeth Schüssler Fiorenza (ed.), *Searching the Scriptures. Volume 2: A Feminist Commentary* (New York and London, 1994), 601–34.

28 Note, too, the correlative argument that knowing Jesus and receiving teaching from him are not in themselves sufficient. The *Gospel of Mary* takes to heart the many Gospel traditions which relate that the disciples around Jesus often did not understand him.

29 See *Gos. Thom.* I 14, *Gos. Phil.* 63.30–64.10; *Pistis Sophia* 11.71.2.

30 See Schüssler Fiorenza, *In Memory of Her* (n. 17), 3–95.

31 Mary of Magdala is not mentioned by name in the Acts of the Apostles, and seems to have disappeared from the scene, overshadowed especially by the male "Twelve" and Paul. We might infer that the reference to "the women" in Acts 1.14 includes Mary, but only Mary the mother of Jesus is named specifically.

32 See Acts 1.14.

33 Acts 1.21.

34 The use of the plural here is important, because an analysis of the texts in which Mary plays a major role shows a variety of theological positions (see Marjanen, *The Woman Jesus Loved* [n. 15]). The same is true, of course, for other apostolic figures as well. Peter, for example, is associated with theological positions supporting the physical resurrection of Jesus (for example, Gospel of John) and supporting a docetic christology (for example, the Apocalypse of Peter).

35 The Gospel of Mary clearly associates its theology with her not only by making her a central character, but also by ascribing the book to her.

36 I have suggested elsewhere that it is possible to identify certain elements that were common to early Christian women's theologizing (see "Prophetic Power and Women's Authority: The Case of the Gospel of Mary (Magdalene)", in Beverly Kienzie and Pamela Walker (eds), *Women Prophets and Preachers* (Berkeley, 1997), 21–41).

20

Exodus-toward-Egypt: Filipino-Americans' Struggle to Realize the Promised Land in America

Eleazar S. Fernandez

In recent years a host of material has been written questioning the biblical exodus-from-Egypt narrative as the paradigmatic narrative for oppressed and marginalized communities. When viewed from the perspective of those who identify with the plight of the Canaanites, this liberating narrative becomes an exodus-conquest narrative and hence a narrative of terror, for the acquisition of the promised land, Canaan, comes by way of conquest of a people, the Canaanites, with the help of Yahweh, the liberator-God turned conqueror-God.

Palestinians in particular, as pointed out by Naim Ateek and Mitri Raheb, find the exodus narrative extremely disturbing.[1] When they read it, they do not identify with the conquering Israelites but with the resident Canaanites. Exodus, for them, becomes a mirror of their oppression as well as of God's identification with the oppressors. For the Palestinians, exodus signifies conquest, not liberation. As such, the exodus narrative becomes a narrative of terror. In resonance with the Palestinians, Robert Allen Warrior argues that American Indians identify with the Canaanites on the land, not with the conquering Israelites, in the exodus narrative.[2] Like the biblical Canaanites, American Indians have also suffered conquest and genocide at the hands of those who escaped from the "Old World" and laid claim to the promised land of the "New World." For American Indians, therefore, the exodus narrative proves a narrative of terror as well, an exodus-conquest narrative.

For a long time I used the exodus-conquest narrative in my Sunday school classes in the land of my birth, the Philippines, without any awareness of or sensitivity to the plight of either the Palestinians or the American Indians. My most crucial ideological blinder in this regard was, I believe, my understanding that the Israelites were

First published in Eleazar S. Fernandez and Fernando F. Segovia, *A Dream Unfinished: Theological Reflections on America from the Margins*. Maryknoll: Orbis Books, 2001, 167–81.

justified in what they had done to the Canaanites, since they were Yahweh's "chosen people" and had been charged by Yahweh to reclaim the promised land. I am not alone in this regard. Even when a biblical narrative of terror is as blatant and as nauseating as that of Yahweh's command to annihilate the inhabitants of Canaan, most readers simply push aside this dimension of the text, as I did, for it is always the well-being of God's elect (the Israelites) that matters, not that of the non-elect (the Canaanites).

Emphasizing the power of narratives, Warrior argues that no amount of critical biblical scholarship, as in the case of Norman Gottwald's *The Tribes of Yahweh*, can change the narrative of "the elect," for "people who read the narratives read them as they are, not as scholars and experts would like them to be read and interpreted. History is no longer with us. The narrative remains."[3] Yes, I agree with Warrior, the narrative remains. Indeed, the impact of the narrative seems more powerful than that of any scholarly account, aside from the fact that only a select few are able to read sophisticated historical, sociological, and theological discourses. Still, critical subaltern scholarship has, at the very least, helped us to hear the muted voices in the text. Nevertheless, what we need far more than scholarly critiques is the articulation of other narratives of liberation, for the God of liberation is not just the liberator of one "elect" people.

That is precisely my aim in this study. I seek to advance a narrative of liberation that, I believe, is more in keeping with the experience of the people to whom I am trying to give a voice – Filipino Americans. I proceed as follows: I begin with an overview of the proposed narrative, which I characterize as one of exodus-toward-Egypt; continue with a critical analysis of the present project of Filipino Americans in the light of their experience in the United States; and conclude with a call for a different project in the light of such experience and the alternative liberation narrative of exodus-toward-Egypt – a historical project for the realization of the promised land in the United States.

Exodus-toward-Egypt: A Narrative Framework for Interpreting the Filipino-American Experience

Filipino Americans find resonance with the views articulated by Palestinian and American Indian theologians. Although many find themselves not just surviving in the country but actually thriving, Filipino Americans have by no means entered the promised land, the United States or America,[4] as jubilant conquerors; to the contrary, they have landed on these shores as a colonial people and have gone on to experience life as second-class citizens. Consequently, instead of the traditional exodus-from-Egypt narrative, with its accompanying themes of conquest and election, I suggest that the narrative that best articulates the Filipino-American experience is that of exodus-toward-Egypt.

Such a narrative framework I see as quite rich, able to conjure up variant messages and thus jar our familiar knowledge of the biblical exodus account. It is a narrative that conveys not a singular notion of liberation and the euphoria that goes with it but an ambiguous nexus of captivity and liberation, of closure and promise, of blessings and alienation. Within such a framework, the term *exodus* carries not

only its ordinary meaning of "flight" or "migration" but also its positive biblical connotations of "release" and "liberation." For Filipino Americans, exodus from their homeland has meant release from poverty and fatalism – an exodus toward a land of wealth and opportunity. The irony, however, is that this exodus has as its destination the homeland of their colonial masters, where they are able to share in the cornucopia of their masters' blessings but also remain colonized in brazen as well as subtle ways every day of their lives.

Unlike the exodus-from-Egypt narrative, which begins in Egypt and then moves outside of Egypt, the exodus-toward-Egypt narrative begins in Canaan and moves toward Egypt. In this framework the exodus starts not with the exploits of Moses in the accounts of the book of Exodus but with the migration of Jacob and his descendants in the book of Genesis, especially with the story revolving around Joseph and the events that led him to Egypt. Consequently, instead of taking the flight out of Egypt as its paradigmatic lens, this narrative casts the exodus in a much broader light, so that the Moses-led exodus constitutes but a moment, though a significant one, in the overall struggle of the people. In this framework, then, Moses does not lead the people out of Egypt but leads them instead in the task of transformation within the geographic confines of Egypt.

Unlike the biblical Israelites, Filipino Americans have no intention of leaving Egypt (the United States); they have made the decision to cast their lot in this new country and have resolved to realize the promised land in Egypt. Yes, realize the promised land in Egypt, not outside of Egypt, not outside of the United States. In this new land they have started to dream dreams, yet this is also a land of unfinished dreams and, at times, of nightmares. In order to avoid any understanding of this exodus-toward-Egypt narrative as involving only movement from one country to another, the experience of emigration from the Philippines to the United States, I want to emphasize that the narrative also takes into account the process of settlement in the new country, the experience of immigration in the United States. Emigration (exodus) and immigration (settlement) should be seen, therefore, as two facets of the one exodus-toward-Egypt narrative. Such a view of the exodus is consistent with that standing interpretation of it not as a one-time event led by the breakthrough figure of Moses but as a continuing struggle for liberation.

My purpose in advancing this alternative narrative of liberation is not to establish a correspondence between the biblical narrative and the Filipino-American experience but to engage in an inter(con)textual reading of the biblical narrative and the Filipino-American experience so that they may enrich each other, opening the way in the process for new horizons of thinking, dwelling, and acting to come. I turn first to the present project of Filipino Americans in the United States.

The Emigration and Immigration of "Mr Pinoy" and "Ms Pinay" to the New Egypt: An Inter(con)textual Reading

In any migratory phenomenon there are always factors that "push" people to migrate; consequently, it is necessary to look at the situation in Canaan that precipitated the migration. According to the biblical narrative, there was famine in the land of Canaan and the sons of Jacob had to look for food. Famine, therefore, was

the triggering factor for the move of Jacob's family from Canaan to Egypt. Given the lack of basic commodities, the members of Joseph's family, in order to survive, had to find food and jobs in other lands. If there was a "push," there was also a "pull" – another set of factors that must not be overlooked when analyzing the phenomenon of migration. Jacob and his family had heard from the caravans that the land of pharaoh had an abundant supply of food. It was thus a question of either going to Egypt or perishing from the famine.

The Filipino exodus to "the land of the free and the home of the brave" resonates with some features of the exodus of Jacob and his family to the biblical Egypt, but it is also different, more complex, textured as it is by a confluence of economic, political, and cultural factors. In fact, the Filipino exodus to the United States can be understood adequately only when seen against the wider framework of global politics and shifting world powers, from Spain to the United States. Since colonization entails political and economic control as well as mental control, the coming of Filipinos to the shores of America has been driven not only by the search for "greener pastures," the primary factor, but also by their image of America. For them, America represents the land of endless opportunities and coming to America the fulfillment of that to which they aspire in life. White America represents what is good and beautiful, noble and laudable, while the brown Philippines represents what they despise in themselves.

Except for those with economic means and those in military service, coming to the United States entails enormous sacrifices for Filipinos. Out of dire need and in the firm belief that plenty of opportunities exist in the States, Filipinos muster every available means at their disposal to come to America. Those who do not have the necessary cash on hand proceed to sell their carabao or water buffalo and, if need be, their small piece of land. Such risks are taken because of the prospect of future rewards; for example, over against the undervalued Filipino peso, a son or daughter in America can send the almighty US dollar – the "God we trust" – to the family "back home." In some instances, again with the exception of families of wealthy professionals, Filipino families, echoing what Joseph's brothers did to him in the biblical narrative, not only sell their carabao and land but also "sell" their family members to US citizens in the hope that they will be taken to the States. An obvious example in this regard, and a booming business in recent times, is the mail-order bride. All such sacrifices finally pay off when the first almighty dollar or box of "goodies" arrives. In the light of our contemporary situation, Filipino Americans can readily envision Joseph's orders to fill his brothers' bags with grain and to put money in their sacks (Gen. 42:25), much as they themselves send money through bank-to-bank transfers or assorted "goodies" by door-to-door delivery.

When the contemporary Filipino-American Joseph goes home to his province, perhaps in time for the barrio fiesta, he brings with him *balikbayan* (literally, "returning to one's country of origin") boxes filled with *pasalubong* (gifts). If he has not been able to save much money, he must make use of his high-interest-rate credit card to pay for travel expenses as well as for entertainment for his long time-no see *barkadas* (peer group), since he has to live up to the expectations on the part of his *kababayan* (country folks) as a "dollar boy." The green-card holder or citizen Joseph is a VIP back home because of his dollar. In fact, the Philippine government regards him, like all Filipino contract workers, as the "new hero." He serves as the

alkansiya (piggy bank) for both his parents and all other family members. Whenever there is a financial problem back home, the "dollar boy" gets a collect call. Because Joseph's parents, brothers, and sisters usually lack health insurance, he also functions as their health-insurance provider whenever folks back home get sick.

Sending money back home is but a first step in helping the immediate family. The ultimate goal is to bring the remaining family members to the States. Joseph's family cannot come at will into the new Egypt; they have to be "petitioned" by Joseph through the Immigration and Naturalization Service (INS). In this regard, the pivotal figures in making it possible for the rest of the family to follow suit are Joseph's parents – Jacob and his wife. Thus, elderly parents, who would be less lonely in their homeland, are forced to come, because it is only through them that other members of the family can be petitioned, though they also prove useful in taking care of the grandchildren (Joseph's children). *Itay* and *Inay* (father and mother) must come to the United States, no matter how frail, since their acquisition of citizenship proves crucial for the immigration of the other family members.

In resonance with the gradual immigration of Jacob and his family, Filipinos have also come to the United States in waves. The earliest group consisted of crewmen aboard the Philippine-made galleon *San Pablo* in the latter half of the eighteenth century and thus at the height of the Manila-Mexico galleon trade (1565–1815). Having suffered maltreatment at the hands of the Spanish on board, they jumped ship in Acapulco, Mexico, and went on to settle in Louisiana in 1763. Since the arrival of this first contingent, four major periods of Filipino immigration into the country can be readily identified: 1763–1906; 1906–34; 1945–65; and 1965 to the present.[5]

Struggling to "make it" in America: Outsiders-insiders of the American dream

Managing to land on the shores of America is only the beginning of a long journey. Newcomers have to deal quickly with the demands of living in a new country, especially in terms of employment. The struggle to "make it" in America cannot wait. After all, this is the main reason why they have come to America: they want to "make it." Again, there is clear resonance here between the plight of Jacob's family and the plight of the Filipino "old timers."

When Jacob and family arrived in Egypt, they were given jobs that, from the masters' point of view, "fit" their occupational background and training. Because of their training as shepherds, Jacob and his family were sent to Goshen to tend sheep (Gen. 47:6). Likewise, Filipino "old timers" were given jobs that, from the perspective of their employers, "fit" not only their occupational background and training but also their physical features. Being small in physical stature, their Euro-American employers thought that they would not suffer from back pain, even if they had to stoop from morning till sunset; they seemed naturally suited, therefore, for the planting and harvesting of such crops as asparagus, iceberg lettuce, spinach, strawberries, and sugar beets.[6] Others found jobs in the sugarcane plantations of Hawaii, the fish canneries of Alaska, and railroad construction on the mainland. Later immigrants were able to find jobs more in keeping with their educational and technical training in the Philippines, although many well-trained and well-educated Filipinos continued to land jobs far below their levels of competence.

Still, "making it" in America remains the goal, no matter what. To be sure, many Filipino Americans have done well and have made a mark in their chosen fields of employment. For example, Filipino-American medical doctors and nurses can be found in hospitals and clinics all over the country; indeed, Filipino Americans represent the largest racial minority group in the health-care industry.[7] Filipino Americans are steadily rising and breaking through the "glass ceiling" in other fields as well, finding their niche in various walks of life.[8] Many, however, are just barely "making it" in America, and this is a story that needs to be told as well. Before coming to "the land of the free and the home of the brave," I had not heard this other side of the Filipino-American experience. In fact, it was not until I came across such Filipino Americans in California and Hawaii that the scales fell from my eyes. Immediately, I felt a fire in my gut.

One group whose plight represents a betrayal of the American Dream is that of World War II veterans, especially the recent arrivals. In 1990, after a long wait and struggle, Filipinos who fought under the banner of the USAFFE (United States Armed Forces in the Far East) were granted US citizenship. For many of these veterans, the granting of citizenship was the fulfillment of their dream, a reward for fighting on the side of the United States against Japan. This dream, however, has become a nightmare for some and an unfinished mission for others. For Ciriaco Punla, time ran out: he died of tuberculosis, having endured the cold, damp weather of San Francisco while waiting for the promised veterans' benefits. Macario Nicdao, another veteran, could only raise these poignant questions: "We offered our blood and lives. What have they done to us? Where is America's heart?"[9]

Another group whose plight portrays the ambiguity of the American Dream includes Filipino Americans who come to the United States by way of marriage to US citizens. Aside from the pursuit of higher education, marrying a US citizen constitutes a ready passport to a better life for many Filipinos. The resultant stories are a mixture of "success" and dreams turning into nightmares. Although many of these Filipinos have found admirable spouses, even willing to help with their families back home, a relationship of subordination is also common. At times they end up in more abusive relationships, which they simply endure and refuse to report to the proper authorities for fear that their bid for a "green card" or US citizenship may be jeopardized.[10] In extreme cases, the dreams have turned into nightmares. This was the case for Emelita Reeves, who came to America with a suitcase full of dreams, thinking that the husband she had found through a pen-pal service was her ticket to the moon. She landed in the hands of a man who murdered her.[11]

Filipinos have thus come to America filled with the hope of participating in the American Dream, and some have "made it" in America. Filipinos have also learned, to their shock, the other side of America: its xenophobia and oppression of racial others. As a Filipino riddle puts it, *Isang magandang señora, libot na libot ng espada* (There is a beautiful lady surrounded with swords).[12] The early Filipino immigrants had to face outright racist violence against them, such as massacres, house-burnings, and beatings.[13] Such violence, moreover, is by no means a thing of the past, certainly not for Filipino-American Derrick Lizardo, a student at Syracuse University, who, along with other Asian-American colleagues, was refused service at a Denny's Restaurant and was subsequently beaten by a group of twenty whites on the evening

of April 11, 1997.[14] Carlos Bulosan captures this outsider-insider experience when he writes to a friend, "I know deep down in my heart that I am an *exile* in America."[15]

Trying hard to be an American: The politics of identity

At present, Filipino Americans rank as the second largest Asian-American ethnic group in the United States and yet we do not hear of Filipinotowns. I do not imagine that there will be Filipinotowns in the near future either, not for Filipino Americans, who have been trained to believe that they are white America's "little brown brothers," even after years of being called "brown monkeys." There will be no Filipinotowns, because Filipino Americans are proud of their effort to blend, not with other people of color in America but with dominant white America, though another factor may be at work here as well, namely, the strong regionalism among Filipino Americans. Filipino Americans have, in general, no aversion to "Americanization," because that is precisely what many aim for. What is the purpose of coming to America if not to be Americanized?

Yet, even as they try hard to be Americanized, many have come to see, as Euro-Americans keep reminding them, the futility of such efforts. "I have been four years in America," a Filipino immigrant in California said sadly, "and I am a stranger. It is not because I want to be. I have tried to be as 'American' as possible. I live like an American, eat like American, and dress the same, and yet everywhere I find Americans who remind me of the fact that I am a stranger."[16] Trying hard to be an American but falling short of the norm – the American as Euro-American – is the plight of Filipino Americans. No matter how hard they try to be Americans, such a task proves impossible, given the identification of the normative American as the Euro-American; Filipino Americans will always fall short of this norm and remain aberrations, forever "missing the mark," like sinners. Indeed, falling short of the norm is rather like falling from grace: outside the norm is hell, a place where an encounter with God is perceived as impossible. Many Filipino-American youth, in an effort to be as American as possible, to be "cool," deny their cultural and ethnic identity and, at times, even blame their parents for their physical features. They want to be just like any white youth, since that is the key to getting out of the hell of non-acceptance. Whites, in turn, often with the best of intentions, respond: "We consider you to be just like us. You don't seem [Filipino]."[17]

"America is a Presence as Huge as God": In the Image of God, in the Image of America

In the story of the garden of Eden, the serpent tempts the first couple with these words: "You will be like God" (Gen. 3:5). The first couple succumb to the temptation because they wanted to be "like God." Filipinos and Filipino Americans, like the first couple in the primeval garden, have also succumbed to this temptation. They, too, desire to be "like God," but this time, more specifically, to be like the "white gods" – their colonial and neocolonial masters. The "fall" of Filipino Americans is brought

about by their desire to be "white," to be an image of the white gods. "Dealing with Filipino-ness," writes Luis Francia, "is to deal with this condition, with a fall from grace, when the twin-headed snake of Spain and America seduced us with the promise of boundless knowledge – we too could be white gods! – even as we reposed in an unimaginably beautiful garden."[18]

Even before coming to "the land of the free and the home of the brave," Filipino Americans know, in the words of Eric Gamalinda, that "America is a presence as huge as God."[19] During my boyhood years on the island of Leyte, I encountered this association of hugeness with Americanness in the literal physical sense through objects, plants, and animals. For example, the largest frog was what the barrio inhabitants called the American frog, and the largest bread I dreamed of eating someday, *hanggang sawa* (eating until I drop), was the American bread, the rectangular loaf of bread. In other words, when something was huge, it had to be American. The hugeness of America, I later realized, was more than what was embodied in that frog or that loaf of bread. "America is a presence as huge as God" insofar as all Filipinos are expected to acquire an exhaustive understanding of America the beautiful and to love America with all their hearts, while denouncing whatever smells Filipino with all their might. Filipinos and Filipino Americans have a term for this, "colonial mentality," which punsters have turned into the more derogatory "mental colony."

The States and stateside (American products) so preoccupy the Filipino mind that they often find their way into common chitchat. Many times, such chitchat is raised to a volume that others can hear:

- *May tia ako sa California* ("I have an aunt in California").
- *Ako? may sister ako*, CPA *sa Nuyork* ("I have a CPA sister in New York").
- My son—*abogado sa Ha-why* ("My son is a lawyer in Hawaii").
- Look at my shoes. PX goods. Stateside '*yan* ("indeed").
- *Kumusta* ("Greetings") to your father, huh? Tell him not to forget us here, huh? Say hello for me. But tell me how's Woodside, Nuyork?
- When is he going to send me my Samsonite? Groovie promised me you know? When is he going to send Yardley and Ivory? They're not too expensive in the States I hear?
- Here in Manila. Here in Manila. Everything, everything too much.[20]

Since "America is a presence as huge as God," without liberation from this God any theological task about the creation of Filipino Americans in the image of God can only mean in the image of the white gods. Without decolonization from their colonial mentality or liberation from their mental colony, Filipino Americans will continue to be an image of white America. Sin for African Americans, declares James Cone, is the desire to be white; the same, I would argue, applies to Filipino Americans.[21] But with a fatal twist. The desire to be white on the part of Filipino Americans often turns against blacks. Deceived into thinking that their lighter skin complexion puts them closer to whites, Filipino Americans often behave as if they were white in relation to blacks. Filipino Americans will find a liberating image of God only when they experience liberation from the mental colony; otherwise, being an image of God will remain being an image of Uncle Sam.

"But the moon was rising and it was bigger than in America": Bursting from the old wineskin

Simeon Dumdum's poem "America" provides a glimpse of a new consciousness that is beginning to seep through the old wineskin, struggling to burst from its encasement:

I listened to him speak
of West Virginia
(he was born in Leyte
but was living in West Virginia).
. . . .
And on that warm evening
I told myself,
That's where I want to be,
in West Virginia, or New York,
or San Francisco,
because cousin says
everything there is big
and cheap—big chickens,
big eggs, big buildings,
and big flowers.
Cousin looked at me
and said, Yes, big roses,
tea roses, and he was
about to name other roses
but the moon was rising
and it was bigger than in
America.[22]

I have traveled long and far from my boyhood home to the heartland of America. There I have come to realize that the big "American" frog I had seen and the big "American" bread I had dreamed of were but glimpses of the hugeness of America's presence in the lives of Filipinos. I have also come to realize that the American Dream itself is a quest for bigness—big houses, big bucks, big appliances, and so on. But the big must also be cheap. "Big and cheap," says the cousin from West Virginia in Dumdum's poem. How can something be big and cheap at the same time? It happens in America, of course, and somebody has to pay for it. Not the corporate welfare mamas, to be sure. Rather, cheap labor must be extracted from both inside the United States and outside in the Two-Thirds World in order to make it possible for Americans to buy "big and cheap." Bigness and cheapness rest, therefore, on the backs of others, both human and ecological.

How can the moon be "bigger than in America" if "America is a presence as huge as God"? How can the moon be "bigger than in America" for someone who aspires to be in America "because cousin says [who lives in West Virginia] everything there is big and cheap—big chickens, big eggs, big buildings, and big flowers"? Such questions defy easy answers, not simply because they are hard to understand but also because they require Filipino Americans to take account of themselves and of their aspirations. The moon is not only small but actually unnoticeable when one is

surrounded by floodlights, streetlights, and neon lights or by the skyscrapers of New York, Los Angeles, and Chicago. When one's days are busy in pursuit of the American Dream, the moon proves small indeed, if not altogether invisible. For those who are busy moonlighting, noticing the moon is an oxymoron, since they have no time even to look at the moon. Nonetheless, the moon is bigger, whether in the Philippines or in the heartland of America, for those who have come to realize that the God that is America is an idol and that the American Dream itself feeds on the blood of many. Filipino Americans, like the characters of Dumdum's poem, need to come to the realization that the moon is bigger than the big chickens, big eggs, big houses, and all the other "bigs" in America. Such consciousness requires, however, a reorientation of their sociopolitical and moral compass.

Encountering God in the adopted land: A God who would be "pissed off" if We Pass by the color purple and not notice it

The experience of exodus involves uprootedness from one's place of origins as well as from one's religious roots. While in exile in Babylon, the Israelites raised the profound issue of God's presence in a foreign land. With voices raised to the heavens, they asked, "How can we sing the Lord's song in a foreign land?" (Ps 137:4). This is a question that all Filipino Americans, whether of the first generation or of later generations, must ask again and again. It is a profound question, insofar as it calls Filipino Americans to reflect on their deep faith in God in the light of their new context and challenges. Not because God has been left behind in the Philippines, for Filipino immigrants know that God travels with them on their journey, but rather because they must learn how to discern God's presence in a new context and in a way that truly speaks to their plight and longings.

In a context where Filipino identity is despised, the God who travels with them must affirm their identity and encounter them in their ethnicity. Elizabeth Tay's confession, "I encounter God in my ethnicity," is one that all Filipino Americans should take to heart.[23] We encounter God in the context of who we are, not outside of who we are. A God who is encountered outside of who we are and who thus calls us to betray our ethnic identity is a God who works for foreign masters.

This twofold experience on the part of Filipino Americans of suffering because of their color and yet encountering a God who affirms their ethnicity can serve as grounds for an analogous construal of a God who is neither colorless nor colorblind; indeed, it is only in a white dominant society that God can be looked upon as colorless and colorblind (read: white). A God who is not cognizant of color is a God who is not cognizant of the pain of those who suffer because of color. One often hears from the pulpit such rhetoric as the following, "In the eyes of God color does not matter." I consider such a statement – no matter how good the intentions behind it may be – to be counterproductive. To speak as if color were of no concern to God is to perpetuate the denigration of color. To be sure, God transcends color, but not because God is colorless (white) but rather because God is colorful and cognizant of the beauty of each color. Such a colorful and color-loving God would be "pissed off," to use the expression of Alice Walker, "if [we] pass by the color purple in the field somewhere and don't notice it."[24]

The God who affirms Filipino-American identity is the same God who raises a prophetic no to any uncritical allegiance to the American Dream. For many Filipino Americans, the American Dream has become an obsession, so much so that their relationships with others both within the Filipino-American community and in the wider society are often measured in terms of success or failure relative to the American Dream. As a result, Filipino-American communities continue to be pestered not only by traditional Philippine regionalism but also by the classism to be found under the canopy of the American Dream. Filipino Americans, like the Israelites of old, need to reflect upon both the blessings and the perils of their new life.

Vomiting one's dream: Breaking silence, breaking the glass ceiling

The descendants of Israel labored hard in the land of the pharaohs. As the years passed, they grew in number and the Egyptians were threatened. The Egyptians, therefore, devised a variety of schemes intended to make the lives of the Israelites in Egypt much more difficult. At first, the Israelites accepted what was demanded of them without complaint, but the situation gradually became unbearable. Finally, they broke their silence.

It is difficult to raise critical comments about America in general and the American Dream in particular in Filipino-American communities. For many, it is simply unthinkable to engage in any type of criticism of America, given their belief in America as the fulfillment of their dreams. Criticism is regarded as tantamount to ungratefulness, rather like vomiting out one's dream and then proceeding to eat back one's vomit. For many Filipino Americans, such an attitude is to be without *utang na loob* (debt of gratitude). Warts and all, one must take America or leave it. This is how many of them think they can repay America – acceptance without question. The challenge, therefore, is to raise the social awareness of Filipino Americans, so that they can come to understand that social criticism is not a betrayal of their dream but a necessary move to realize the America of their dreams. Filipino Americans must move beyond *tinikling* (native bamboo dance) solidarity during ethnic cultural events to a solidarity that deals with the sociopolitical issues faced by society as a whole.

Again, there are Filipino Americans who have broken through the glass ceiling, but one must remember that this was possible only because other Filipino Americans had broken their silence before them. This is what contemporary Filipino Americans need to realize. Whatever success stories there may be in our communities at present have come out of the struggles of the past. Breaking silence is thus a part of the Filipino-American legacy that needs to be reclaimed. Filipino Americans must realize that it does not pay to remain silent and that silence, to paraphrase José Comblin, is a lie when the truth needs to be spoken.[25] From the early days of their settlement in America, a number of Filipino Americans have broken their silence. The Filipino *sacadas* in Hawaii, for example, organized a union and broke their silence against unfair treatment. At first, they raised their voices as an ethnic group, but later on they realized that they had to establish common cause with other minorities and form an interracial union.[26] It is very encouraging to see that new generations of Filipino Americans have reclaimed this legacy of breaking silence.

Going public and acting on the vision: Taking account of one's location in a globalized context

I have focused throughout on the Israelite narrative as if the Israelites had been the only ethnic group in Egypt besides the dominant group, the Egyptians. There is no empire, however, that does not gather a variety of marginalized groups within its shadow, and each of these groups has its own narrative to tell. It is important, therefore, that, even as one such narrative is foregrounded, others also be taken into account. Filipino Americans need to realize that their presence and plight in America represents a microcosm of the plight of the Two-Thirds World in general. Here I quite agree with Robert Blauner to the effect that "the economic, social, and political subordination of third world groups in America is a microcosm of the position of all peoples of color in the world order of stratification."[27] Such subordination, Blauner continues, is not an accident but "part of a world historical drama in which the culture, economic system, and political power of the white West has spread throughout virtually the entire globe."[28] It is in the context of this global drama, then, that Filipino Americans must take account of their presence in the United States and, in so doing, contribute to the birthing of a better tomorrow, not only for the United States but also for their country of origin as well as for the world in general.

They must not only give words to their pain but also go public with their vision. Beyond sending the almighty dollar to the folks back home, Filipino Americans need to understand the interweaving of the global and the local. Once they do, they will cease to be unequivocally happy about their relative advantage over Filipinos back home, because they will come to see that this advantage of theirs is predicated on the disadvantage of others. Filipino Americans embody in their lives this interweaving of the global and the local, between a home "over here" and a home "back there." However, they must also learn to articulate what they embody, if they are to be of help in making the larger US society understand the interconnecting dynamics between the plight of the Two-Thirds World and the plight of marginalized people in the United States. They must break their silence, if they want to avert the easy scapegoating of the weakest members of American society in times of crisis.

When Filipino Americans see themselves in this interweaving of the global and the local, they will also see their ethnic identity in a broader light. Their struggle to understand who they are as well as their plight will lead them to issues that transcend specific ethnic concerns. As people who have experienced marginalization and who have known what it means to cross geographical and cultural divides, Filipino Americans can help to build bridges of connections. As people who have known what it means to suffer as a result of one's color, they can also help to articulate a vision of a just, colorful, and sustainable tomorrow. Filipino Americans must not remain passive bystanders in America, busying themselves in pursuit of all the "bigs" of the American Dream; they must live up instead to the calling of responsible citizenship.

Realizing the Promised Land in Egypt: A Historical Project

While the exiled Israelites longed for an eventual return to their homeland, Filipino Americans, except for some first-generation immigrants who long to spend their

retirement years in the Philippines, have resolved to stay in America. They have resolved to realize the promised land in Egypt.[29] The "success" stories of Filipino Americans who break through the glass ceiling certainly call for a *fiesta* – a celebration with dances and *lechon* (roasted young pig). At the same time, we should always remember that such stories are possible only because others before us have broken their silence or have had their bodies broken by the forces of death. If the new generations are to express their *utang na loob* to those who broke their silence, they must do so by turning these monuments of past accomplishments into movements of today – movements of transformation, movements to forge a colorful tomorrow. America is in the hearts of Filipino Americans, and they have not given up the America of their dreams. The task is not only to understand America, as Carlos Bulosan put it, but also to make America a just society. This is to realize the America of one's heart.[30] The America that Filipino Americans desire in their hearts can only become a reality through a historical project – a project of breaking silence, of naming the pains, of articulating a colorful society, of acting on dreams so that the promised land may be realized in Egypt.

NOTES

1 Naim S. Ateek, *Justice and Only Justice: Towards a Palestinian Theology of Liberation* (Maryknoll, NY: Orbis Books, 1989); Mitri Raheb, *I Am a Palestinian Christian* (Minneapolis, Minn.: Fortress Press, 1995). See Marc H. Ellis, *Toward a Jewish Theology of Liberation* (Maryknoll, NY: Orbis Books, 1987).
2 Robert Allen Warrior, "A Native American Perspective: Canaanites, Cowboys, and Indians," in *Voices from the Margin: Interpreting the Bible in the Third World*, ed. R. S. Sugirtharajah (Maryknoll, NY: Orbis Books, 1991), 287–95.
3 Ibid., 290. See Norman K. Gottwald, *The Tribes of Yahweh: A Sociology of the Religion of Liberated Israel, 1250–1050* BCE (Maryknoll, NY: Orbis Books, 1979).
4 I should note that when Filipinos say "America," they basically mean the United States, not the rest of North America (Canada or Mexico) or Central America or South America; it is in that sense that I use "America" in this chapter.
5 Aurora Tompar-Tiu and Juliana Sustento-Seneriches, *Depression and Other Mental Health Issues: The Filipino American Experience* (San Francisco: Jossey-Bass Publishers, 1995), 8. With the last major wave of Filipino newcomers, the Filipino-American population has increased tremendously. The 1990 census counted 1.4 million Filipino Americans. Most are first-generation immigrants. If this growth rate continues, it is estimated that in the next ten years the Filipino-American population will reach over 2 million, becoming the largest Asian immigrant group.
6 Brandy Tuzon, "The War in Salinas," *Filipinas* (October 1996): 66.
7 David Bacon, "Living the Legacy of Unionism," *Filipinas* (January 1997): 18–21.
8 The following are salient examples: military (Major General Edward Soriano and Brigadier General Antonio Taguba of the Army); business (Diosdado Banatao and other Silicon Valley success stories); sports (Tiffany Roberts); journalism (Carlos Bulosan, Jessica Hagedorn, Byron Acohido, Alex Tizon); show business/entertainment (Paulo Montalban, Tia Carrere, Jocelyn Enriquez, Enrico Labayen); politics (Gov. Benjamin Cayetano of Hawaii and Mayor Peter Fajardo of Carson City, California). See Ely Barros, "The U.S. Army's First Filipino Generals," *Filipinas* (October 1997): 27–8; Emil Guillermo, "Tiffany Roberts: Gold Mettle," *Filipinas* (March 1997): 38–9, 41; "Jocelyn Enriquez: Dance

Music Diva," *Filipinas* (June 1998): 40; Laura Schiff, "She's Just Drawn That Way," *Filipinas* (August 1997): 38–42.

9 Rick Rocamora, "Unfinished Mission: The American Journey of Filipino World War II Veterans," *Filipinas* (June 1998): 22–5.

10 Tompar-Tiu and Sustento-Seneriches, *Depression and Other Mental Health Issues*, 47.

11 Jocelyn Alvarez Allgood, "A Death in Texas: The Emelita Reeves Murder Case," *Filipinas* (March 1997): 21–2.

12 Ronald Takaki, *Strangers from a Different Shore: A History of Asian Americans* (New York: Penguin, 1989), 316.

13 Dean Alegado, "Blood in the Fields," *Filipinas* (October 1997): 62–4, 76, 90.

14 Rachelle Ayuyang, "Violence on the Menu," *Filipinas* (October 1997): 31–2.

15 Cited in Takaki, *Strangers from a Different Shore*, 344.

16 Cited in Takaki, *Strangers from a Different Shore*, 316.

17 Grace Sangkok Kim, "Asian North American Youth: A Ministry of Self-Identity and Pastoral Care," in David Ng (ed.), *People on the Way: Asian North Americans Discovering Christ, Culture, and Community*, (Valley Forge, Pa.: Judson Press, 1996), 203.

18 Luis Francia, "The Other Side of the American Coin," in *Flippin': Filipinos on America*, eds Luis Francia and Eric Gamalinda (New York: The Asian American Writers' Workshop, 1996), 6.

19 Eric Gamalinda, "Myth, Memory, Myopia: Or, I May Be Brown But I Hear America Singin'," in Francia and Gamalinda, *Flippin'*, 3.

20 Bino Realuyo, "States of Being," in Francia and Gamalinda, *Flippin'*, 160.

21 James Cone, *A Black Theology of Liberation*, twentieth anniversary edn (Maryknoll, NY: Orbis Books, 1986), 108.

22 Simeon Dumdum, "America," in Francia and Gamalinda, *Flippin'*, 238–9.

23 Elizabeth Tay, as cited in Fumitaka Matsuoka, *Out of Silence: Emerging Themes in Asian American Churches* (Cleveland, Ohio: United Church Press, 1995), 134.

24 Alice Walker, *The Color Purple* (New York: Washington Square Press, 1978), 178.

25 José Comblin, *The Church and the National Security State* (Maryknoll, NY: Orbis Books, 1979), 15.

26 Algado, "Blood in the Fields," 63–4, 76, 90.

27 Robert Blauner, "Colonized and Immigrant Minorities," in *From Different Shores: Perspectives on Race and Ethnicity in America*, ed. Ronald Takaki (New York and Oxford: Oxford University Press, 1987), 159.

28 Ibid.

29 Therese Hermosisima Finnegan, "An Endless Search for Home," *Filipinas* (July 1996): 70.

30 Carlos Bulosan, *America Is in the Heart: A Personal History* (Seattle, Wash.: University of Washington Press, 1973; orig. publ., 1946).

Index of Biblical References

Index of Names and Subjects